Planet Ladder

Other 100% Authentic Manga Available from TOKYOPOP®:

COWBOY BEBOP 1-3 (of 3)
All-new adventures of interstellar bounty hunting, based on the hit anime seen on Cartoon Network.

MARMALADE BOY 1-3 (of 8)
A tangled teen romance for the new millennium.

REAL BOUT HIGH SCHOOL 1-3 (of 4+)
At Daimon High, teachers don't break up fights…they grade them.

MARS 1-3 (of 15)
Biker Rei and artist Kira are as different as night and day, but fate binds them in this angst-filled romance.

GTO 1-5 (of 23+)
Biker gang member Onizuka is going back to school…as a teacher!

CHOBITS 1-2 (of 5+)
In the future, boys will be boys and girls will be…robots? The newest hit series from CLAMP!

SKULL MAN 1-3 (of 7+)
They took his family. They took his face. They took his soul. Now, he's going to take his revenge.

DRAGON KNIGHTS 1-3 (of 17)
Part dragon, part knight, ALL glam. The most inept knights on the block are out to kick some demon butt.

INITIAL D 1-3 (of 23+)
Delivery boy Tak has a gift for driving, but can he compete in the high-stakes world of street racing?

PARADISE KISS 1-2 (of 3+)
High fashion and deep passion collide in this hot new shojo series!

KODOCHA: Sana's Stage 1-2 (of 10)
There's a rumble in the jungle gym when child star Sana Kurata and bully Akito Hayama collide.

ANGELIC LAYER 1-2 (of 5)
In the future, the most popular game is Angelic Layer, where hand-raised robots battle for supremacy.

LOVE HINA 1-5 (of 14)
Can Keitaro handle living in a dorm with five cute girls…and still make it through school?

Also Available from TOKYOPOP®:

PRIEST 1 (of 10+)
The quick and the u ndead in one macabre manga.

RAGNAROK 1-3 (of 9+)
In the final battle between gods and men, only a small band of heros stands in the way
of total annihilation.

Planet Ladder

Volume 2

Written and Illustrated by
Yuri Narushima

Los Angeles . Tokyo

Translator – Gabi Blumberg
Retouch and Lettering – Kyle Plummer
Cover Designer – Akemi Imafuku
Graphic Designer – Anna Kernbaum
English Adaptation – Elizabeth Hurchalla
Senior Editor – Julie Taylor

Production Manager – Mario Rodriguez
Art Director – Matt Alford
VP Production – Ron Klamert
Publisher – Stuart Levy

Email: editor@TOKYOPOP.com
Come visit us online at www.TOKYOPOP.com

A TOKYOPOP® manga
TOKYOPOP® is an imprint of Mixx Entertainment, Inc.
5900 Wilshire Blvd. Ste 2000, Los Angeles, CA 90036

ISBN: 1-931514-63-1

First TOKYOPOP® printing: July 2002

10 9 8 7 6 5 4 3 2

Manufactured in the USA

Planet Ladder

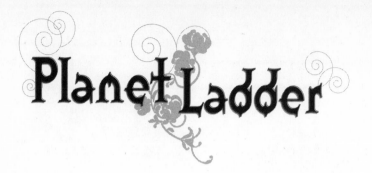

CONTENTS

GOLD
ORGANIC GOLD CREATED BY
SEEU, ITS OWNER.

KAGUYA HARUYMA
DARK-HAIRED, BLUE-EYED GIRL WHO HAS
NO MEMORIES BEFORE THE AGE OF FOUR.

THE STORY SO FAR...

KAGUYA IS A YOUNG ORPHAN GIRL WHO'S BEEN ADOPTED BY THE
HARUYAMA FAMILY. STRANGELY, THE ONLY MEMORY SHE POSSESSES
BEFORE THE AGE OF FOUR IS FEELING FRIGHTENED AS SHE WATCHED A
BOY'S HAND REACH OUT FROM INSIDE A FLAME TO HELP HER.

BUT THEN ONE NIGHT, HER WHOLE WORLD COMPLETELY CHANGED.
RIGHT BEFORE KAGUYA'S EYES, A MAN KNOWN AS PRINCE SEEU AND HIS
RAVEN-HAIRED ENEMY, IDOU, CAME TO TAKE HER AWAY. HER MOTHER AND
BROTHER TRIED TO HELP, BUT SEEU MANAGED TO ABDUCT KAGUYA WITH THE
MYSTERIOUS ORGANIC GOLD. SEEU STARTED TO TRANSPORT KAGUYA AND
HIMSELF TO ANOTHER DIMENSION, BUT WAS ATTACKED BY IDOU BEFORE HE
REACHED HIS DESTINATION. IN THE END, ONLY KAGUYA AND GOLD MADE IT.

THE PAIR WANDERED THE UNKNOWN WORLD UNTIL THEY ENCOUN-
TERED A COVERED WAGON WITH A GROUP OF PEOPLE INSIDE. ALTHOUGH SHE
WAS INITIALLY RELIEVED TO MEET OTHER HUMANS, KAGUYA SOON SENSED
DANGER AND TRIED TO FLEE WITH GOLD. BUT THEN...

CAST OF CHARACTERS

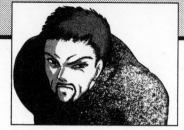

THE MAD PRINCE SEEU

A SOLDIER FROM ANOTHER WORLD WHO'S COME TO MEET KAGUYA. OWNER OF THE LUNATO MERCURY.

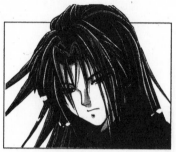

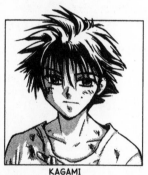

KAGAMI

HIS WEAPON IS THE ORGANIC GOLD. AS A SOLDIER IN THE GREAT WAR, HE'S THOUGHT TO BE DEAD, LEAVING BEHIND ONLY HIS WEAPON. BUT IS HE?

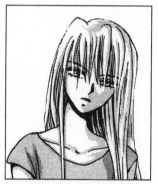

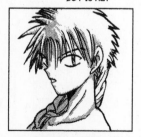

MEISHIE LARACOTTE

A GREAT SAGE IN ANOTHER WORLD.

IDOU

THREE HUNDRED YEARS AGO, HE AND SEEU FOUGHT TOGETHER AS SOLDIERS. NOW THEY ARE ENEMIES. IDOU HOLDS THE ZENITH CRIO.

SHEENA MORU BANVIVIRIE

A BEAUTIFUL BLONDE KAGUYA MEETS IN THE OTHER WORLD.

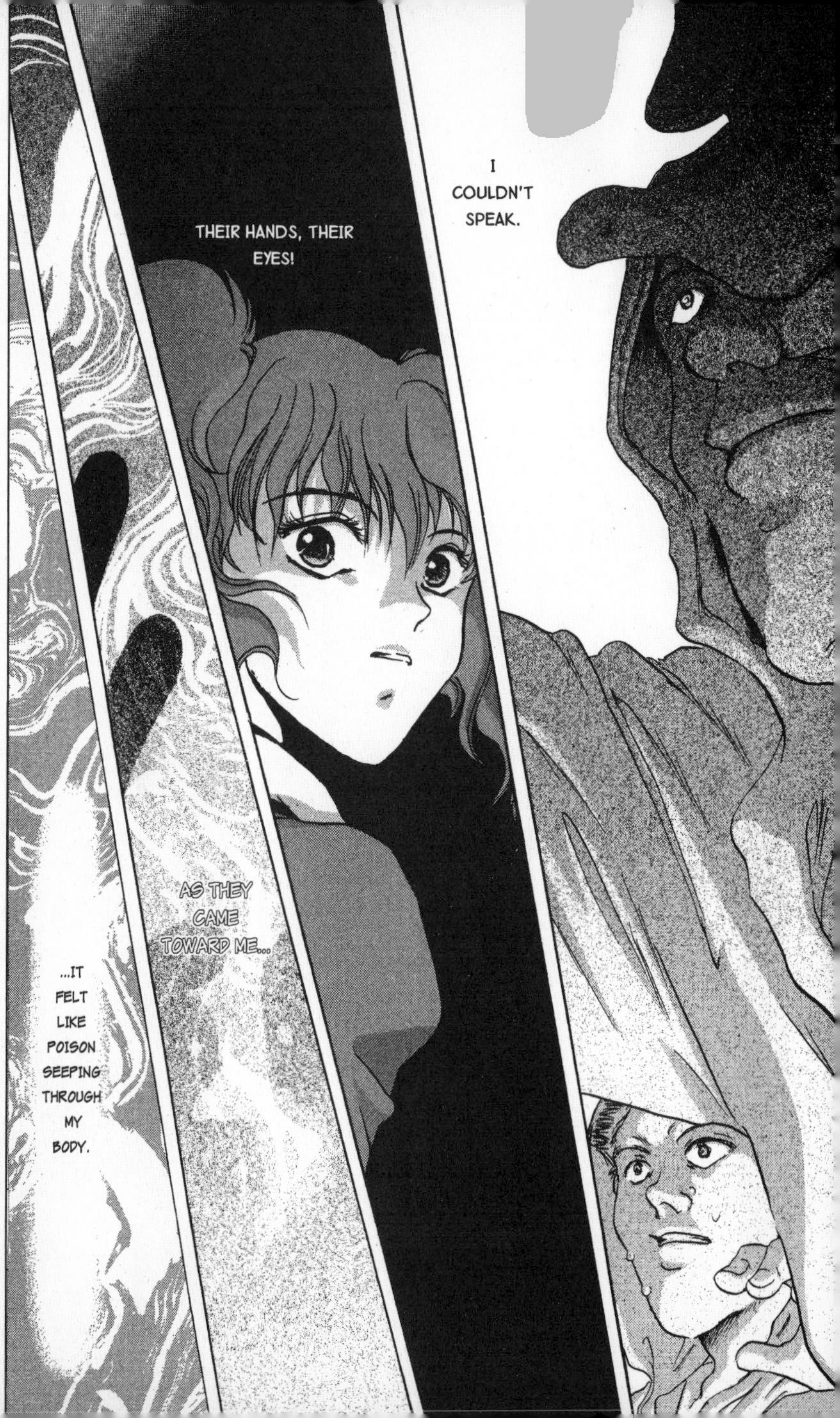
I COULDN'T SPEAK.
THEIR HANDS, THEIR EYES!
AS THEY CAME TOWARD ME...
...IT FELT LIKE POISON SEEPING THROUGH MY BODY.

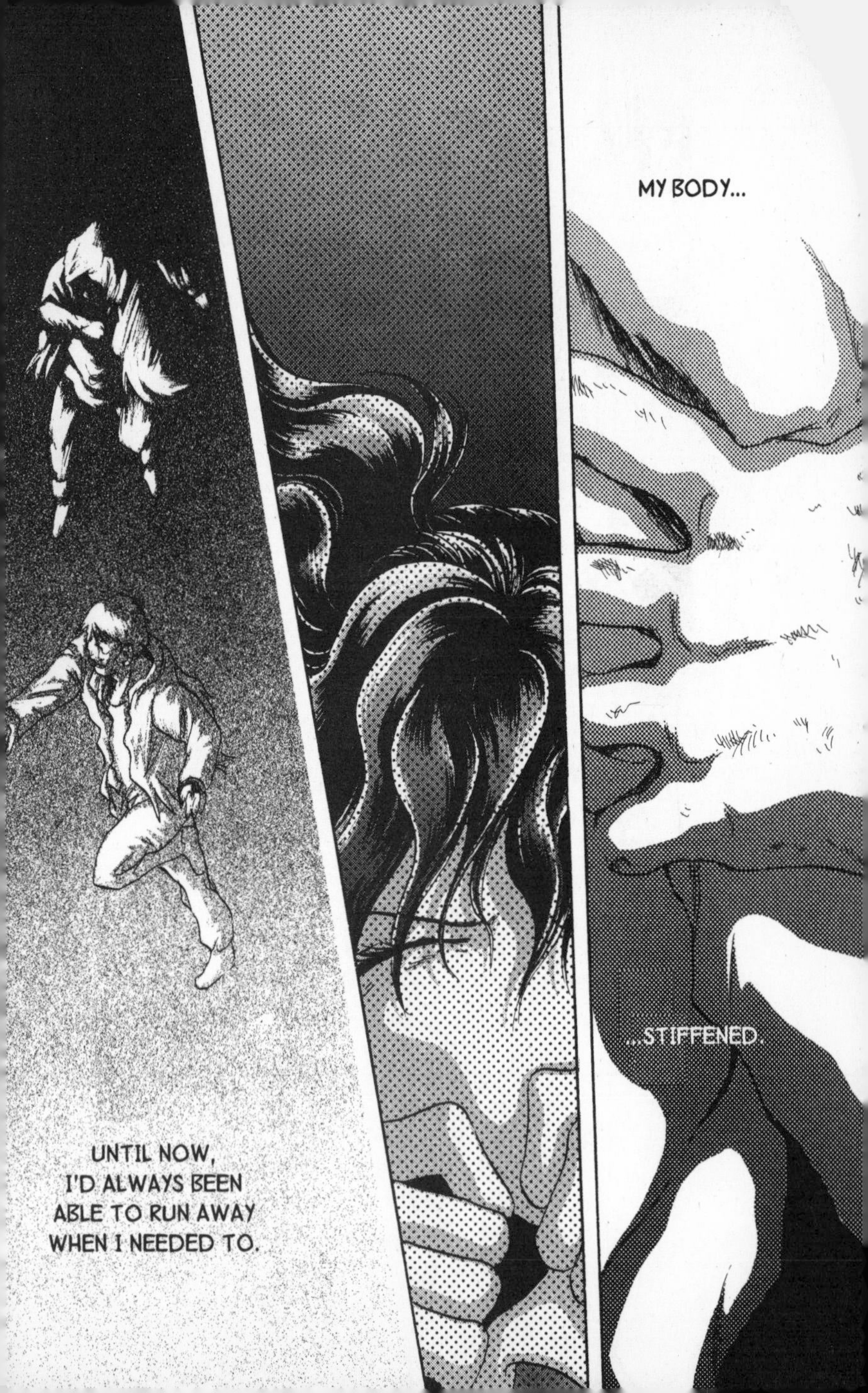
MY BODY...
...STIFFENED.
UNTIL NOW, I'D ALWAYS BEEN ABLE TO RUN AWAY WHEN I NEEDED TO.

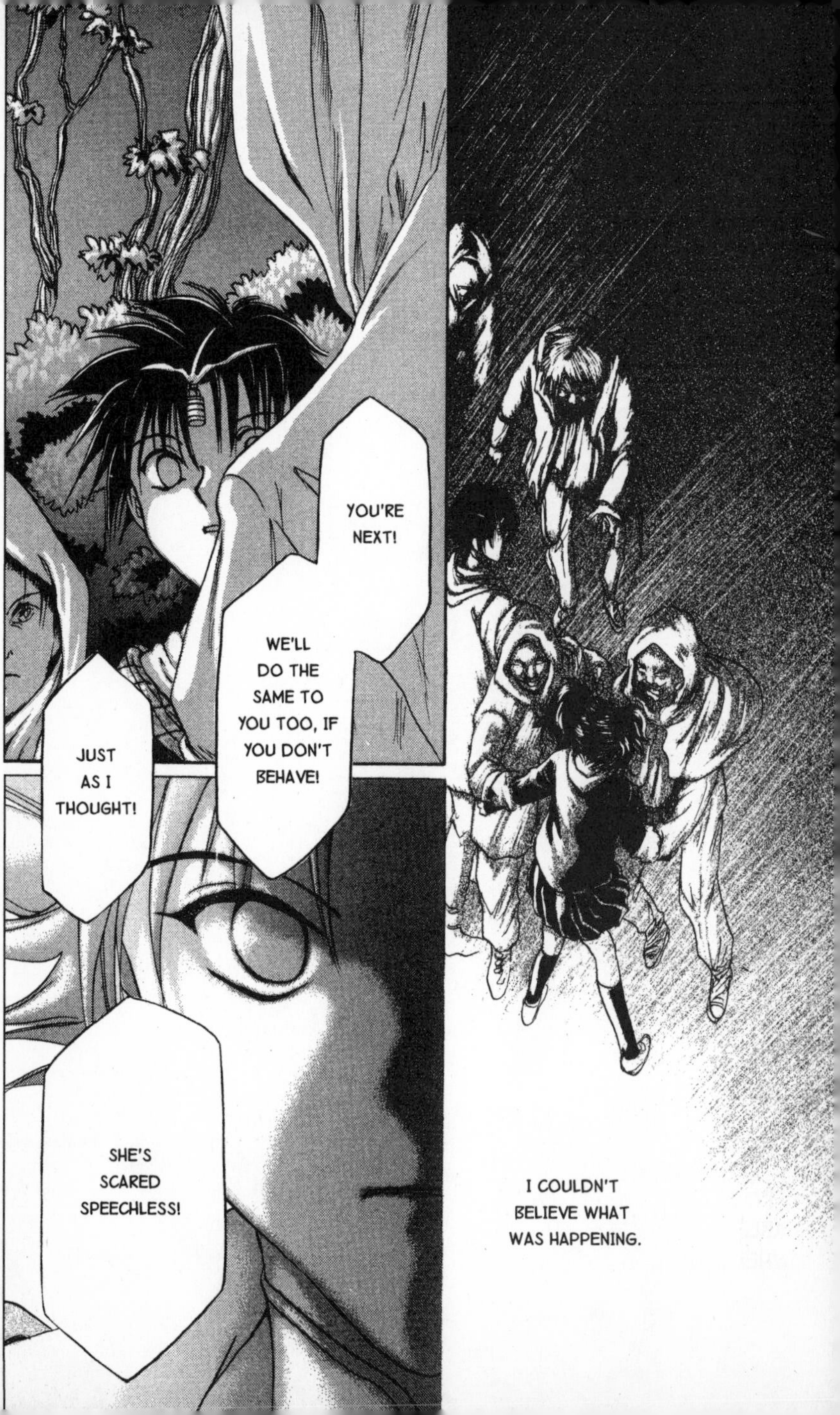
I COULDN'T BELIEVE WHAT WAS HAPPENING.
YOU'RE NEXT!
WE'LL DO THE SAME TO YOU TOO, IF YOU DON'T BEHAVE!
JUST AS I THOUGHT!
SHE'S SCARED SPEECHLESS!

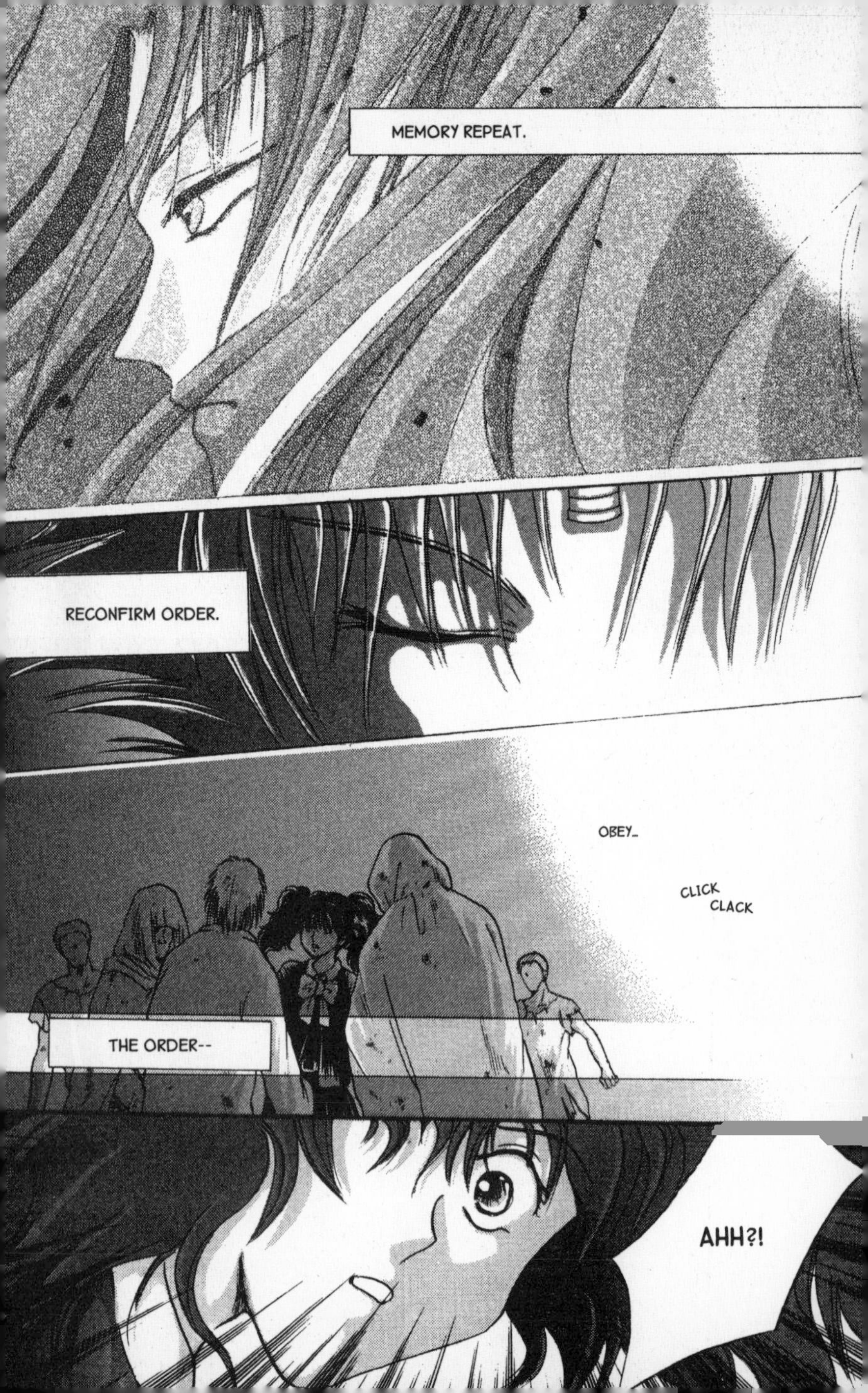
MEMORY REPEAT.
RECONFIRM ORDER.
OBEY..
CLICK
CLACK
THE ORDER--
AHH?!

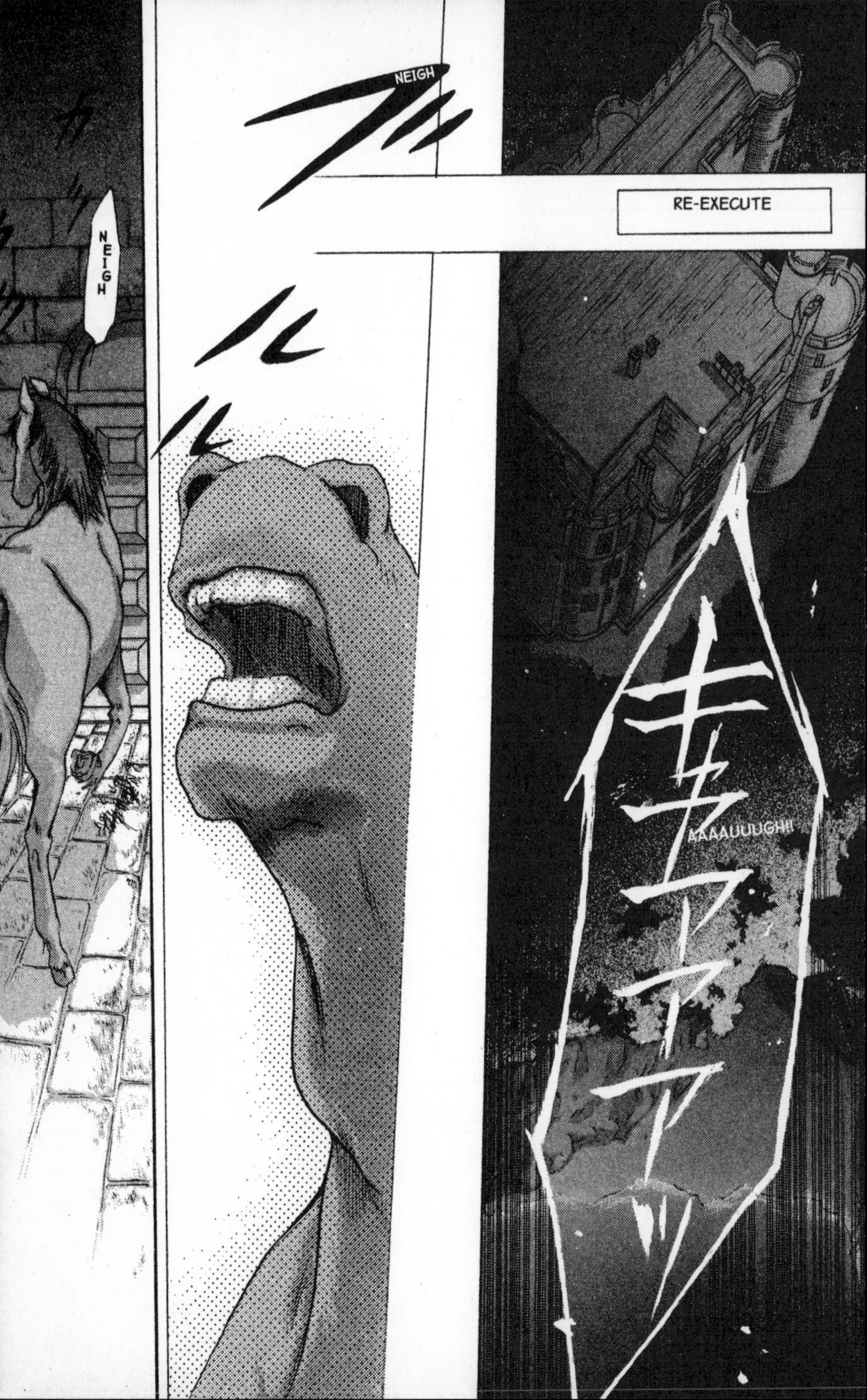
RE-EXECUTE
AAAAUUUGH!!
NEIGH
NEIGH

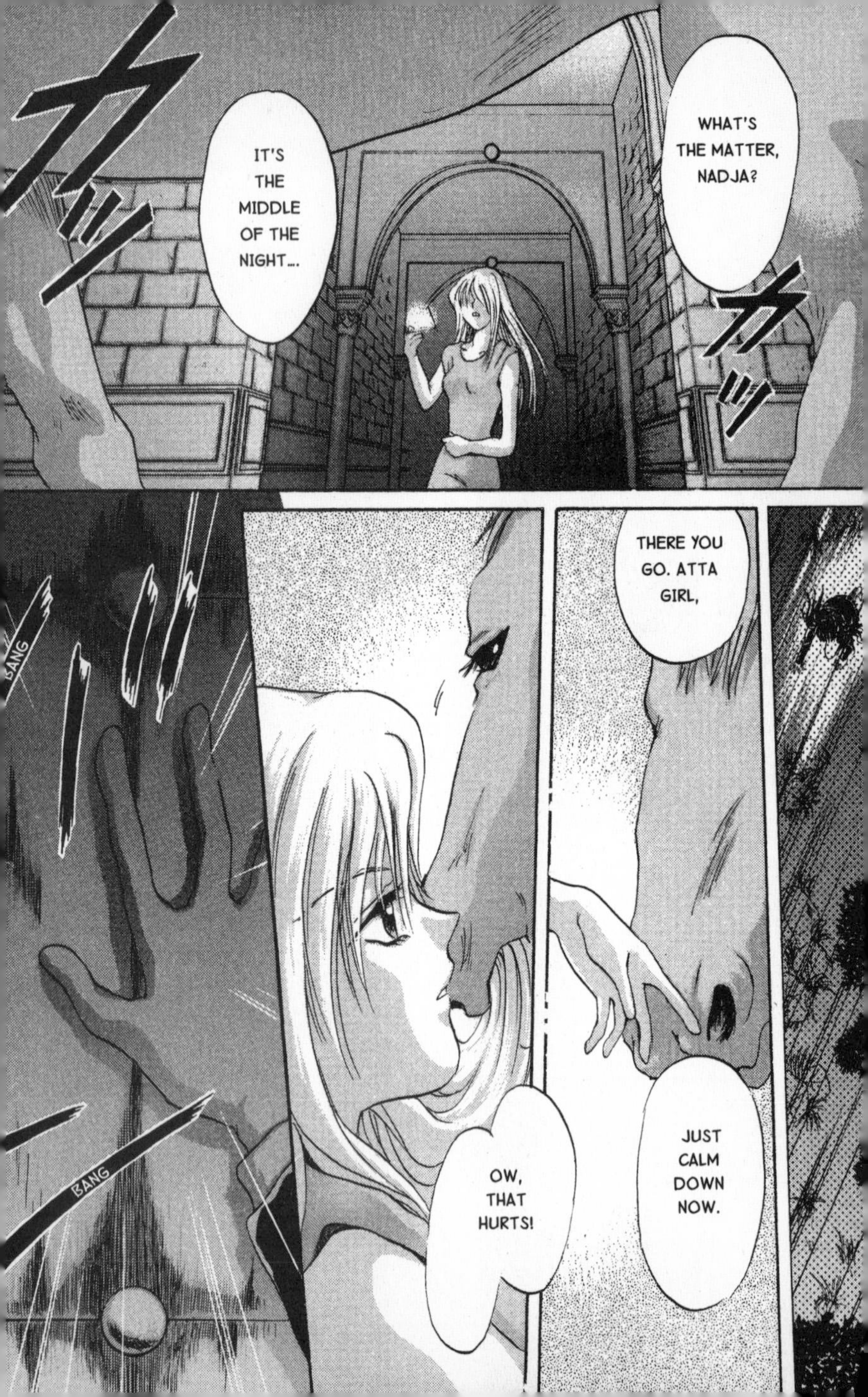
カッ
WHAT'S THE MATTER, NADJA?
IT'S THE MIDDLE OF THE NIGHT....
カッ
THERE YOU GO. ATTA GIRL,
JUST CALM DOWN NOW.
OW, THAT HURTS!
BANG
BANG

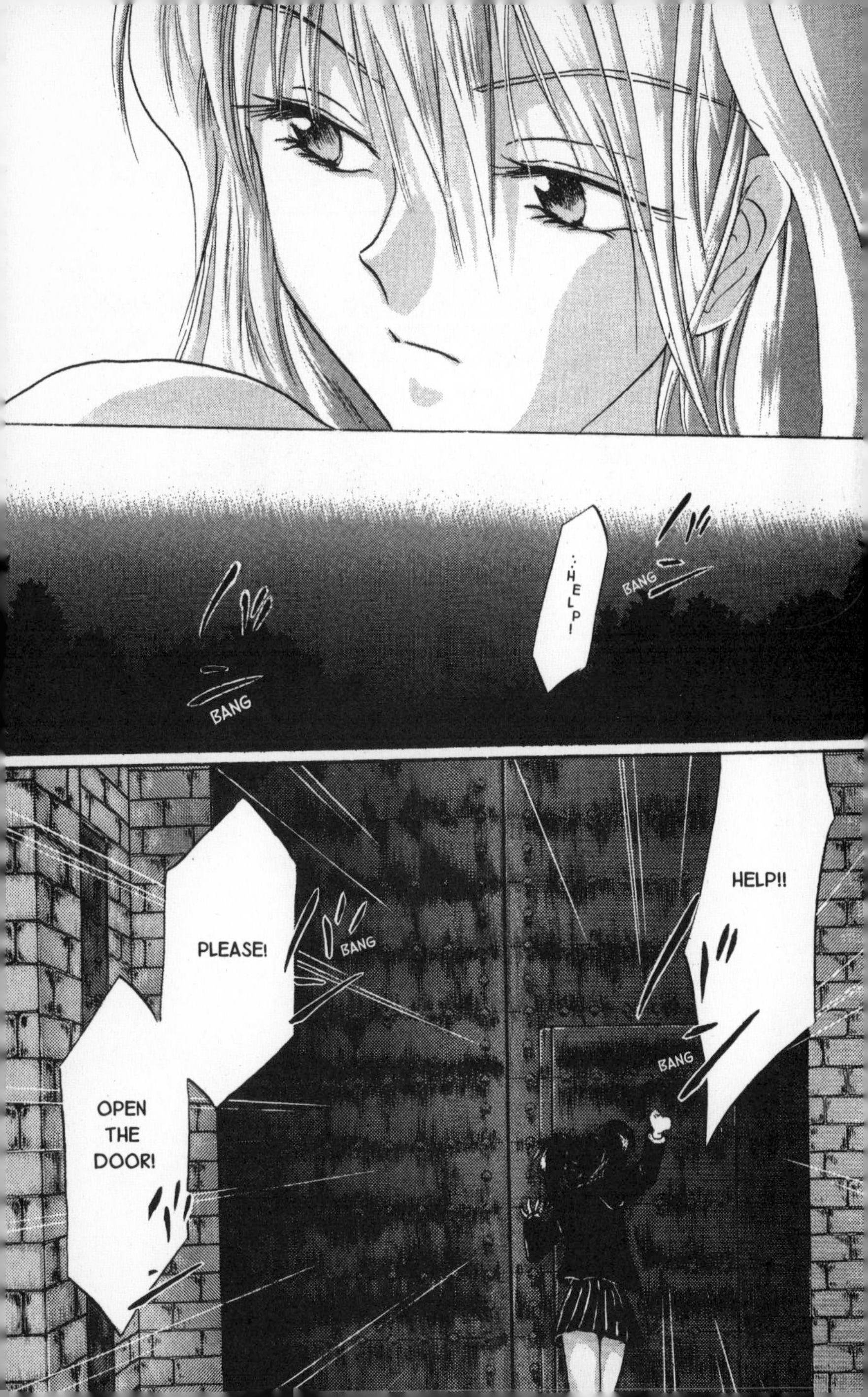
BANG
...HELP!
BANG
HELP!!
BANG
PLEASE!
BANG
OPEN THE DOOR!

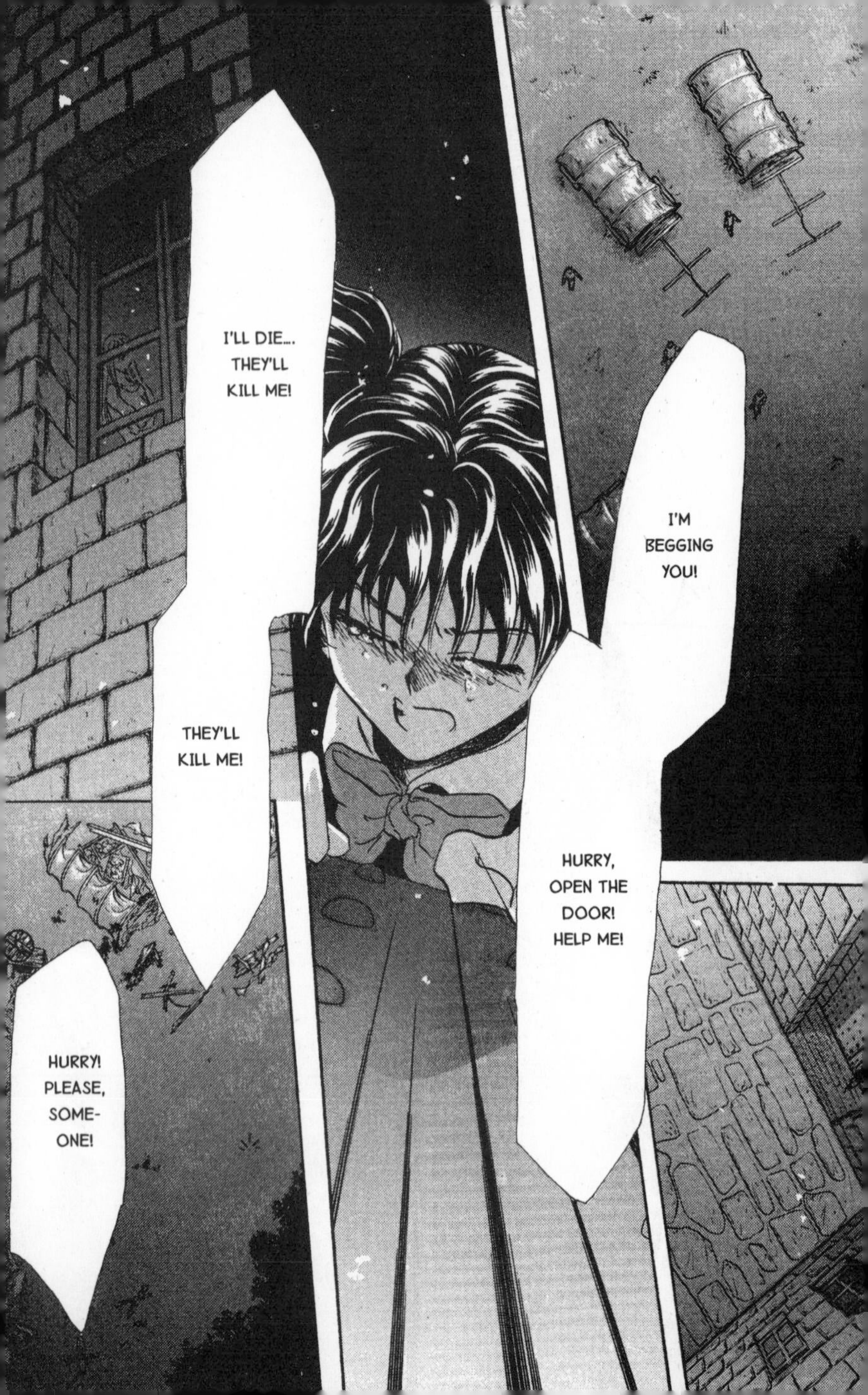
I'M BEGGING YOU!
HURRY, OPEN THE DOOR! HELP ME!
I'LL DIE.... THEY'LL KILL ME!
THEY'LL KILL ME!
HURRY! PLEASE, SOME-ONE!

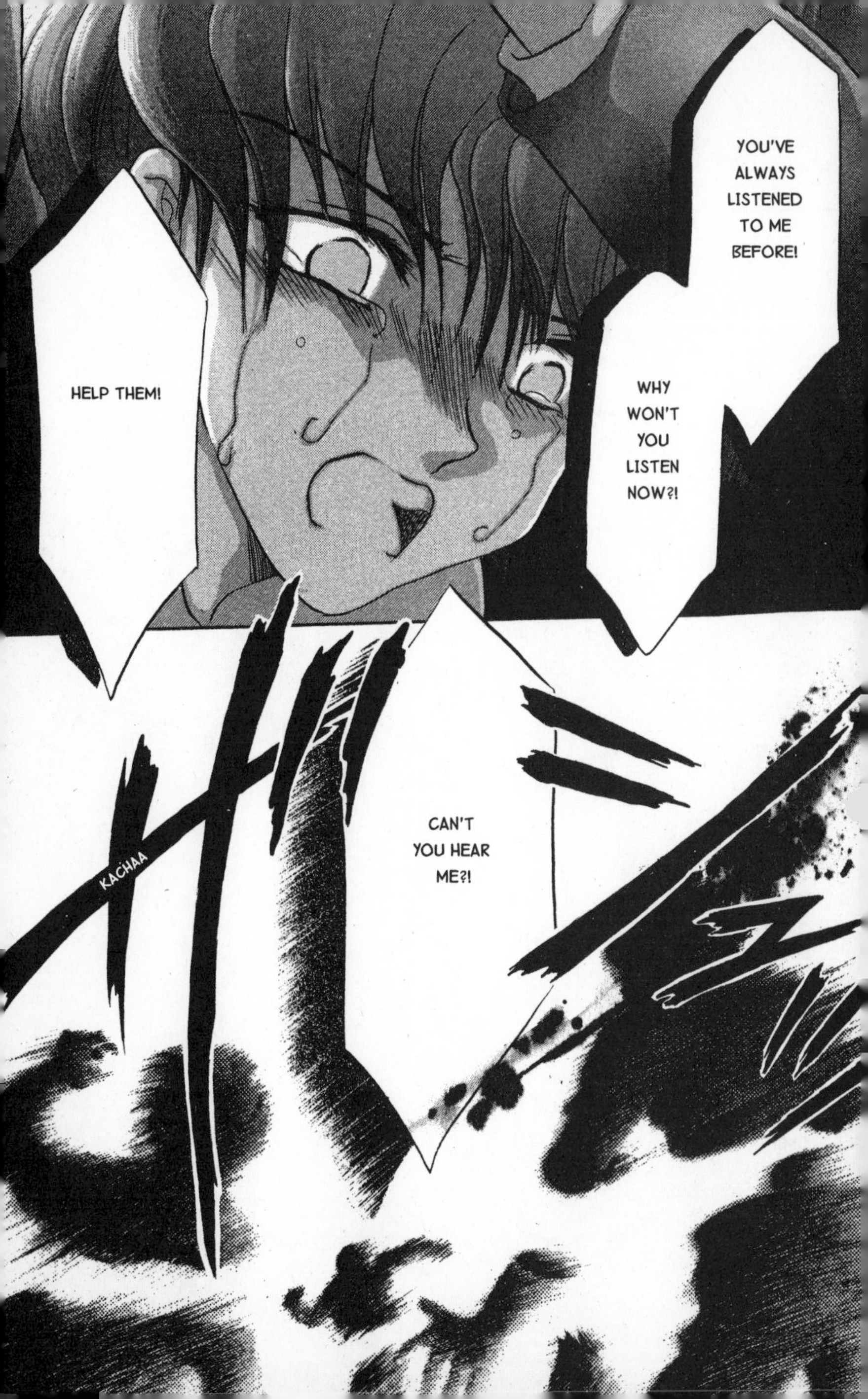
YOU'VE ALWAYS LISTENED TO ME BEFORE!
WHY WON'T YOU LISTEN NOW?!
HELP THEM!
CAN'T YOU HEAR ME?!
KACHAA

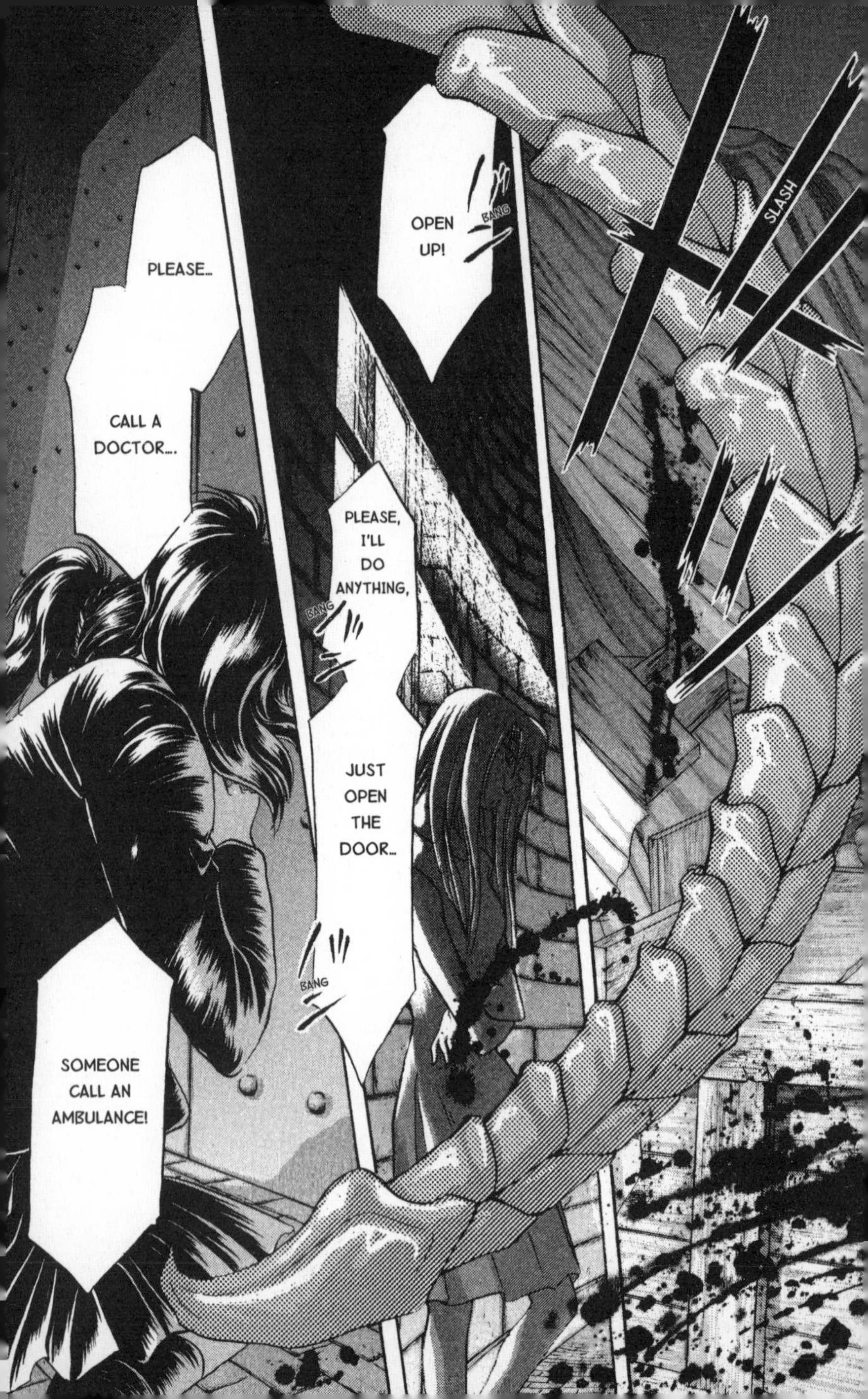
SLASH
OPEN UP!
BANG
PLEASE, I'LL DO ANYTHING,
BANG
JUST OPEN THE DOOR...
BANG
PLEASE...
CALL A DOCTOR...
SOMEONE CALL AN AMBULANCE!

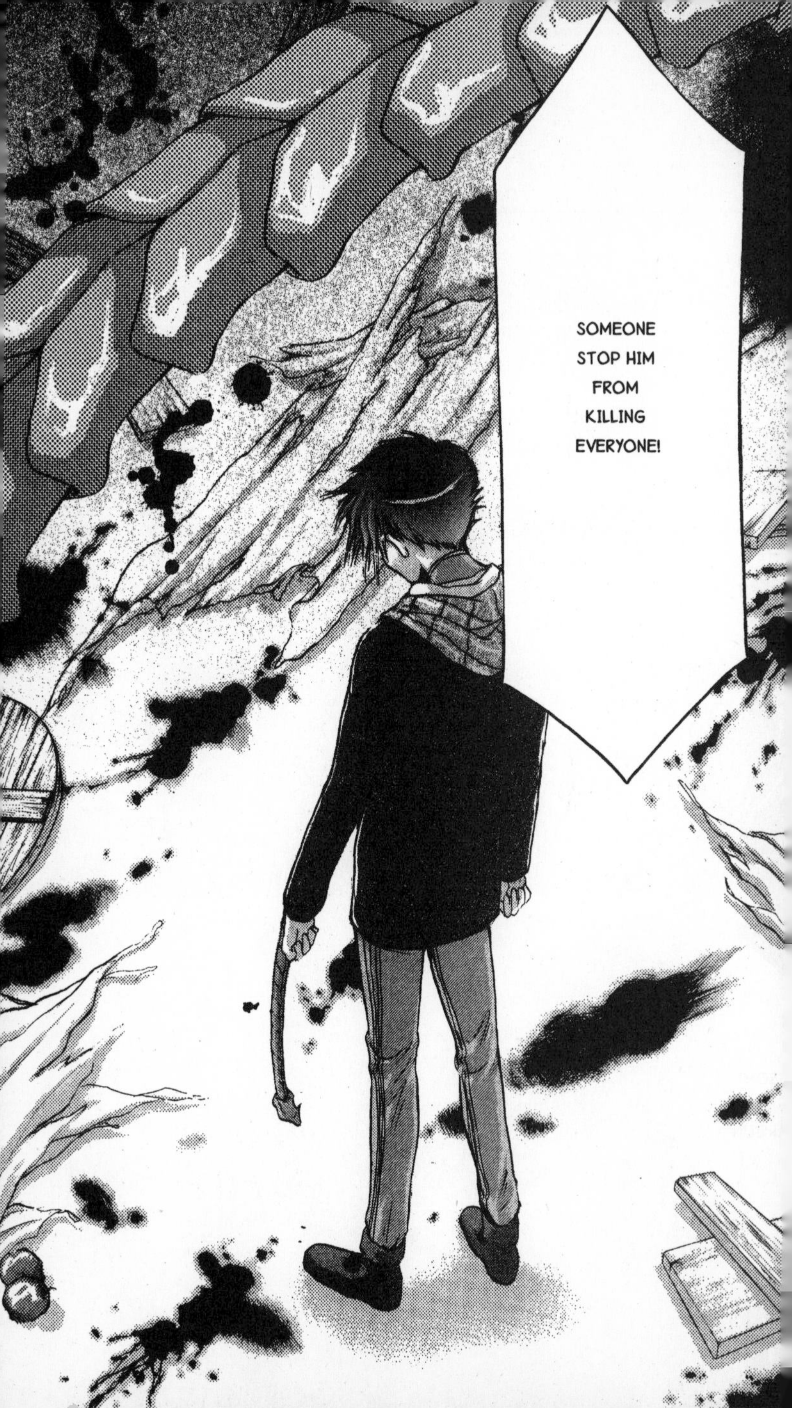
SOMEONE STOP HIM FROM KILLING EVERYONE!

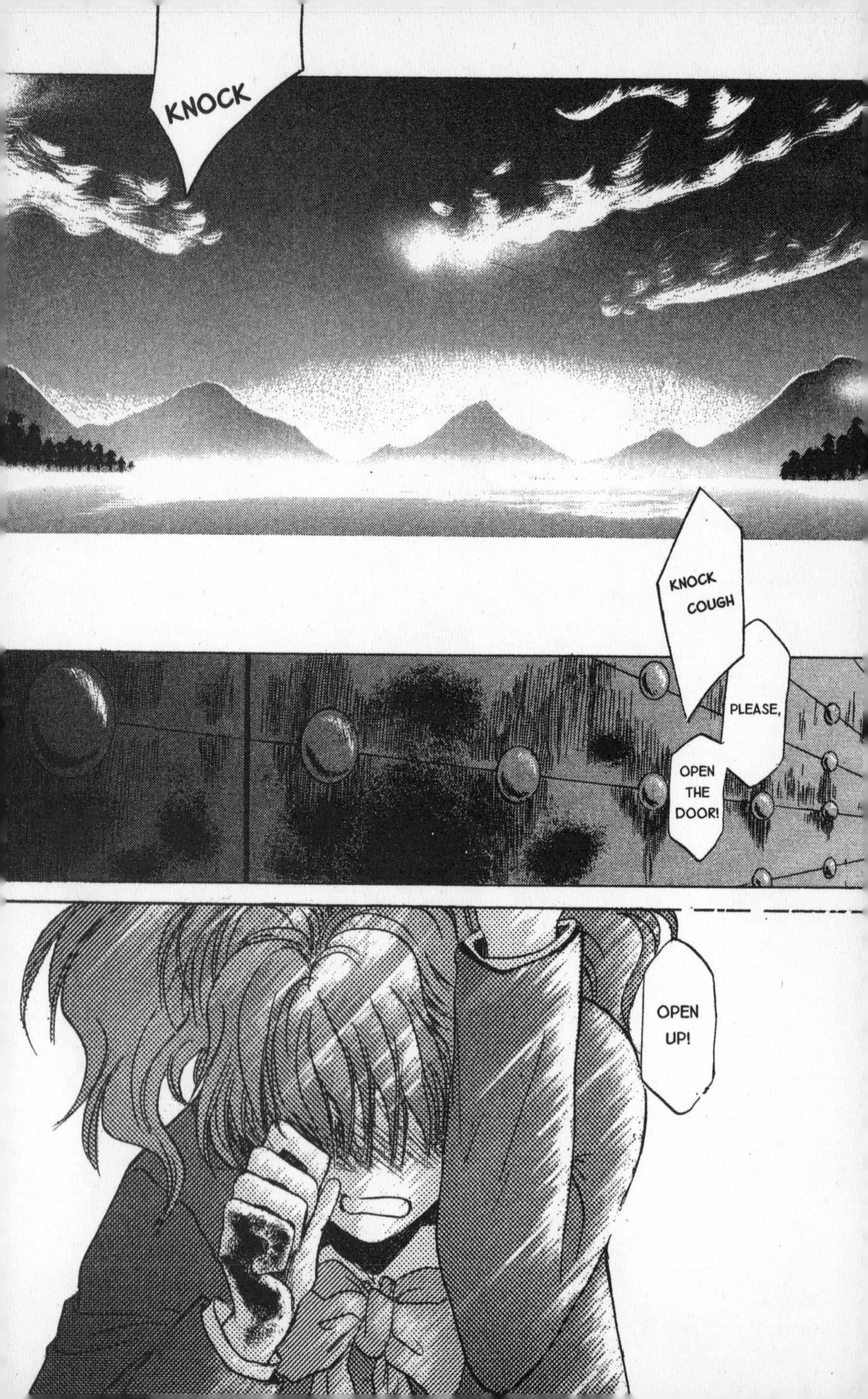
KNOCK
KNOCK COUGH
PLEASE,
OPEN THE DOOR!
OPEN UP!

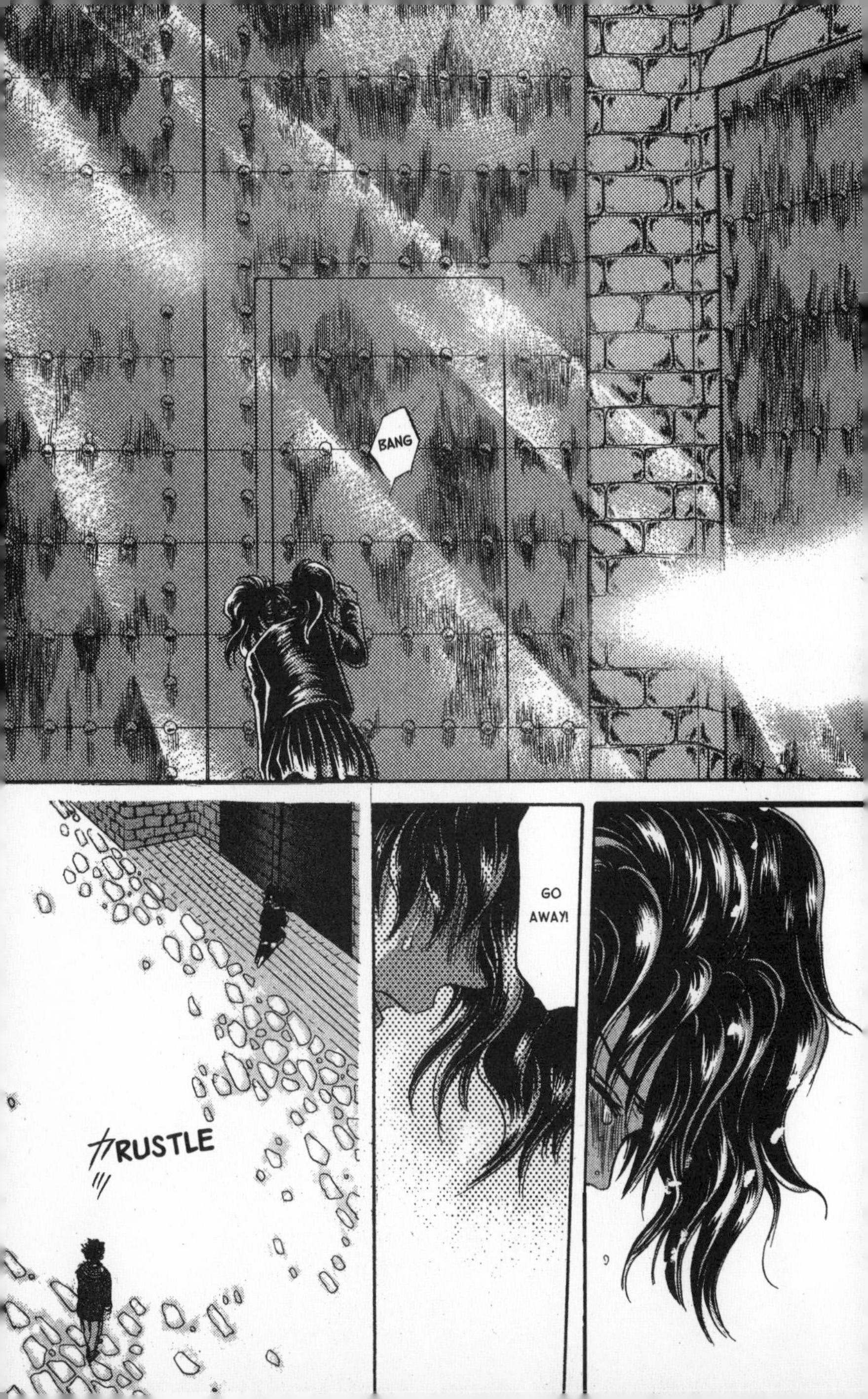
BANG
GO AWAY!
RUSTLE

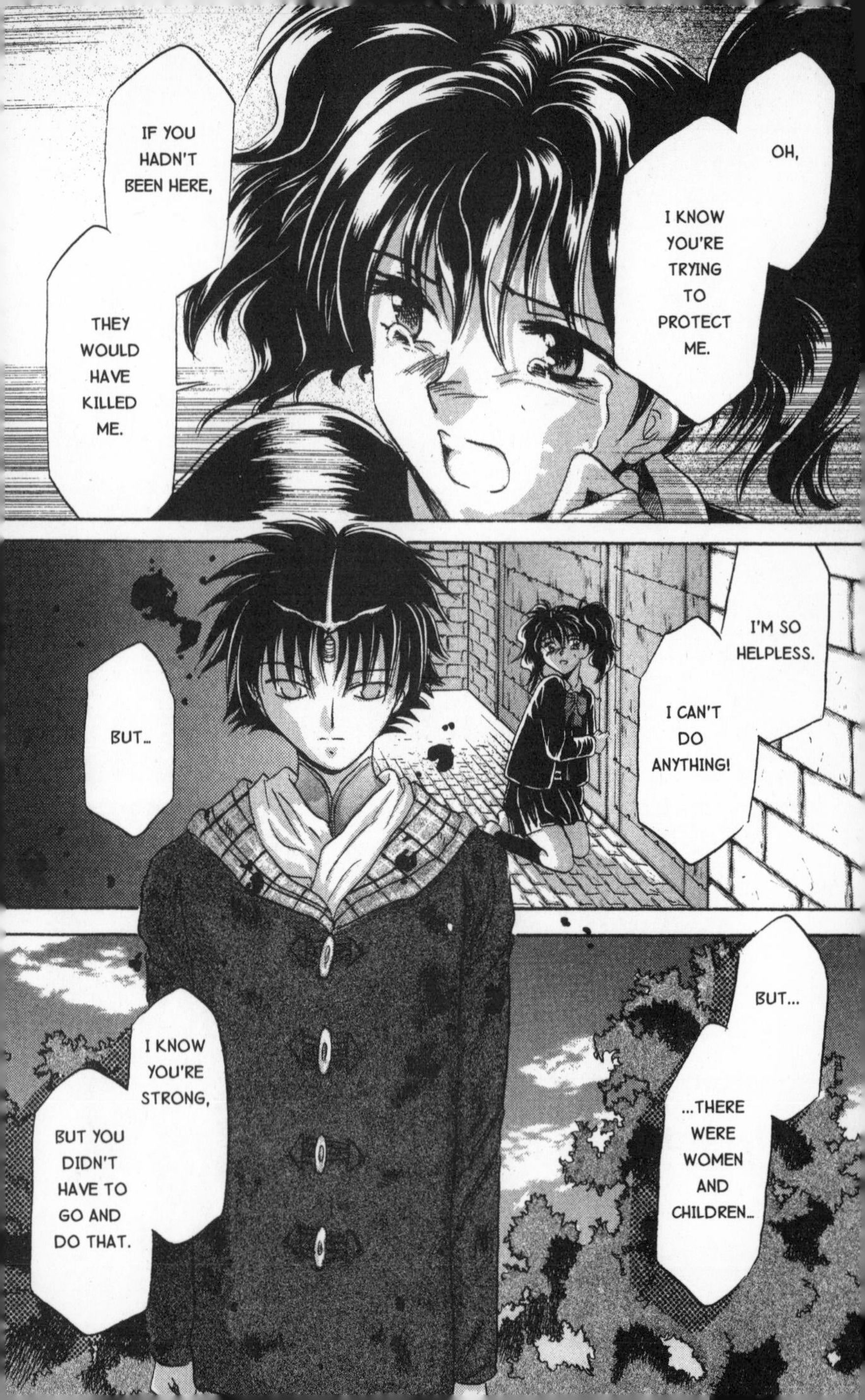
OH,
I KNOW YOU'RE TRYING TO PROTECT ME.
IF YOU HADN'T BEEN HERE,
THEY WOULD HAVE KILLED ME.
I'M SO HELPLESS.
I CAN'T DO ANYTHING!
BUT...
BUT...
...THERE WERE WOMEN AND CHILDREN...
I KNOW YOU'RE STRONG,
BUT YOU DIDN'T HAVE TO GO AND DO THAT.

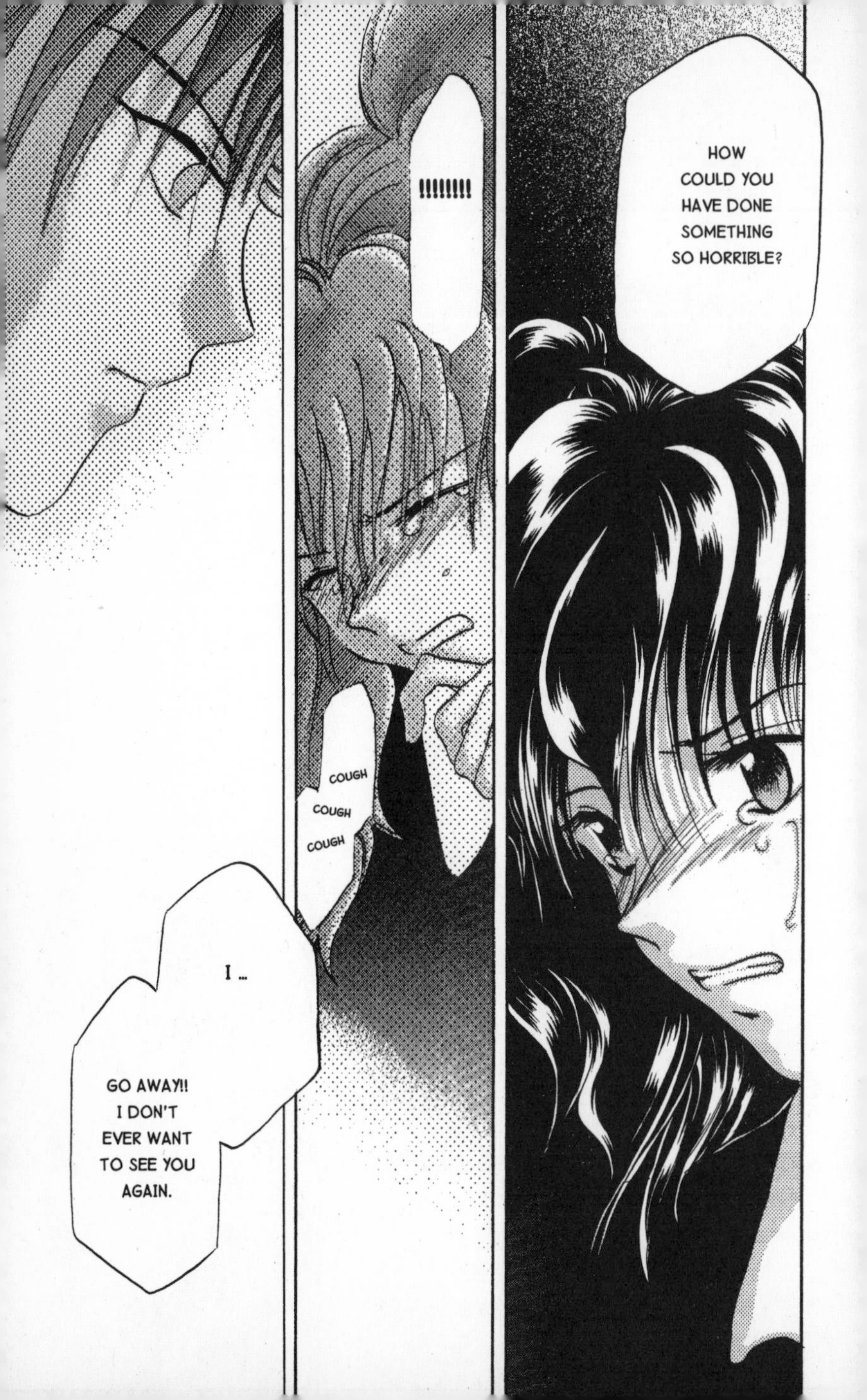
HOW COULD YOU HAVE DONE SOMETHING SO HORRIBLE?
!!!!!!!!
COUGH COUGH COUGH
I ...
GO AWAY!! I DON'T EVER WANT TO SEE YOU AGAIN.

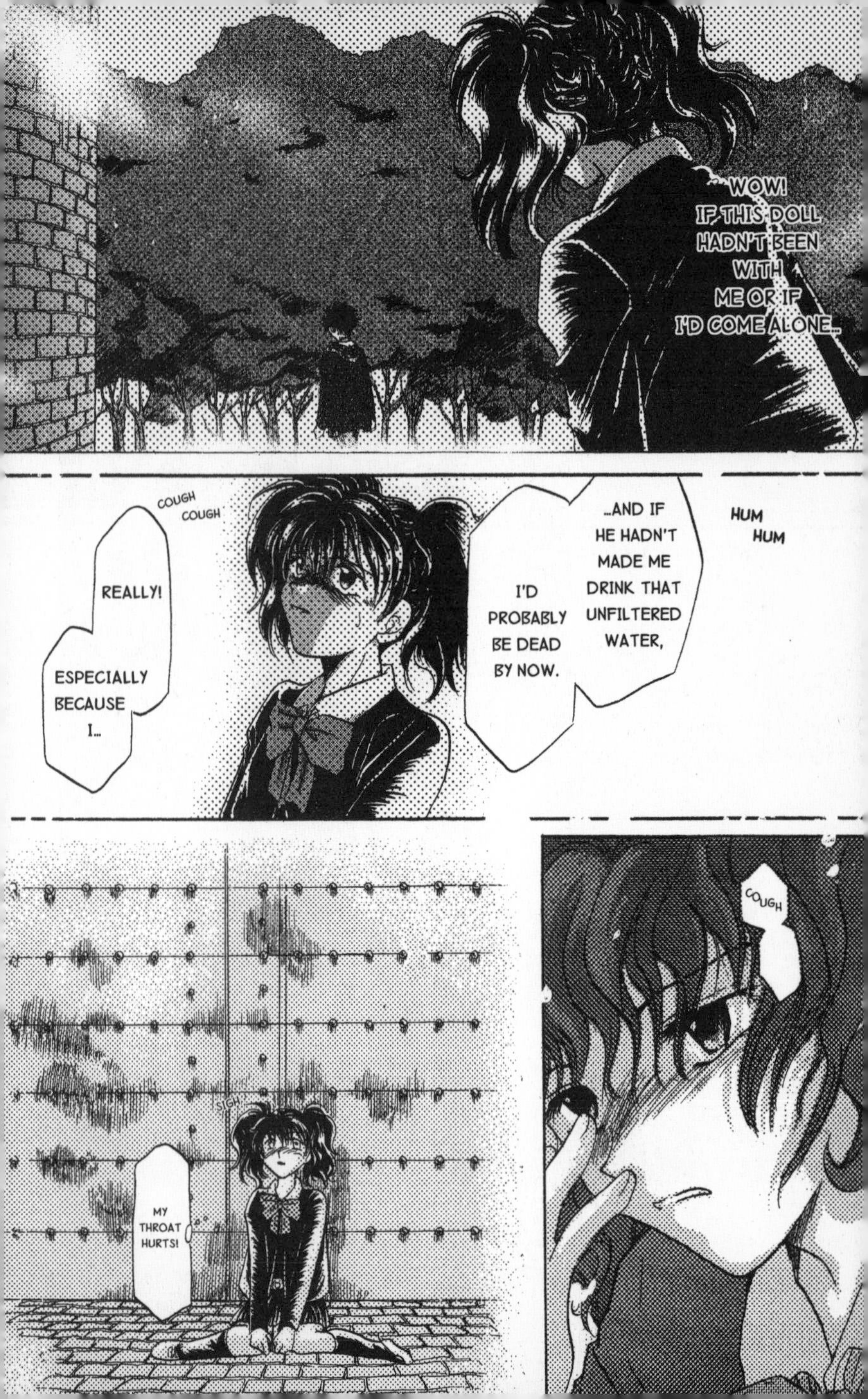
WOW! IF THIS DOLL HADN'T BEEN WITH ME OR IF I'D COME ALONE...
HUM HUM
...AND IF HE HADN'T MADE ME DRINK THAT UNFILTERED WATER,
I'D PROBABLY BE DEAD BY NOW.
COUGH COUGH
REALLY!
ESPECIALLY BECAUSE I...
COUGH
SIGH
MY THROAT HURTS!

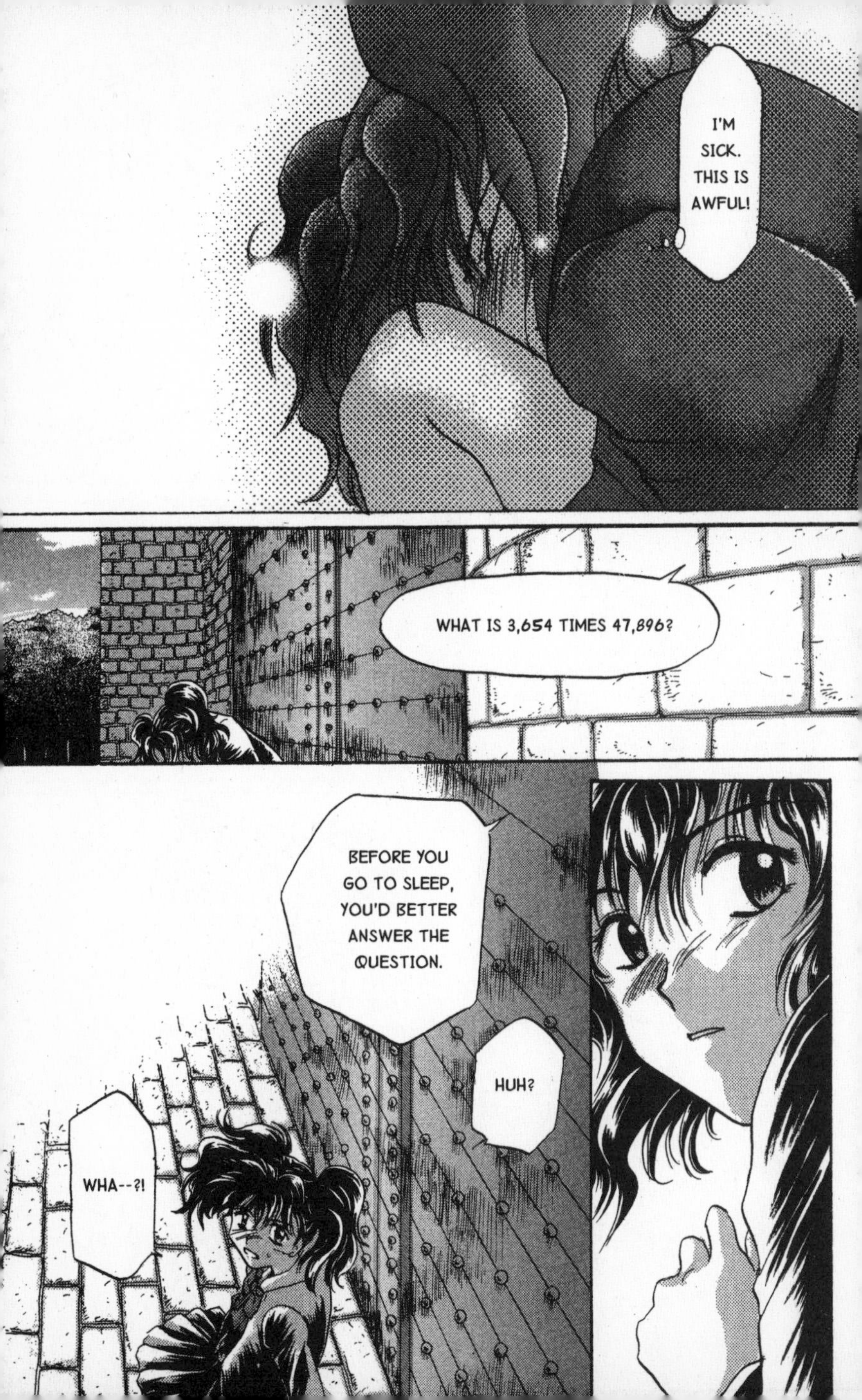
I'M SICK. THIS IS AWFUL!
WHAT IS 3,654 TIMES 47,896?
BEFORE YOU GO TO SLEEP, YOU'D BETTER ANSWER THE QUESTION.
HUH?
WHA--?!

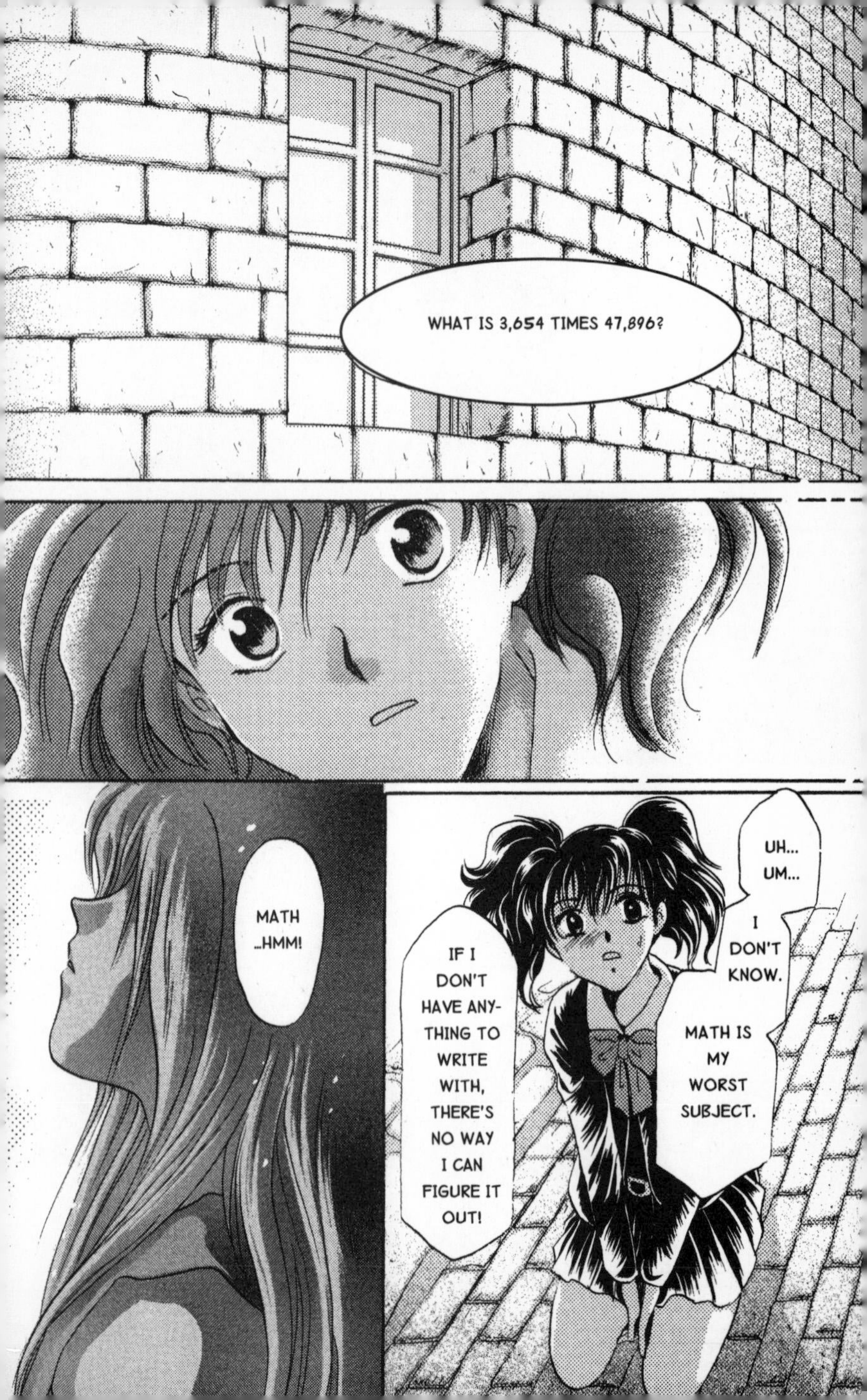
WHAT IS 3,654 TIMES 47,896?
UH... UM...
I DON'T KNOW.
MATH IS MY WORST SUBJECT.
IF I DON'T HAVE ANYTHING TO WRITE WITH, THERE'S NO WAY I CAN FIGURE IT OUT!
MATH ...HMM!

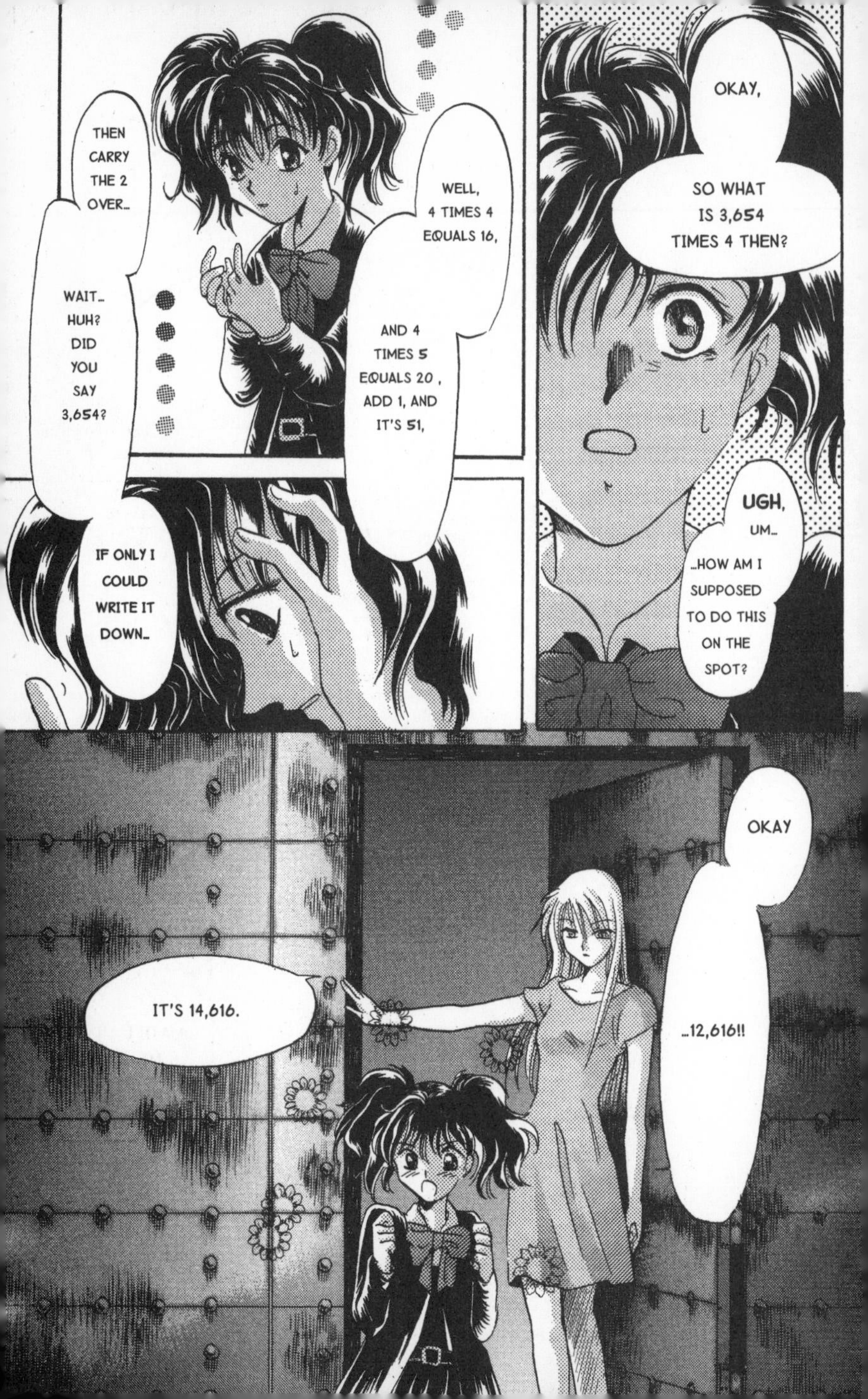
OKAY,
SO WHAT IS 3,654 TIMES 4 THEN?
UGH, UM...
...HOW AM I SUPPOSED TO DO THIS ON THE SPOT?
WELL, 4 TIMES 4 EQUALS 16,
AND 4 TIMES 5 EQUALS 20 , ADD 1, AND IT'S 51,
THEN CARRY THE 2 OVER...
WAIT... HUH? DID YOU SAY 3,654?
IF ONLY I COULD WRITE IT DOWN...
OKAY
...12,616!!
IT'S 14,616.

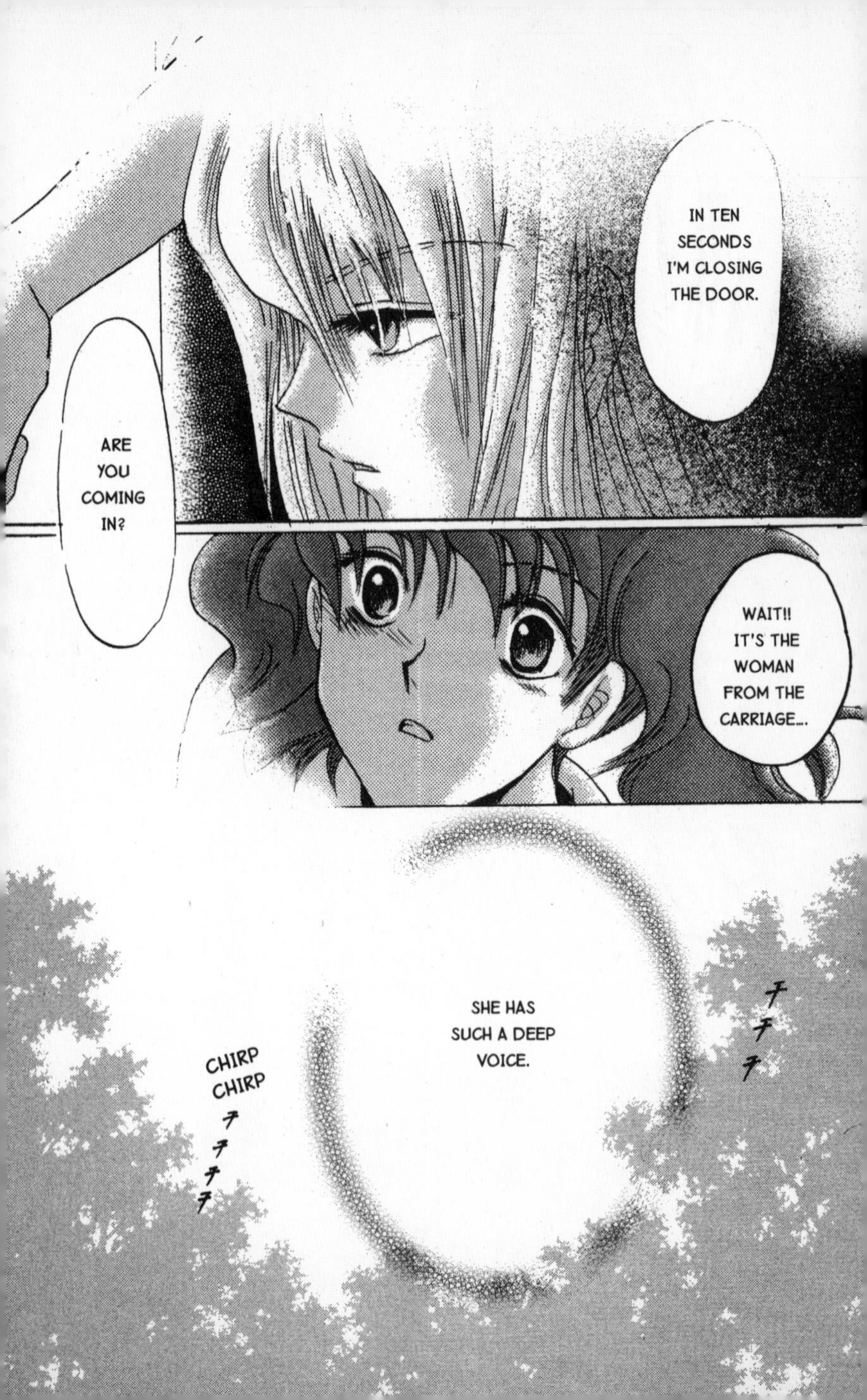
IN TEN SECONDS I'M CLOSING THE DOOR.
ARE YOU COMING IN?
WAIT!! IT'S THE WOMAN FROM THE CARRIAGE...
チチチ
SHE HAS SUCH A DEEP VOICE.
CHIRP CHIRP
チチチチ

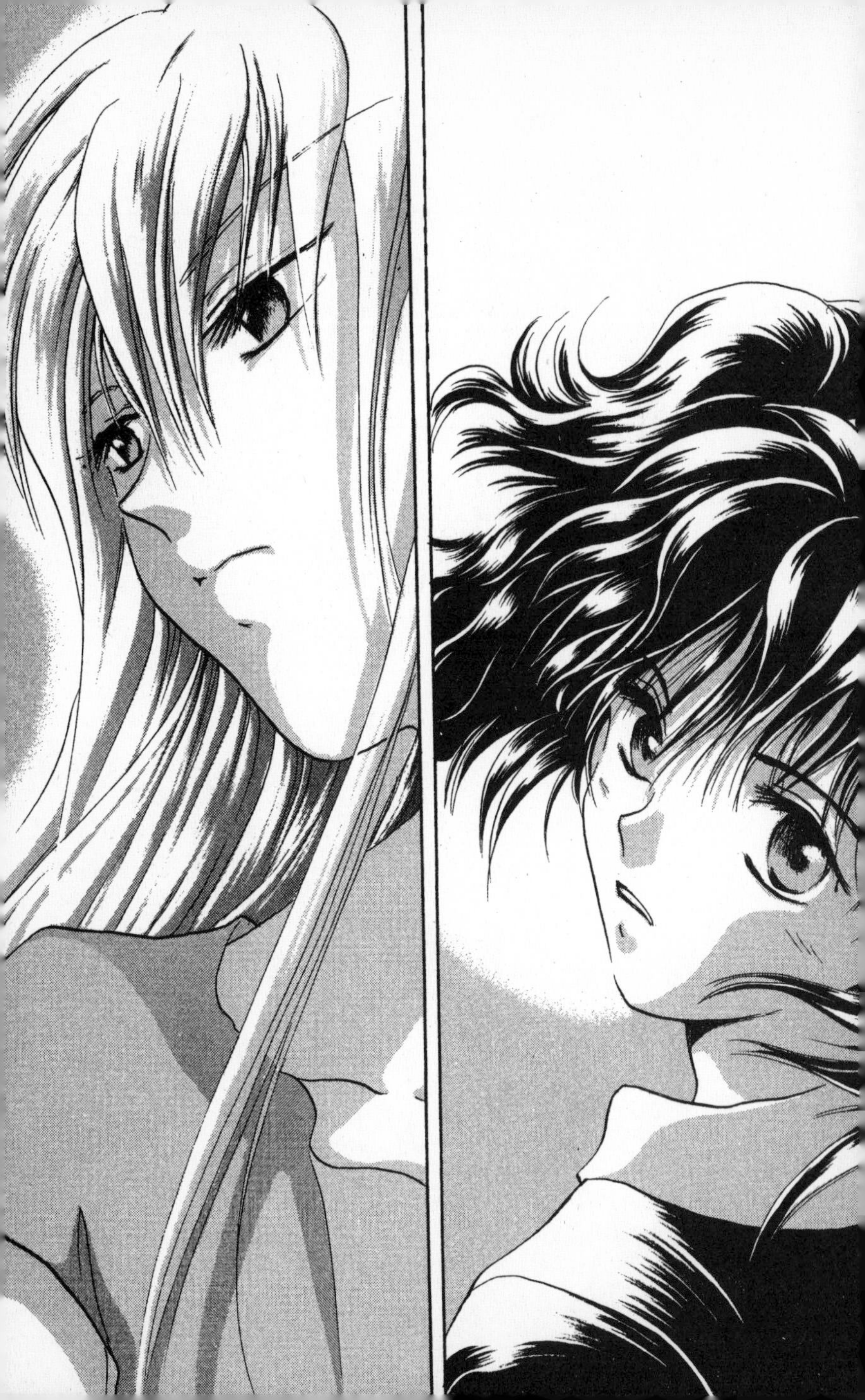

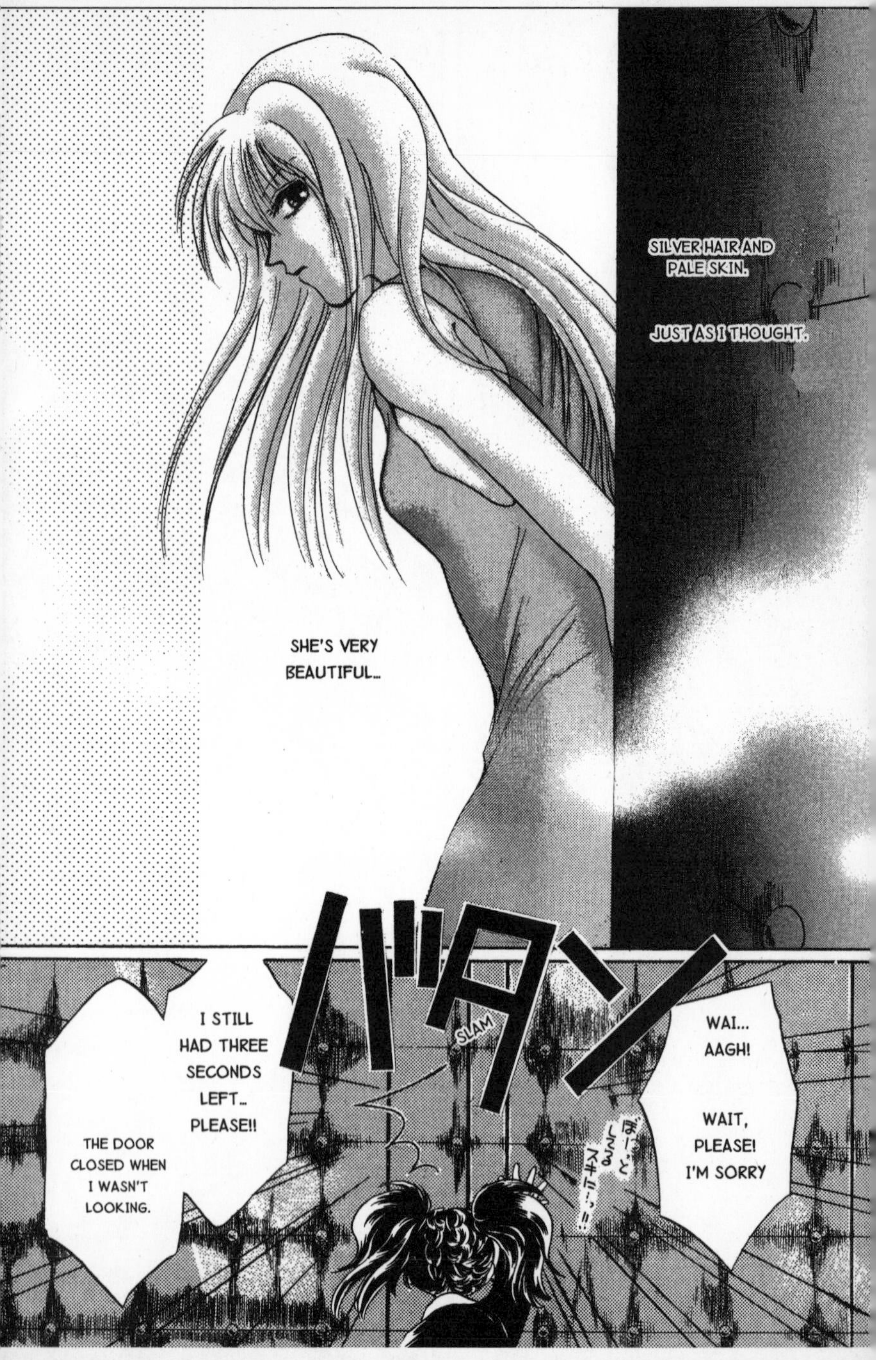
SILVER HAIR AND PALE SKIN.
JUST AS I THOUGHT.
SHE'S VERY BEAUTIFUL...
WAI... AAGH!
WAIT, PLEASE! I'M SORRY
ぼーっとしてるスキに…!!
バタン
SLAM
I STILL HAD THREE SECONDS LEFT... PLEASE!!
THE DOOR CLOSED WHEN I WASN'T LOOKING.

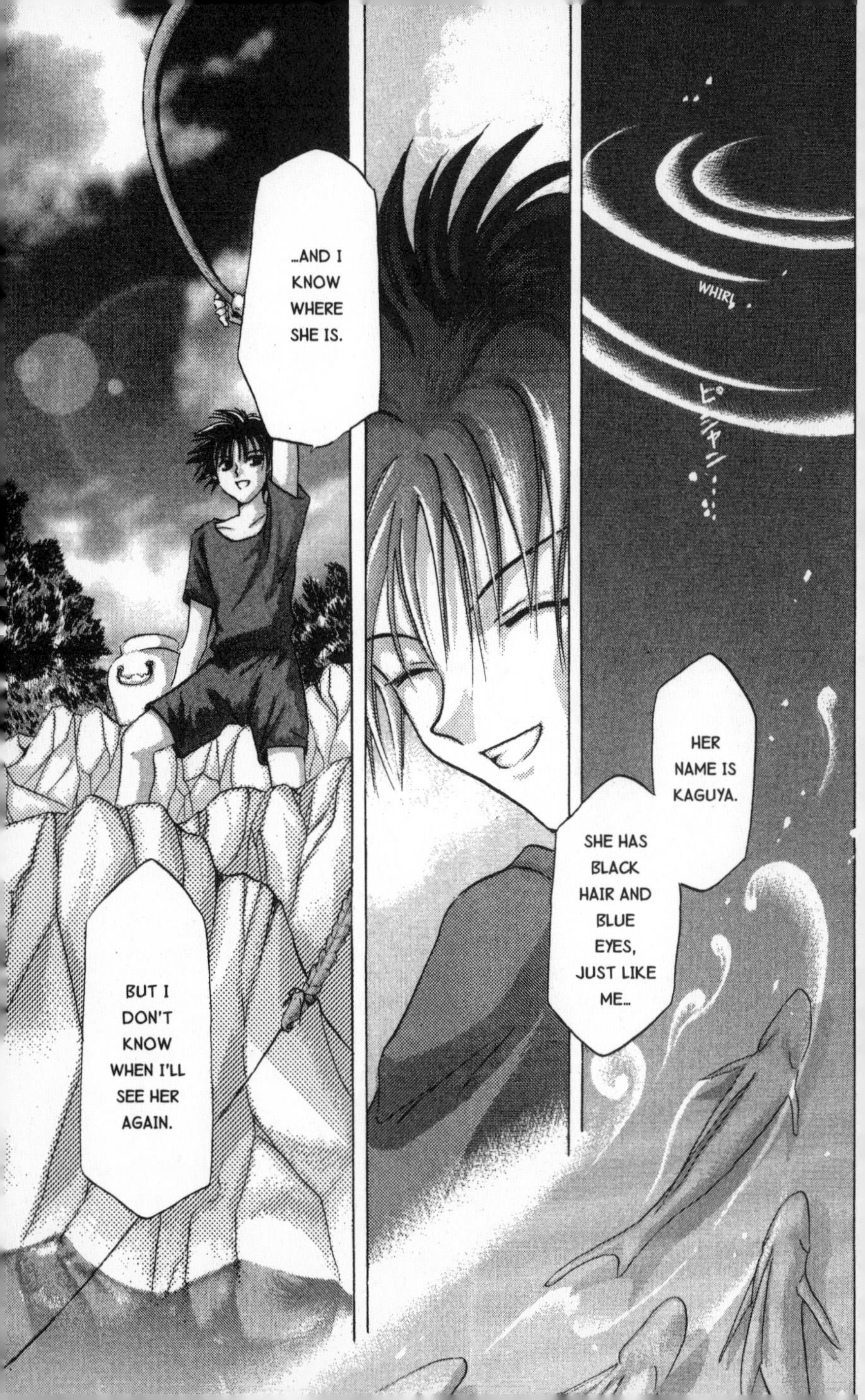
WHIRL
ピシャン…
HER NAME IS KAGUYA.
SHE HAS BLACK HAIR AND BLUE EYES, JUST LIKE ME…
…AND I KNOW WHERE SHE IS.
BUT I DON'T KNOW WHEN I'LL SEE HER AGAIN.

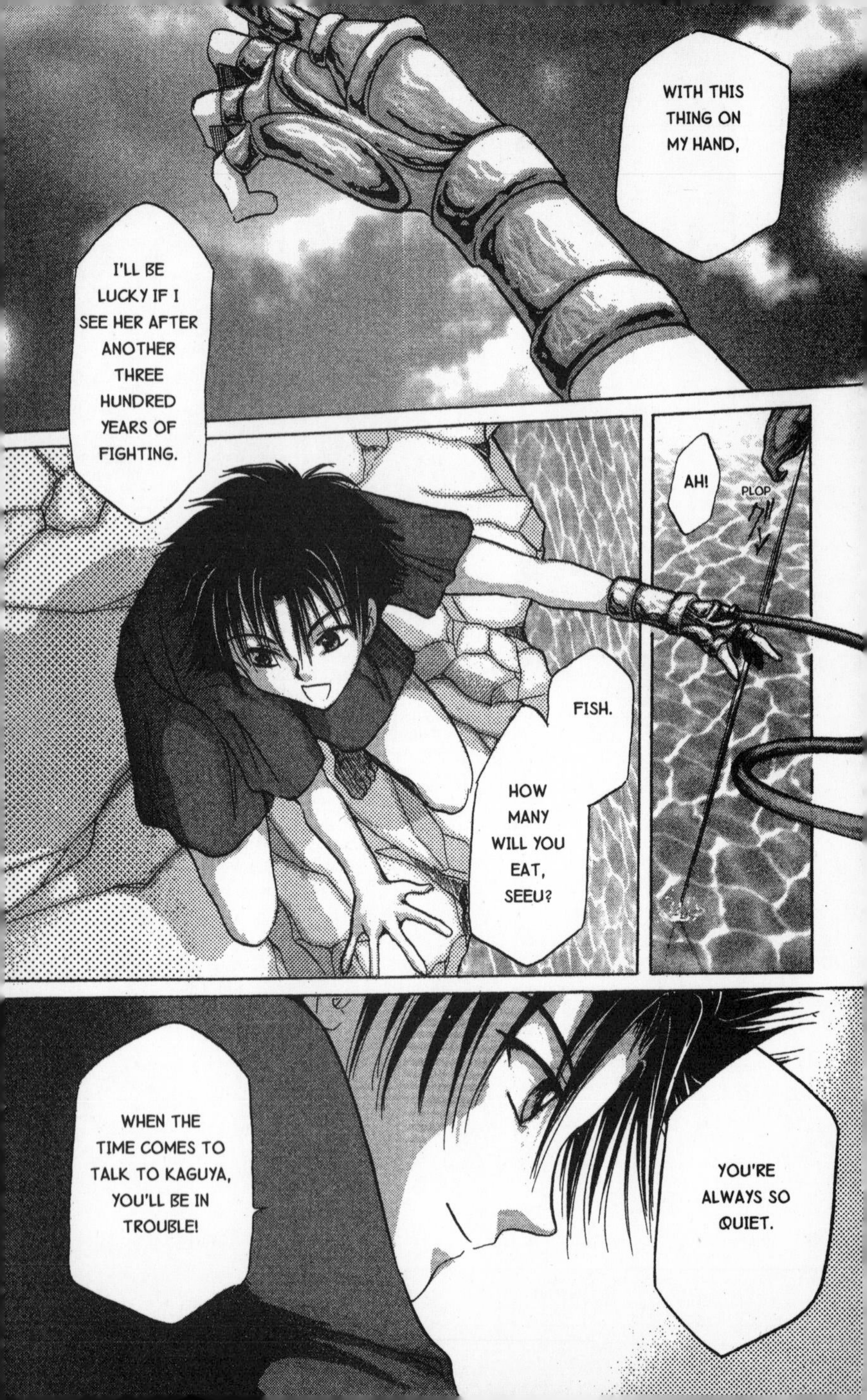
WITH THIS THING ON MY HAND,
I'LL BE LUCKY IF I SEE HER AFTER ANOTHER THREE HUNDRED YEARS OF FIGHTING.
AH!
PLOP
FISH.
HOW MANY WILL YOU EAT, SEEU?
YOU'RE ALWAYS SO QUIET.
WHEN THE TIME COMES TO TALK TO KAGUYA, YOU'LL BE IN TROUBLE!

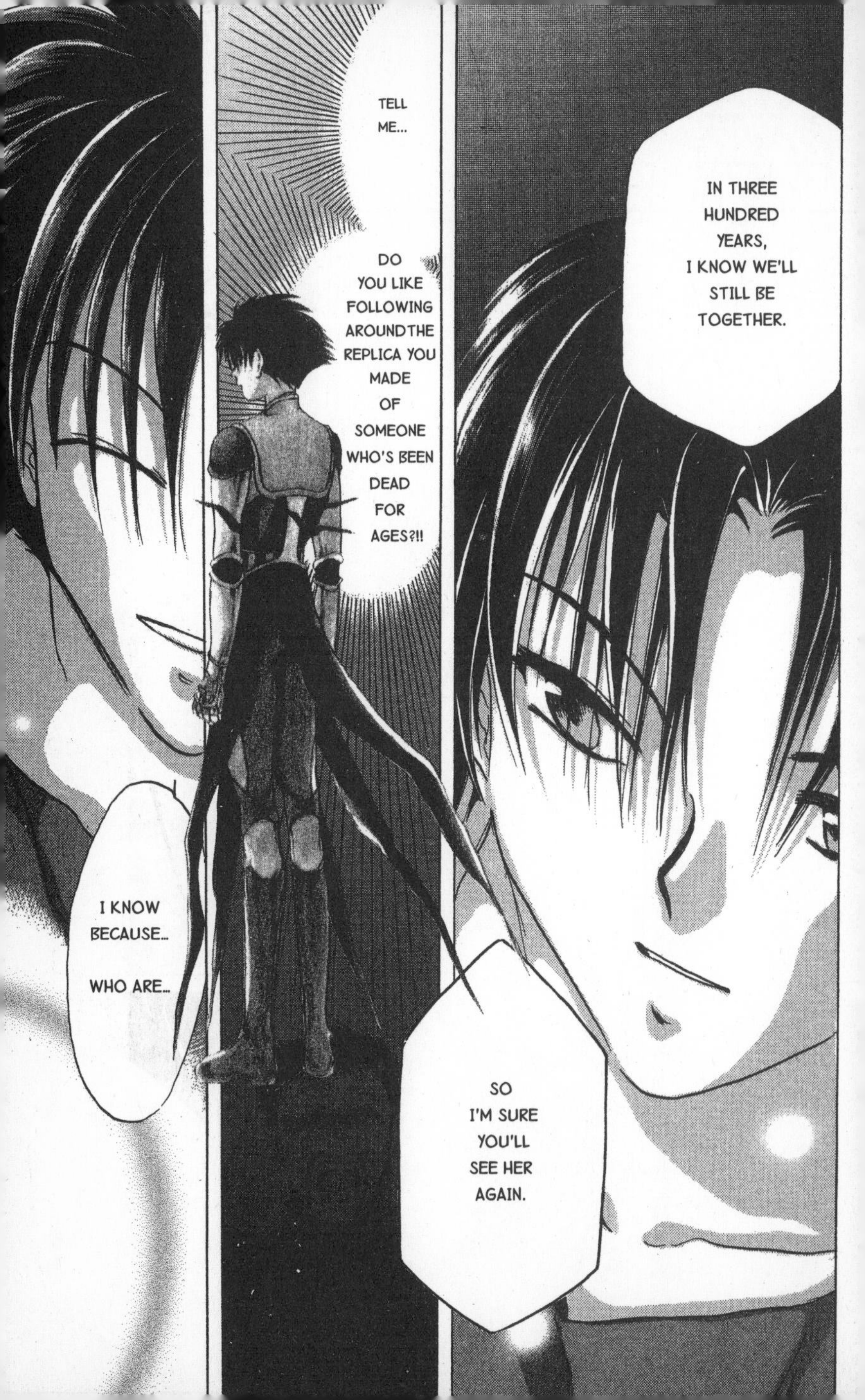
IN THREE HUNDRED YEARS, I KNOW WE'LL STILL BE TOGETHER.
SO I'M SURE YOU'LL SEE HER AGAIN.
TELL ME...
DO YOU LIKE FOLLOWING AROUND THE REPLICA YOU MADE OF SOMEONE WHO'S BEEN DEAD FOR AGES?!!
I KNOW BECAUSE...
WHO ARE...

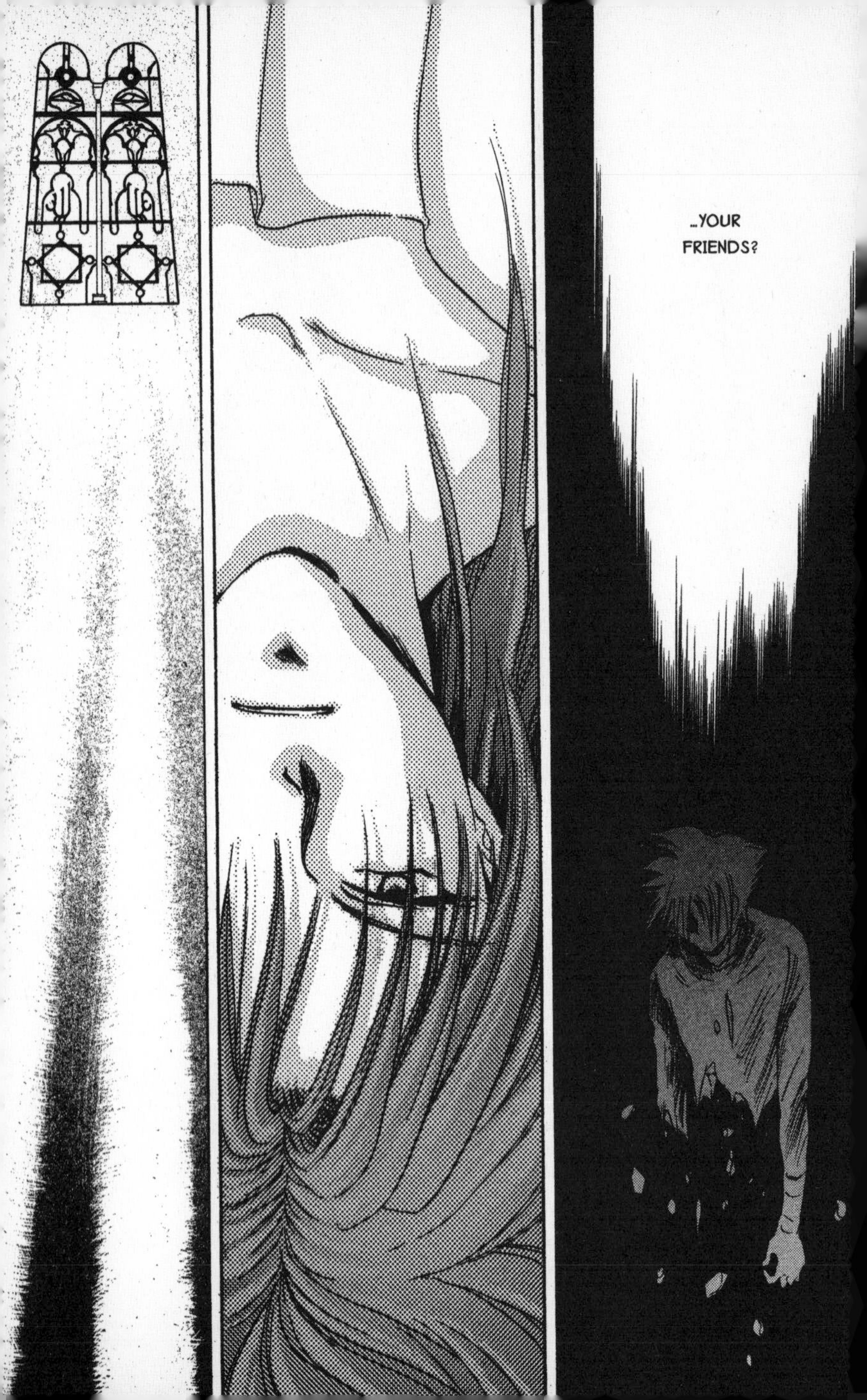
...YOUR FRIENDS?

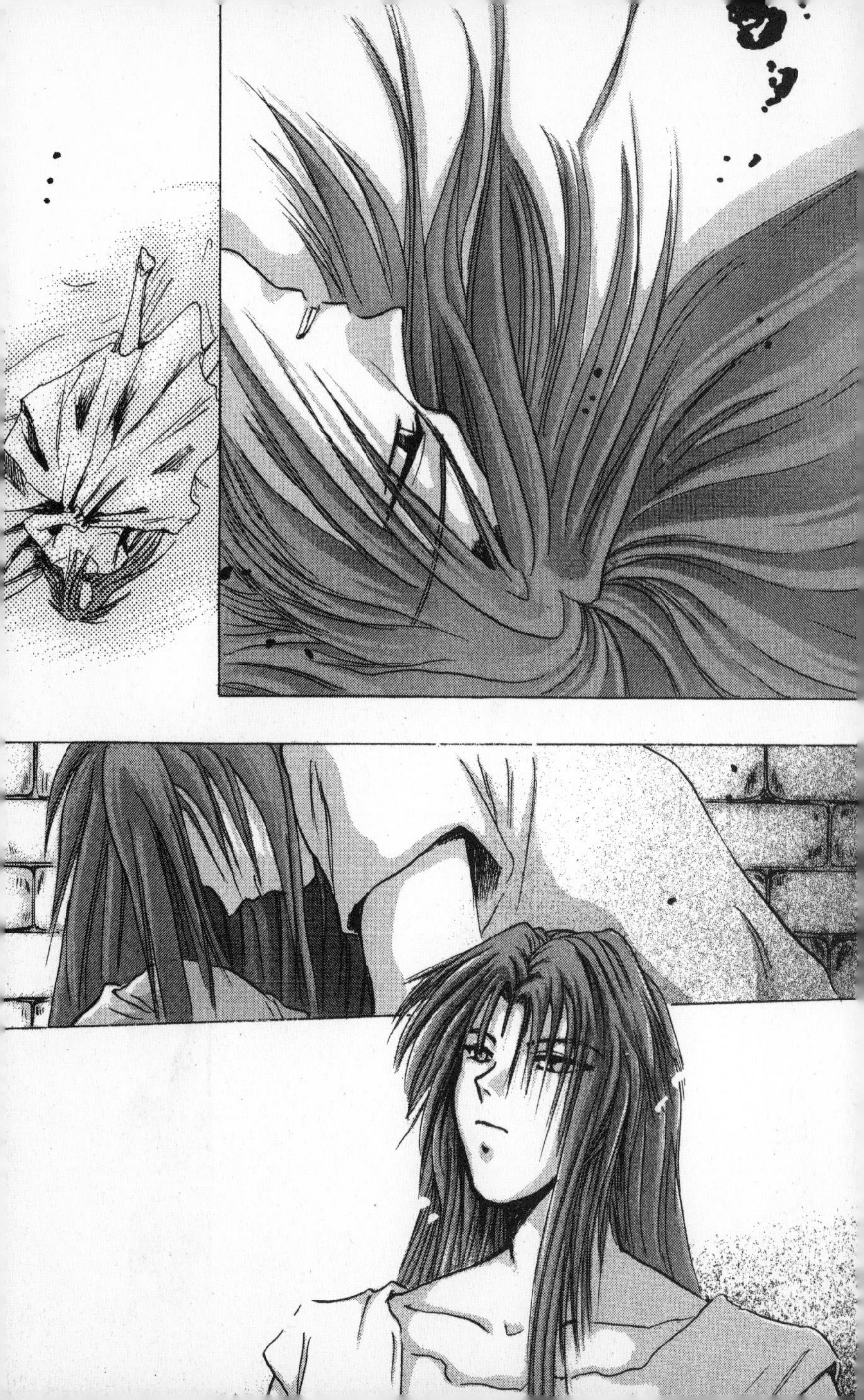

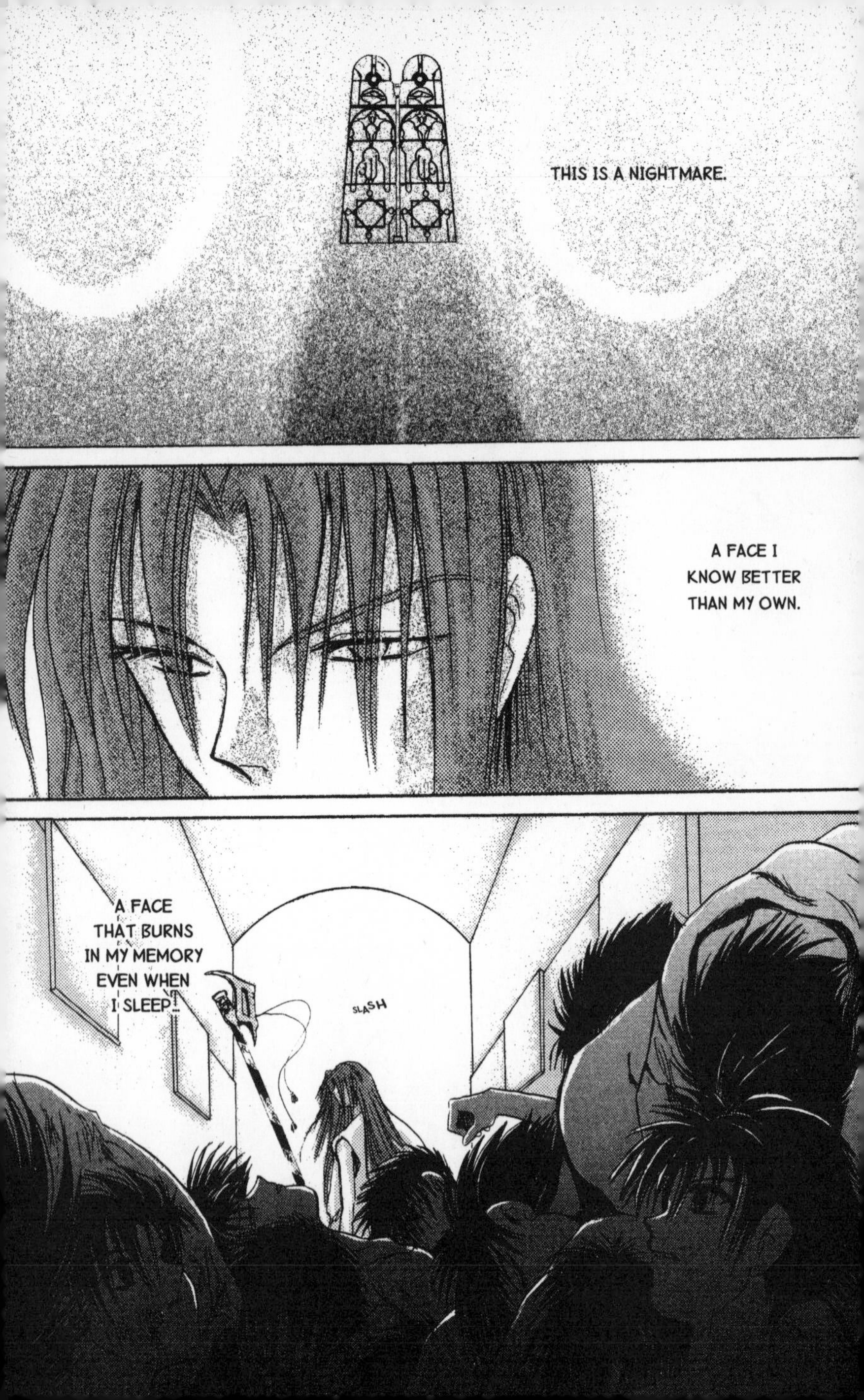
THIS IS A NIGHTMARE.
A FACE I KNOW BETTER THAN MY OWN.
A FACE THAT BURNS IN MY MEMORY EVEN WHEN I SLEEP...
SLASH

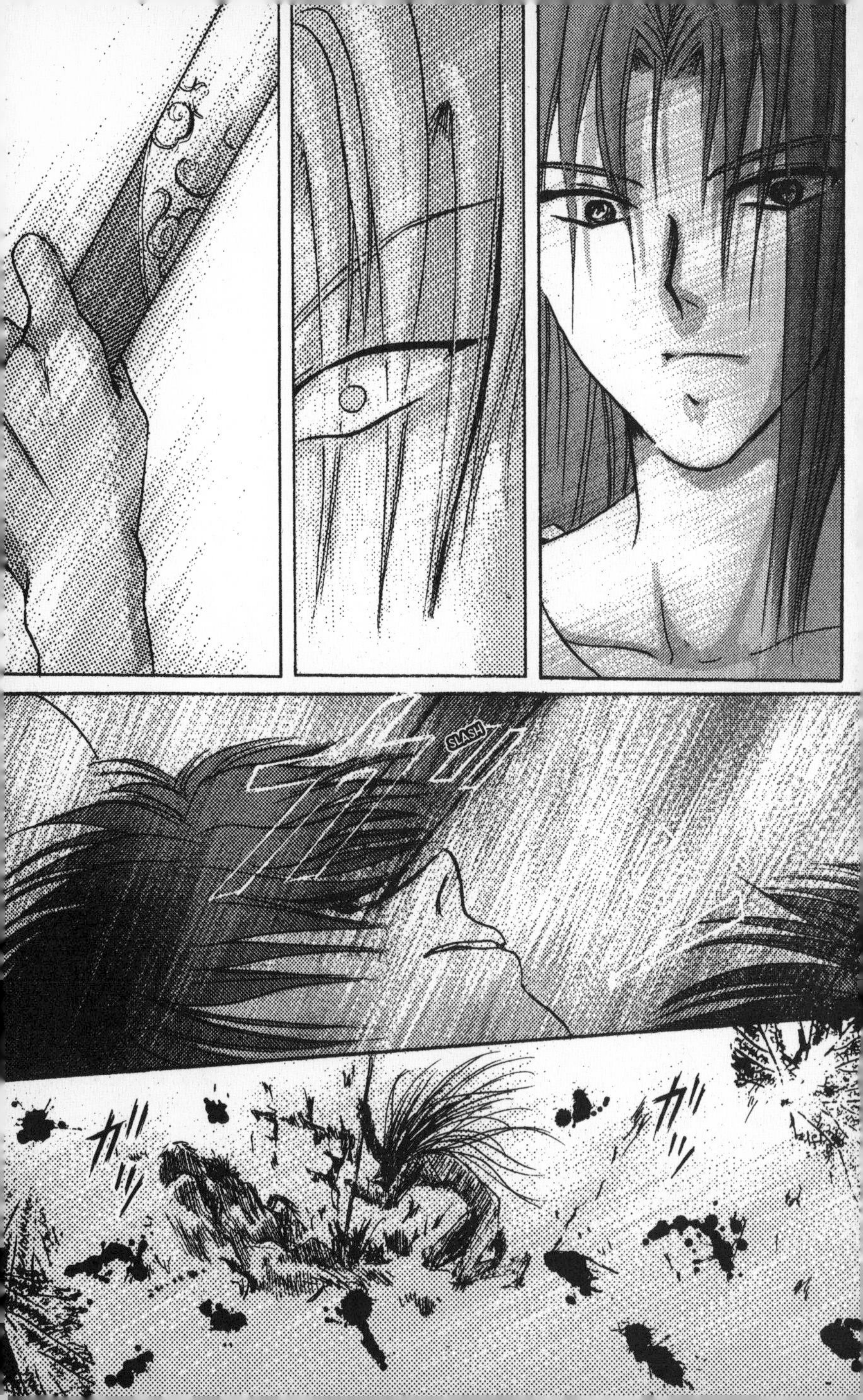
SLASH

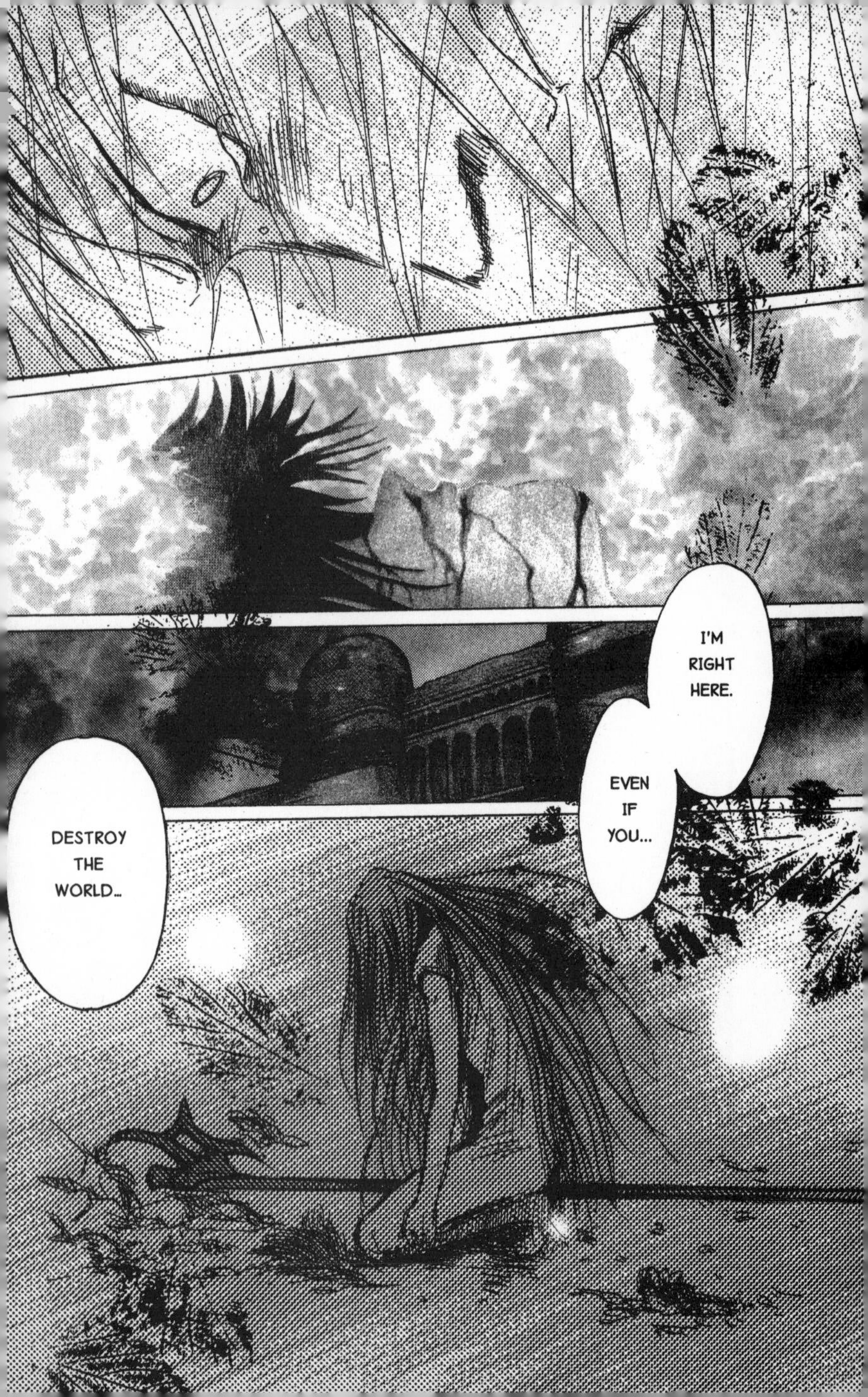
I'M RIGHT HERE.
EVEN IF YOU...
DESTROY THE WORLD...

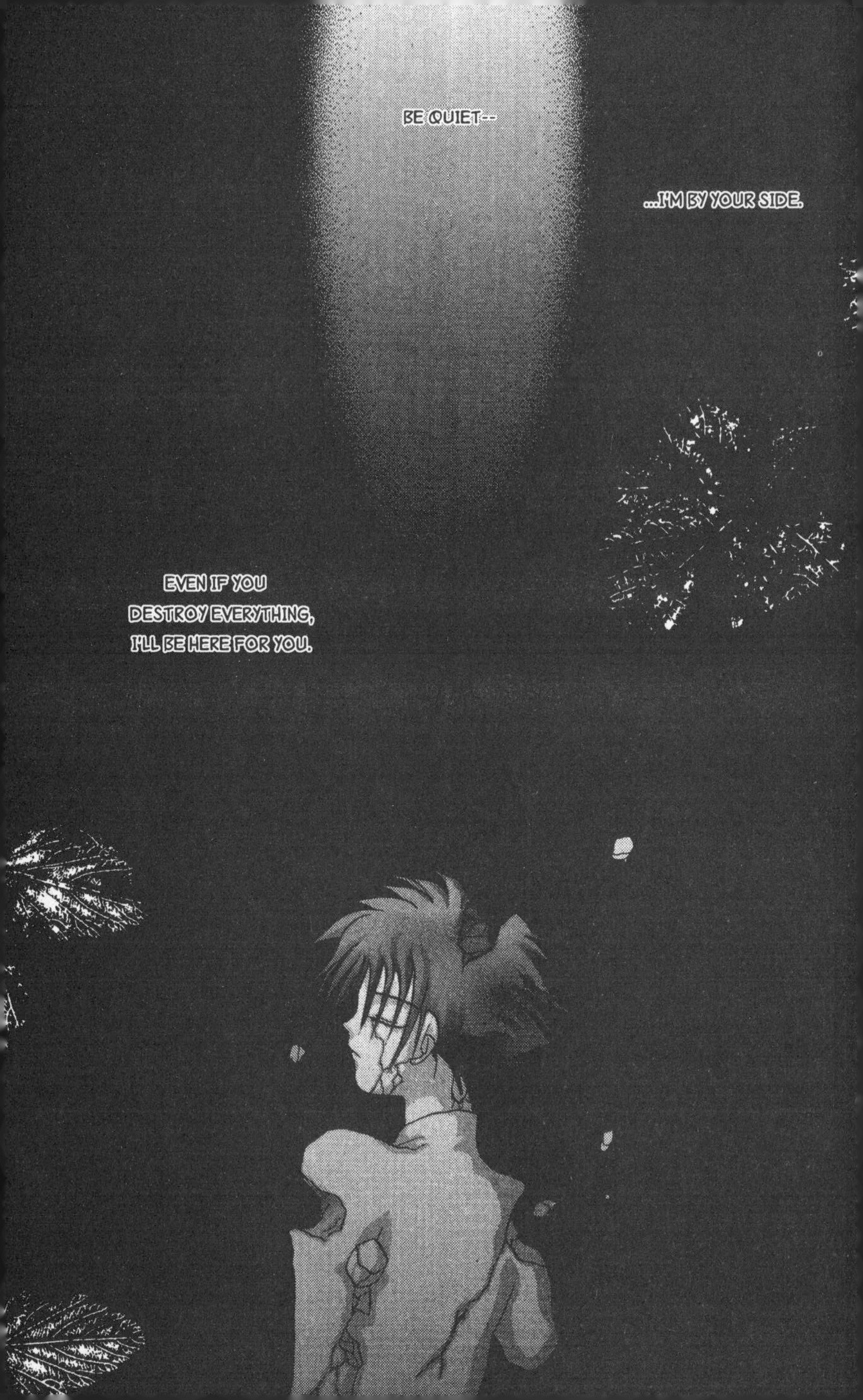
BE QUIET--
...I'M BY YOUR SIDE.
EVEN IF YOU DESTROY EVERYTHING, I'LL BE HERE FOR YOU.

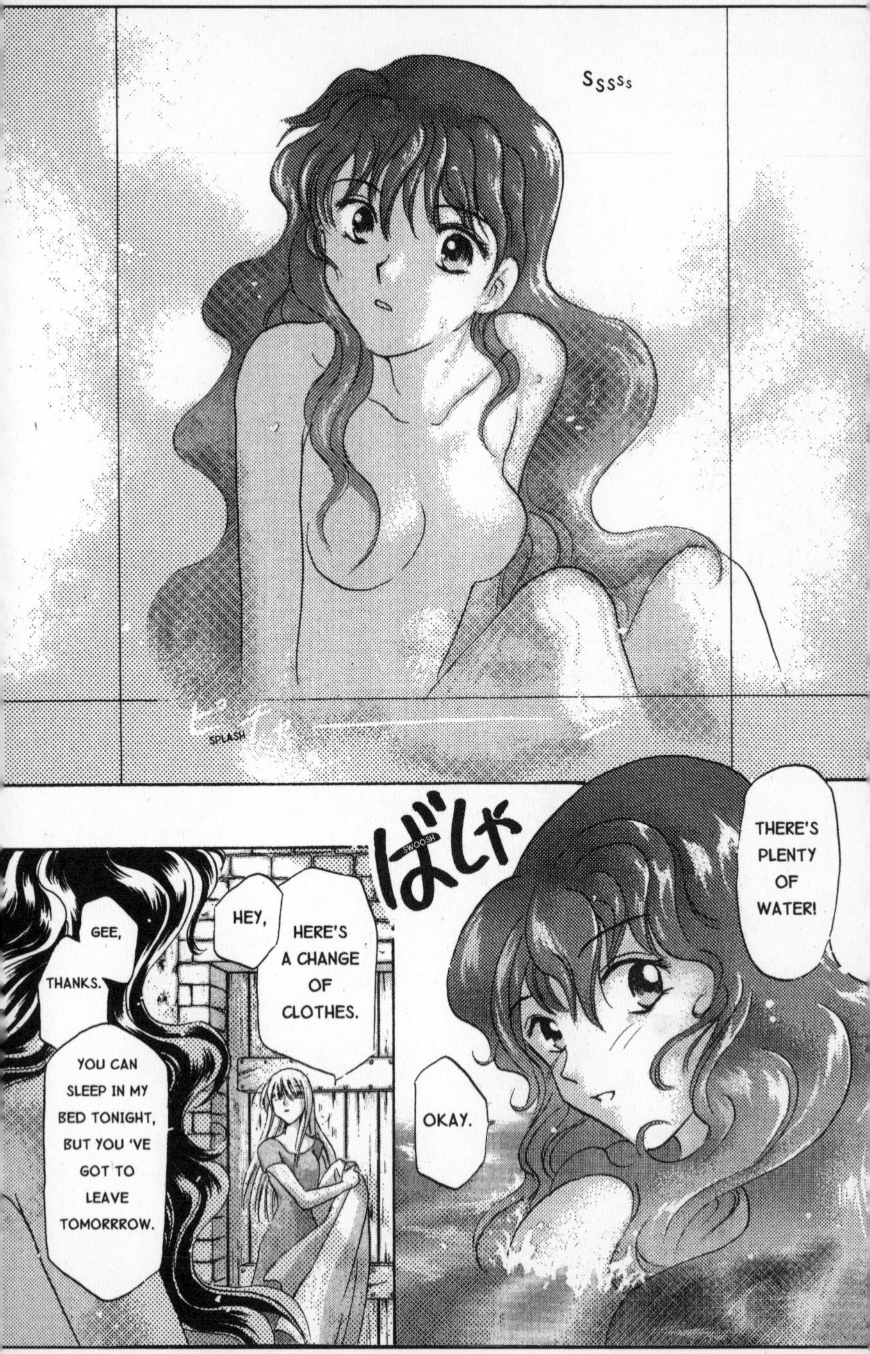
Sssss
SPLASH
ばしゃ
SWOOSH
THERE'S PLENTY OF WATER!
OKAY.
HEY,
HERE'S A CHANGE OF CLOTHES.
GEE,
THANKS.
YOU CAN SLEEP IN MY BED TONIGHT, BUT YOU 'VE GOT TO LEAVE TOMORRROW.

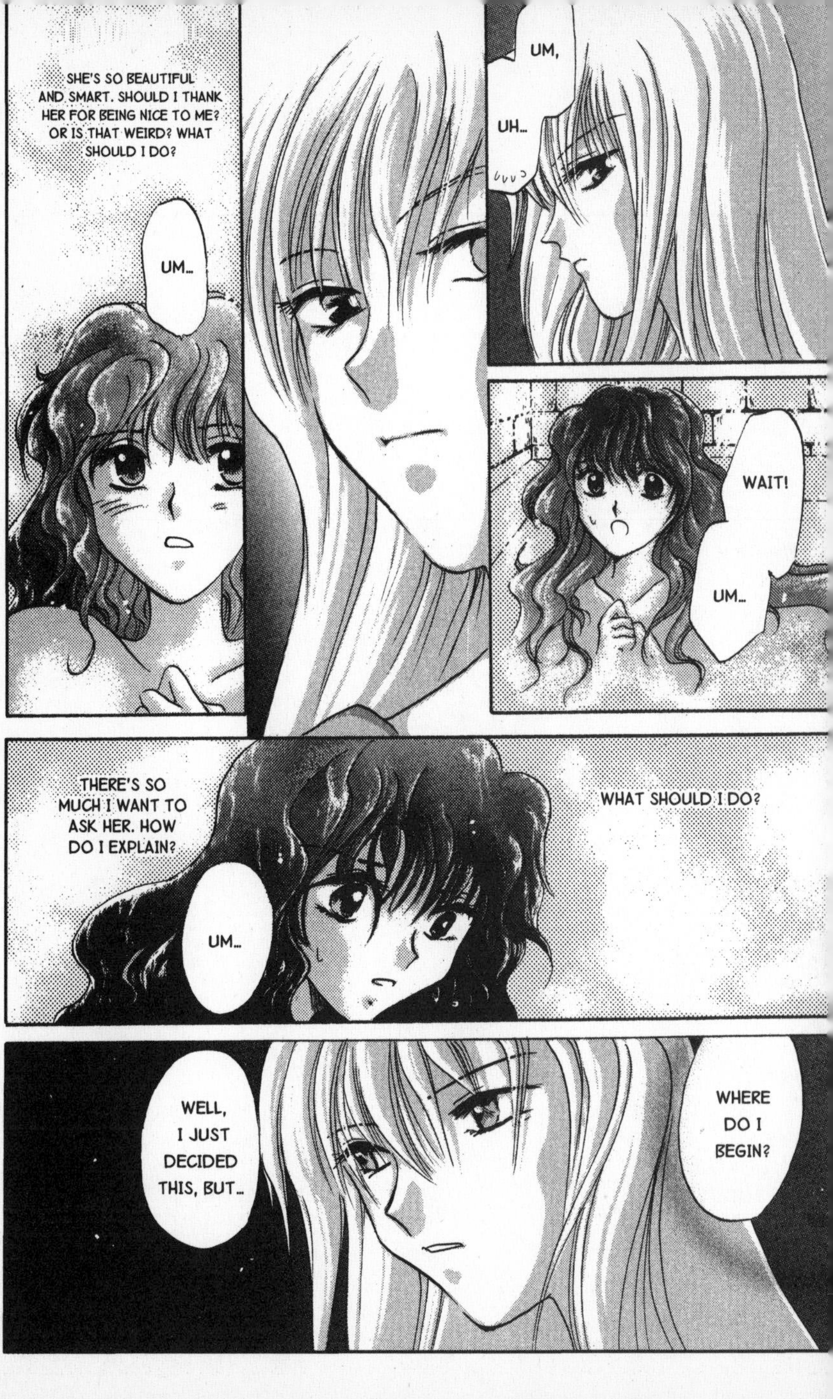
UM,
UH...
WAIT!
UM...
SHE'S SO BEAUTIFUL AND SMART. SHOULD I THANK HER FOR BEING NICE TO ME? OR IS THAT WEIRD? WHAT SHOULD I DO?
UM...
WHAT SHOULD I DO?
THERE'S SO MUCH I WANT TO ASK HER. HOW DO I EXPLAIN?
UM...
WHERE DO I BEGIN?
WELL, I JUST DECIDED THIS, BUT...

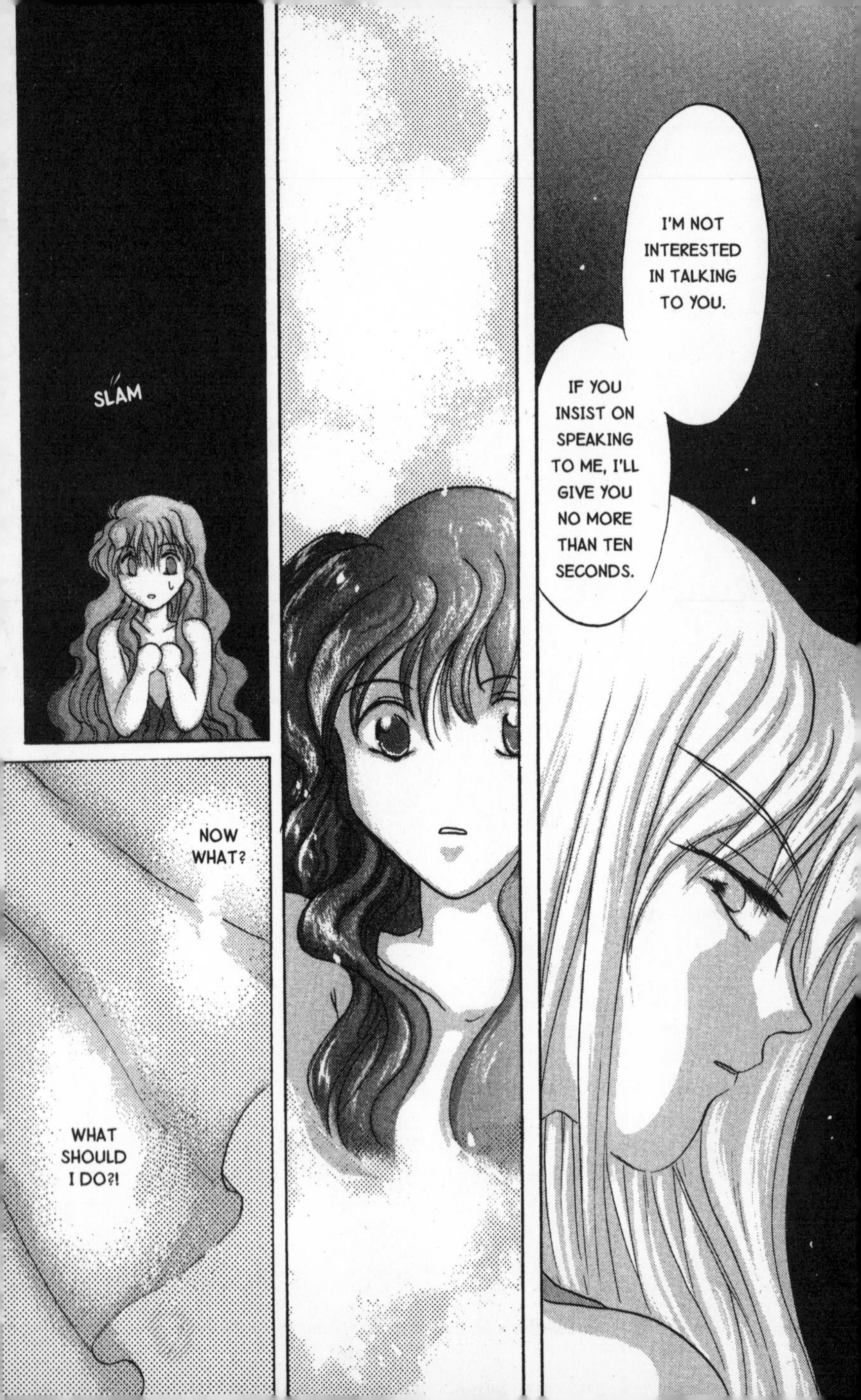
I'M NOT INTERESTED IN TALKING TO YOU.
IF YOU INSIST ON SPEAKING TO ME, I'LL GIVE YOU NO MORE THAN TEN SECONDS.
SLAM
NOW WHAT?
WHAT SHOULD I DO?!

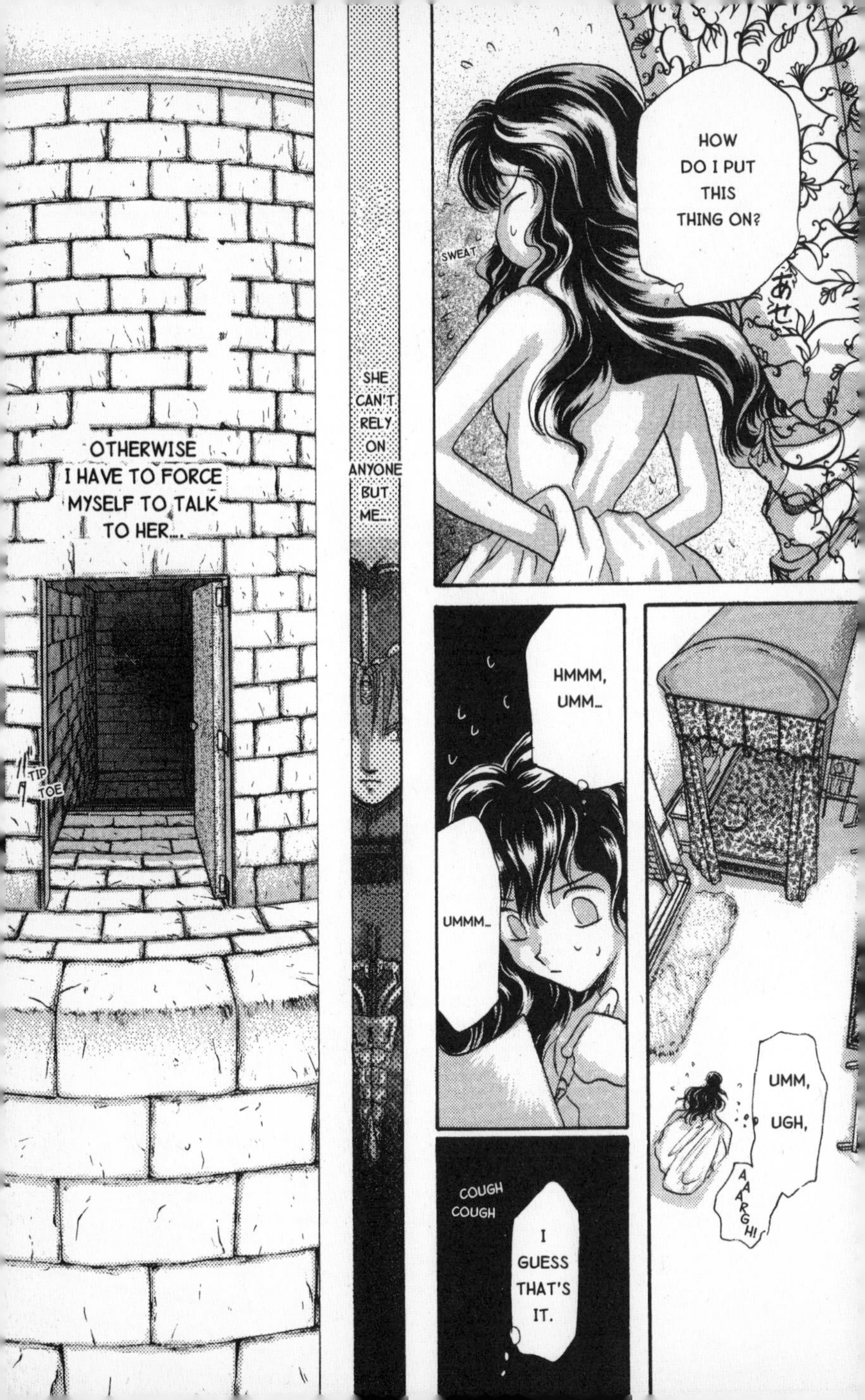
HOW DO I PUT THIS THING ON?
SWEAT
あせ
UMM, UGH,
AAARGH!
HMMM, UMM...
UMMM...
COUGH COUGH
I GUESS THAT'S IT.
SHE CAN'T RELY ON ANYONE BUT ME...
OTHERWISE I HAVE TO FORCE MYSELF TO TALK TO HER...
TIP TOE

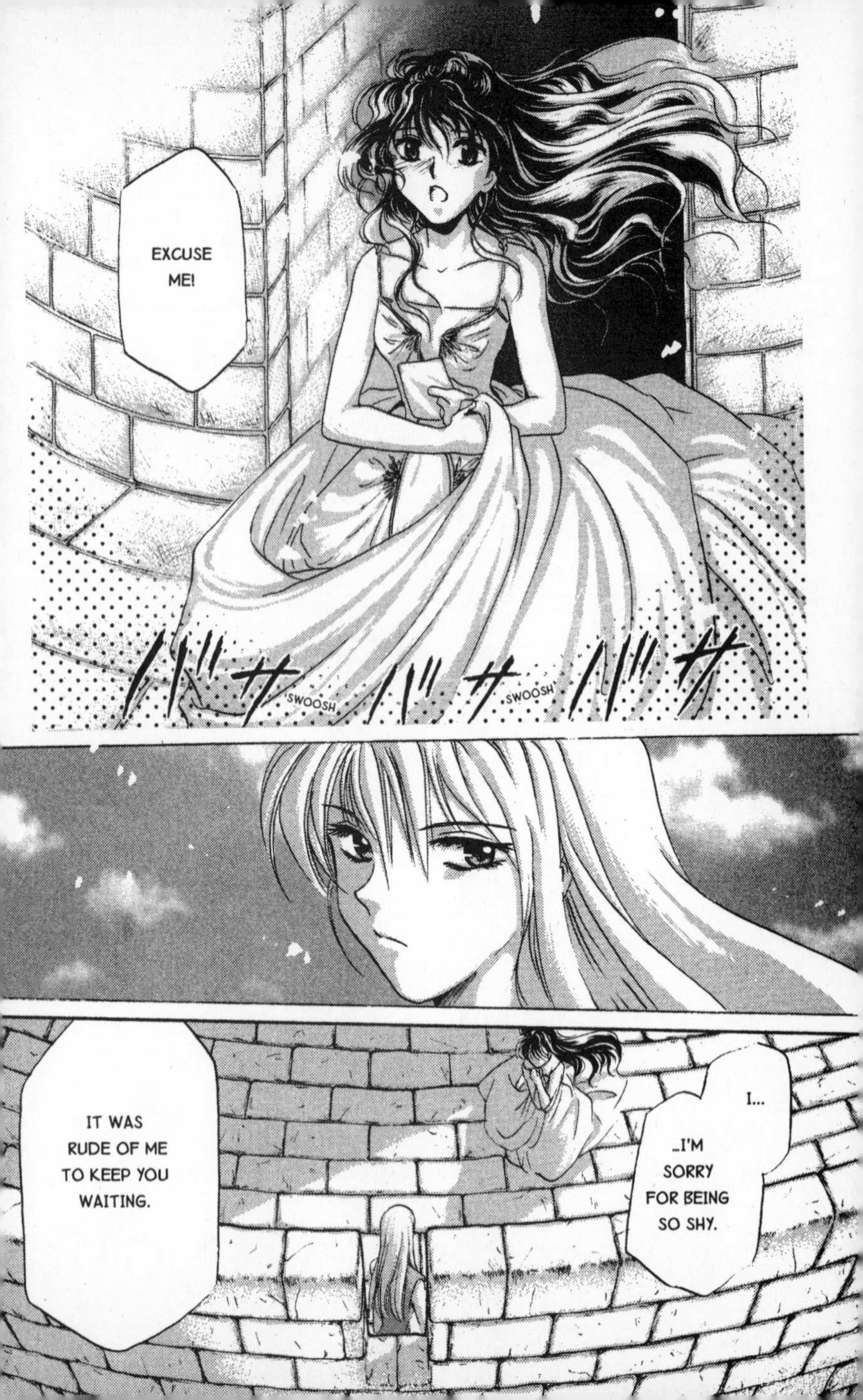
EXCUSE ME!
SWOOSH
SWOOSH
I...
...I'M SORRY FOR BEING SO SHY.
IT WAS RUDE OF ME TO KEEP YOU WAITING.

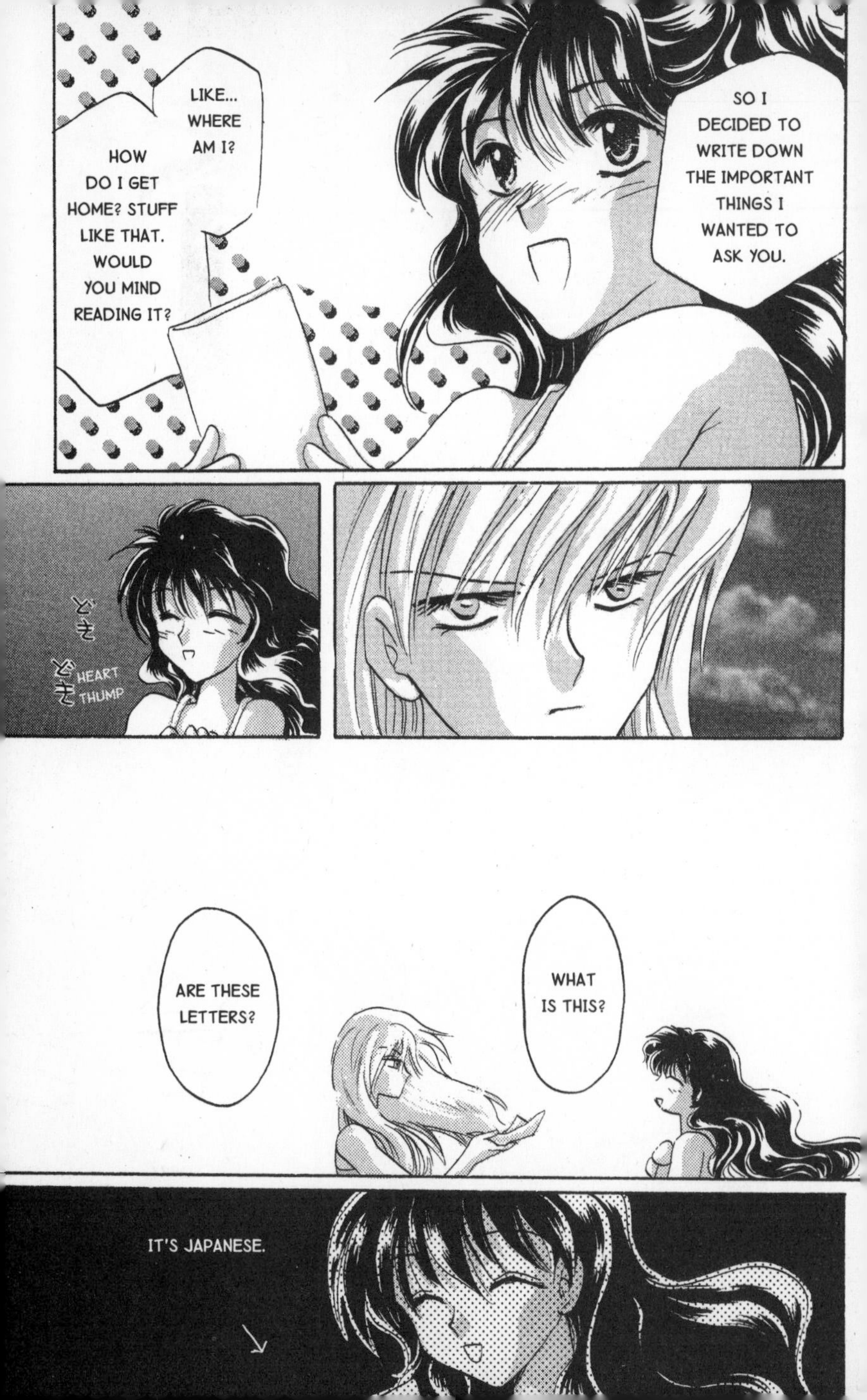
SO I DECIDED TO WRITE DOWN THE IMPORTANT THINGS I WANTED TO ASK YOU.
LIKE... WHERE AM I?
HOW DO I GET HOME? STUFF LIKE THAT. WOULD YOU MIND READING IT?
どき どき
HEART THUMP
WHAT IS THIS?
ARE THESE LETTERS?
IT'S JAPANESE.

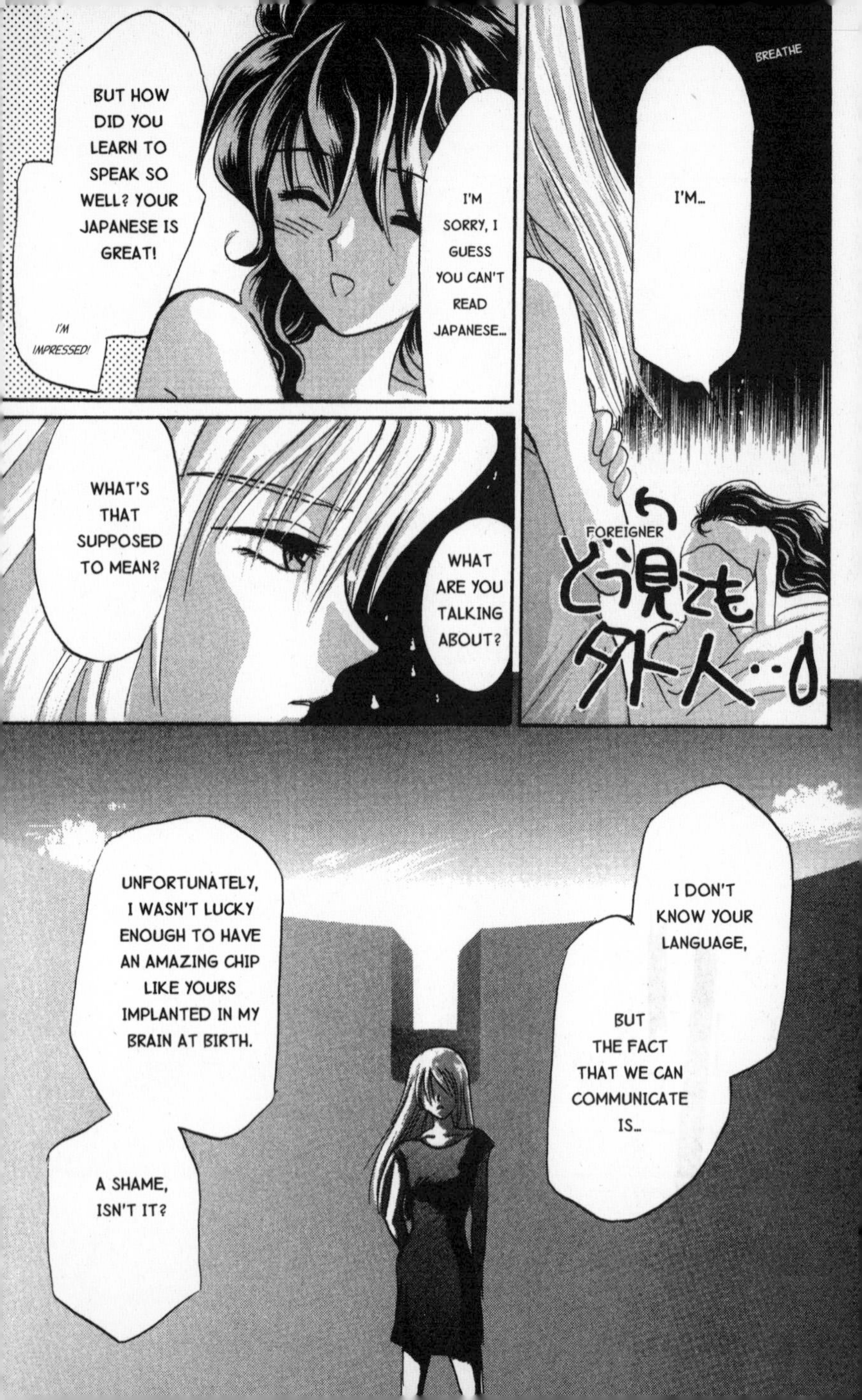
BREATHE
I'M...
FOREIGNER
どう見ても外人‥
I'M SORRY, I GUESS YOU CAN'T READ JAPANESE...
BUT HOW DID YOU LEARN TO SPEAK SO WELL? YOUR JAPANESE IS GREAT!
I'M IMPRESSED!
WHAT ARE YOU TALKING ABOUT?
WHAT'S THAT SUPPOSED TO MEAN?
I DON'T KNOW YOUR LANGUAGE,
BUT THE FACT THAT WE CAN COMMUNICATE IS...
UNFORTUNATELY, I WASN'T LUCKY ENOUGH TO HAVE AN AMAZING CHIP LIKE YOURS IMPLANTED IN MY BRAIN AT BIRTH.
A SHAME, ISN'T IT?

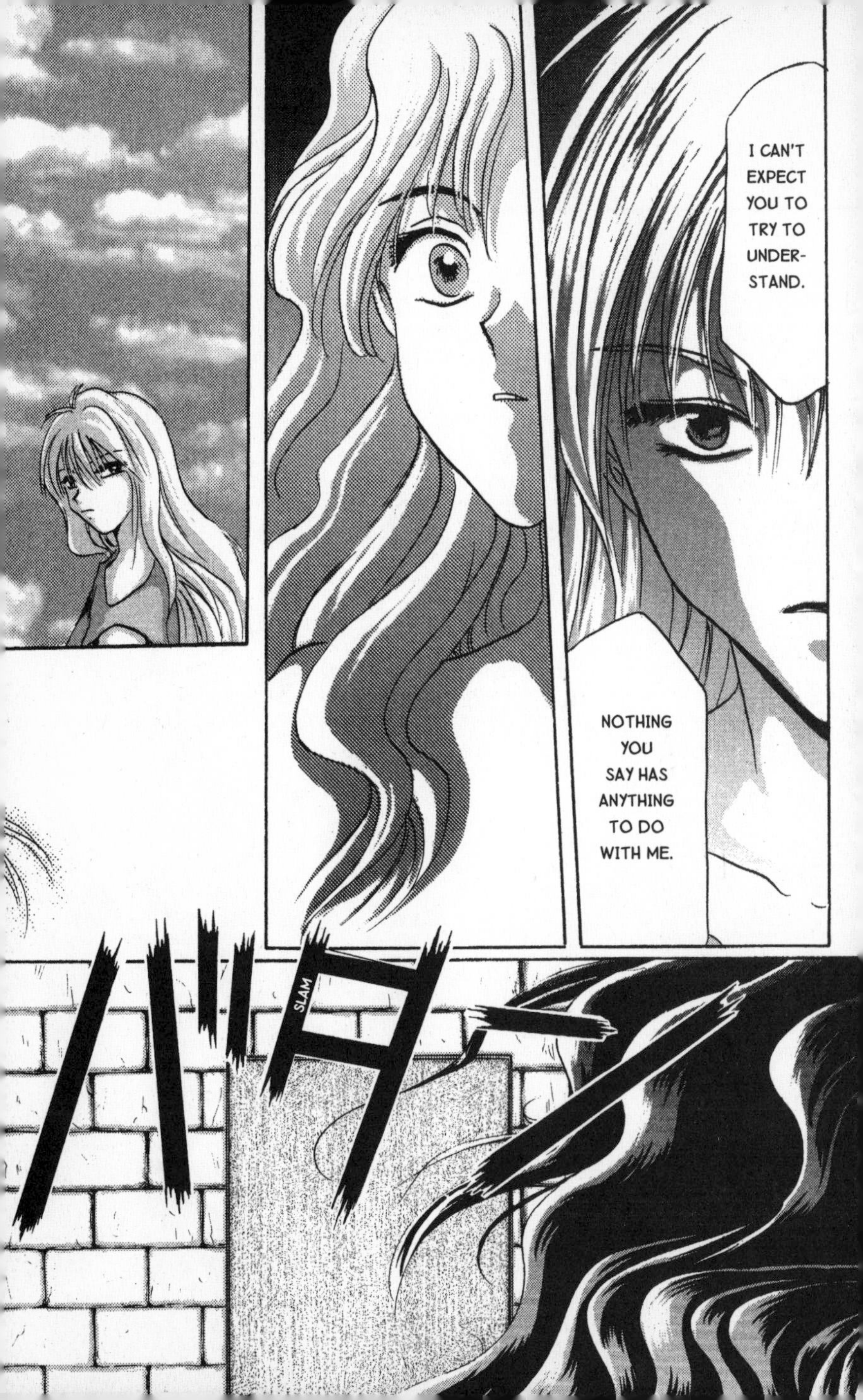
I CAN'T EXPECT YOU TO TRY TO UNDER-STAND.
NOTHING YOU SAY HAS ANYTHING TO DO WITH ME.
SLAM

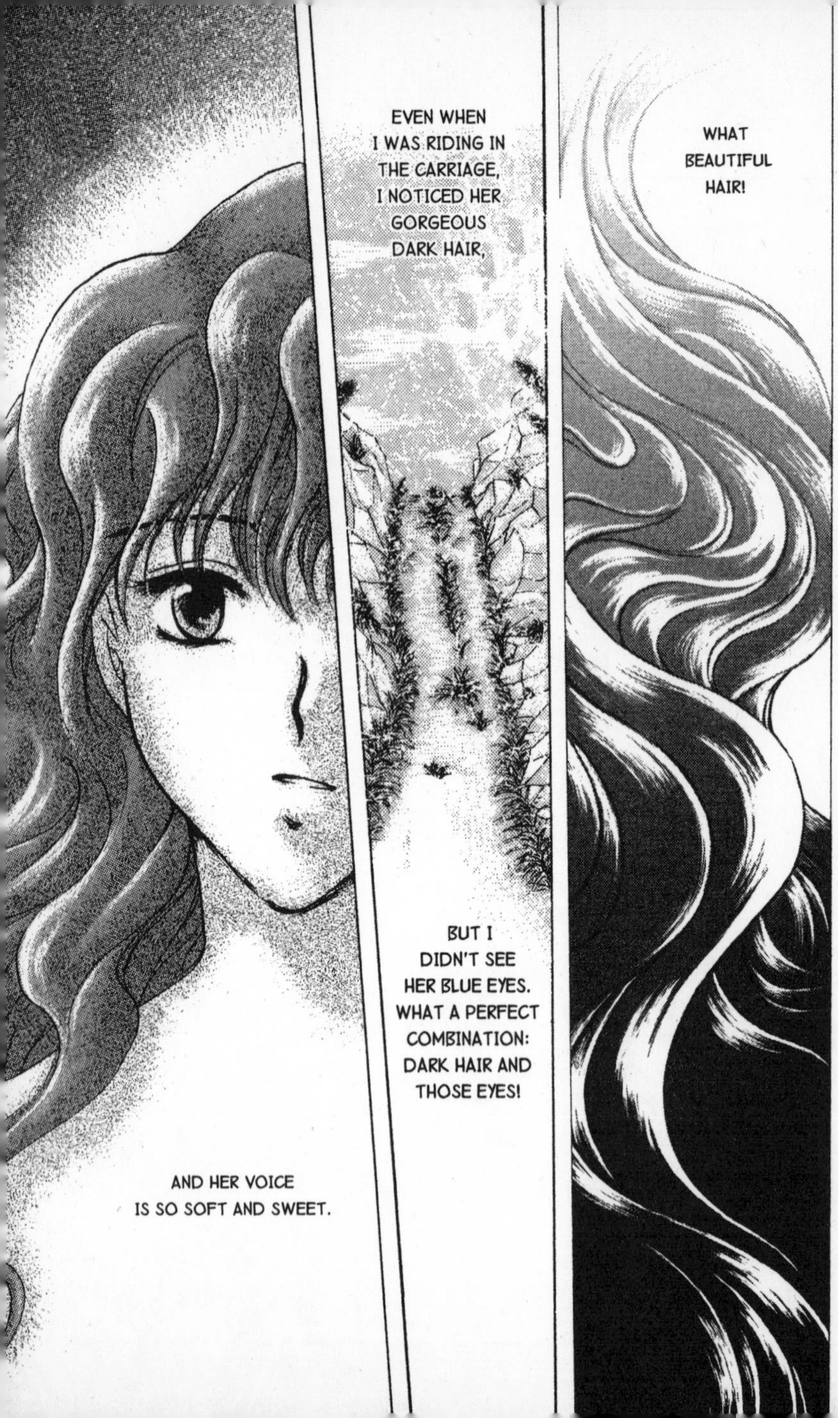
WHAT BEAUTIFUL HAIR!
EVEN WHEN I WAS RIDING IN THE CARRIAGE, I NOTICED HER GORGEOUS DARK HAIR,
BUT I DIDN'T SEE HER BLUE EYES. WHAT A PERFECT COMBINATION: DARK HAIR AND THOSE EYES!
AND HER VOICE IS SO SOFT AND SWEET.

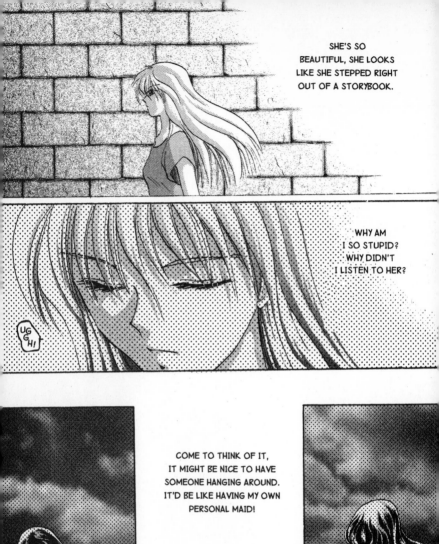

SHE'S SO BEAUTIFUL, SHE LOOKS LIKE SHE STEPPED RIGHT OUT OF A STORYBOOK.

WHY AM I SO STUPID? WHY DIDN'T I LISTEN TO HER?

UGGH!

COME TO THINK OF IT, IT MIGHT BE NICE TO HAVE SOMEONE HANGING AROUND. IT'D BE LIKE HAVING MY OWN PERSONAL MAID!

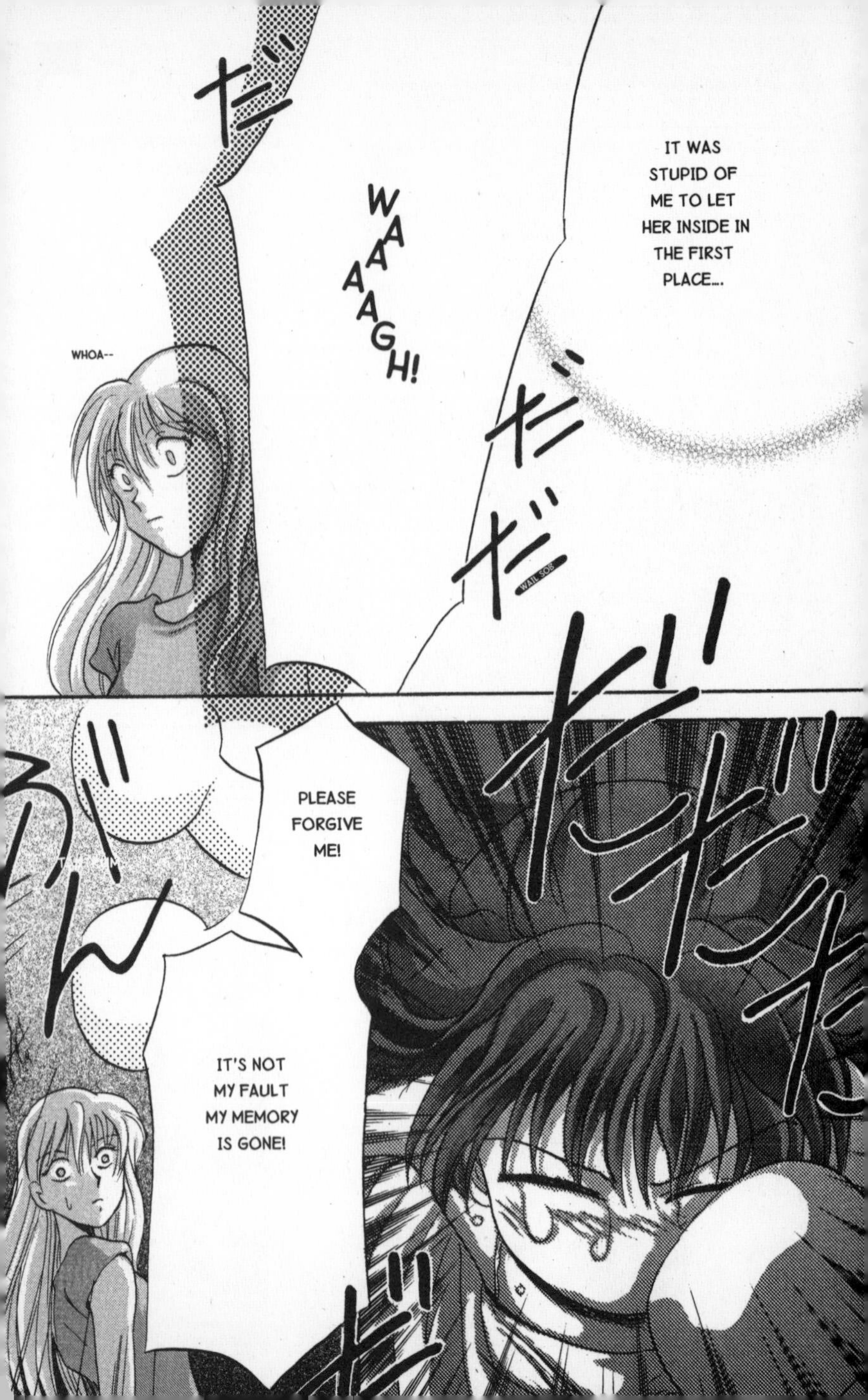
IT WAS STUPID OF ME TO LET HER INSIDE IN THE FIRST PLACE...
WAAAAAGH!
WHOA--
WAIL SOB
PLEASE FORGIVE ME!
IT'S NOT MY FAULT MY MEMORY IS GONE!

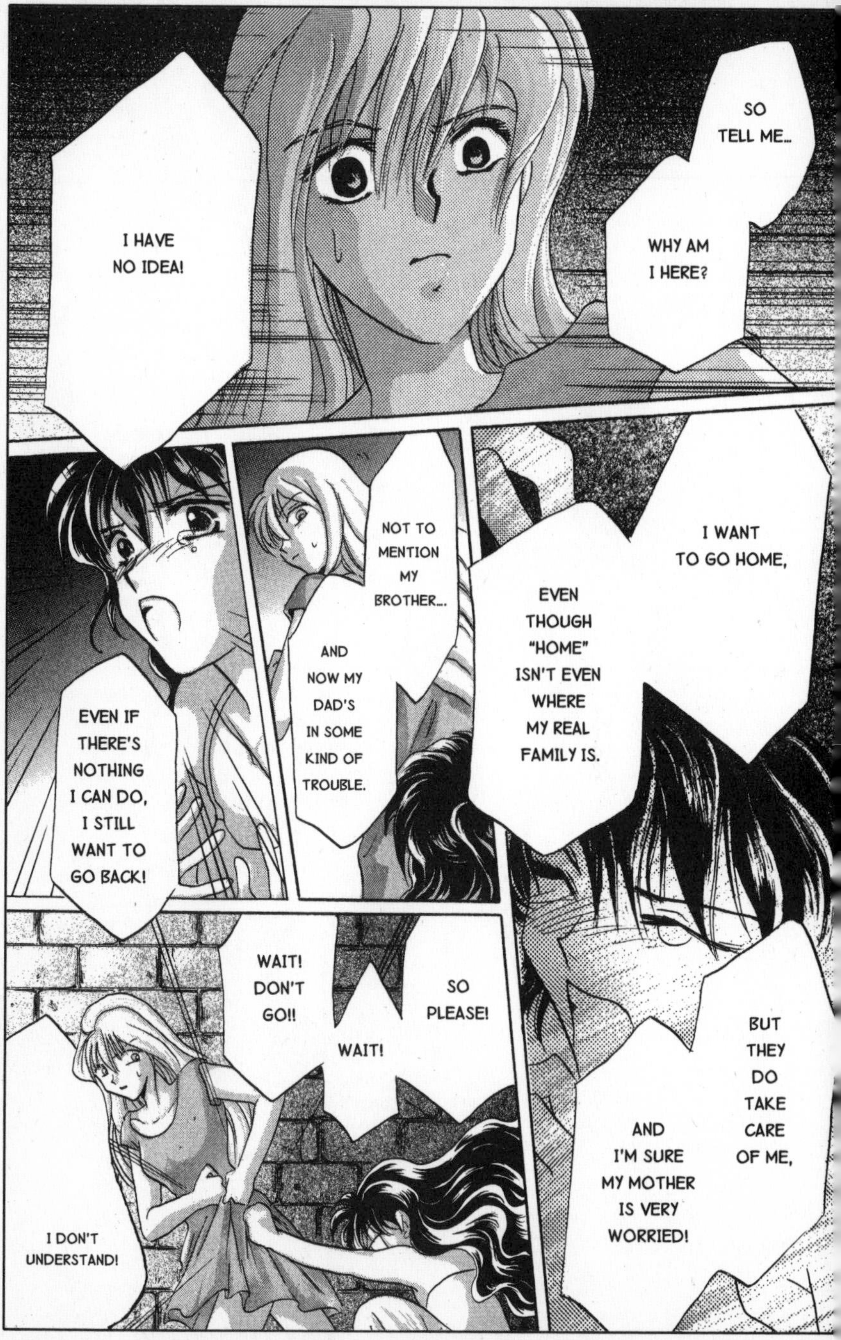
SO TELL ME...
WHY AM I HERE?
I HAVE NO IDEA!
I WANT TO GO HOME,
EVEN THOUGH "HOME" ISN'T EVEN WHERE MY REAL FAMILY IS.
BUT THEY DO TAKE CARE OF ME,
AND I'M SURE MY MOTHER IS VERY WORRIED!
NOT TO MENTION MY BROTHER...
AND NOW MY DAD'S IN SOME KIND OF TROUBLE.
EVEN IF THERE'S NOTHING I CAN DO, I STILL WANT TO GO BACK!
SO PLEASE!
WAIT! DON'T GO!!
WAIT!
I DON'T UNDERSTAND!

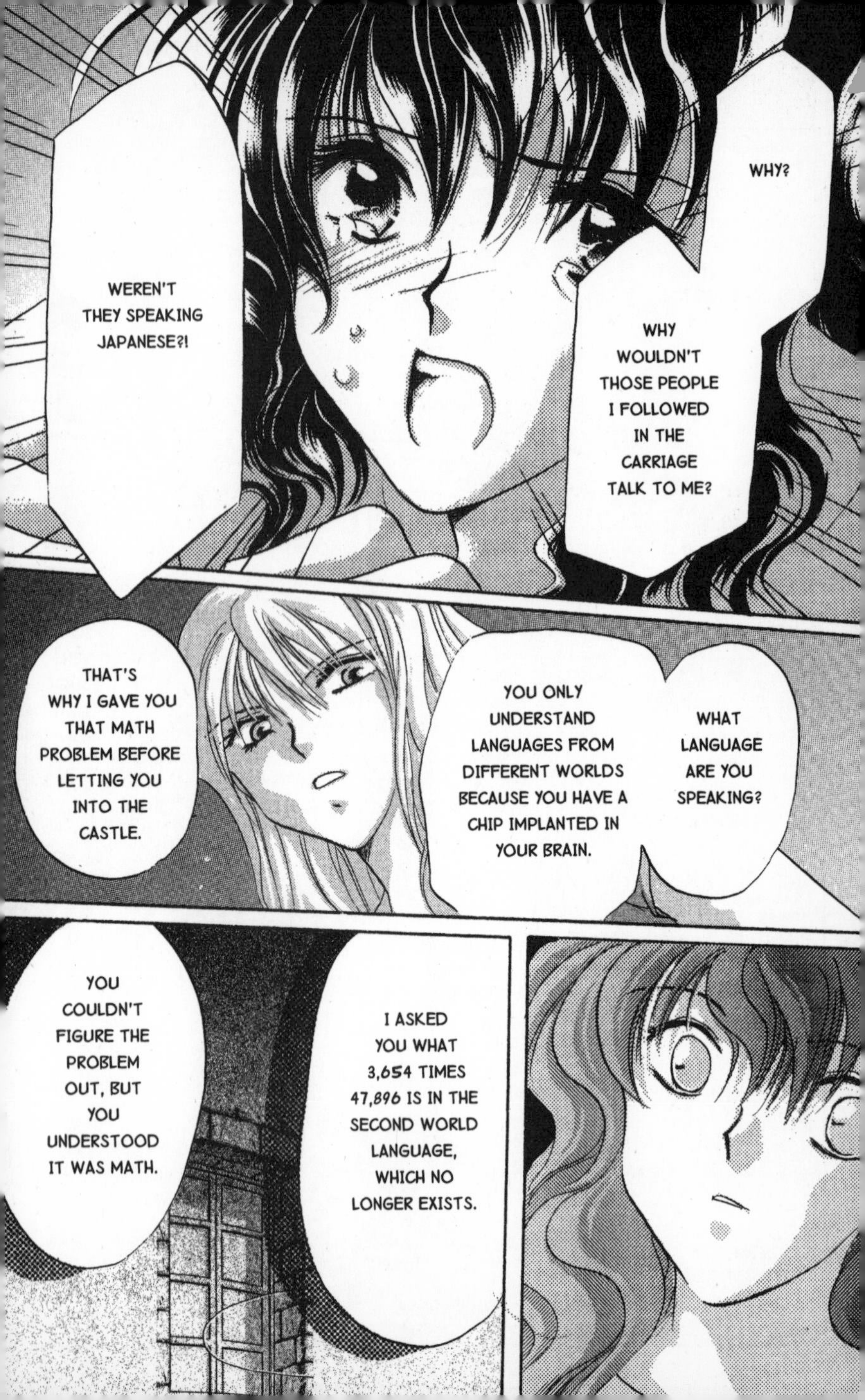
WHY?
WHY WOULDN'T THOSE PEOPLE I FOLLOWED IN THE CARRIAGE TALK TO ME?
WEREN'T THEY SPEAKING JAPANESE?!
WHAT LANGUAGE ARE YOU SPEAKING?
YOU ONLY UNDERSTAND LANGUAGES FROM DIFFERENT WORLDS BECAUSE YOU HAVE A CHIP IMPLANTED IN YOUR BRAIN.
THAT'S WHY I GAVE YOU THAT MATH PROBLEM BEFORE LETTING YOU INTO THE CASTLE.
I ASKED YOU WHAT 3,654 TIMES 47,896 IS IN THE SECOND WORLD LANGUAGE, WHICH NO LONGER EXISTS.
YOU COULDN'T FIGURE THE PROBLEM OUT, BUT YOU UNDERSTOOD IT WAS MATH.

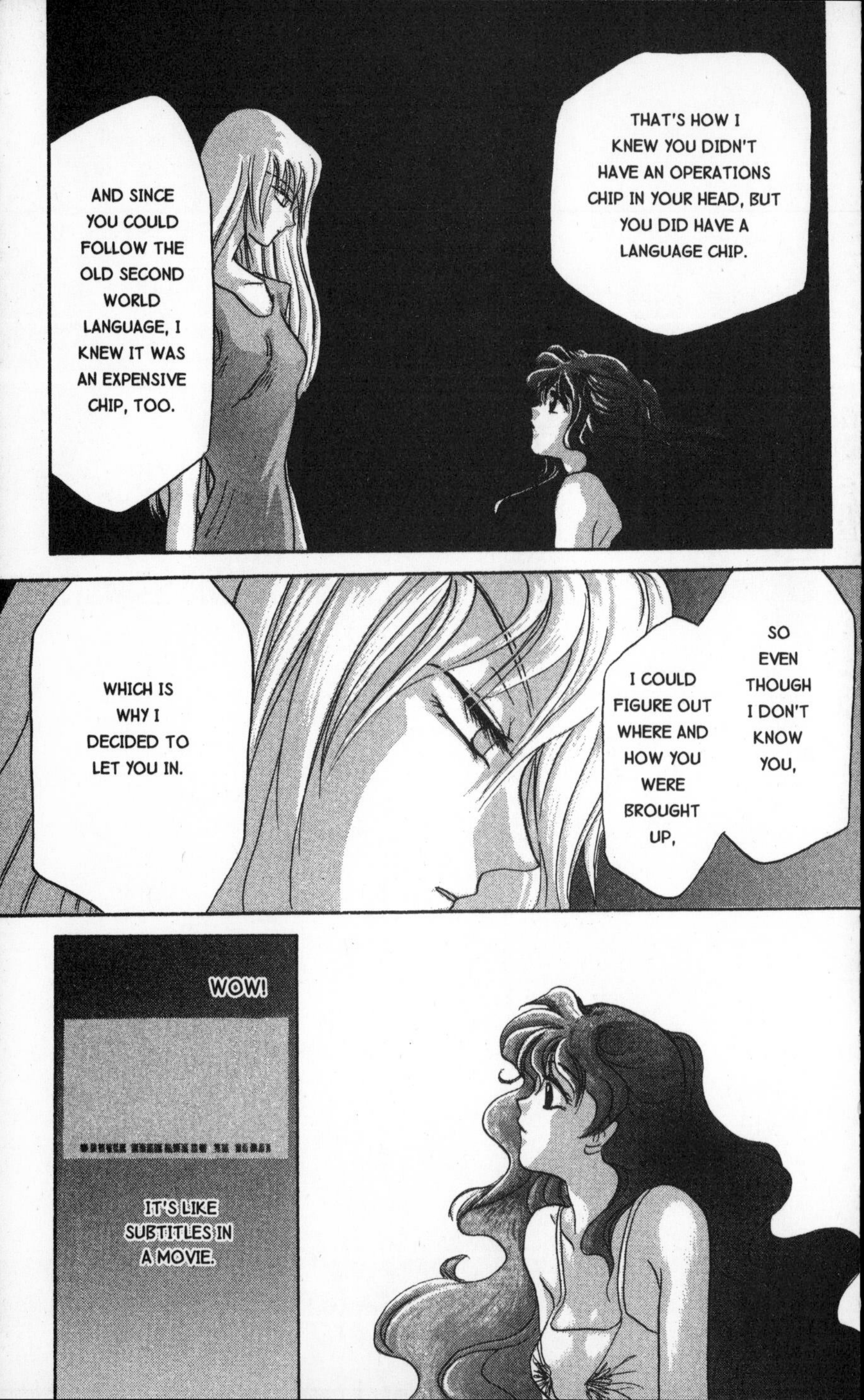
THAT'S HOW I KNEW YOU DIDN'T HAVE AN OPERATIONS CHIP IN YOUR HEAD, BUT YOU DID HAVE A LANGUAGE CHIP.
AND SINCE YOU COULD FOLLOW THE OLD SECOND WORLD LANGUAGE, I KNEW IT WAS AN EXPENSIVE CHIP, TOO.
SO EVEN THOUGH I DON'T KNOW YOU,
I COULD FIGURE OUT WHERE AND HOW YOU WERE BROUGHT UP,
WHICH IS WHY I DECIDED TO LET YOU IN.
WOW!
IT'S LIKE SUBTITLES IN A MOVIE.

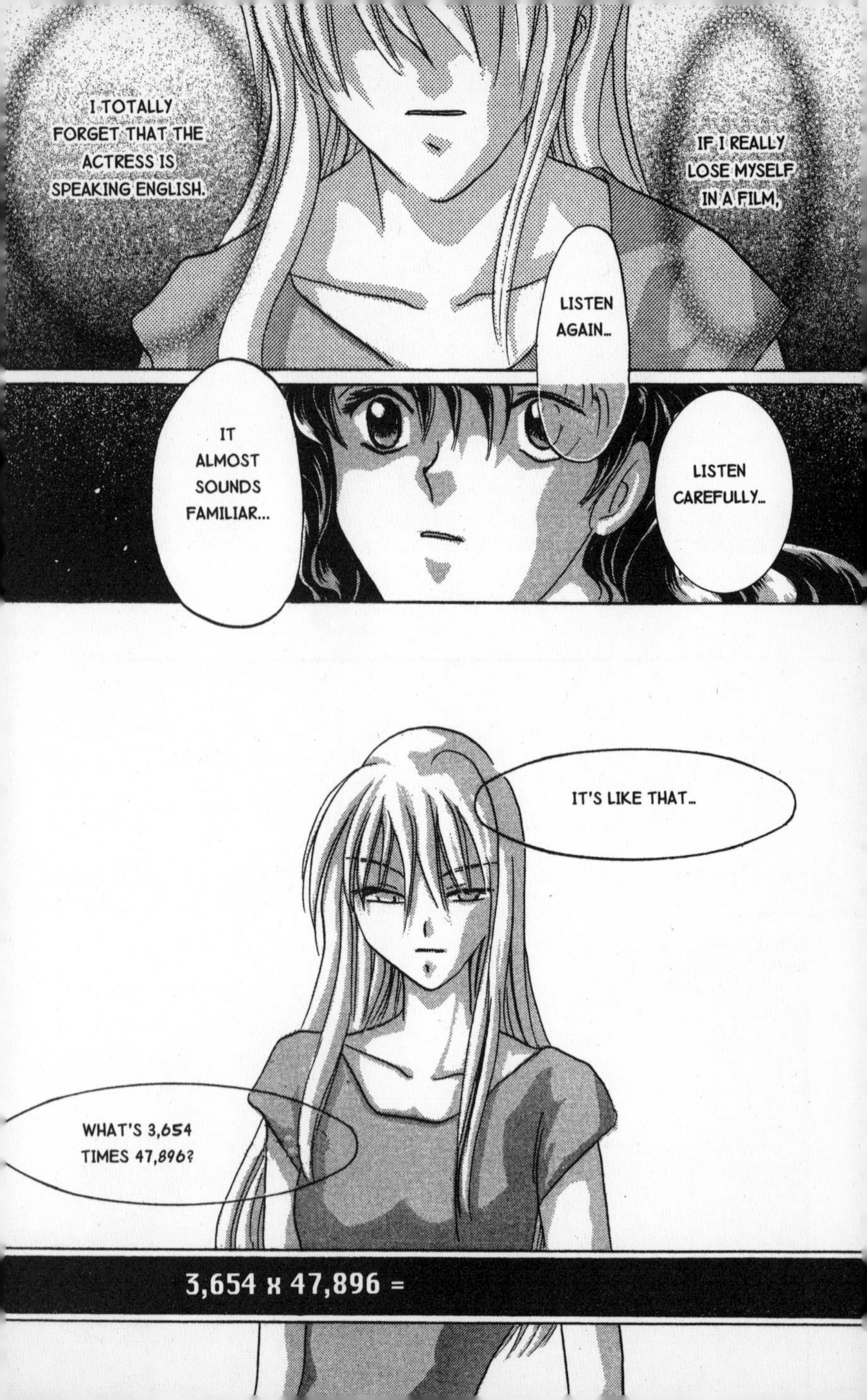

IF I REALLY LOSE MYSELF IN A FILM,
I TOTALLY FORGET THAT THE ACTRESS IS SPEAKING ENGLISH.
LISTEN AGAIN...
LISTEN CAREFULLY...
IT ALMOST SOUNDS FAMILIAR...
IT'S LIKE THAT...
WHAT'S 3,654 TIMES 47,896?
3,654 x 47,896 =

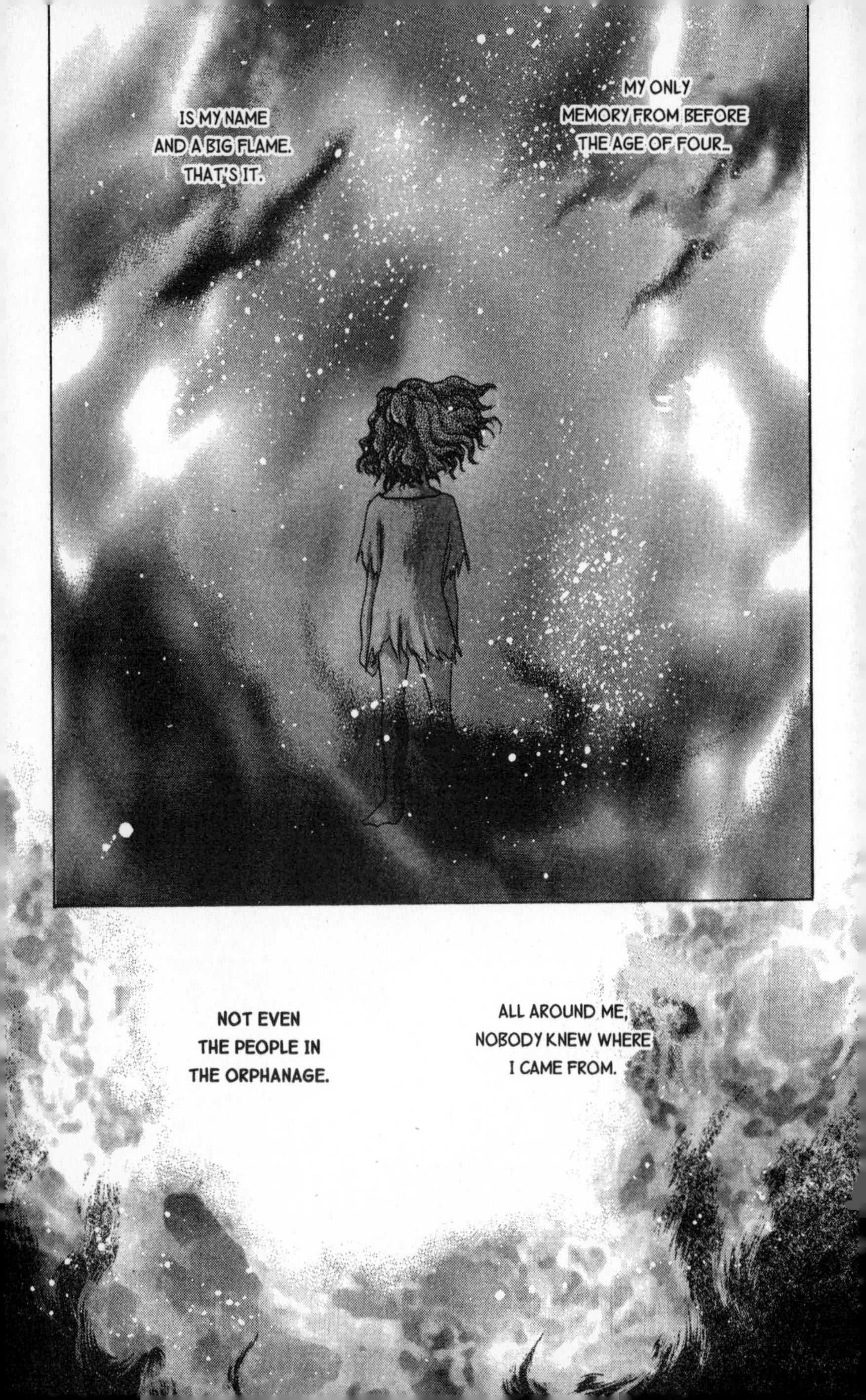
MY ONLY MEMORY FROM BEFORE THE AGE OF FOUR..
IS MY NAME AND A BIG FLAME. THAT'S IT.
ALL AROUND ME, NOBODY KNEW WHERE I CAME FROM.
NOT EVEN THE PEOPLE IN THE ORPHANAGE.

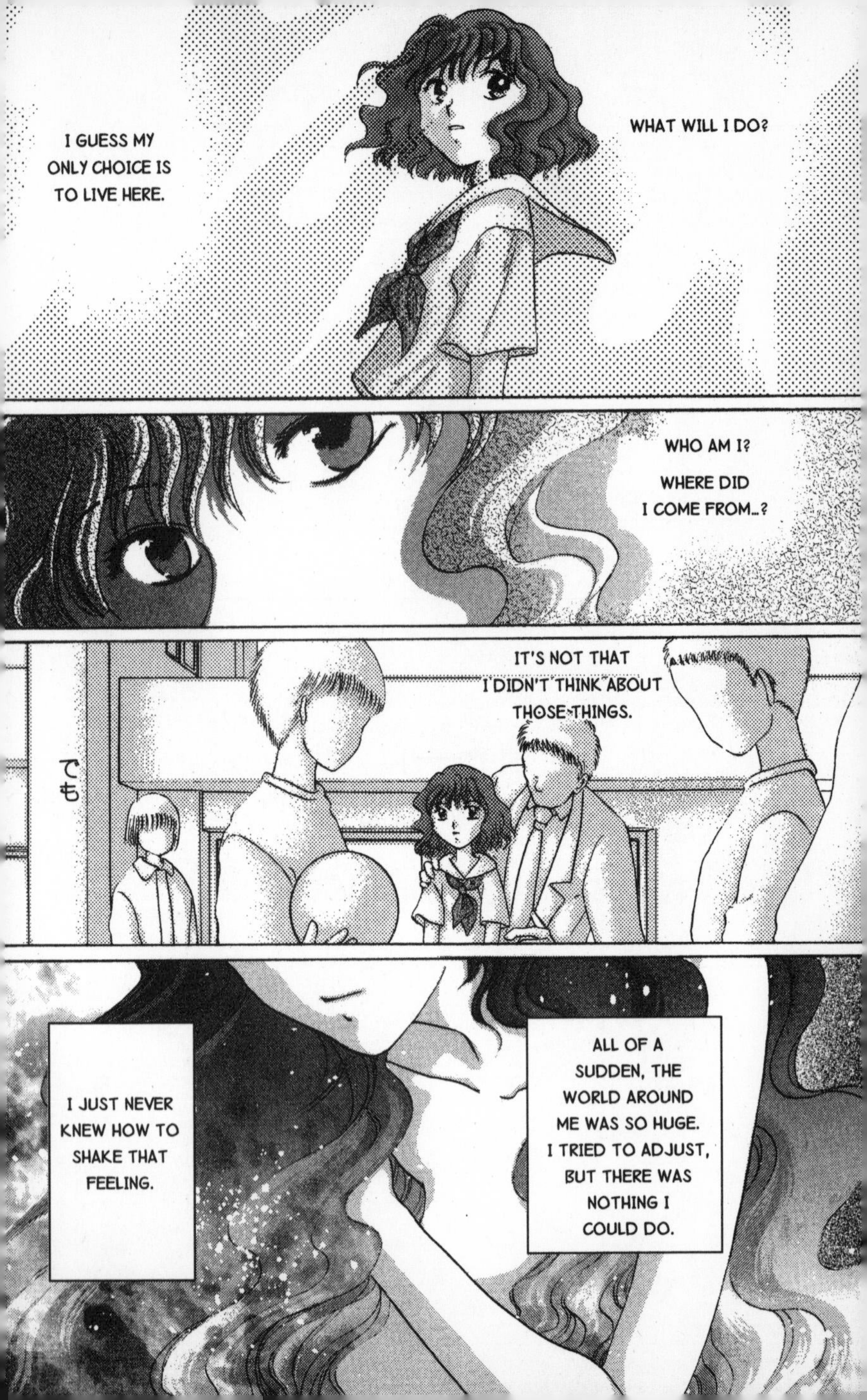
WHAT WILL I DO?
I GUESS MY ONLY CHOICE IS TO LIVE HERE.
WHO AM I?
WHERE DID I COME FROM...?
IT'S NOT THAT I DIDN'T THINK ABOUT THOSE THINGS.
でも
ALL OF A SUDDEN, THE WORLD AROUND ME WAS SO HUGE. I TRIED TO ADJUST, BUT THERE WAS NOTHING I COULD DO.
I JUST NEVER KNEW HOW TO SHAKE THAT FEELING.

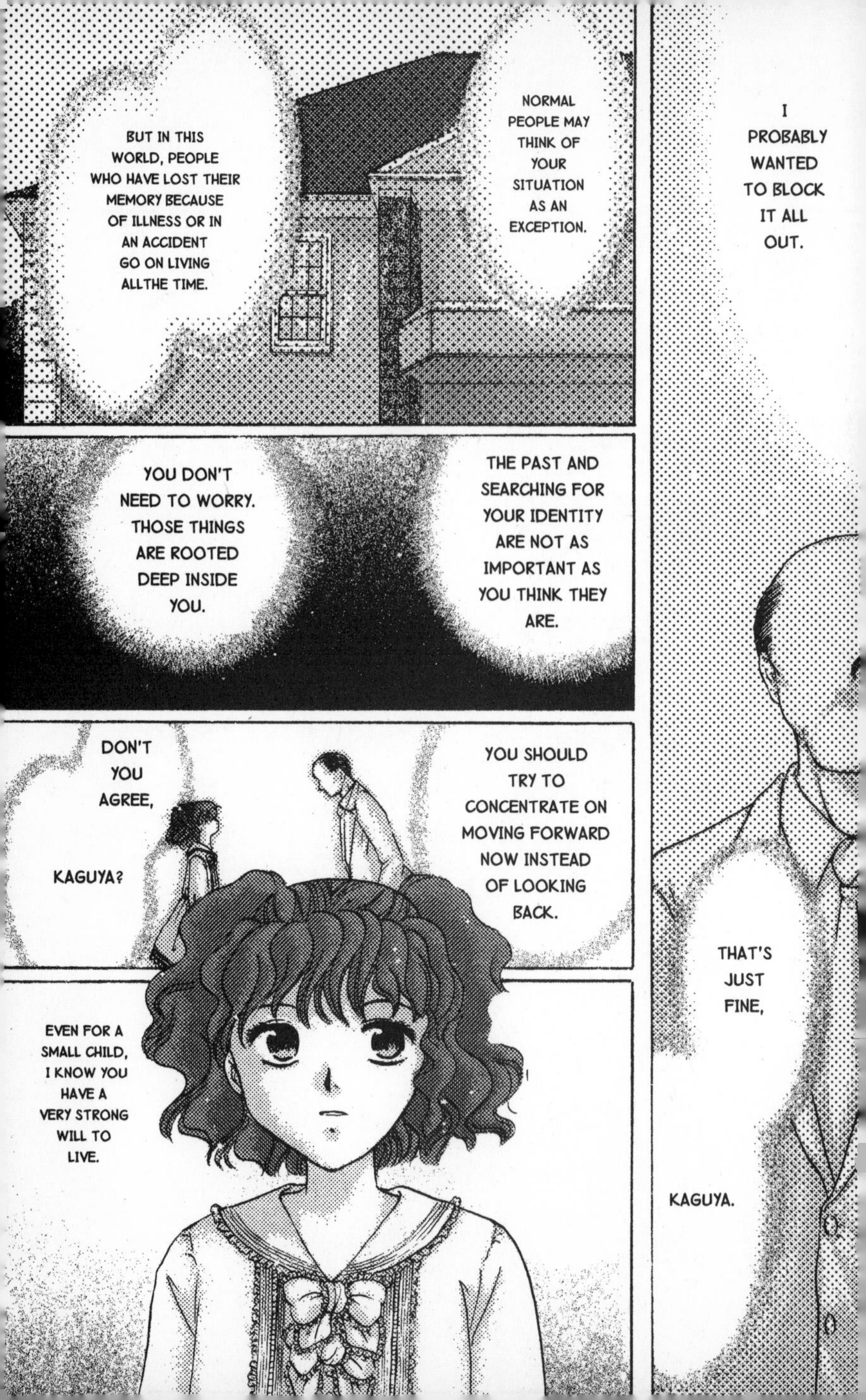
I PROBABLY WANTED TO BLOCK IT ALL OUT.
THAT'S JUST FINE,
KAGUYA.
NORMAL PEOPLE MAY THINK OF YOUR SITUATION AS AN EXCEPTION.
BUT IN THIS WORLD, PEOPLE WHO HAVE LOST THEIR MEMORY BECAUSE OF ILLNESS OR IN AN ACCIDENT GO ON LIVING ALLTHE TIME.
THE PAST AND SEARCHING FOR YOUR IDENTITY ARE NOT AS IMPORTANT AS YOU THINK THEY ARE.
YOU DON'T NEED TO WORRY. THOSE THINGS ARE ROOTED DEEP INSIDE YOU.
YOU SHOULD TRY TO CONCENTRATE ON MOVING FORWARD NOW INSTEAD OF LOOKING BACK.
DON'T YOU AGREE,
KAGUYA?
EVEN FOR A SMALL CHILD, I KNOW YOU HAVE A VERY STRONG WILL TO LIVE.

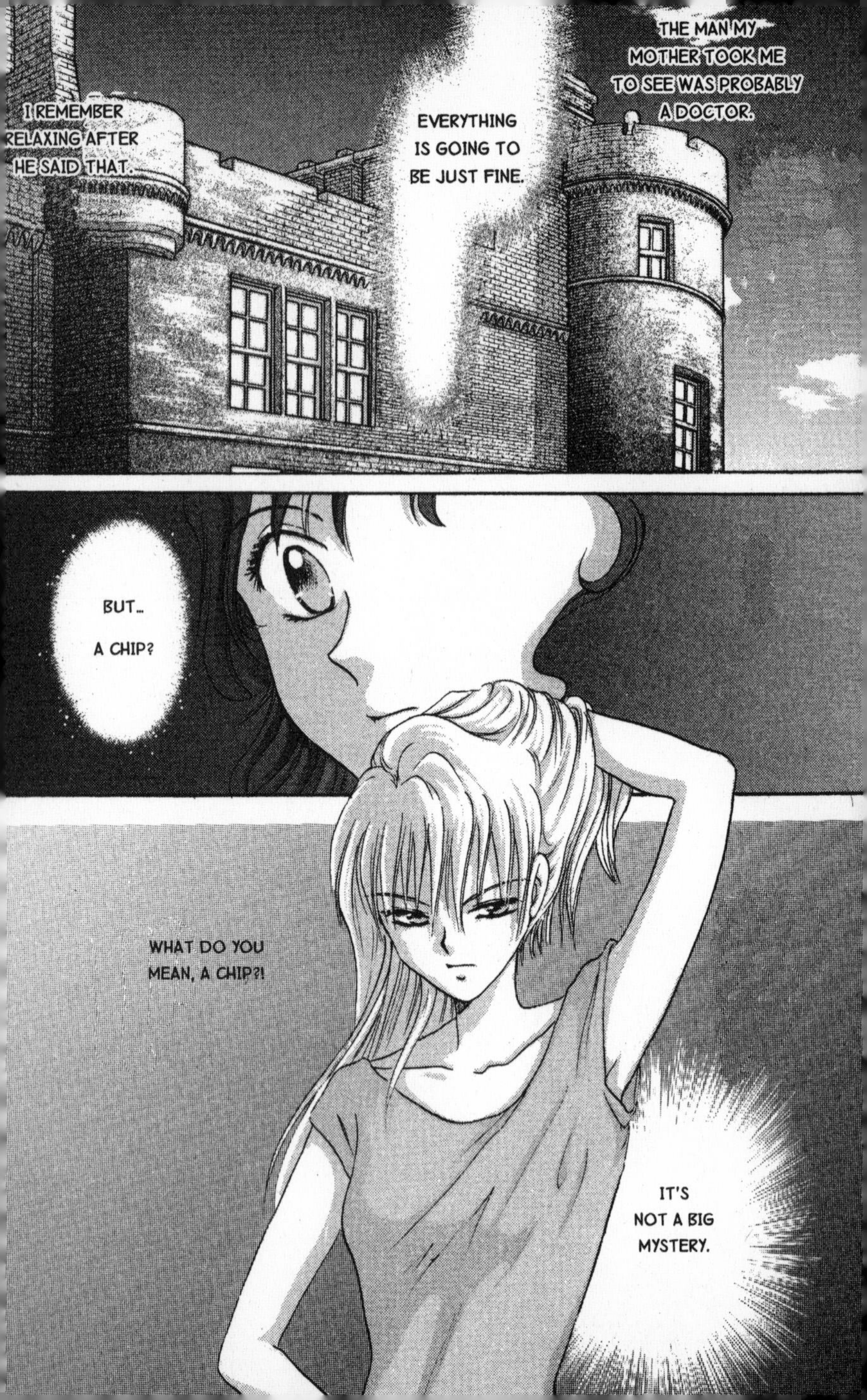
THE MAN MY MOTHER TOOK ME TO SEE WAS PROBABLY A DOCTOR.
EVERYTHING IS GOING TO BE JUST FINE.
I REMEMBER RELAXING AFTER HE SAID THAT.
BUT... A CHIP?
WHAT DO YOU MEAN, A CHIP?!
IT'S NOT A BIG MYSTERY.

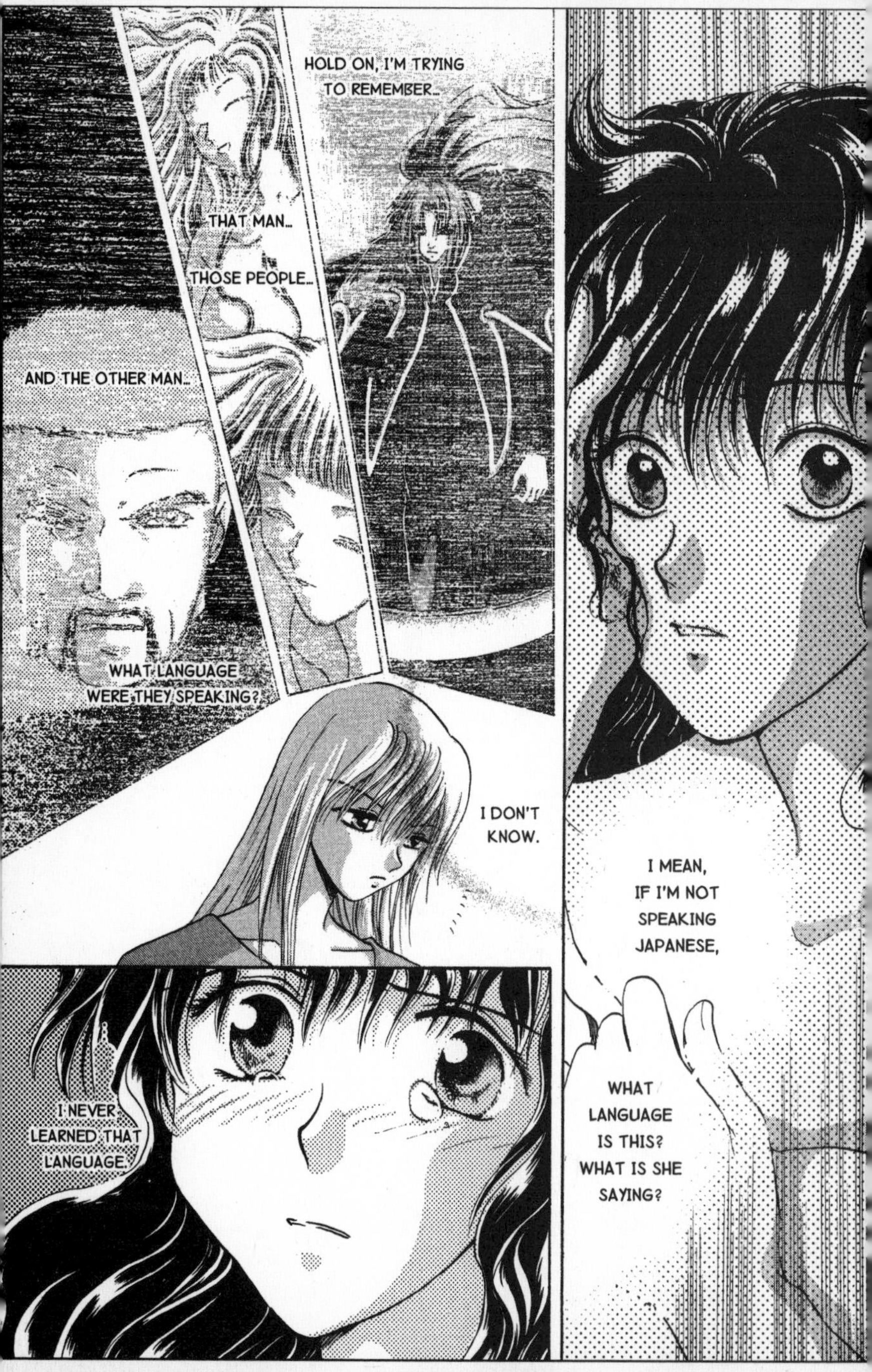
I MEAN, IF I'M NOT SPEAKING JAPANESE,
WHAT LANGUAGE IS THIS? WHAT IS SHE SAYING?
HOLD ON, I'M TRYING TO REMEMBER..
THAT MAN..
THOSE PEOPLE..
AND THE OTHER MAN..
WHAT LANGUAGE WERE THEY SPEAKING?
I DON'T KNOW.
I NEVER LEARNED THAT LANGUAGE.

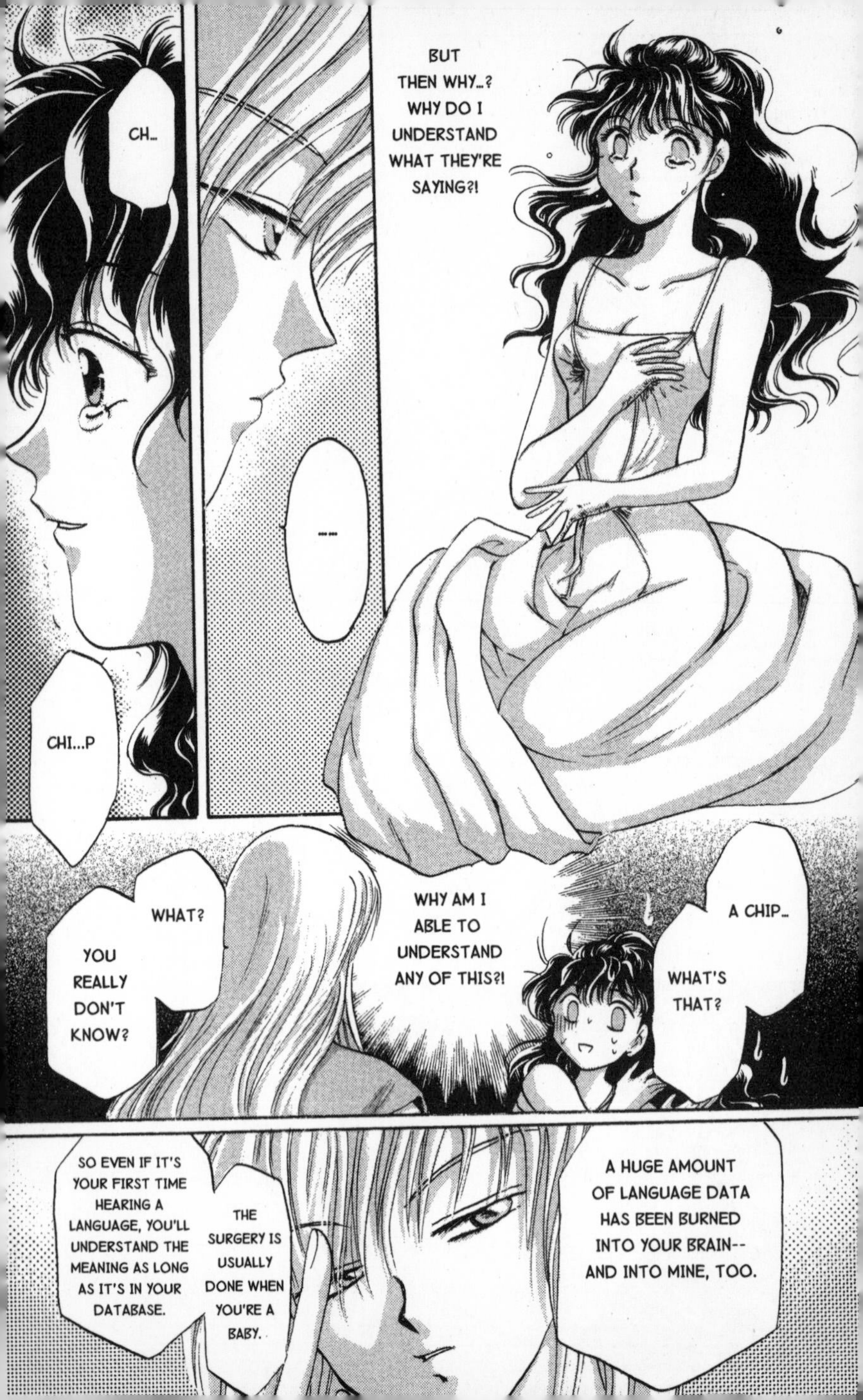
BUT THEN WHY...? WHY DO I UNDERSTAND WHAT THEY'RE SAYING?!
......
CH...
CHI...P
A CHIP...
WHAT'S THAT?
WHY AM I ABLE TO UNDERSTAND ANY OF THIS?!
WHAT?
YOU REALLY DON'T KNOW?
A HUGE AMOUNT OF LANGUAGE DATA HAS BEEN BURNED INTO YOUR BRAIN-- AND INTO MINE, TOO.
THE SURGERY IS USUALLY DONE WHEN YOU'RE A BABY.
SO EVEN IF IT'S YOUR FIRST TIME HEARING A LANGUAGE, YOU'LL UNDERSTAND THE MEANING AS LONG AS IT'S IN YOUR DATABASE.

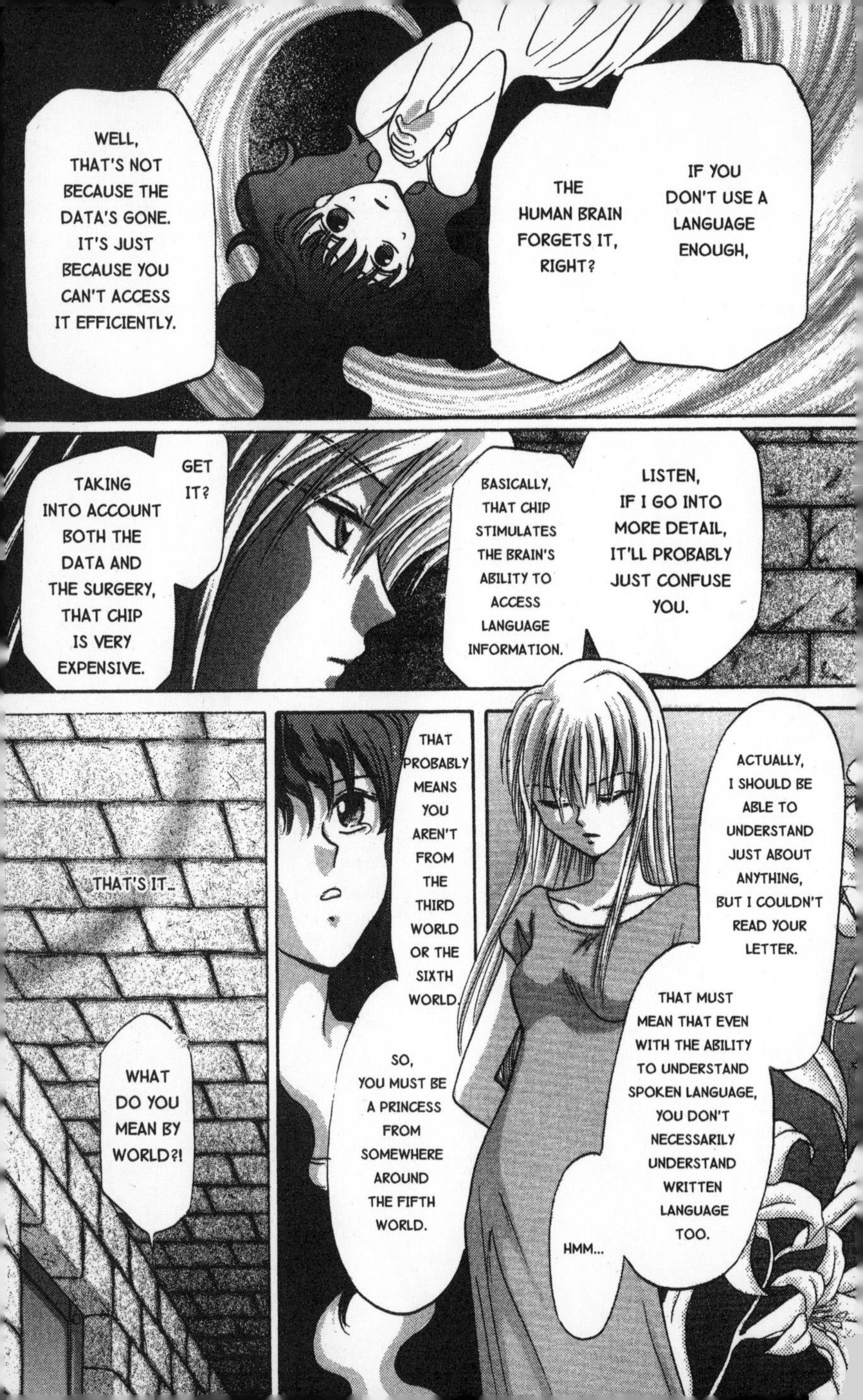
IF YOU DON'T USE A LANGUAGE ENOUGH,
THE HUMAN BRAIN FORGETS IT, RIGHT?
WELL, THAT'S NOT BECAUSE THE DATA'S GONE. IT'S JUST BECAUSE YOU CAN'T ACCESS IT EFFICIENTLY.
LISTEN, IF I GO INTO MORE DETAIL, IT'LL PROBABLY JUST CONFUSE YOU.
BASICALLY, THAT CHIP STIMULATES THE BRAIN'S ABILITY TO ACCESS LANGUAGE INFORMATION.
GET IT?
TAKING INTO ACCOUNT BOTH THE DATA AND THE SURGERY, THAT CHIP IS VERY EXPENSIVE.
ACTUALLY, I SHOULD BE ABLE TO UNDERSTAND JUST ABOUT ANYTHING, BUT I COULDN'T READ YOUR LETTER.
THAT MUST MEAN THAT EVEN WITH THE ABILITY TO UNDERSTAND SPOKEN LANGUAGE, YOU DON'T NECESSARILY UNDERSTAND WRITTEN LANGUAGE TOO.
HMM...
THAT PROBABLY MEANS YOU AREN'T FROM THE THIRD WORLD OR THE SIXTH WORLD.
SO, YOU MUST BE A PRINCESS FROM SOMEWHERE AROUND THE FIFTH WORLD.
THAT'S IT...
WHAT DO YOU MEAN BY WORLD?!

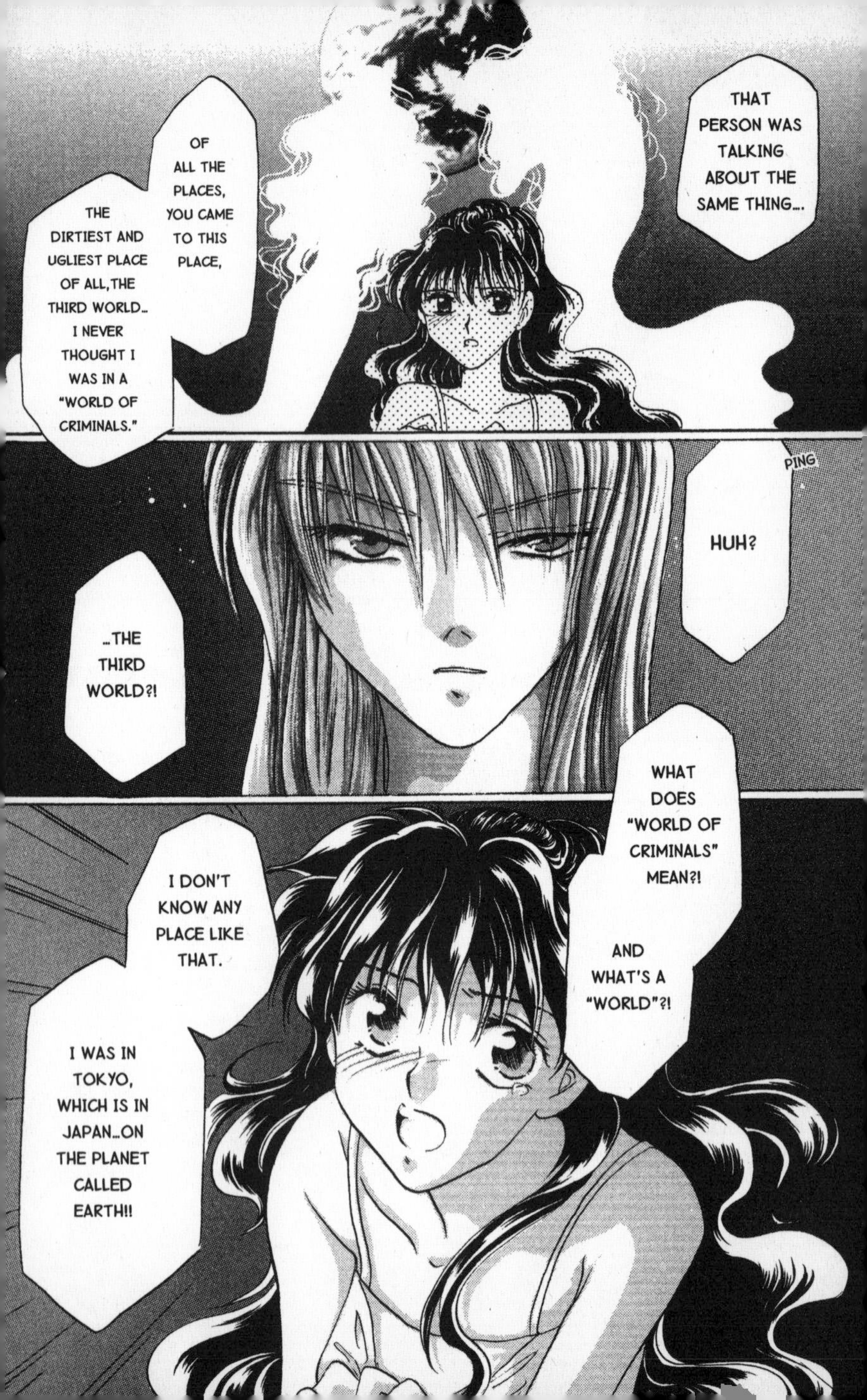
THAT PERSON WAS TALKING ABOUT THE SAME THING....
OF ALL THE PLACES, YOU CAME TO THIS PLACE,
THE DIRTIEST AND UGLIEST PLACE OF ALL, THE THIRD WORLD... I NEVER THOUGHT I WAS IN A "WORLD OF CRIMINALS."
PING
HUH?
...THE THIRD WORLD?!
WHAT DOES "WORLD OF CRIMINALS" MEAN?!
AND WHAT'S A "WORLD"?!
I DON'T KNOW ANY PLACE LIKE THAT.
I WAS IN TOKYO, WHICH IS IN JAPAN...ON THE PLANET CALLED EARTH!!

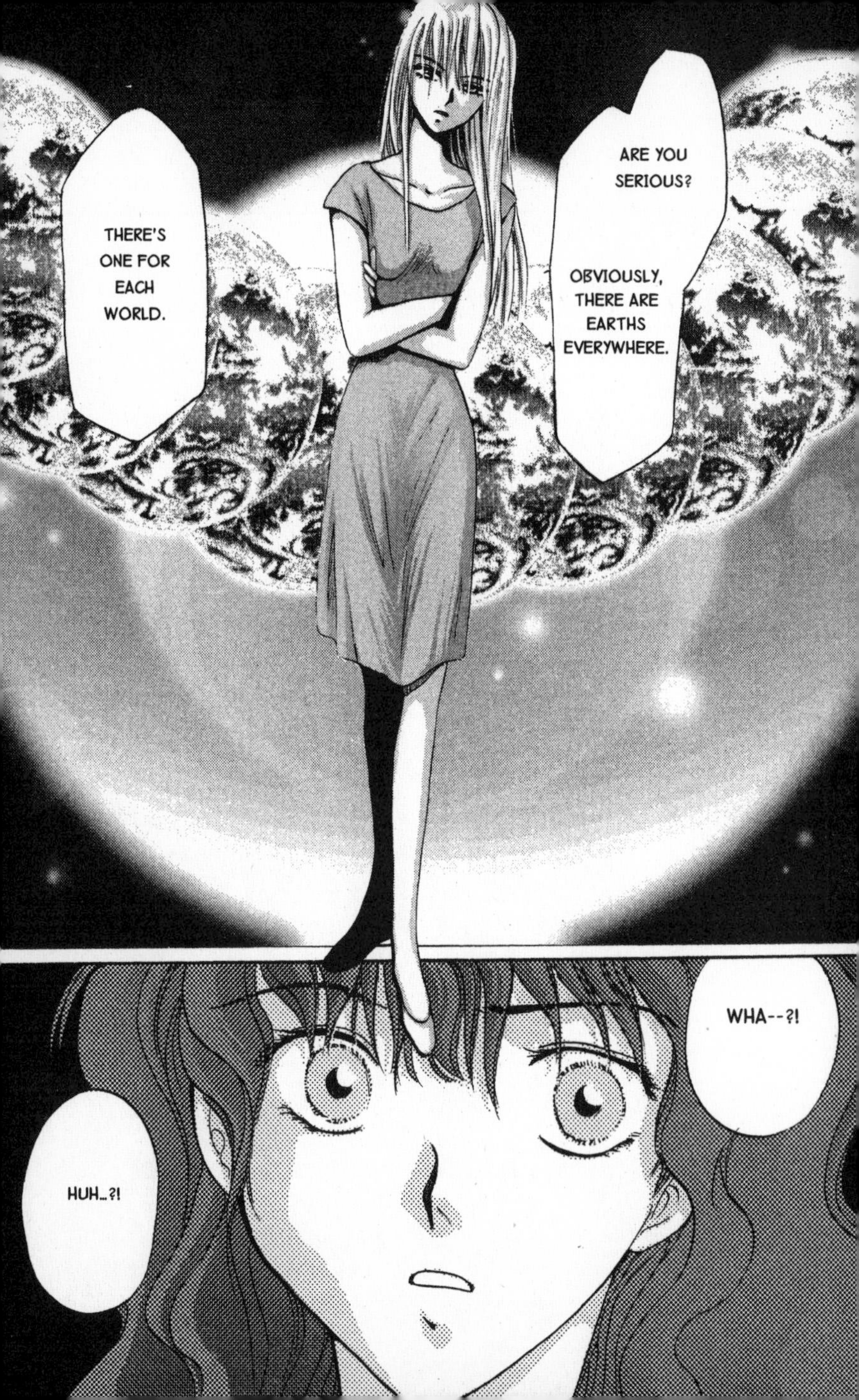
ARE YOU SERIOUS?
OBVIOUSLY, THERE ARE EARTHS EVERYWHERE.
THERE'S ONE FOR EACH WORLD.
WHA--?!
HUH...?!

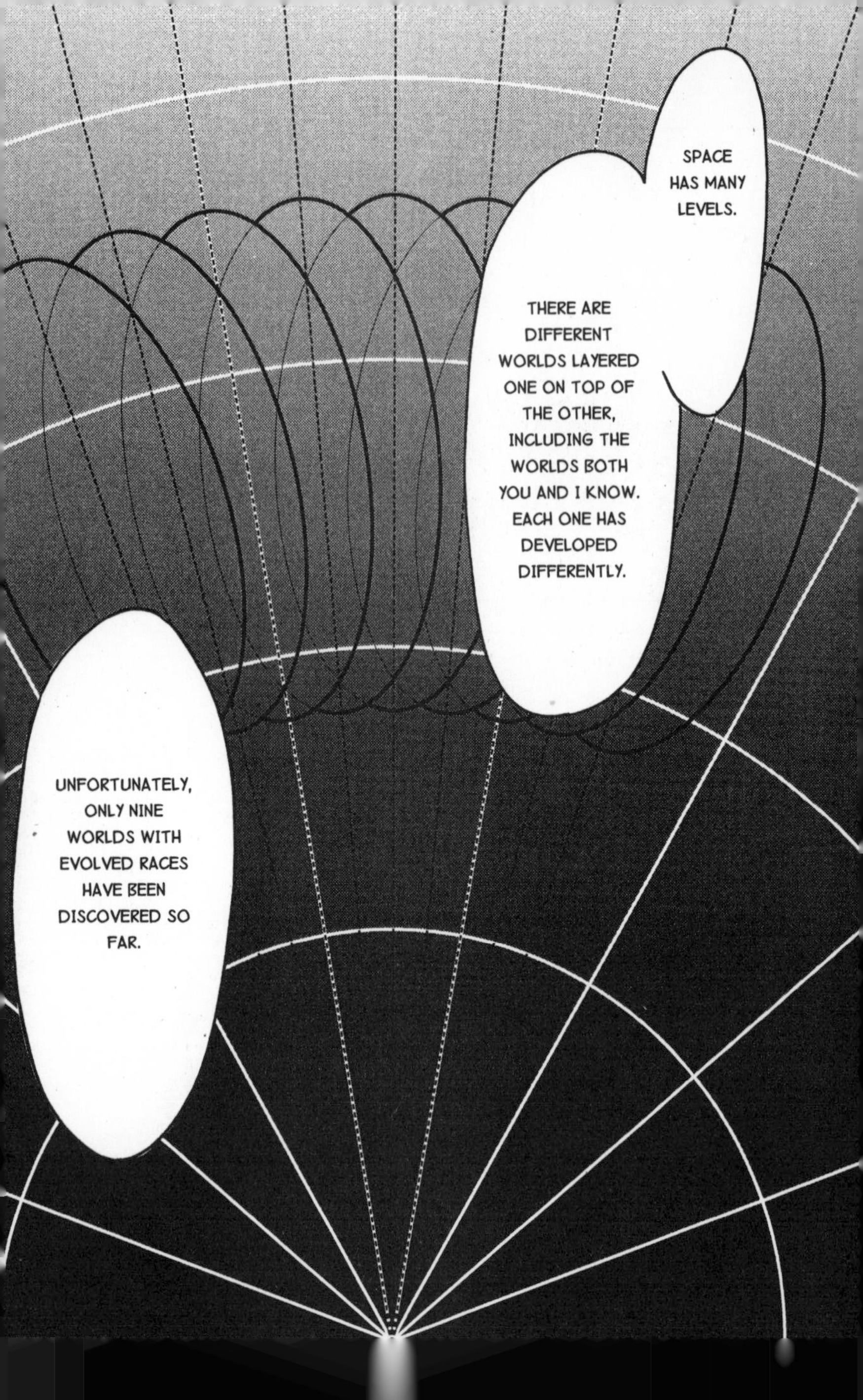
SPACE HAS MANY LEVELS.
THERE ARE DIFFERENT WORLDS LAYERED ONE ON TOP OF THE OTHER, INCLUDING THE WORLDS BOTH YOU AND I KNOW. EACH ONE HAS DEVELOPED DIFFERENTLY.
UNFORTUNATELY, ONLY NINE WORLDS WITH EVOLVED RACES HAVE BEEN DISCOVERED SO FAR.

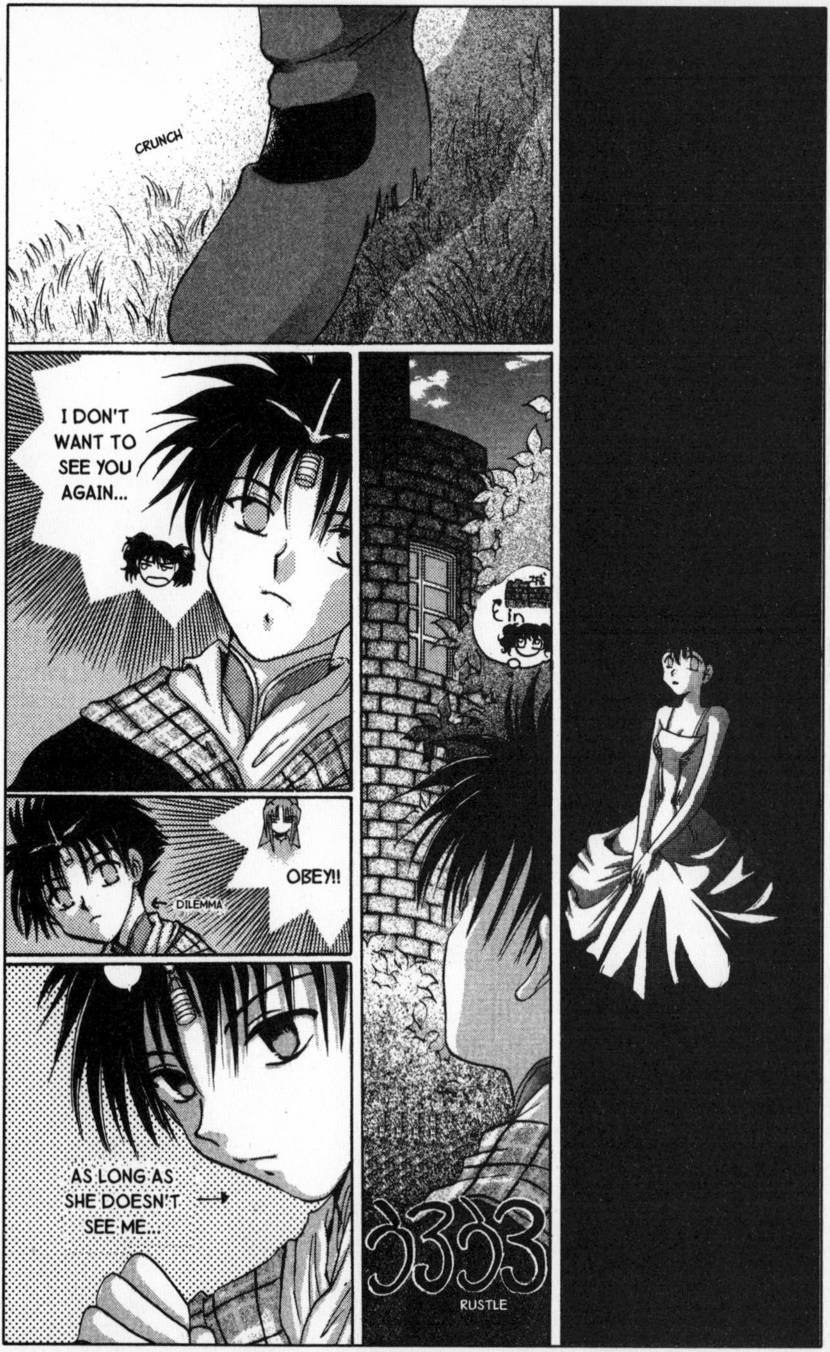
CRUNCH
RUSTLE
I DON'T WANT TO SEE YOU AGAIN...
OBEY!!
DILEMMA
AS LONG AS SHE DOESN'T SEE ME...

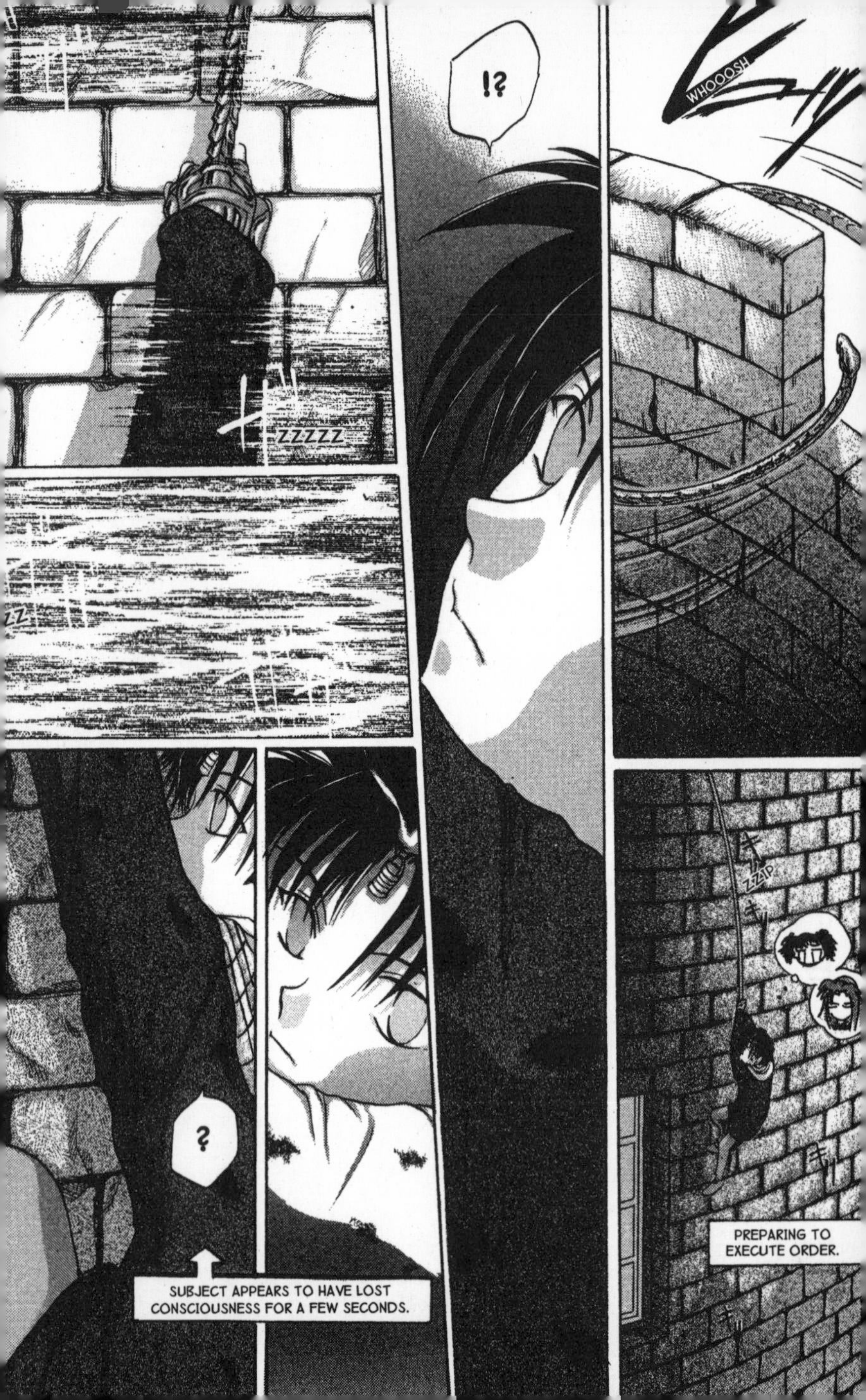
WHOOOSH
ZZIP
PREPARING TO EXECUTE ORDER.
!?
ZZZZZ
ZZ
?
SUBJECT APPEARS TO HAVE LOST CONSCIOUSNESS FOR A FEW SECONDS.

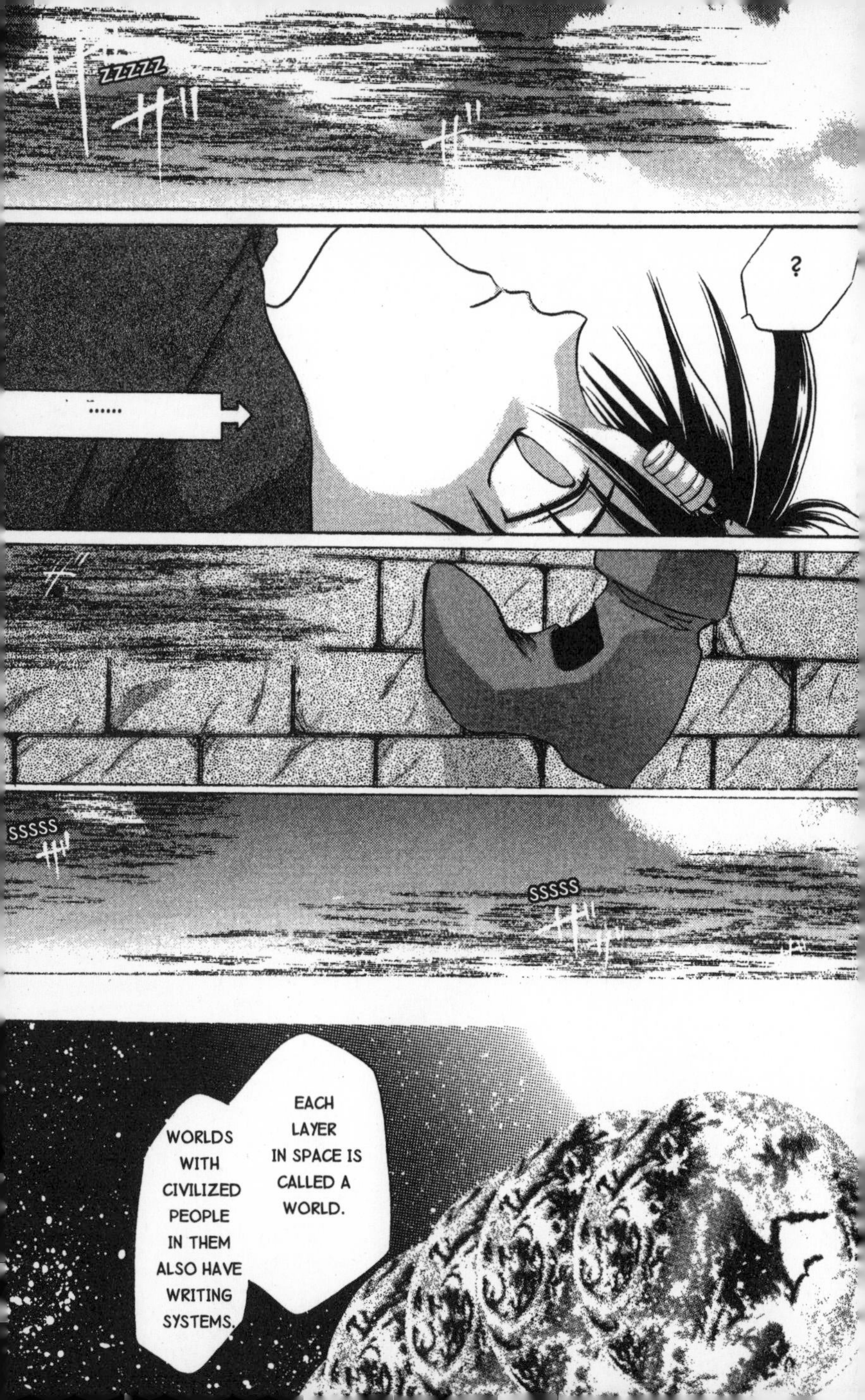
ZZ·ZZ·Z
?
......
SSSSS
SSSSS
EACH LAYER IN SPACE IS CALLED A WORLD.
WORLDS WITH CIVILIZED PEOPLE IN THEM ALSO HAVE WRITING SYSTEMS.

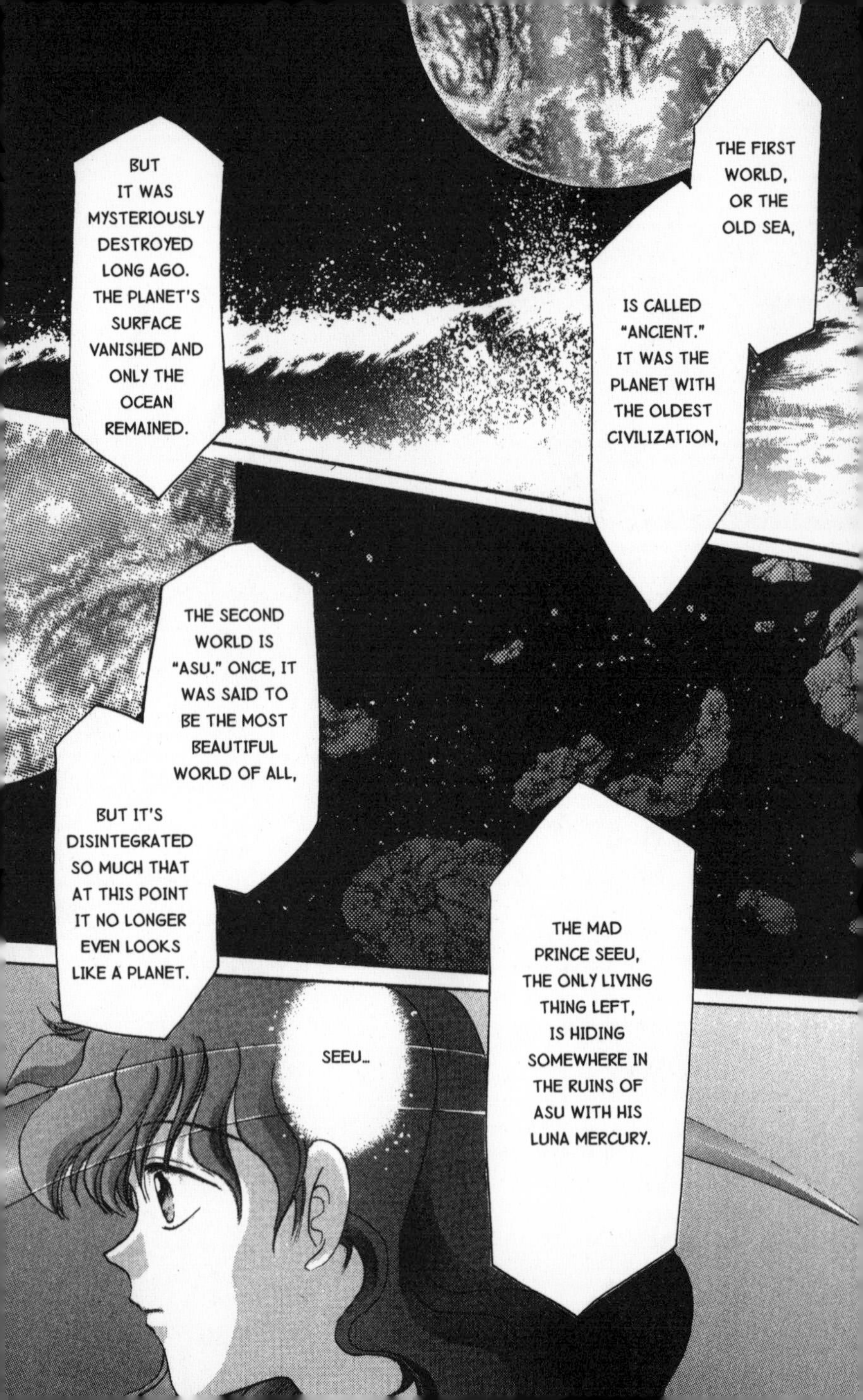
THE FIRST WORLD, OR THE OLD SEA,
IS CALLED "ANCIENT." IT WAS THE PLANET WITH THE OLDEST CIVILIZATION,
BUT IT WAS MYSTERIOUSLY DESTROYED LONG AGO. THE PLANET'S SURFACE VANISHED AND ONLY THE OCEAN REMAINED.
THE SECOND WORLD IS "ASU." ONCE, IT WAS SAID TO BE THE MOST BEAUTIFUL WORLD OF ALL,
BUT IT'S DISINTEGRATED SO MUCH THAT AT THIS POINT IT NO LONGER EVEN LOOKS LIKE A PLANET.
THE MAD PRINCE SEEU, THE ONLY LIVING THING LEFT, IS HIDING SOMEWHERE IN THE RUINS OF ASU WITH HIS LUNA MERCURY.
SEEU...

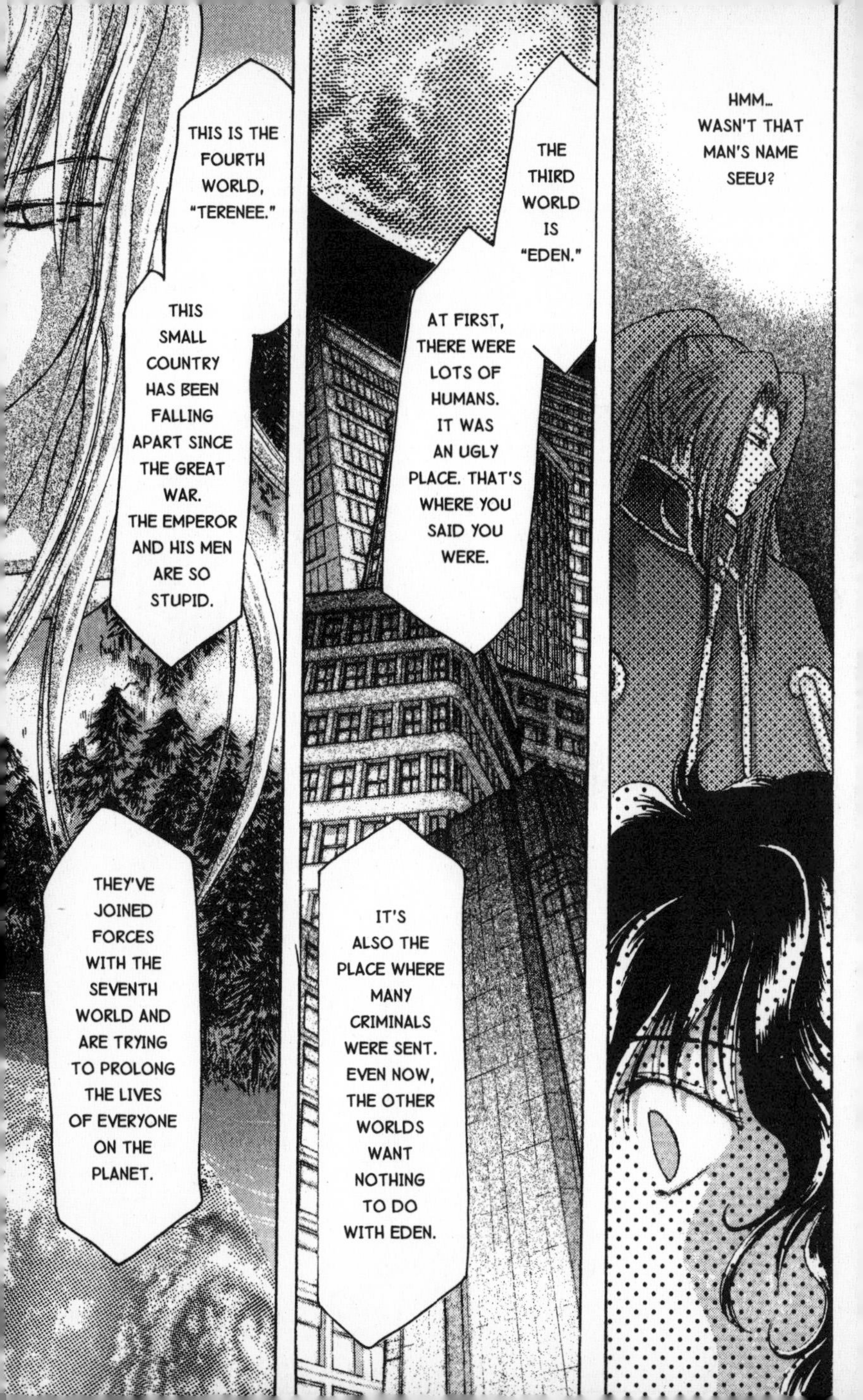
HMM... WASN'T THAT MAN'S NAME SEEU?
THE THIRD WORLD IS "EDEN."
AT FIRST, THERE WERE LOTS OF HUMANS. IT WAS AN UGLY PLACE. THAT'S WHERE YOU SAID YOU WERE.
IT'S ALSO THE PLACE WHERE MANY CRIMINALS WERE SENT. EVEN NOW, THE OTHER WORLDS WANT NOTHING TO DO WITH EDEN.
THIS IS THE FOURTH WORLD, "TERENEE."
THIS SMALL COUNTRY HAS BEEN FALLING APART SINCE THE GREAT WAR. THE EMPEROR AND HIS MEN ARE SO STUPID.
THEY'VE JOINED FORCES WITH THE SEVENTH WORLD AND ARE TRYING TO PROLONG THE LIVES OF EVERYONE ON THE PLANET.

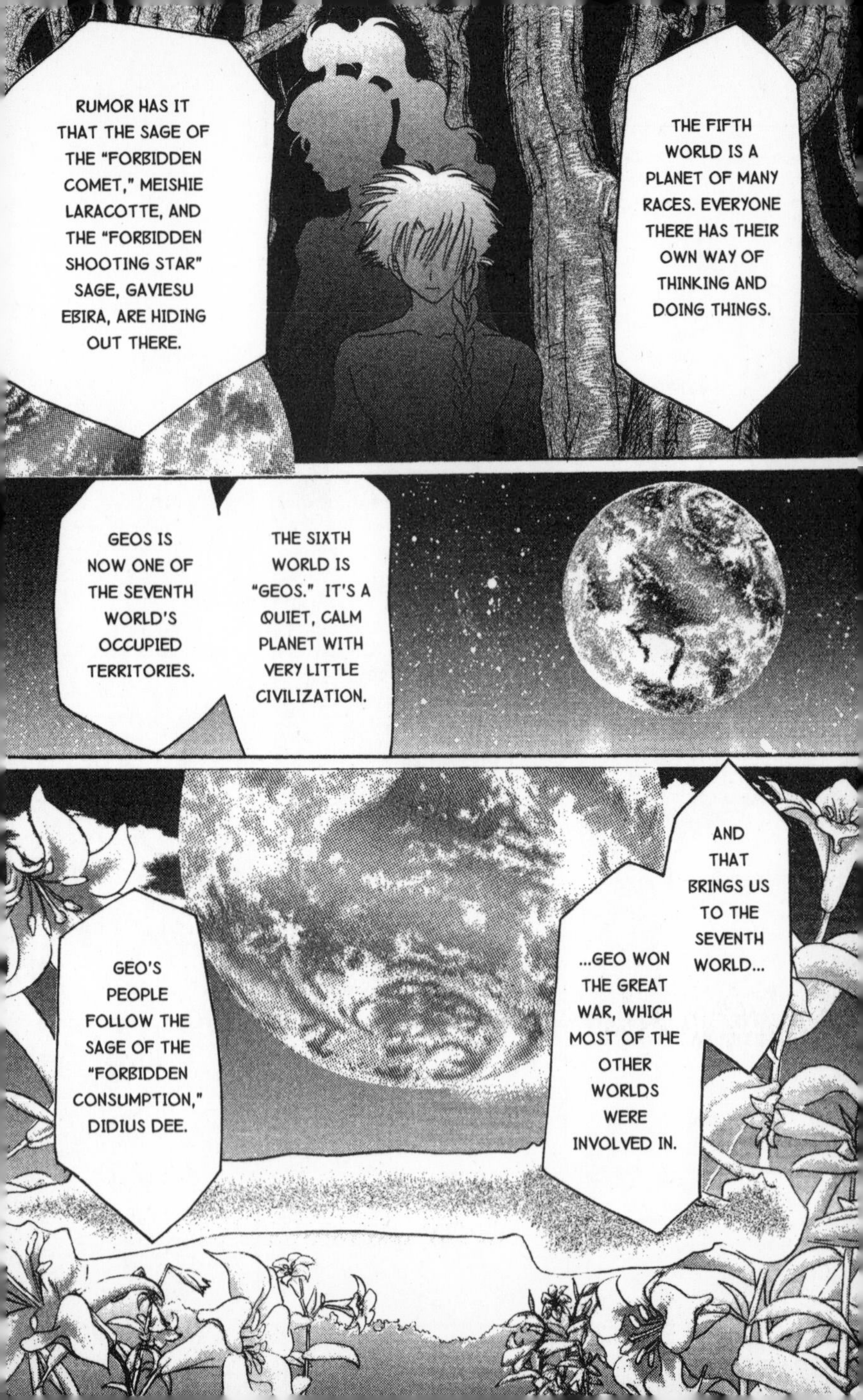
THE FIFTH WORLD IS A PLANET OF MANY RACES. EVERYONE THERE HAS THEIR OWN WAY OF THINKING AND DOING THINGS.
RUMOR HAS IT THAT THE SAGE OF THE "FORBIDDEN COMET," MEISHIE LARACOTTE, AND THE "FORBIDDEN SHOOTING STAR" SAGE, GAVIESU EBIRA, ARE HIDING OUT THERE.
THE SIXTH WORLD IS "GEOS." IT'S A QUIET, CALM PLANET WITH VERY LITTLE CIVILIZATION.
GEOS IS NOW ONE OF THE SEVENTH WORLD'S OCCUPIED TERRITORIES.
AND THAT BRINGS US TO THE SEVENTH WORLD...
...GEO WON THE GREAT WAR, WHICH MOST OF THE OTHER WORLDS WERE INVOLVED IN.
GEO'S PEOPLE FOLLOW THE SAGE OF THE "FORBIDDEN CONSUMPTION," DIDIUS DEE.

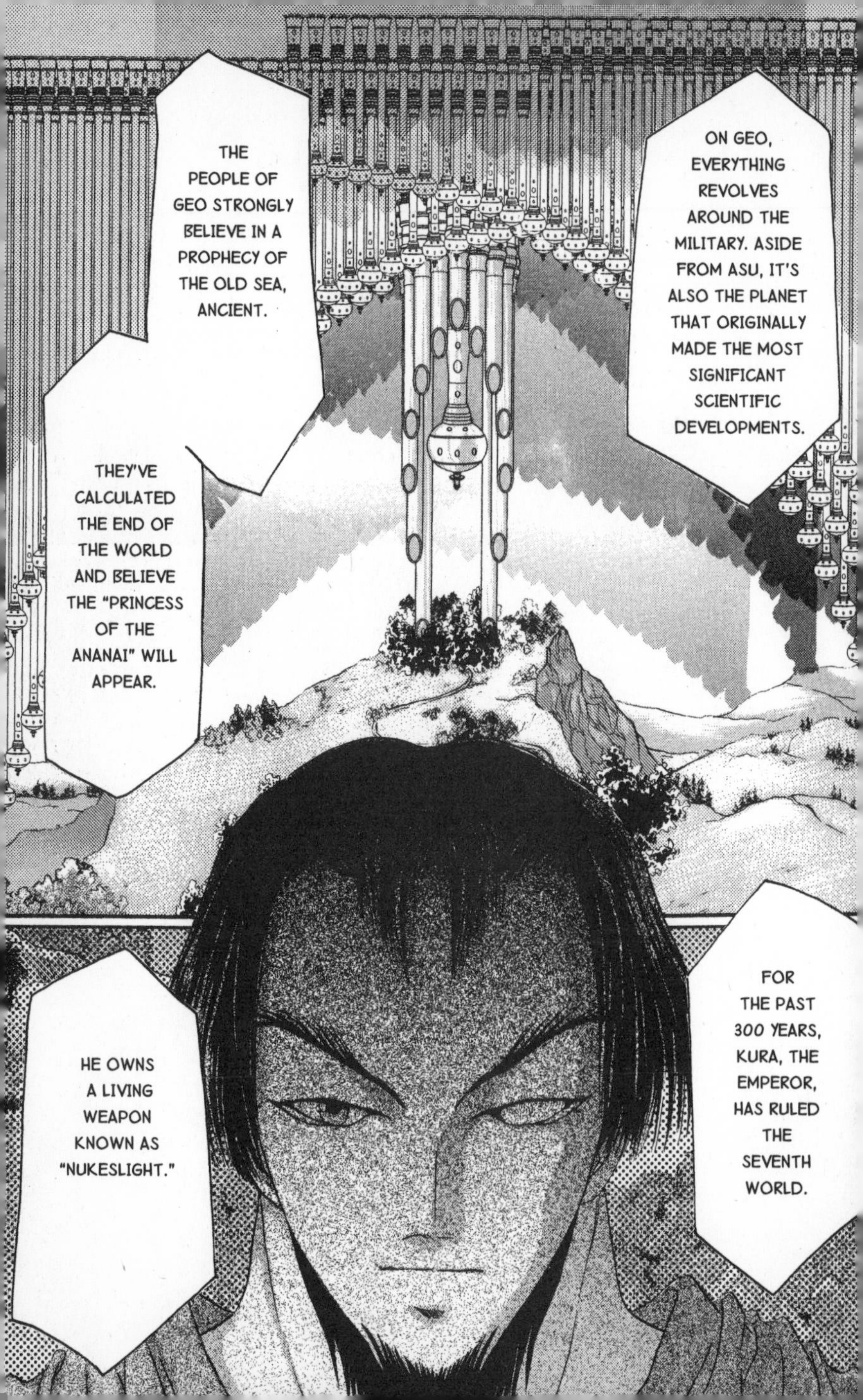
ON GEO, EVERYTHING REVOLVES AROUND THE MILITARY. ASIDE FROM ASU, IT'S ALSO THE PLANET THAT ORIGINALLY MADE THE MOST SIGNIFICANT SCIENTIFIC DEVELOPMENTS.
THE PEOPLE OF GEO STRONGLY BELIEVE IN A PROPHECY OF THE OLD SEA, ANCIENT.
THEY'VE CALCULATED THE END OF THE WORLD AND BELIEVE THE "PRINCESS OF THE ANANAI" WILL APPEAR.
FOR THE PAST 300 YEARS, KURA, THE EMPEROR, HAS RULED THE SEVENTH WORLD.
HE OWNS A LIVING WEAPON KNOWN AS "NUKESLIGHT."

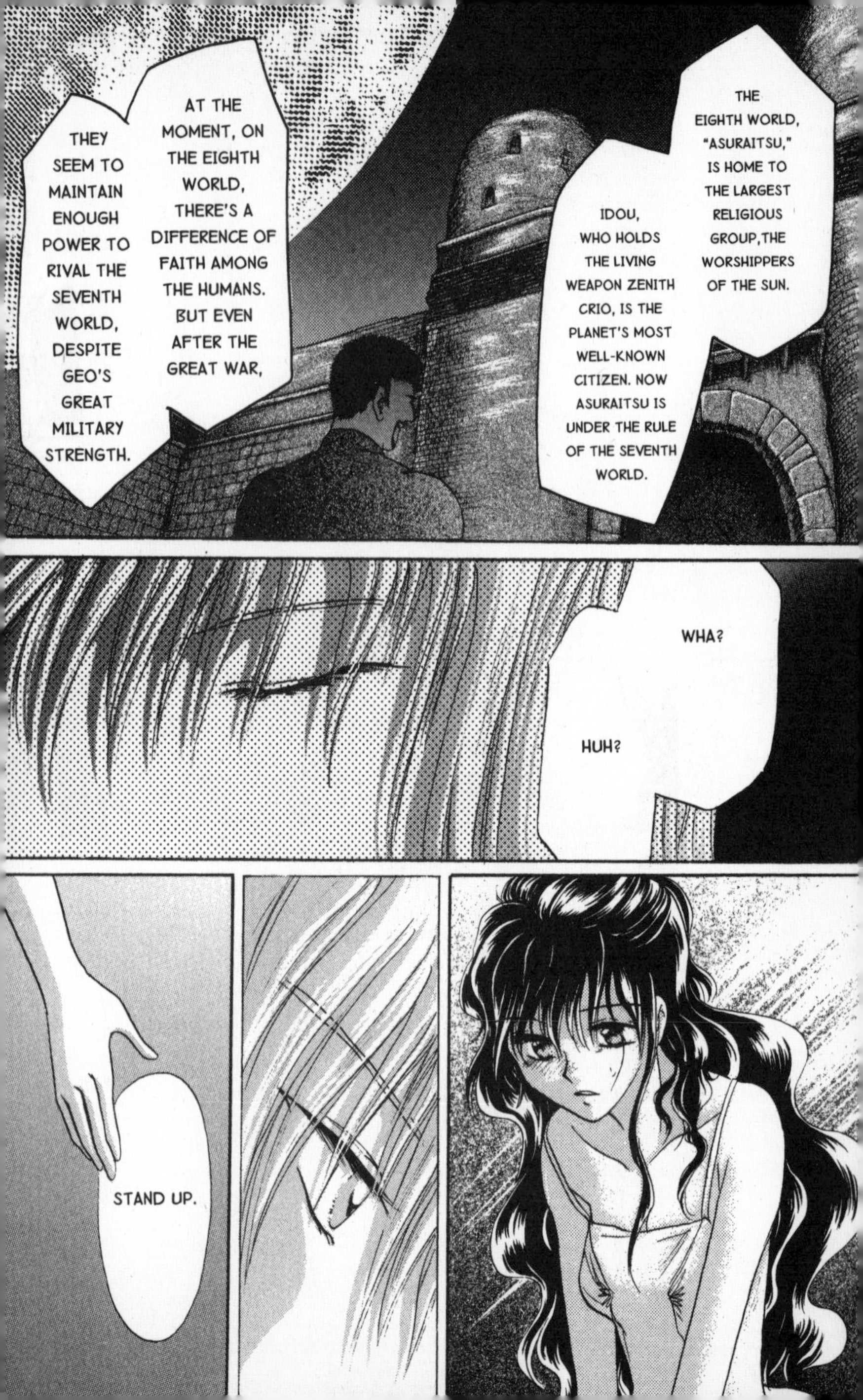
THE EIGHTH WORLD, "ASURAITSU," IS HOME TO THE LARGEST RELIGIOUS GROUP, THE WORSHIPPERS OF THE SUN.
IDOU, WHO HOLDS THE LIVING WEAPON ZENITH CRIO, IS THE PLANET'S MOST WELL-KNOWN CITIZEN. NOW ASURAITSU IS UNDER THE RULE OF THE SEVENTH WORLD.
AT THE MOMENT, ON THE EIGHTH WORLD, THERE'S A DIFFERENCE OF FAITH AMONG THE HUMANS. BUT EVEN AFTER THE GREAT WAR,
THEY SEEM TO MAINTAIN ENOUGH POWER TO RIVAL THE SEVENTH WORLD, DESPITE GEO'S GREAT MILITARY STRENGTH.
WHA?
HUH?
STAND UP.

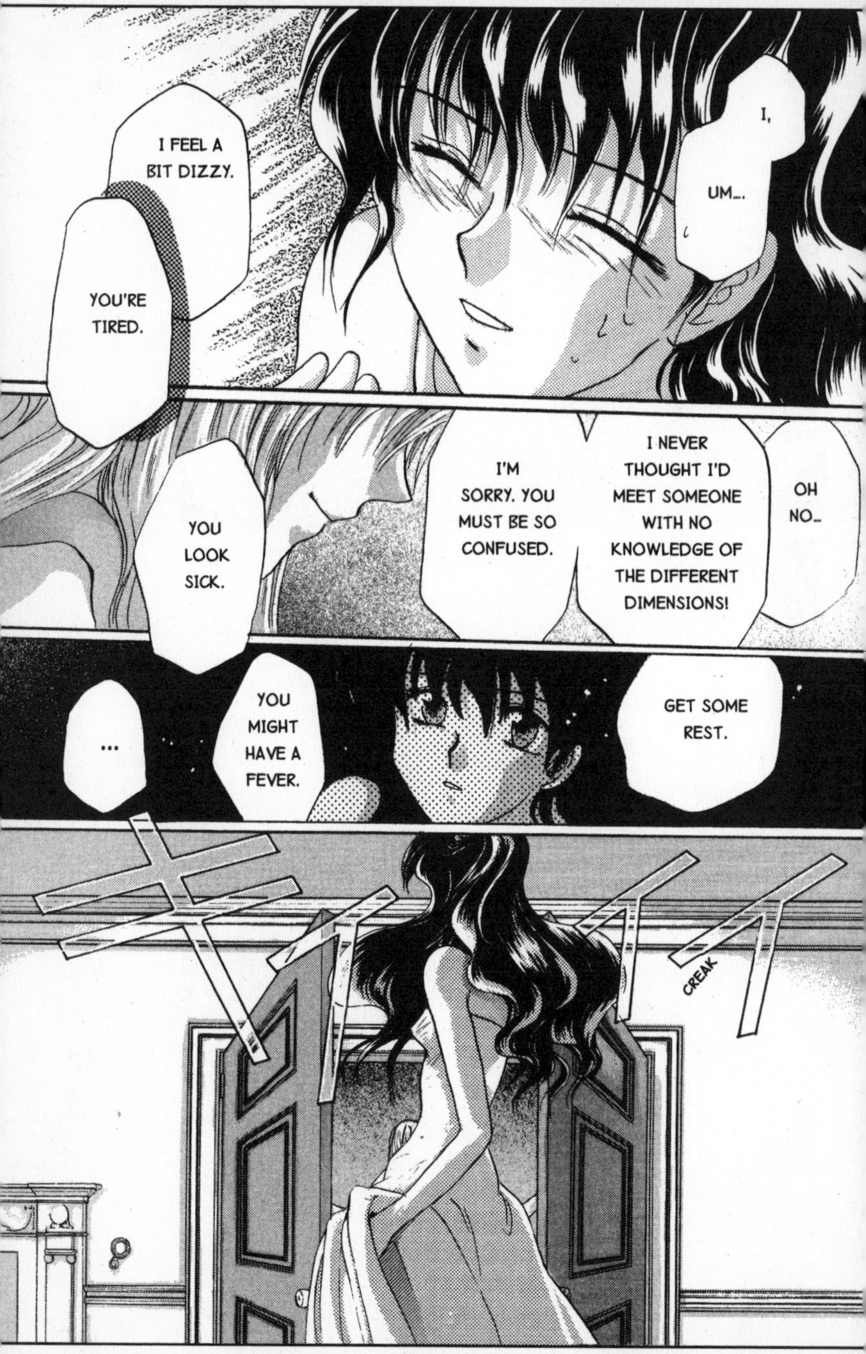

I,
UM...
I FEEL A BIT DIZZY.
YOU'RE TIRED.
OH NO...
I NEVER THOUGHT I'D MEET SOMEONE WITH NO KNOWLEDGE OF THE DIFFERENT DIMENSIONS!
I'M SORRY. YOU MUST BE SO CONFUSED.
YOU LOOK SICK.
GET SOME REST.
YOU MIGHT HAVE A FEVER.
...
CREAK

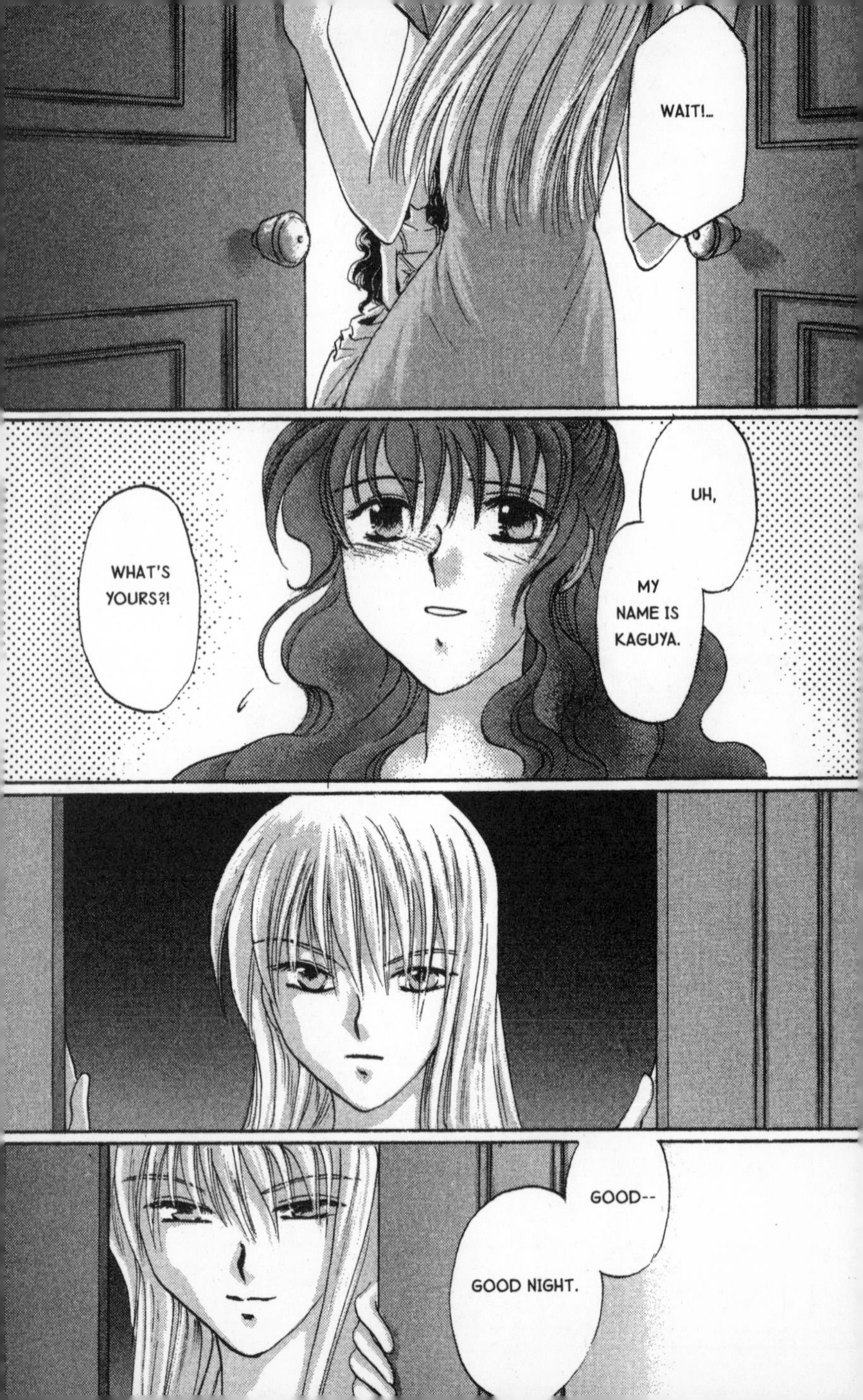
WAIT!..
UH,
MY NAME IS KAGUYA.
WHAT'S YOURS?!
GOOD--
GOOD NIGHT.

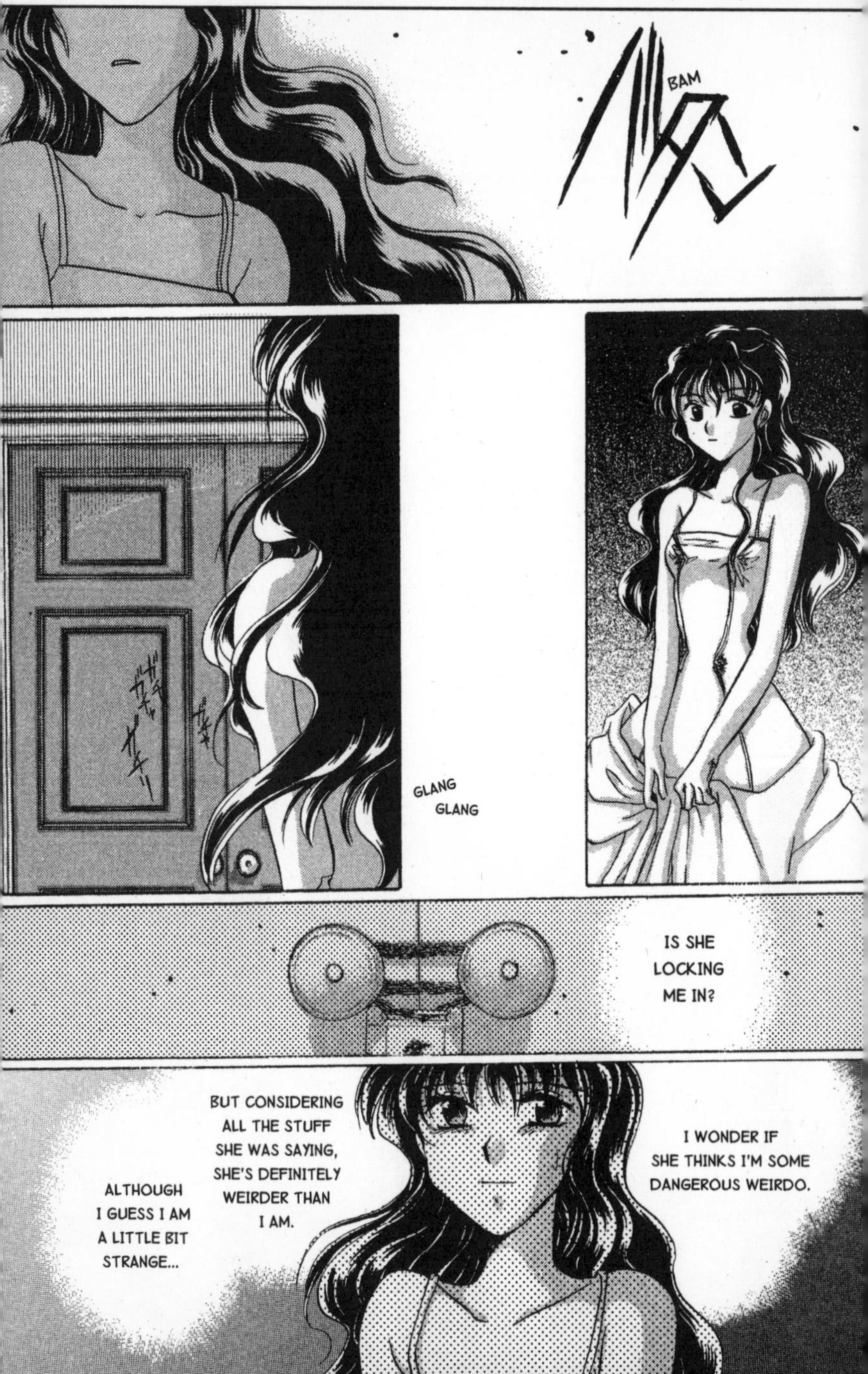
BAM
GLANG GLANG
IS SHE LOCKING ME IN?
I WONDER IF SHE THINKS I'M SOME DANGEROUS WEIRDO.
BUT CONSIDERING ALL THE STUFF SHE WAS SAYING, SHE'S DEFINITELY WEIRDER THAN I AM.
ALTHOUGH I GUESS I AM A LITTLE BIT STRANGE...

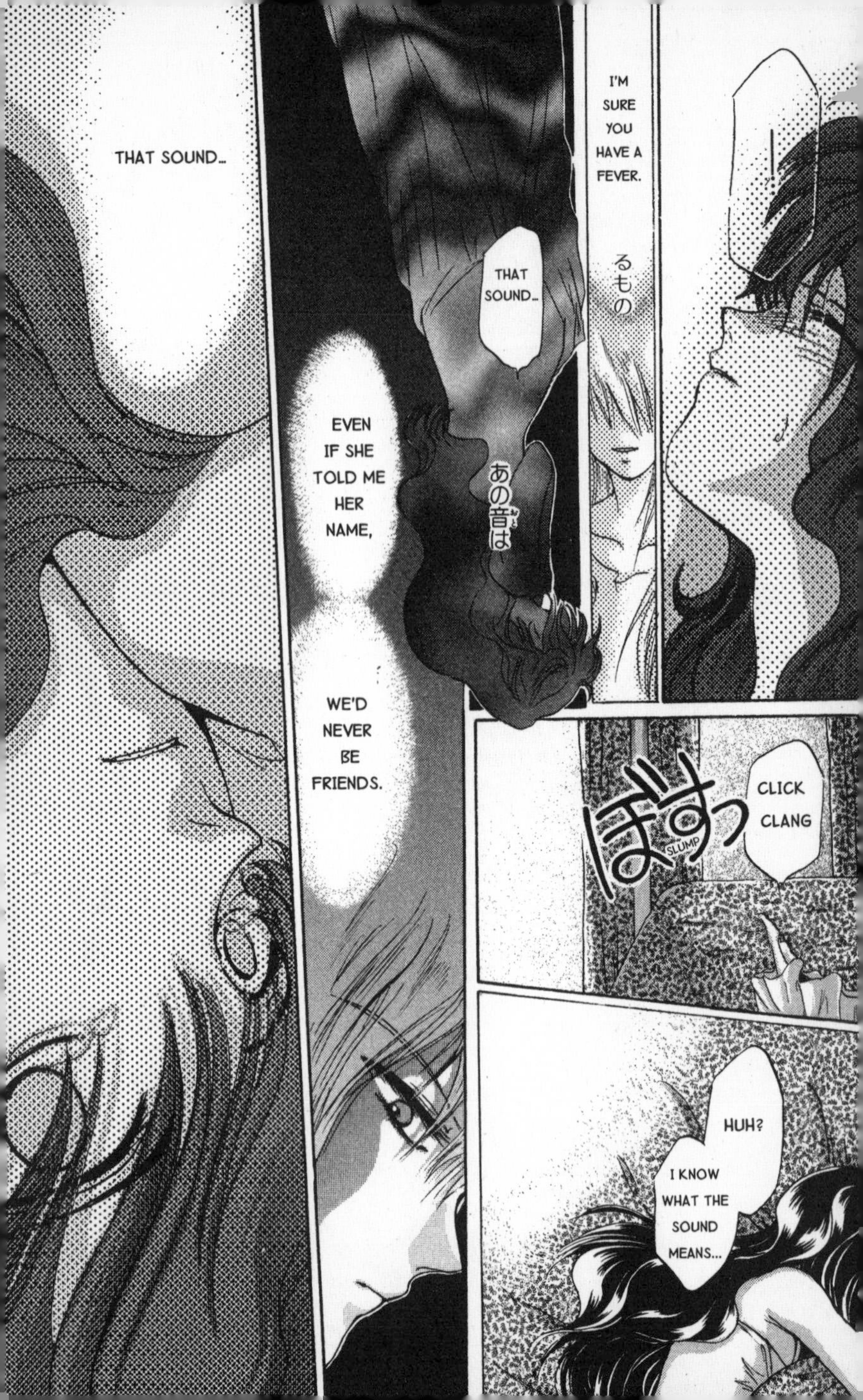
!
I'M SURE YOU HAVE A FEVER.
るもの
THAT SOUND...
あの音は
EVEN IF SHE TOLD ME HER NAME,
WE'D NEVER BE FRIENDS.
CLICK CLANG
ぼすっ
SLUMP
HUH?
I KNOW WHAT THE SOUND MEANS...
THAT SOUND...

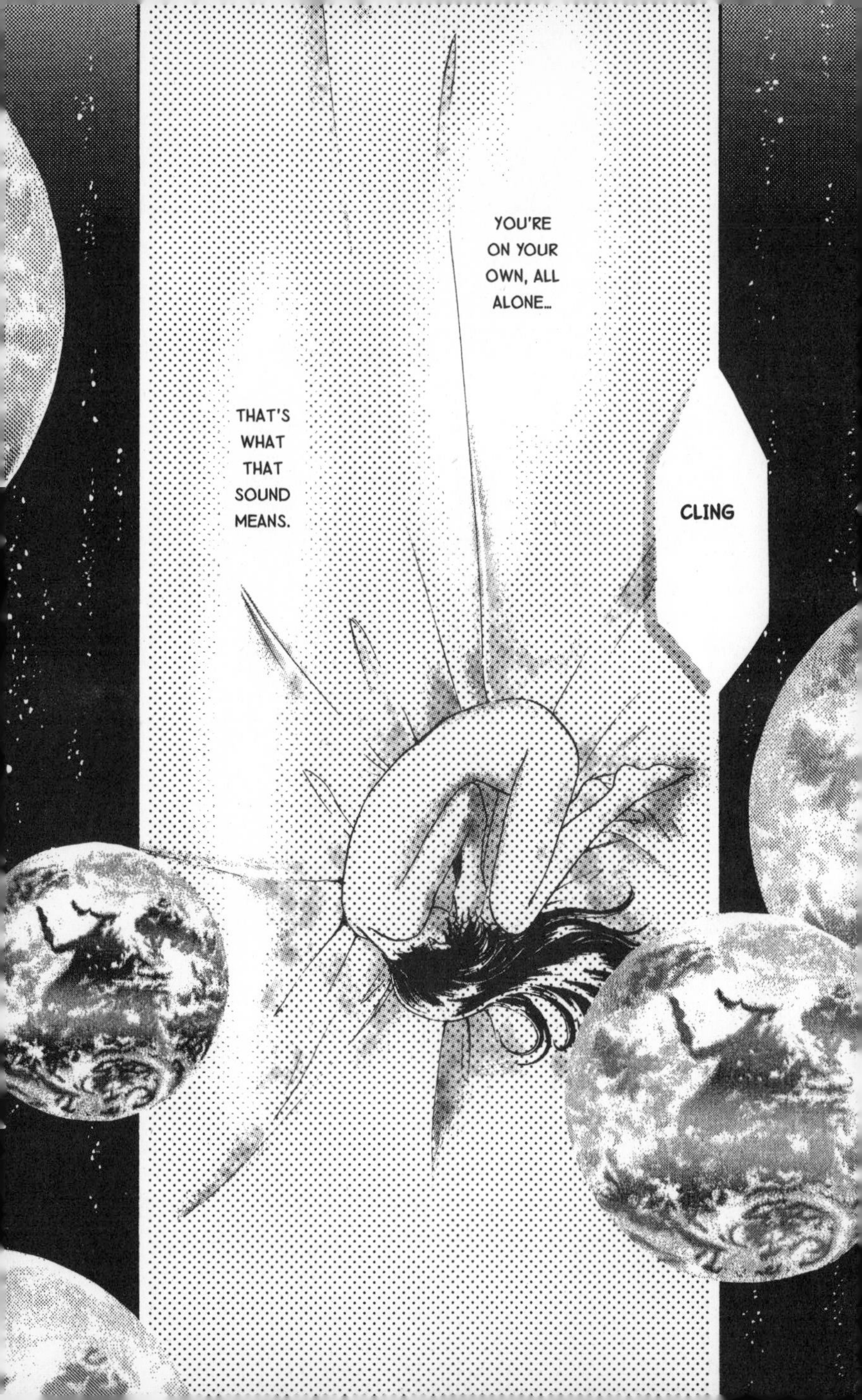
CLING
YOU'RE ON YOUR OWN, ALL ALONE...
THAT'S WHAT THAT SOUND MEANS.

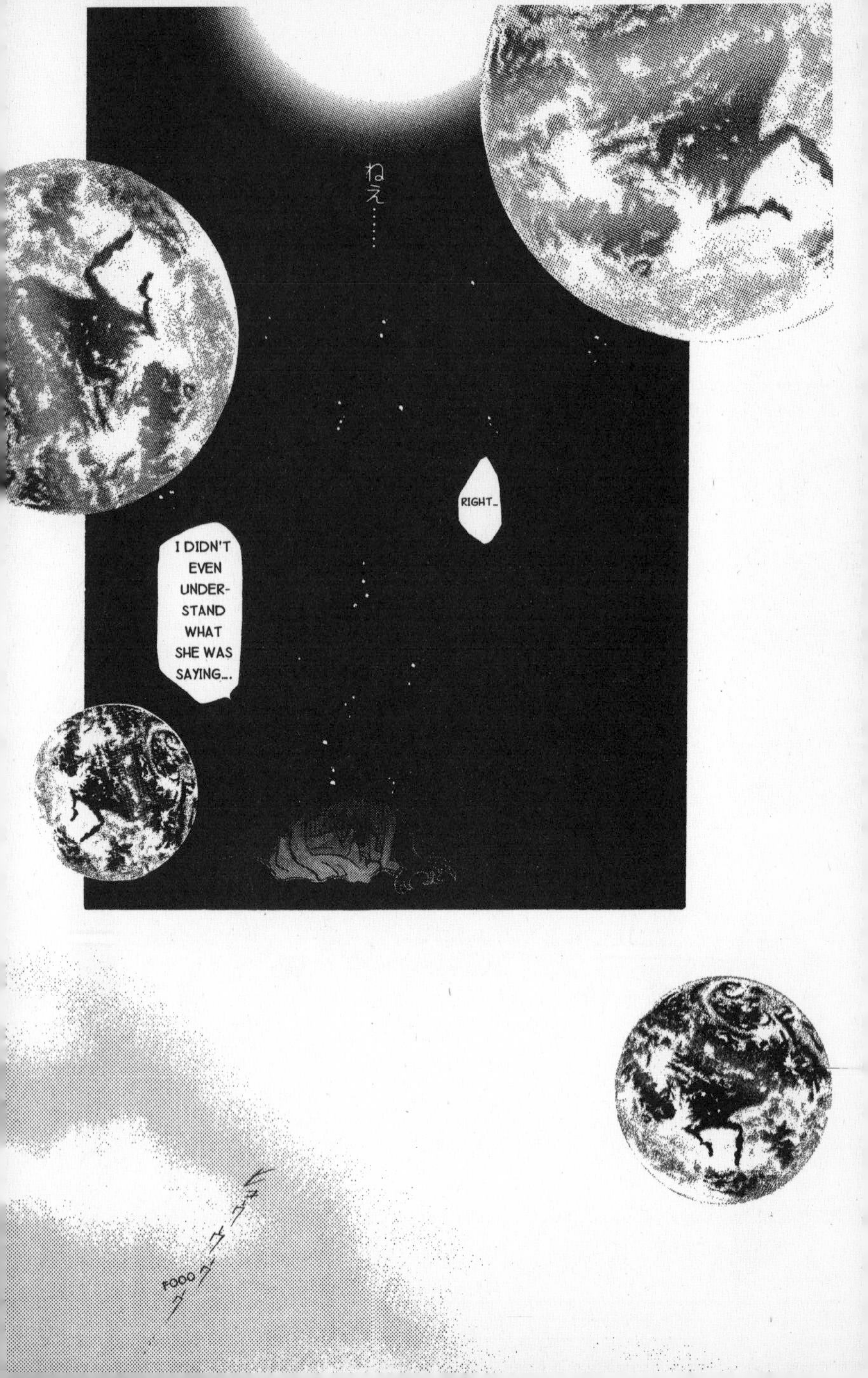
ねえ……
RIGHT…
I DIDN'T EVEN UNDER-STAND WHAT SHE WAS SAYING….
FOOO

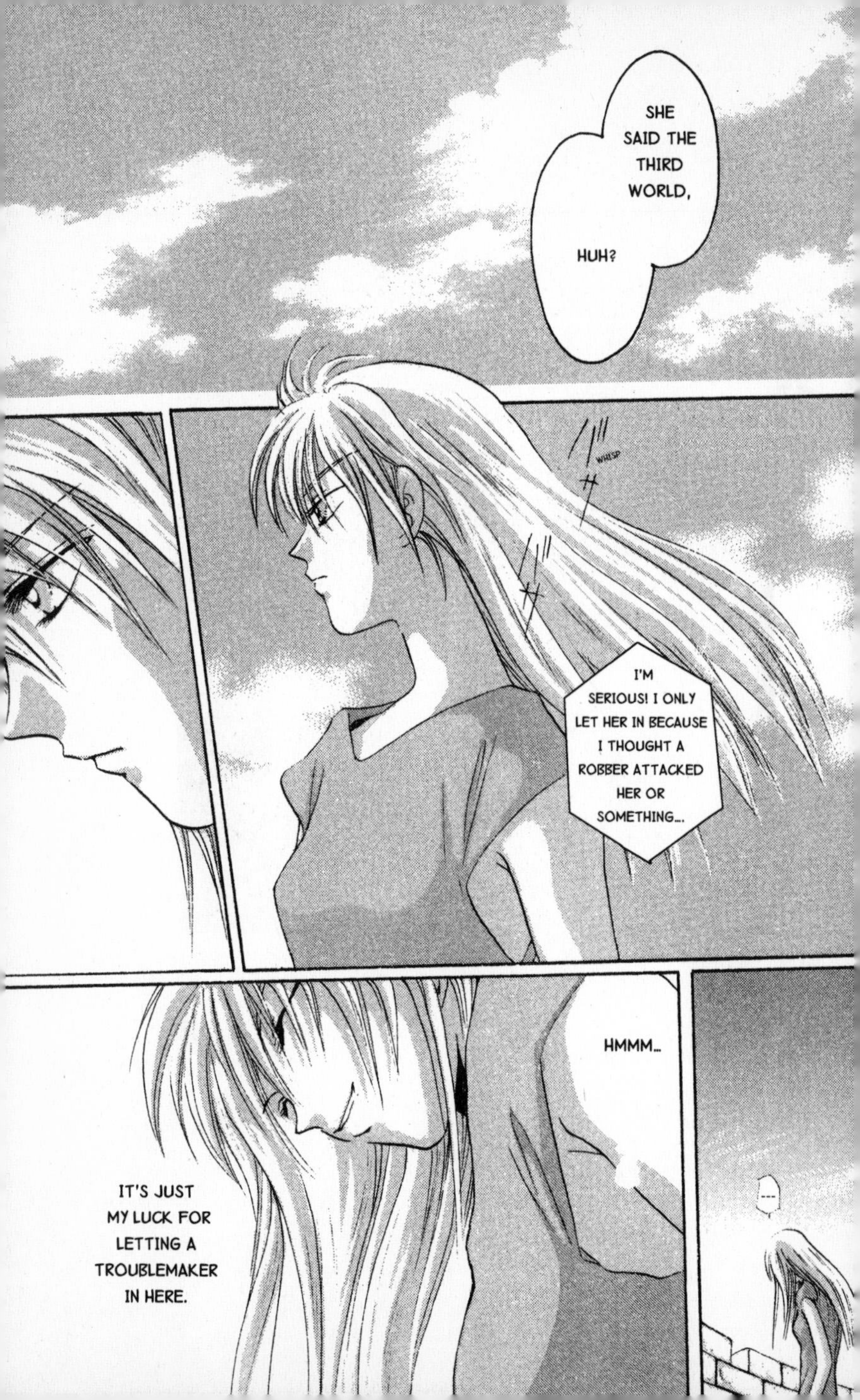
SHE SAID THE THIRD WORLD,
HUH?
WHISP
I'M SERIOUS! I ONLY LET HER IN BECAUSE I THOUGHT A ROBBER ATTACKED HER OR SOMETHING...
HMMM...
IT'S JUST MY LUCK FOR LETTING A TROUBLEMAKER IN HERE.

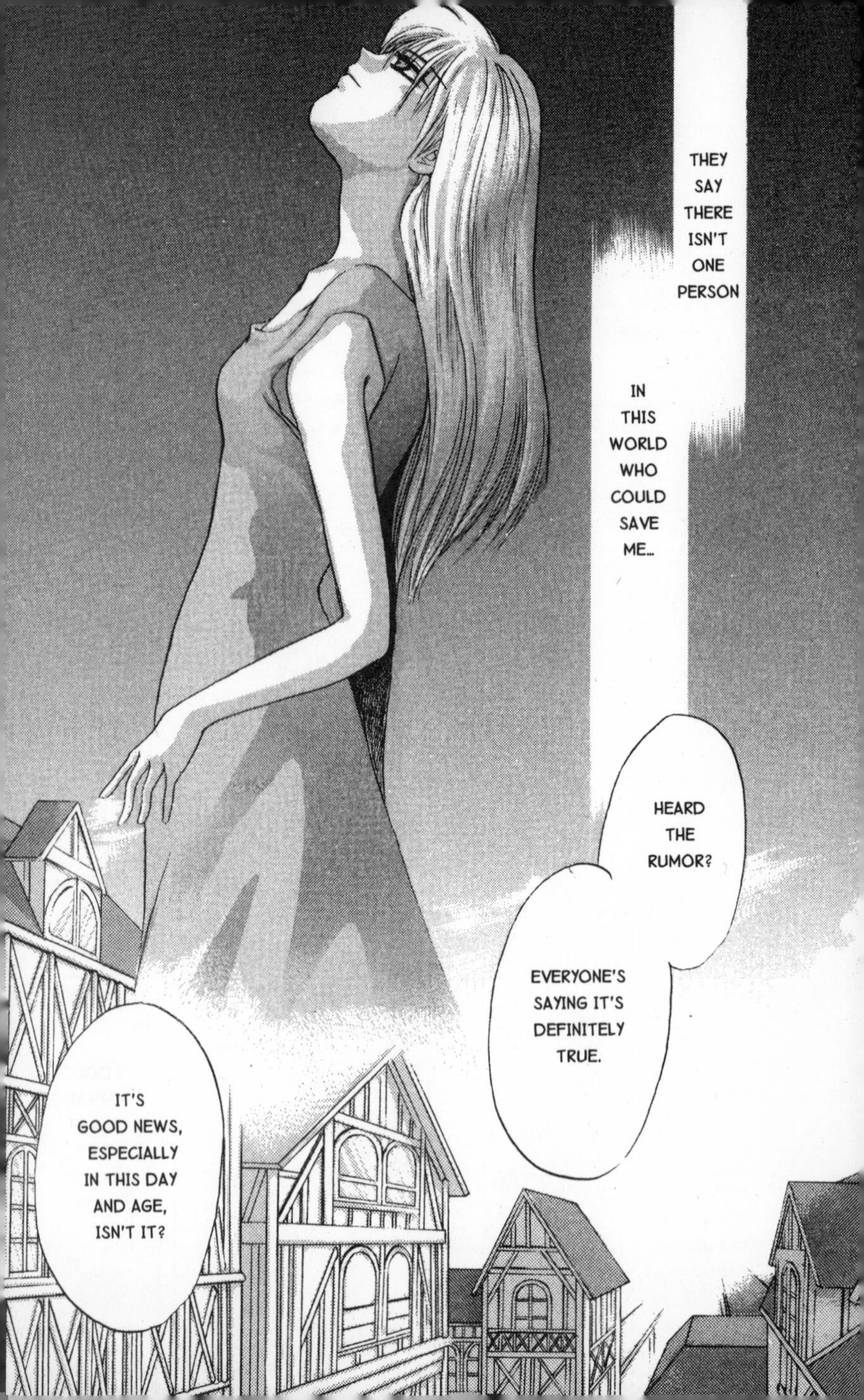
THEY SAY THERE ISN'T ONE PERSON
IN THIS WORLD WHO COULD SAVE ME...
HEARD THE RUMOR?
EVERYONE'S SAYING IT'S DEFINITELY TRUE.
IT'S GOOD NEWS, ESPECIALLY IN THIS DAY AND AGE, ISN'T IT?

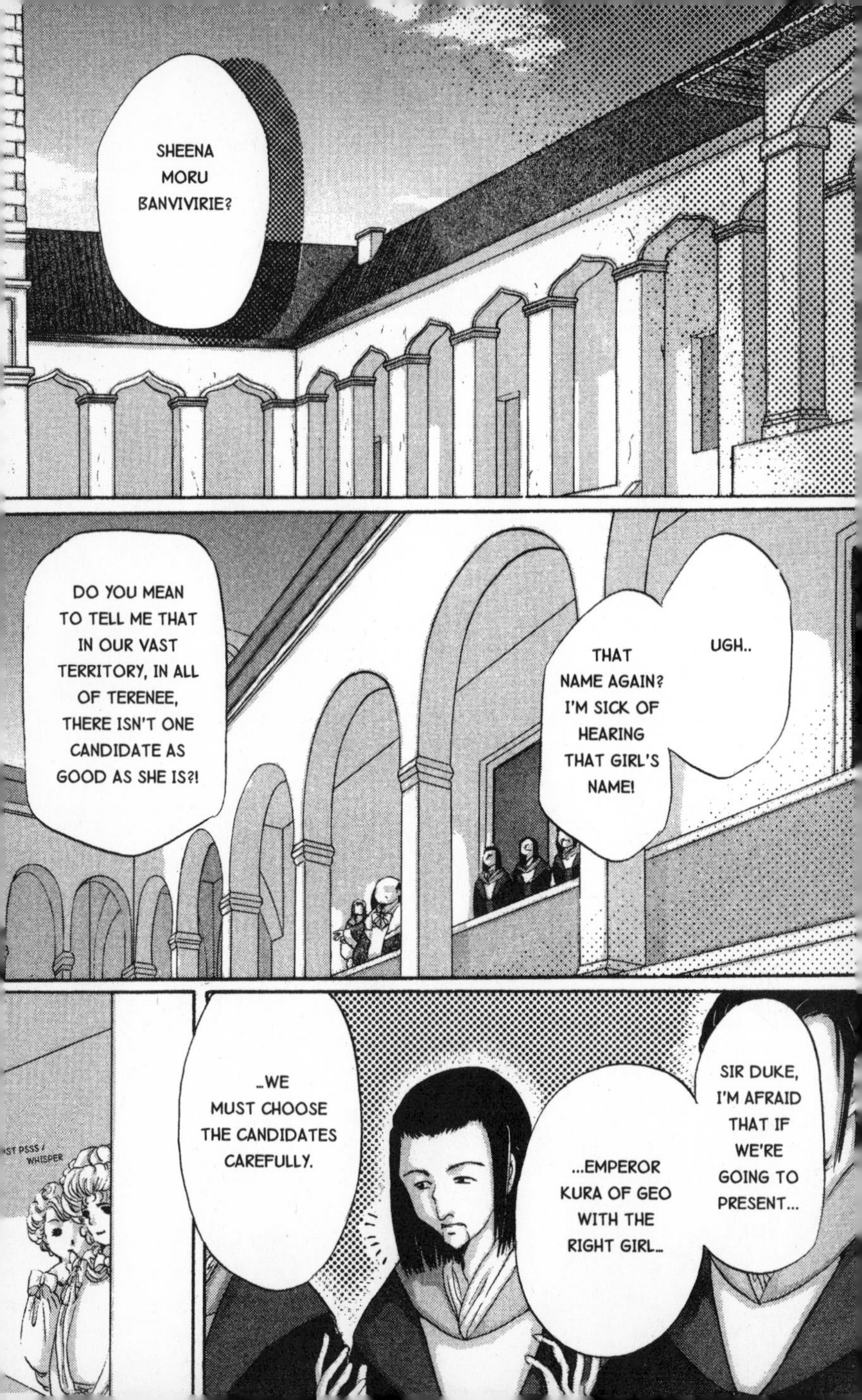
SHEENA MORU BANVIVIRIE?
UGH..
THAT NAME AGAIN? I'M SICK OF HEARING THAT GIRL'S NAME!
DO YOU MEAN TO TELL ME THAT IN OUR VAST TERRITORY, IN ALL OF TERENEE, THERE ISN'T ONE CANDIDATE AS GOOD AS SHE IS?!
SIR DUKE, I'M AFRAID THAT IF WE'RE GOING TO PRESENT...
...EMPEROR KURA OF GEO WITH THE RIGHT GIRL...
...WE MUST CHOOSE THE CANDIDATES CAREFULLY.
PSSS / WHISPER

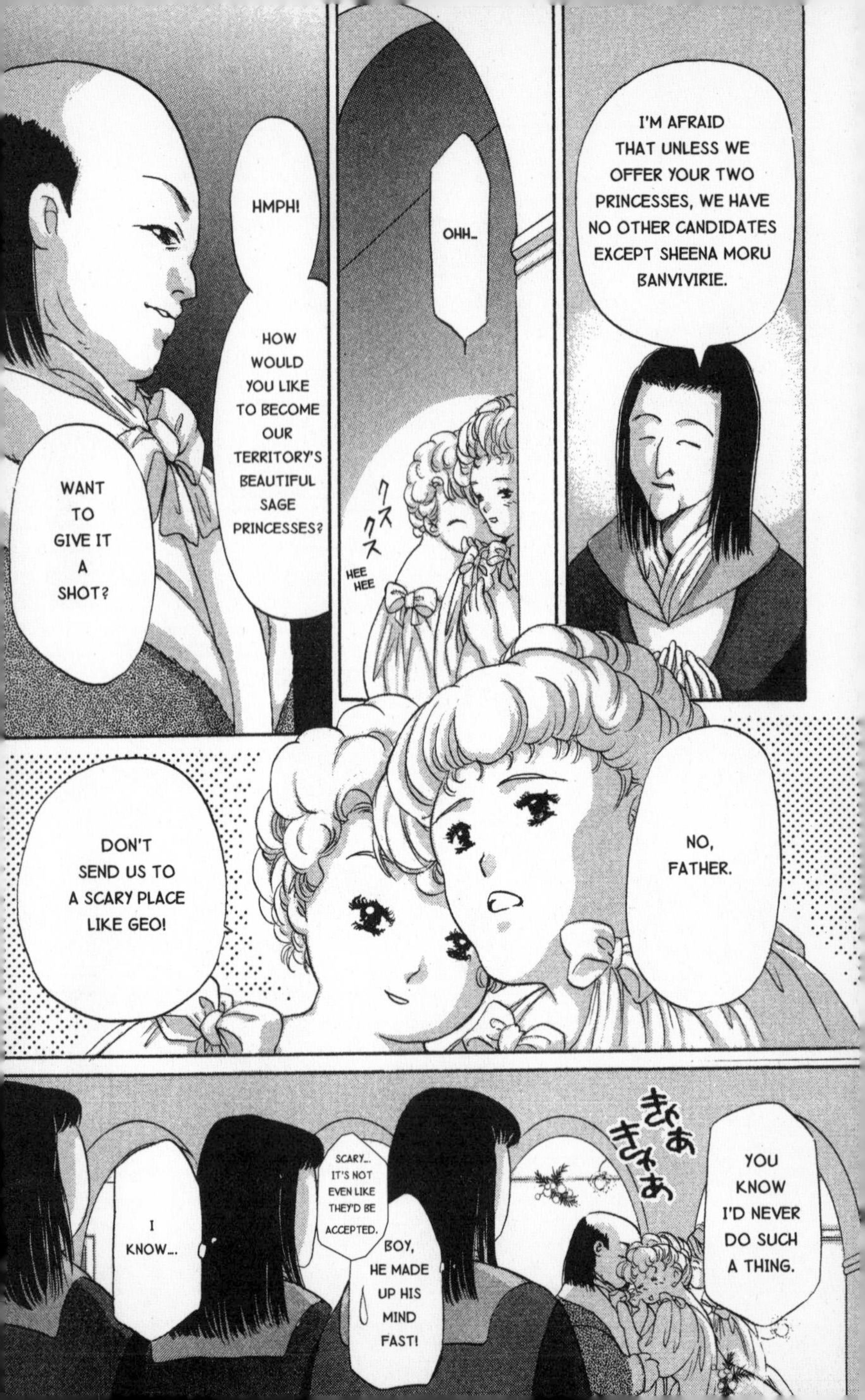
I'M AFRAID THAT UNLESS WE OFFER YOUR TWO PRINCESSES, WE HAVE NO OTHER CANDIDATES EXCEPT SHEENA MORU BANVIVIRIE.
OHH..
クスクス
HEE HEE
HMPH!
HOW WOULD YOU LIKE TO BECOME OUR TERRITORY'S BEAUTIFUL SAGE PRINCESSES?
WANT TO GIVE IT A SHOT?
NO, FATHER.
DON'T SEND US TO A SCARY PLACE LIKE GEO!
きゃあきゃあ
YOU KNOW I'D NEVER DO SUCH A THING.
BOY, HE MADE UP HIS MIND FAST!
SCARY... IT'S NOT EVEN LIKE THEY'D BE ACCEPTED.
I KNOW...

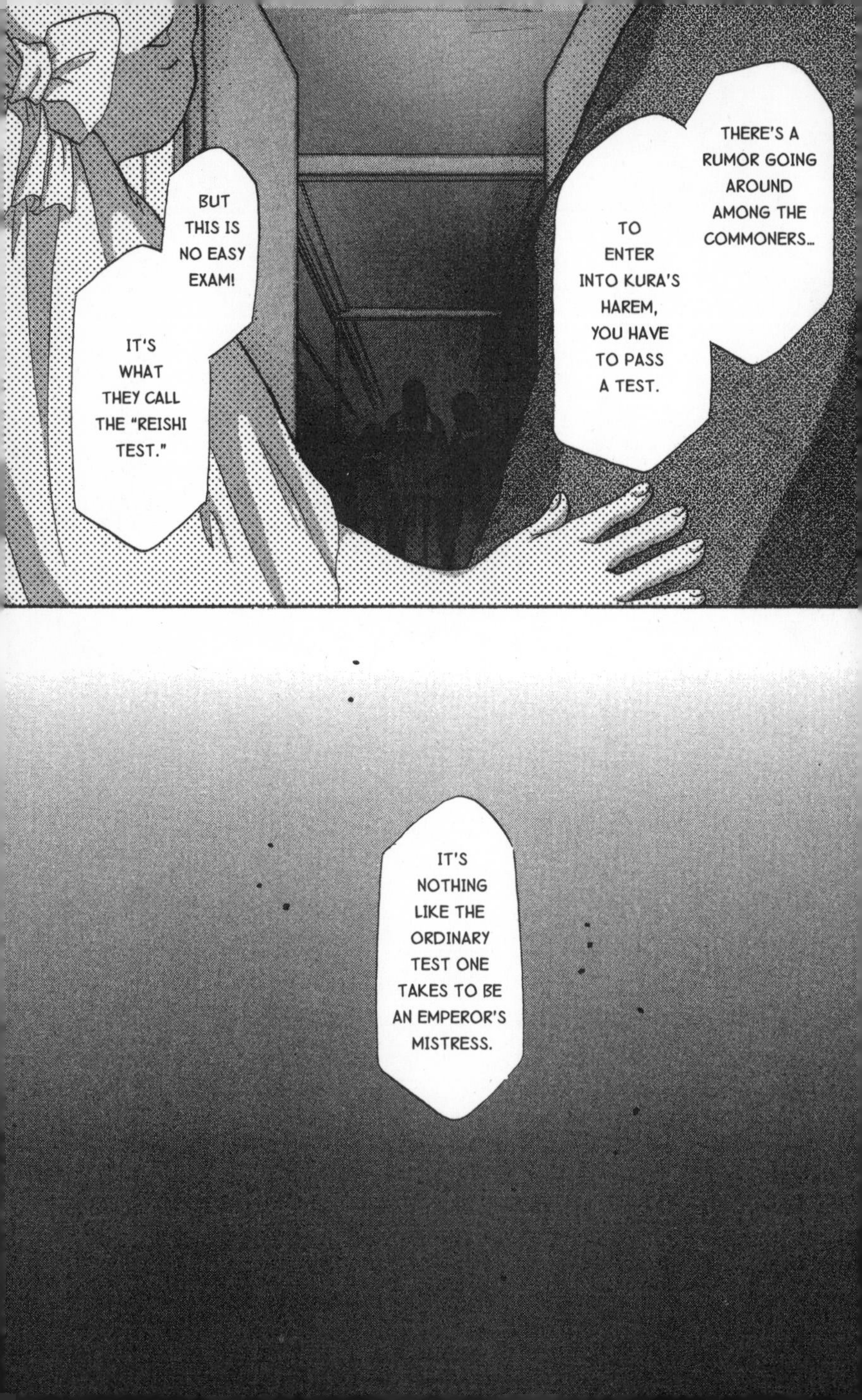
THERE'S A RUMOR GOING AROUND AMONG THE COMMONERS...
TO ENTER INTO KURA'S HAREM, YOU HAVE TO PASS A TEST.
BUT THIS IS NO EASY EXAM!
IT'S WHAT THEY CALL THE "REISHI TEST."
IT'S NOTHING LIKE THE ORDINARY TEST ONE TAKES TO BE AN EMPEROR'S MISTRESS.

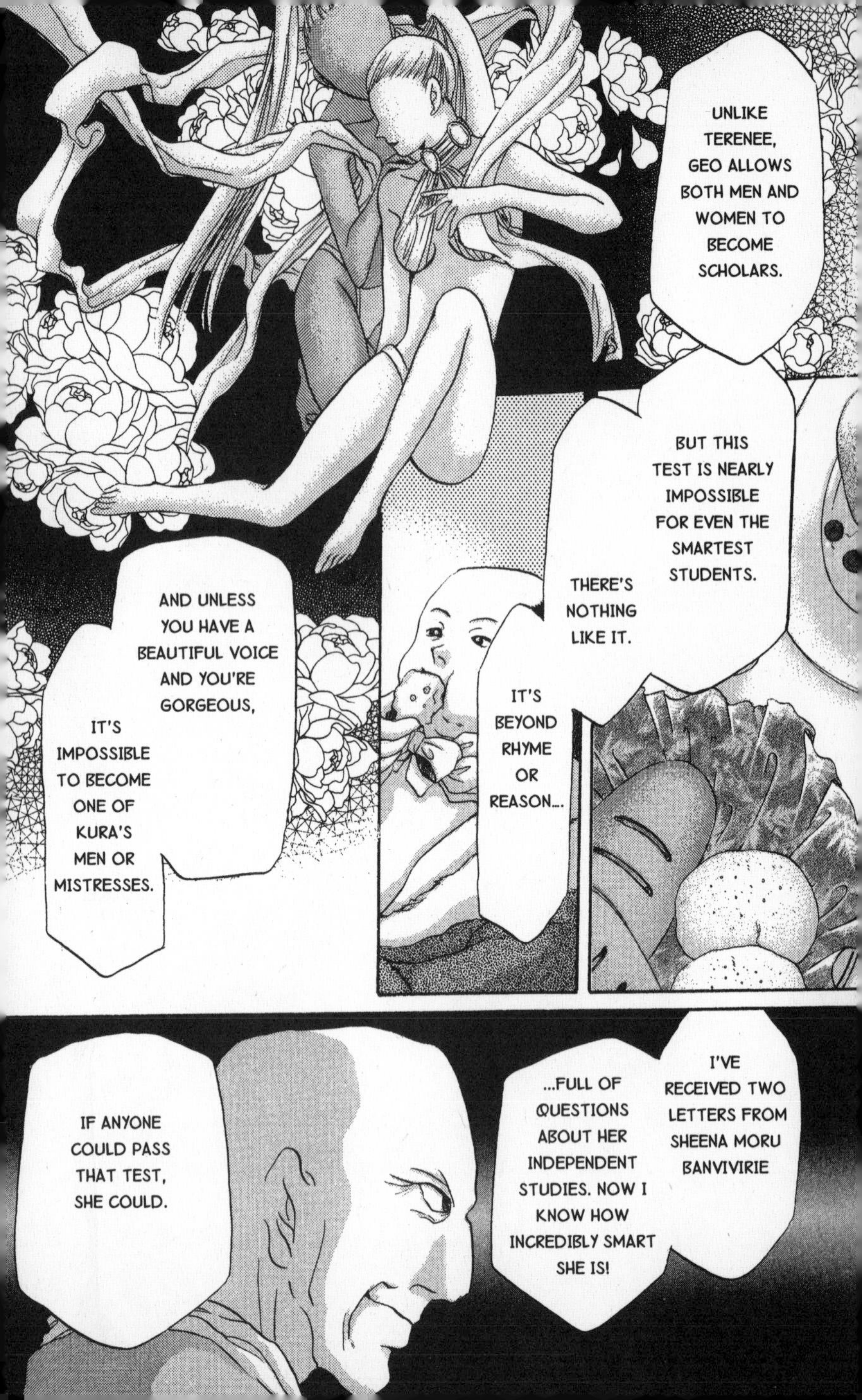
UNLIKE TERENEE, GEO ALLOWS BOTH MEN AND WOMEN TO BECOME SCHOLARS.
AND UNLESS YOU HAVE A BEAUTIFUL VOICE AND YOU'RE GORGEOUS,
IT'S IMPOSSIBLE TO BECOME ONE OF KURA'S MEN OR MISTRESSES.
BUT THIS TEST IS NEARLY IMPOSSIBLE FOR EVEN THE SMARTEST STUDENTS.
THERE'S NOTHING LIKE IT.
IT'S BEYOND RHYME OR REASON....
I'VE RECEIVED TWO LETTERS FROM SHEENA MORU BANVIVIRIE
...FULL OF QUESTIONS ABOUT HER INDEPENDENT STUDIES. NOW I KNOW HOW INCREDIBLY SMART SHE IS!
IF ANYONE COULD PASS THAT TEST, SHE COULD.

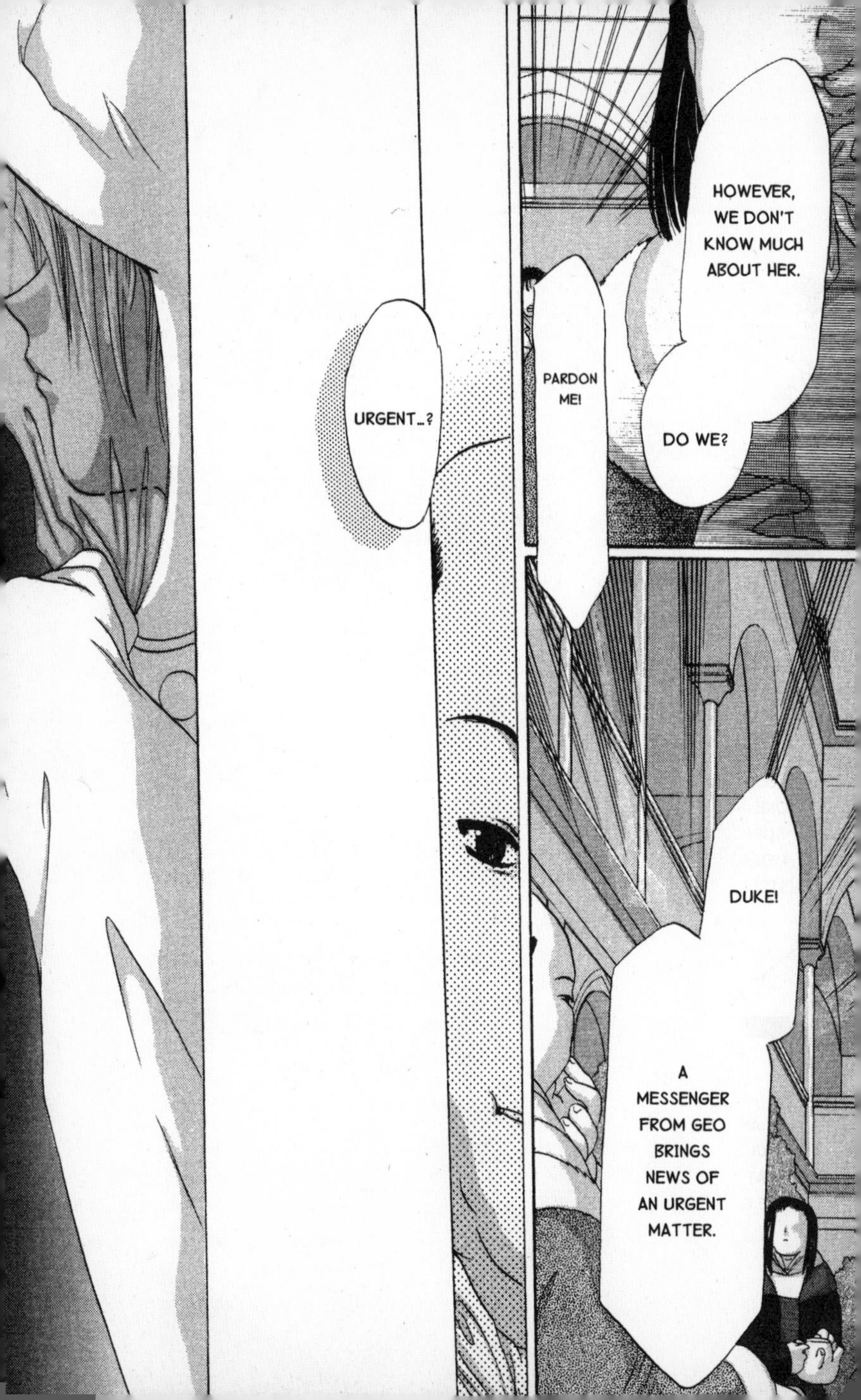
HOWEVER, WE DON'T KNOW MUCH ABOUT HER.
DO WE?
PARDON ME!
DUKE!
A MESSENGER FROM GEO BRINGS NEWS OF AN URGENT MATTER.
URGENT...?

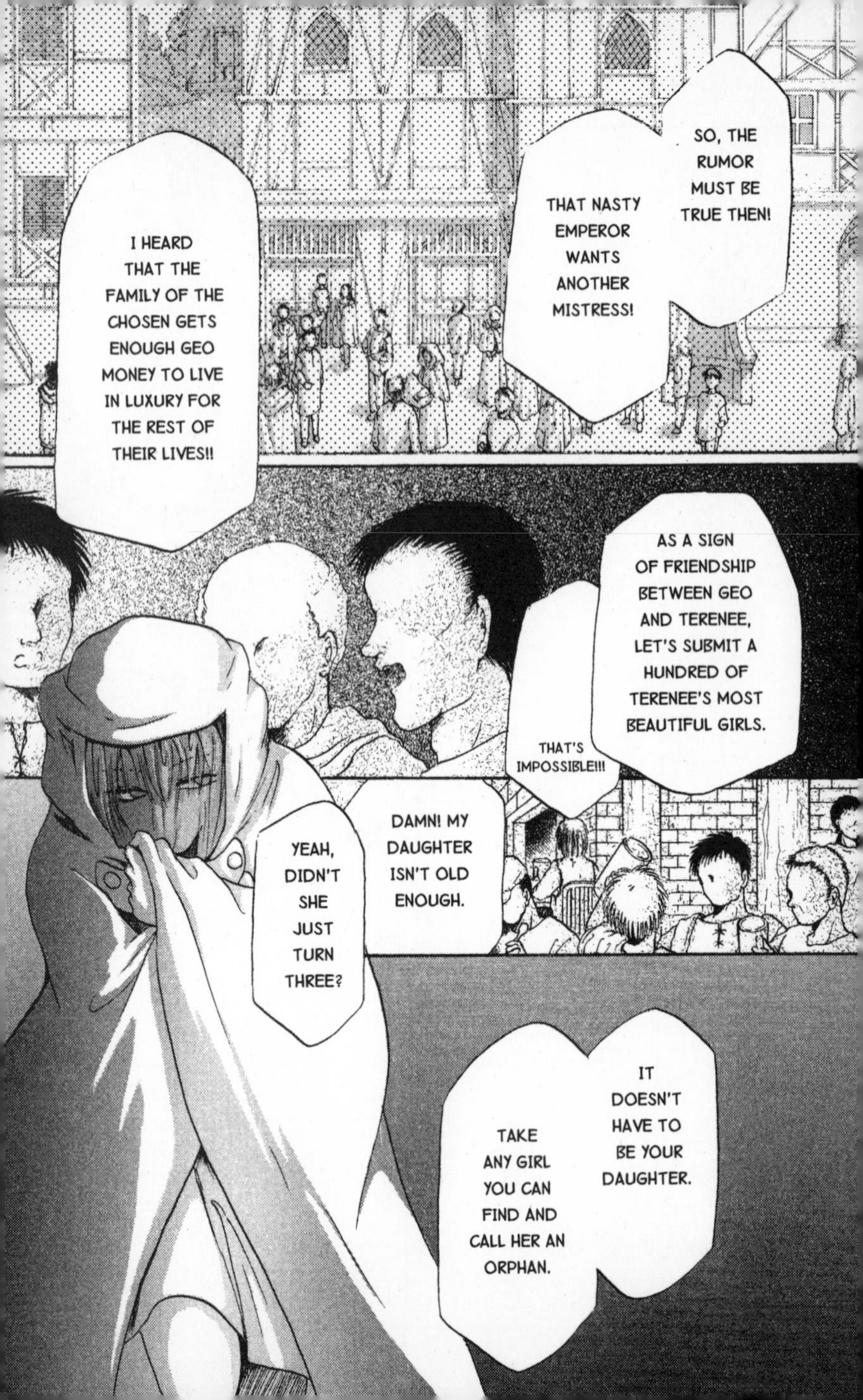
SO, THE RUMOR MUST BE TRUE THEN!
THAT NASTY EMPEROR WANTS ANOTHER MISTRESS!
I HEARD THAT THE FAMILY OF THE CHOSEN GETS ENOUGH GEO MONEY TO LIVE IN LUXURY FOR THE REST OF THEIR LIVES!!
AS A SIGN OF FRIENDSHIP BETWEEN GEO AND TERENEE, LET'S SUBMIT A HUNDRED OF TERENEE'S MOST BEAUTIFUL GIRLS.
THAT'S IMPOSSIBLE!!!
DAMN! MY DAUGHTER ISN'T OLD ENOUGH.
YEAH, DIDN'T SHE JUST TURN THREE?
IT DOESN'T HAVE TO BE YOUR DAUGHTER.
TAKE ANY GIRL YOU CAN FIND AND CALL HER AN ORPHAN.

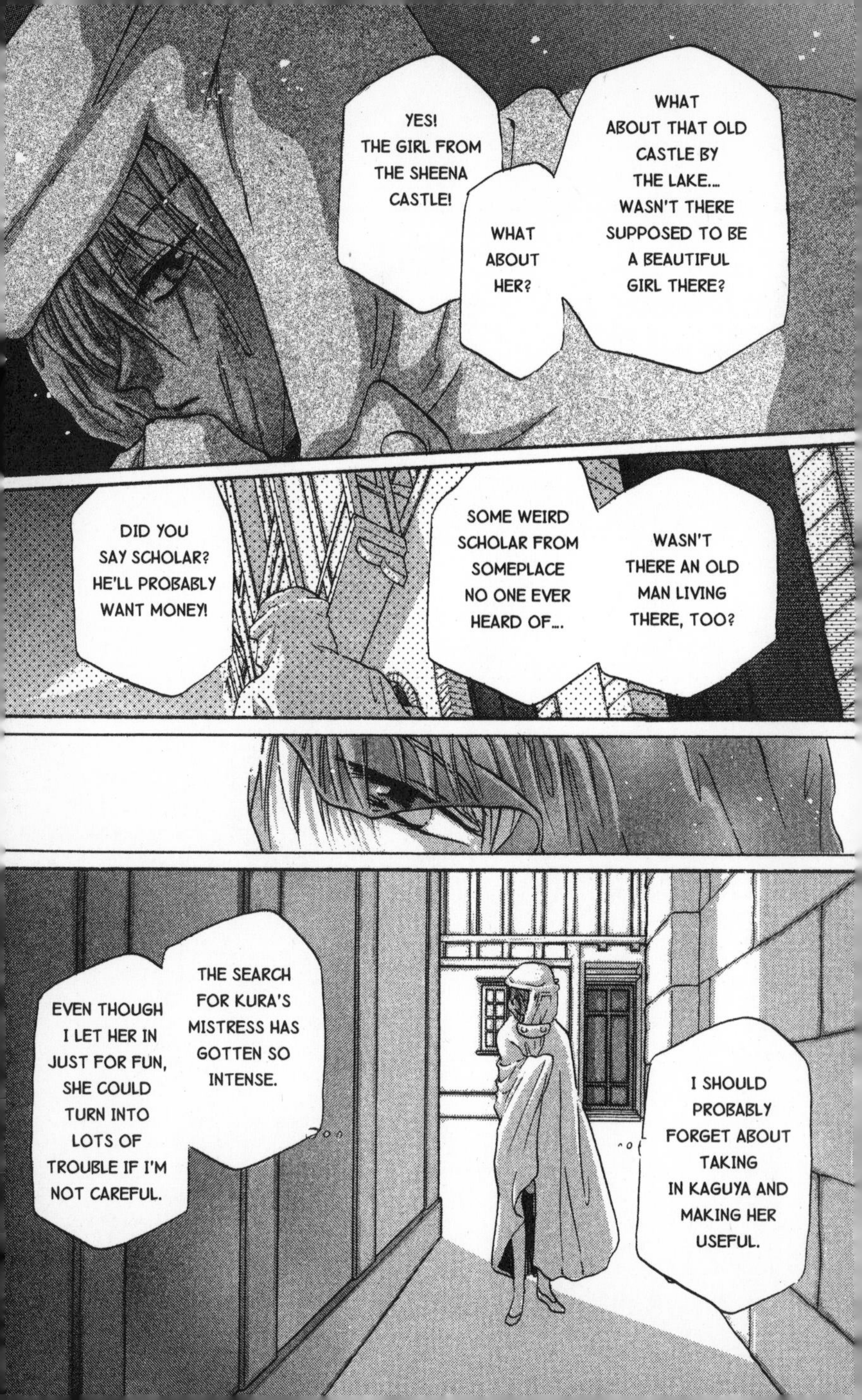
WHAT ABOUT THAT OLD CASTLE BY THE LAKE.... WASN'T THERE SUPPOSED TO BE A BEAUTIFUL GIRL THERE?
WHAT ABOUT HER?
YES! THE GIRL FROM THE SHEENA CASTLE!
WASN'T THERE AN OLD MAN LIVING THERE, TOO?
SOME WEIRD SCHOLAR FROM SOMEPLACE NO ONE EVER HEARD OF....
DID YOU SAY SCHOLAR? HE'LL PROBABLY WANT MONEY!
I SHOULD PROBABLY FORGET ABOUT TAKING IN KAGUYA AND MAKING HER USEFUL.
THE SEARCH FOR KURA'S MISTRESS HAS GOTTEN SO INTENSE.
EVEN THOUGH I LET HER IN JUST FOR FUN, SHE COULD TURN INTO LOTS OF TROUBLE IF I'M NOT CAREFUL.

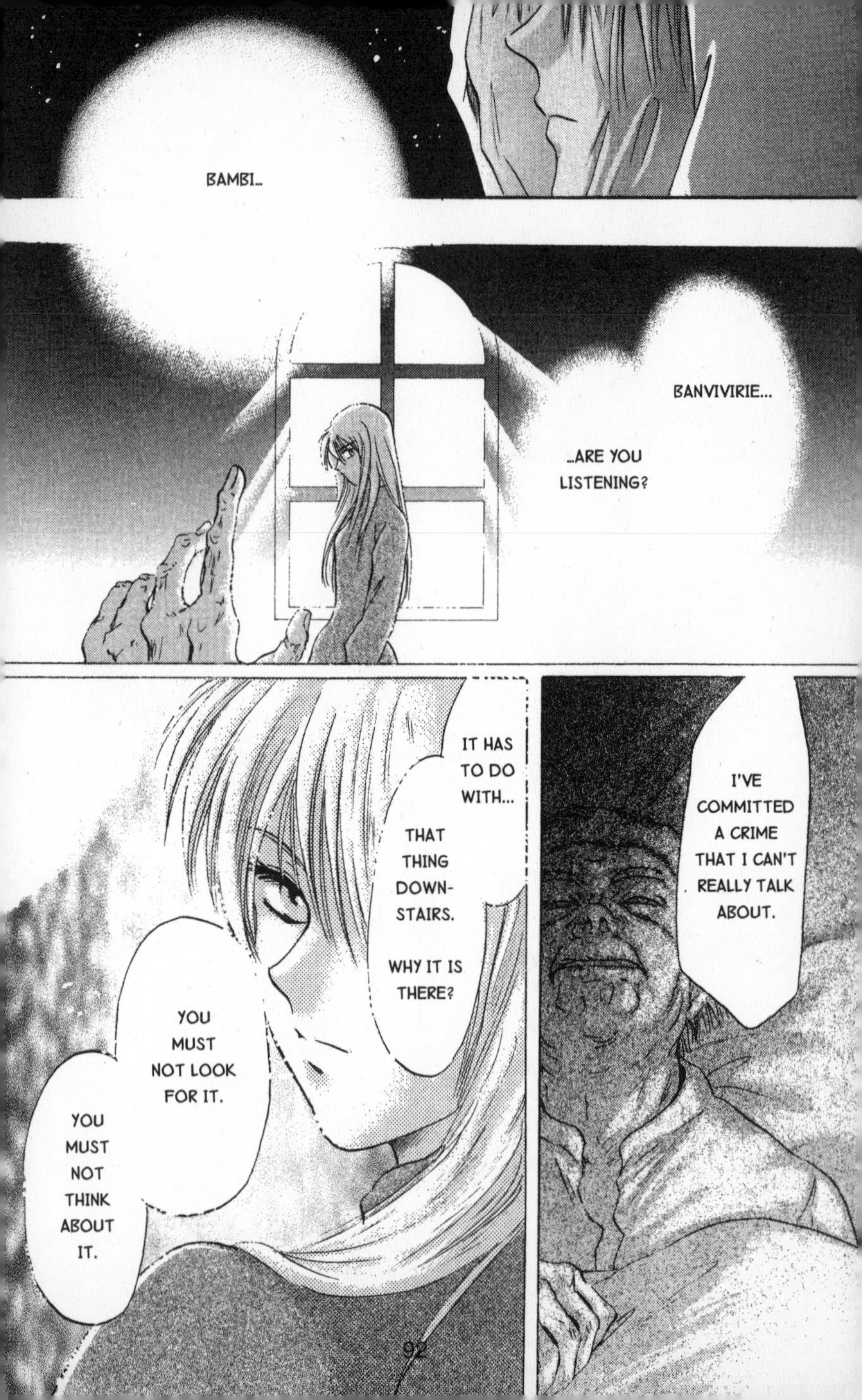
BAMBI...
BANVIVIRIE...
...ARE YOU LISTENING?
I'VE COMMITTED A CRIME THAT I CAN'T REALLY TALK ABOUT.
IT HAS TO DO WITH...
THAT THING DOWN-STAIRS.
WHY IT IS THERE?
YOU MUST NOT LOOK FOR IT.
YOU MUST NOT THINK ABOUT IT.

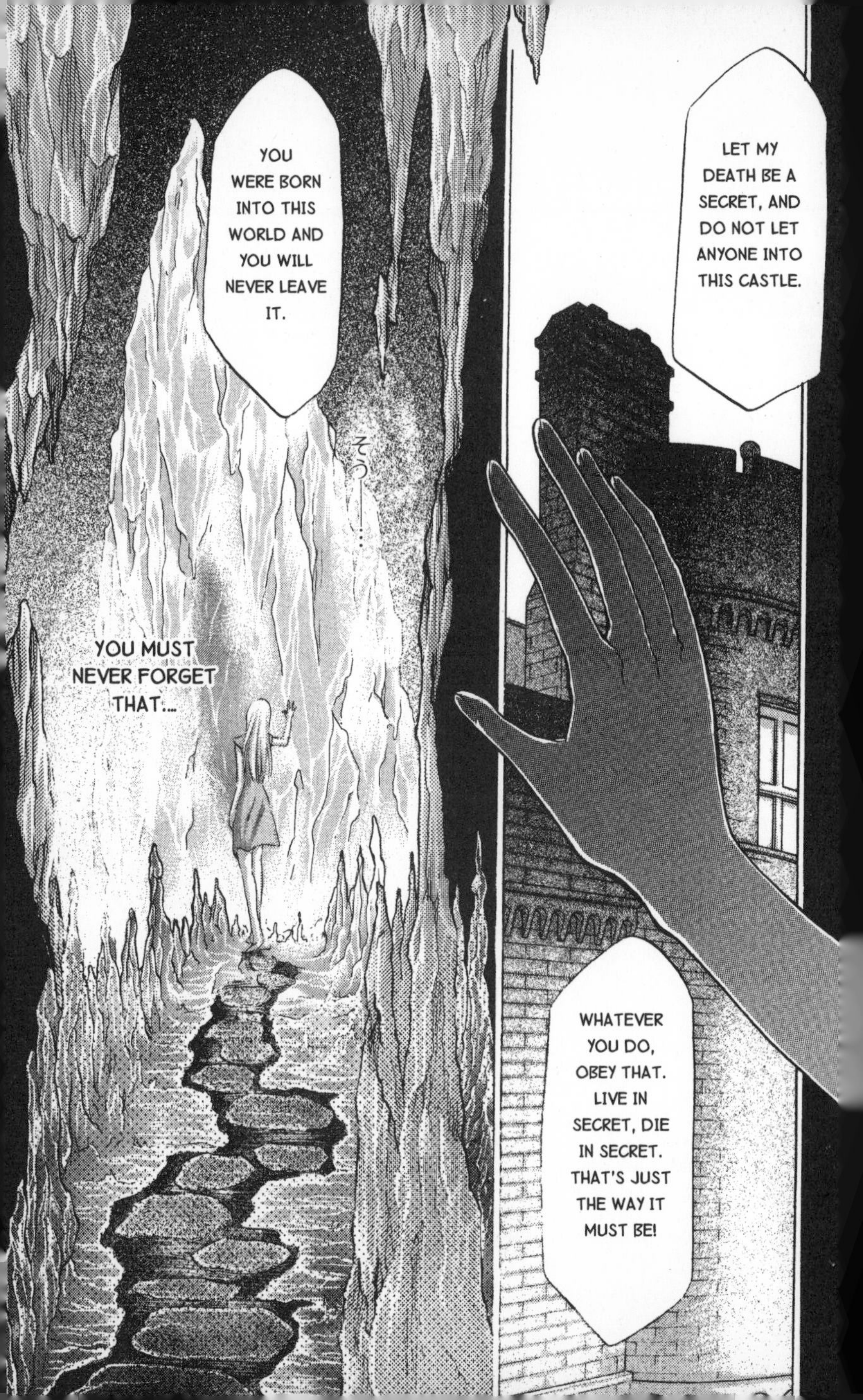
LET MY DEATH BE A SECRET, AND DO NOT LET ANYONE INTO THIS CASTLE.
WHATEVER YOU DO, OBEY THAT. LIVE IN SECRET, DIE IN SECRET. THAT'S JUST THE WAY IT MUST BE!
YOU WERE BORN INTO THIS WORLD AND YOU WILL NEVER LEAVE IT.
YOU MUST NEVER FORGET THAT....

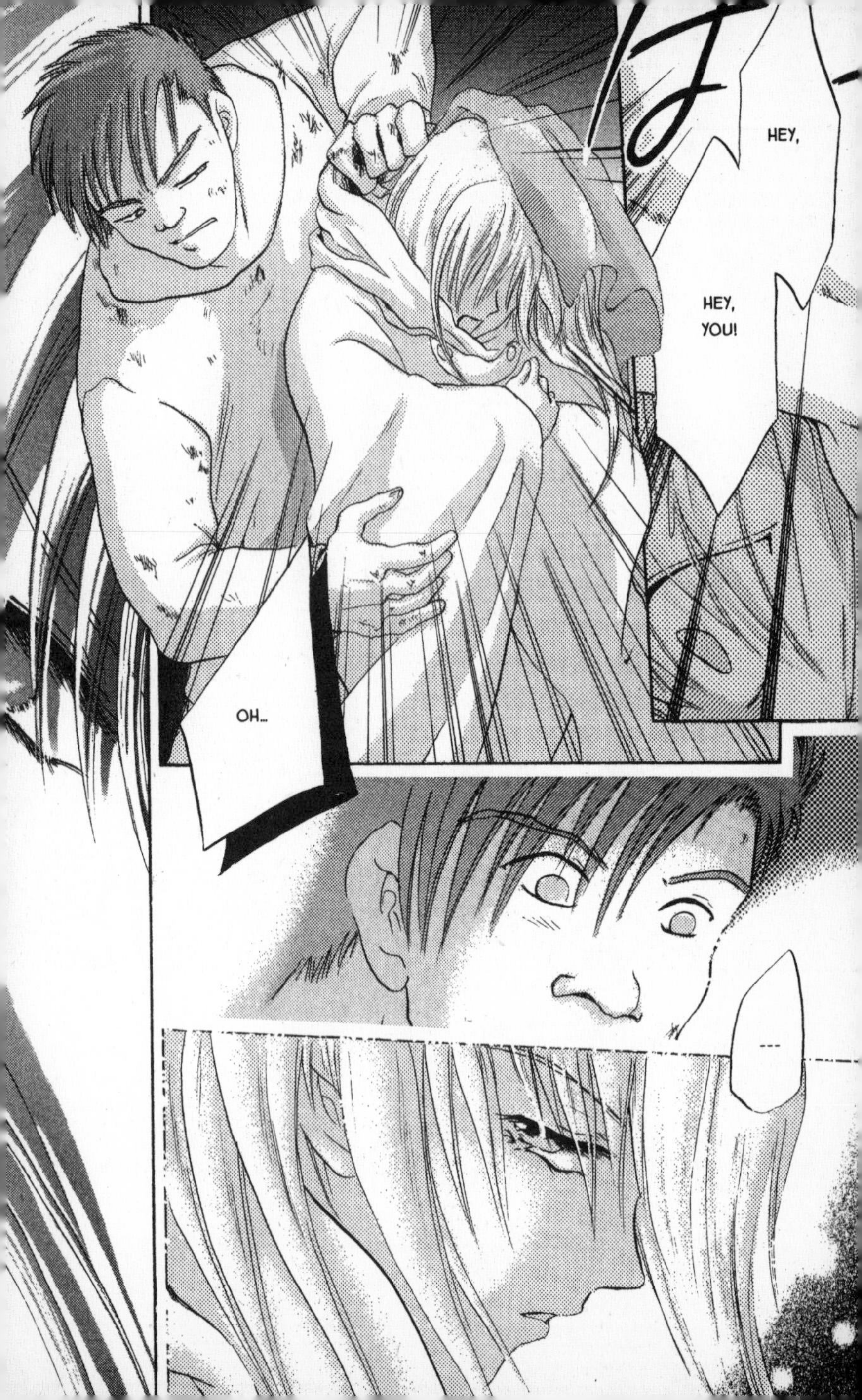
は
HEY,
HEY, YOU!
OH...

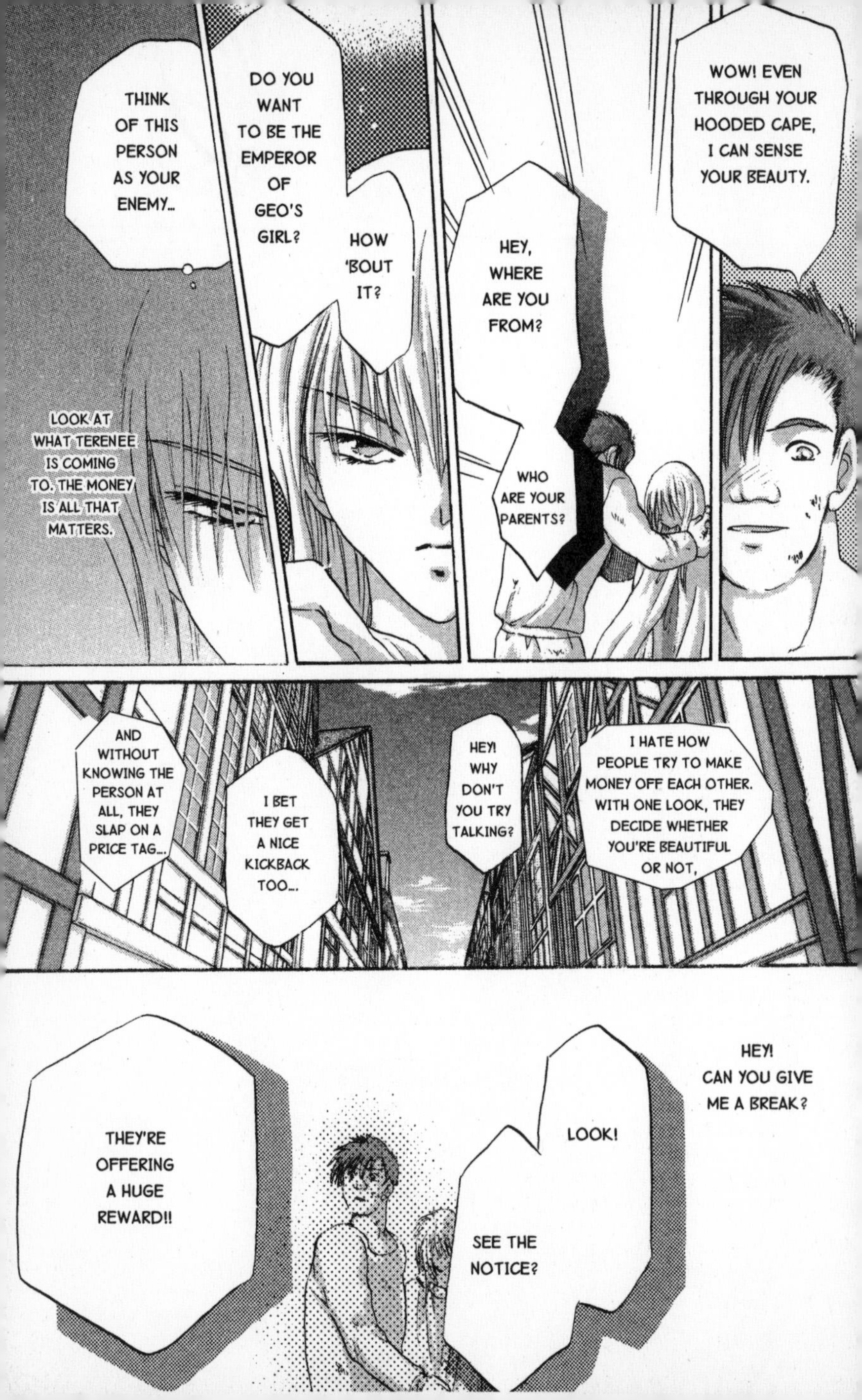
WOW! EVEN THROUGH YOUR HOODED CAPE, I CAN SENSE YOUR BEAUTY.
HEY, WHERE ARE YOU FROM?
WHO ARE YOUR PARENTS?
DO YOU WANT TO BE THE EMPEROR OF GEO'S GIRL?
HOW 'BOUT IT?
THINK OF THIS PERSON AS YOUR ENEMY...
LOOK AT WHAT TERENEE IS COMING TO. THE MONEY IS ALL THAT MATTERS.
I HATE HOW PEOPLE TRY TO MAKE MONEY OFF EACH OTHER. WITH ONE LOOK, THEY DECIDE WHETHER YOU'RE BEAUTIFUL OR NOT,
HEY! WHY DON'T YOU TRY TALKING?
AND WITHOUT KNOWING THE PERSON AT ALL, THEY SLAP ON A PRICE TAG...
I BET THEY GET A NICE KICKBACK TOO...
HEY! CAN YOU GIVE ME A BREAK?
LOOK!
SEE THE NOTICE?
THEY'RE OFFERING A HUGE REWARD!!

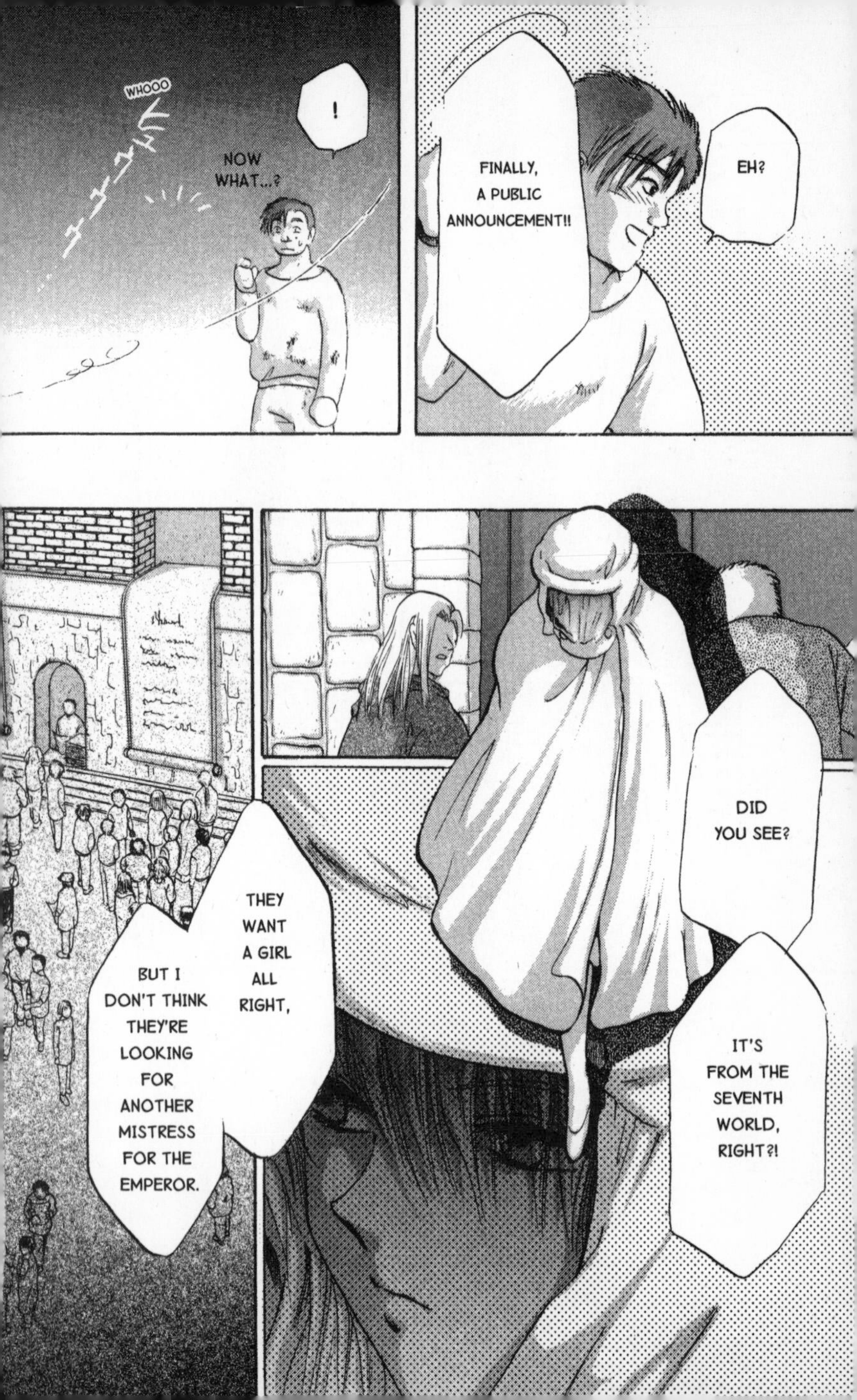
EH?
FINALLY, A PUBLIC ANNOUNCEMENT!!
!
NOW WHAT...?
WHOOO
DID YOU SEE?
IT'S FROM THE SEVENTH WORLD, RIGHT?!
THEY WANT A GIRL ALL RIGHT,
BUT I DON'T THINK THEY'RE LOOKING FOR ANOTHER MISTRESS FOR THE EMPEROR.

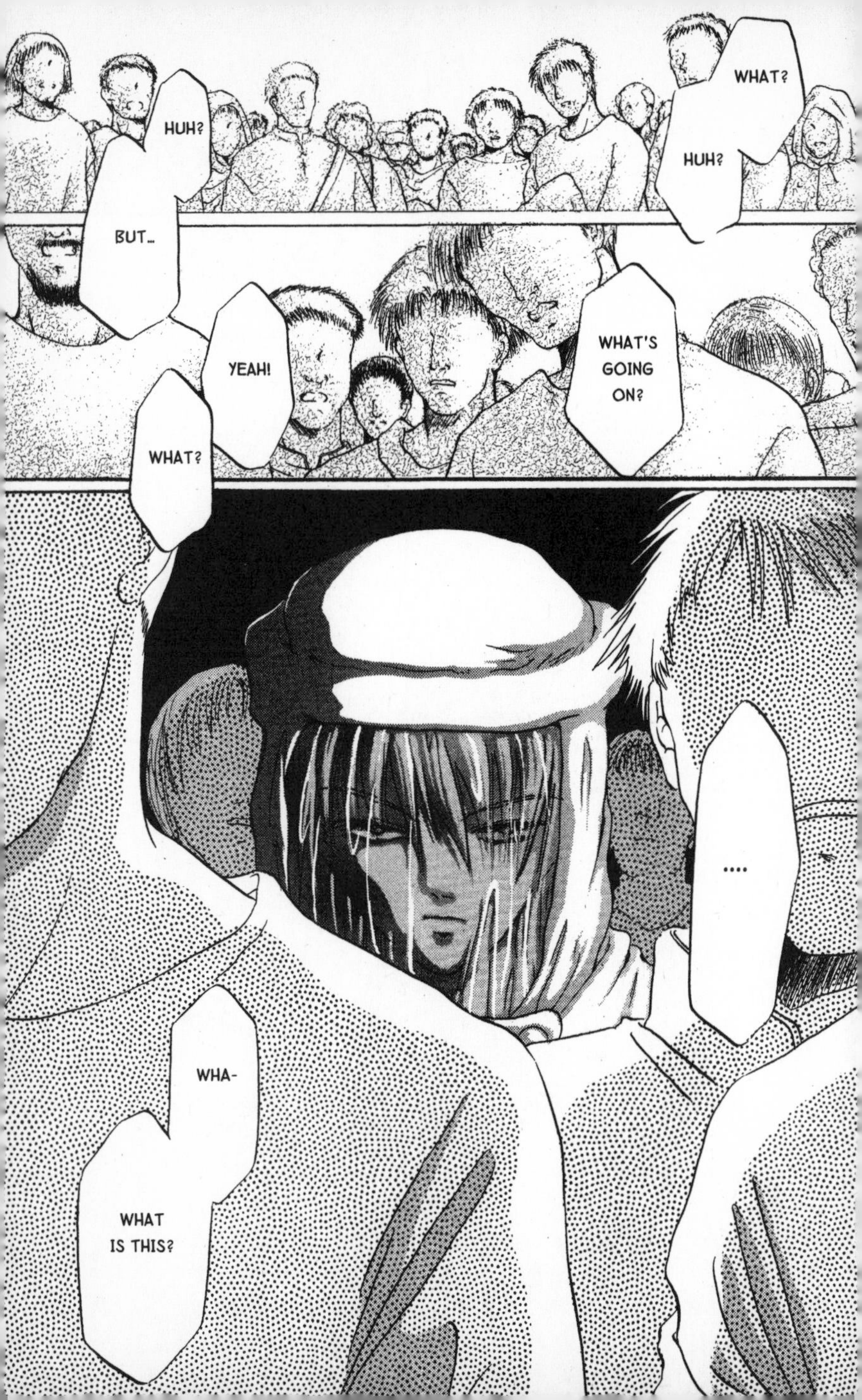
WHAT?
HUH?
HUH?
WHAT'S GOING ON?
YEAH!
BUT...
WHAT?
....
WHA-
WHAT IS THIS?

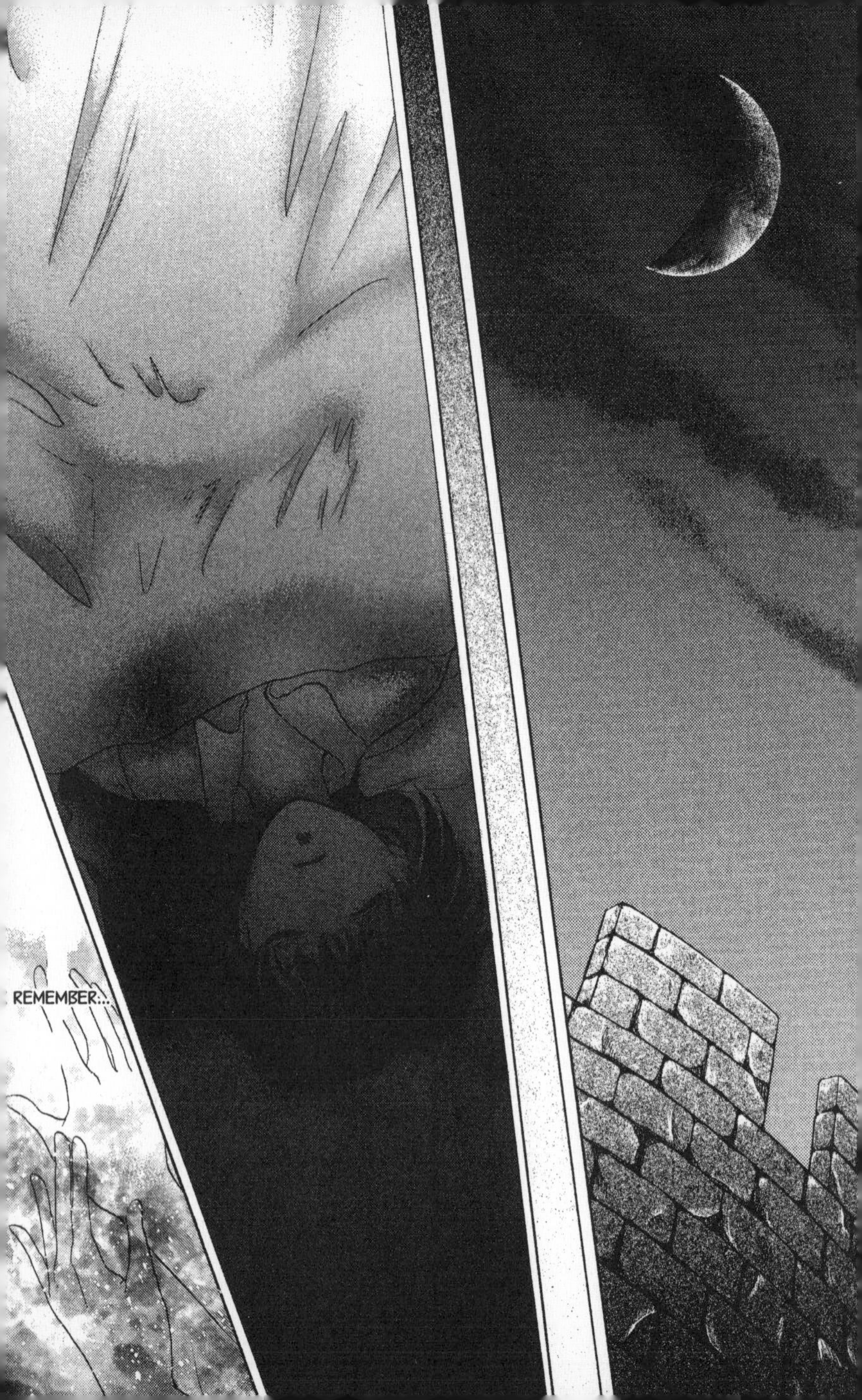
REMEMBER...

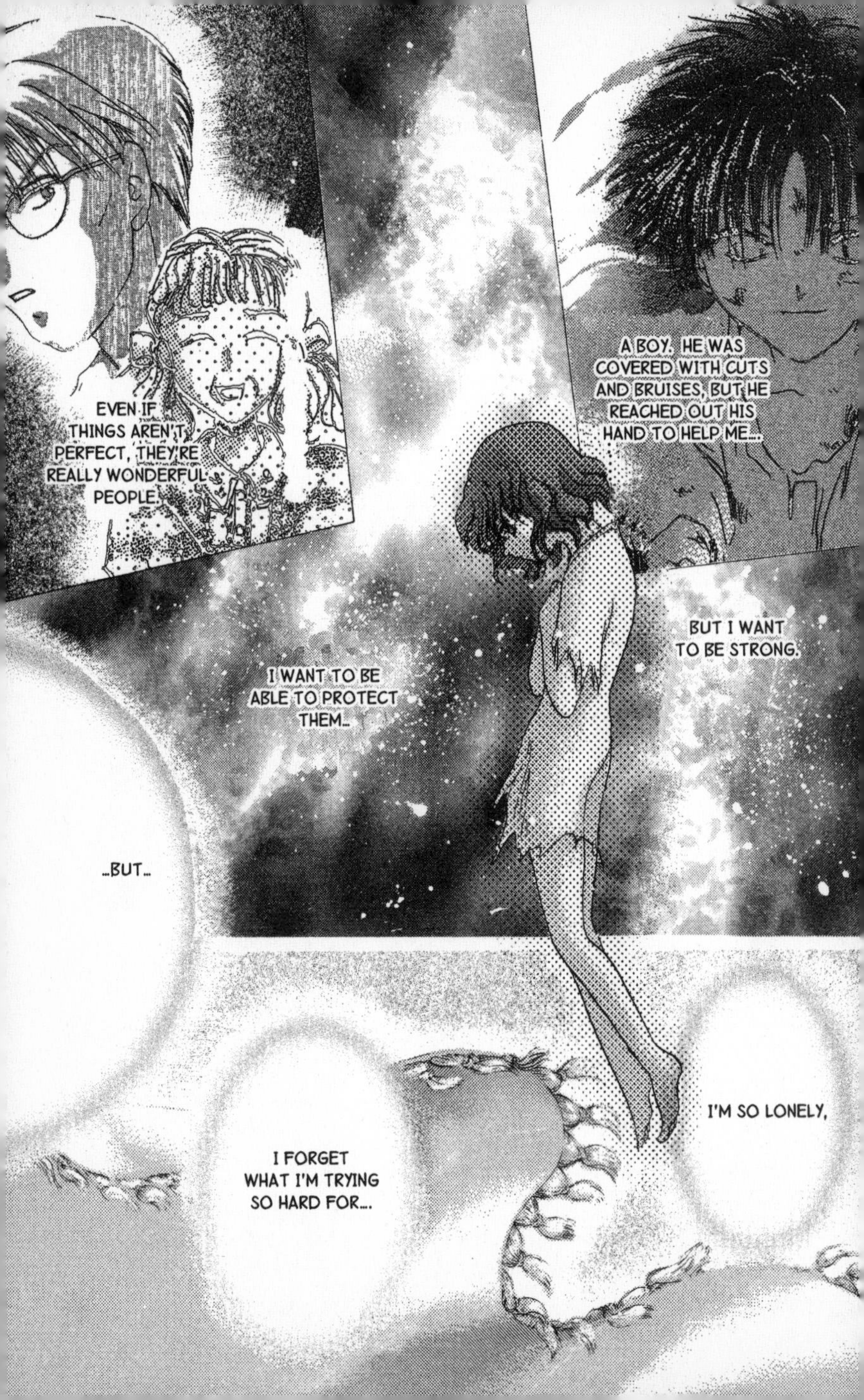
A BOY. HE WAS COVERED WITH CUTS AND BRUISES, BUT HE REACHED OUT HIS HAND TO HELP ME...
EVEN IF THINGS AREN'T PERFECT, THEY'RE REALLY WONDERFUL PEOPLE.
BUT I WANT TO BE STRONG.
I WANT TO BE ABLE TO PROTECT THEM..
..BUT..
I'M SO LONELY,
I FORGET WHAT I'M TRYING SO HARD FOR....

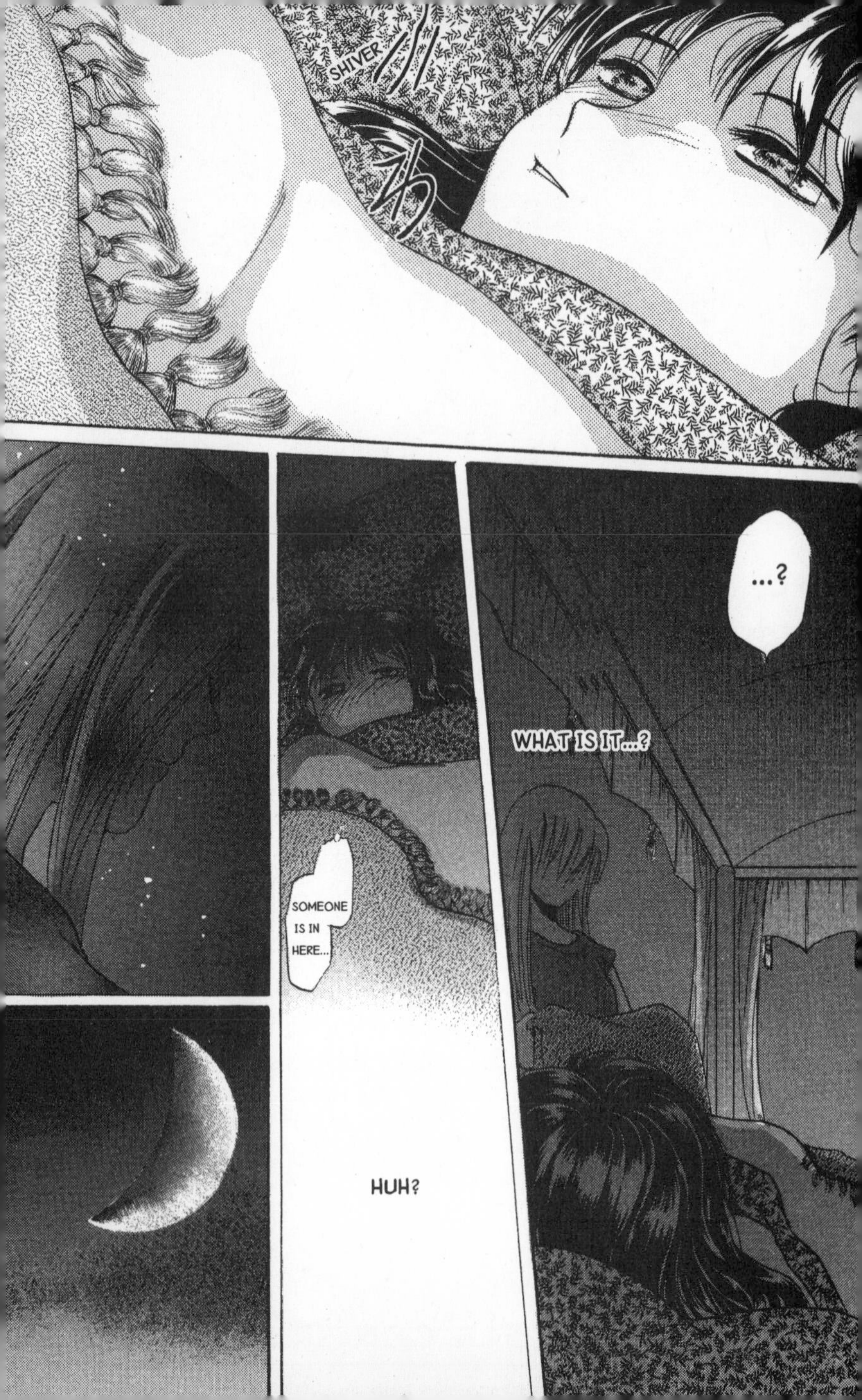
SHIVER
...?
WHAT IS IT...?
SOMEONE IS IN HERE...
HUH?

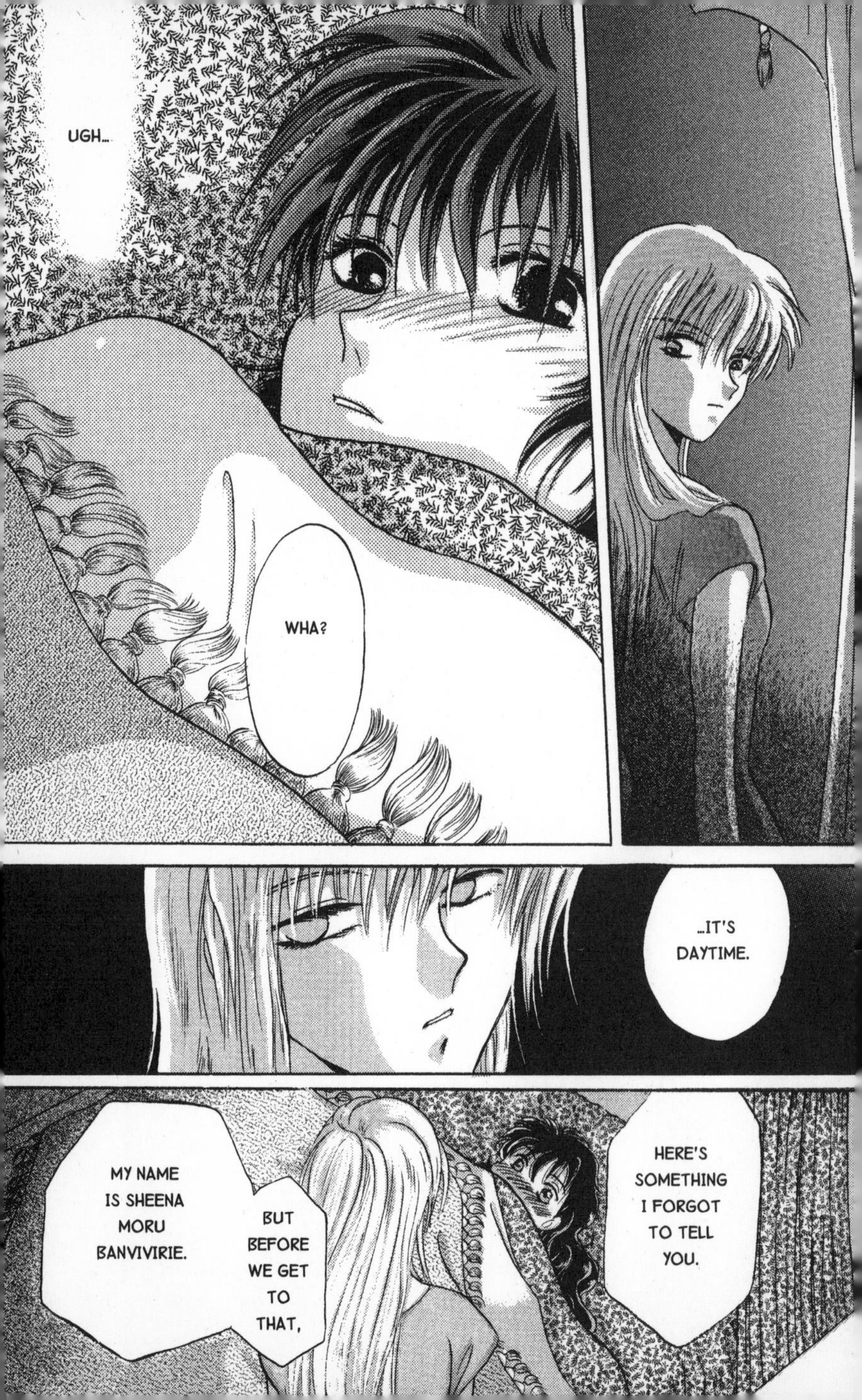
UGH...
WHA?
...IT'S DAYTIME.
HERE'S SOMETHING I FORGOT TO TELL YOU.
MY NAME IS SHEENA MORU BANVIVIRIE.
BUT BEFORE WE GET TO THAT,

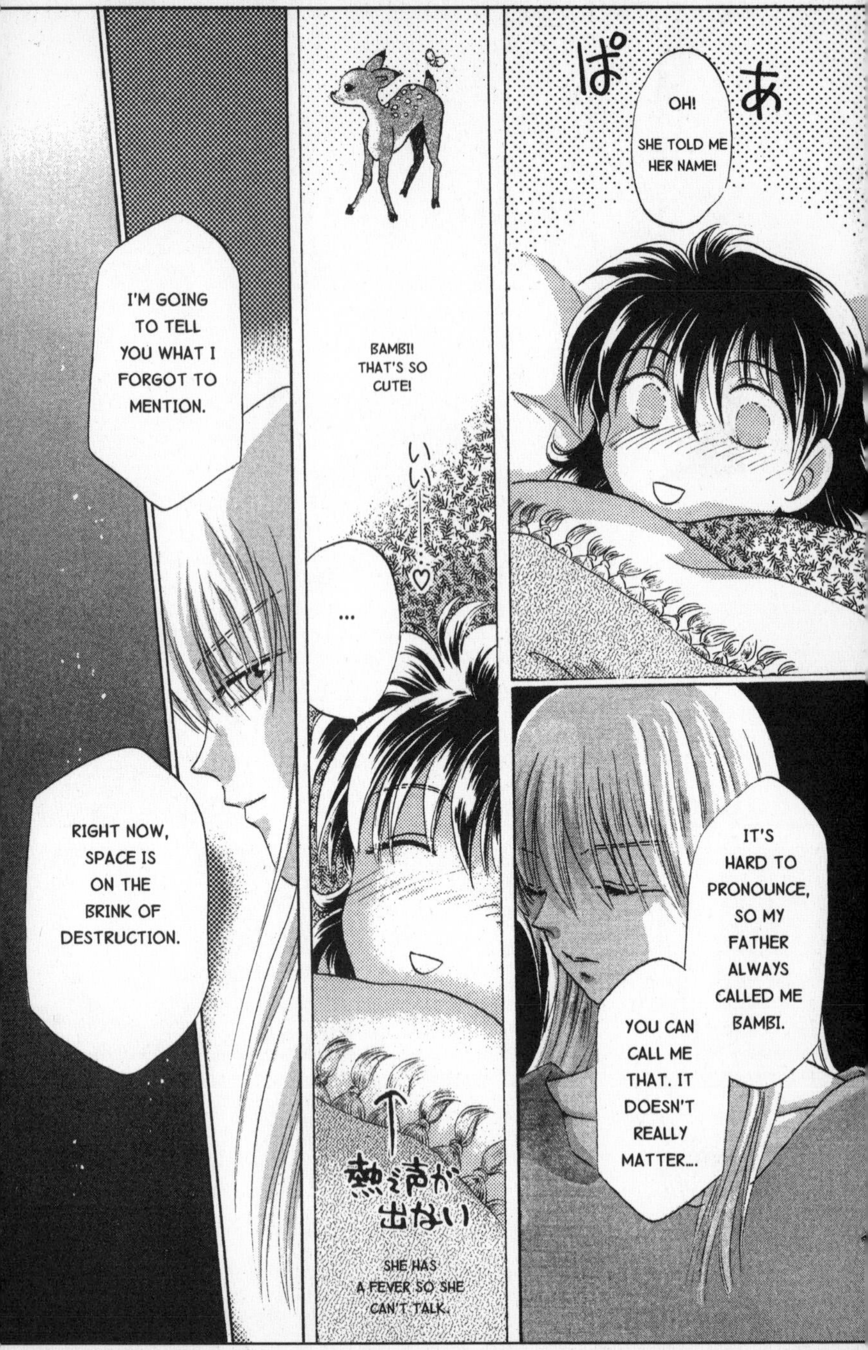
ぱあ
OH!
SHE TOLD ME HER NAME!
IT'S HARD TO PRONOUNCE, SO MY FATHER ALWAYS CALLED ME BAMBI.
YOU CAN CALL ME THAT. IT DOESN'T REALLY MATTER...
BAMBI! THAT'S SO CUTE!
いい……♡
...
熱で声が出ない
SHE HAS A FEVER SO SHE CAN'T TALK.
I'M GOING TO TELL YOU WHAT I FORGOT TO MENTION.
RIGHT NOW, SPACE IS ON THE BRINK OF DESTRUCTION.

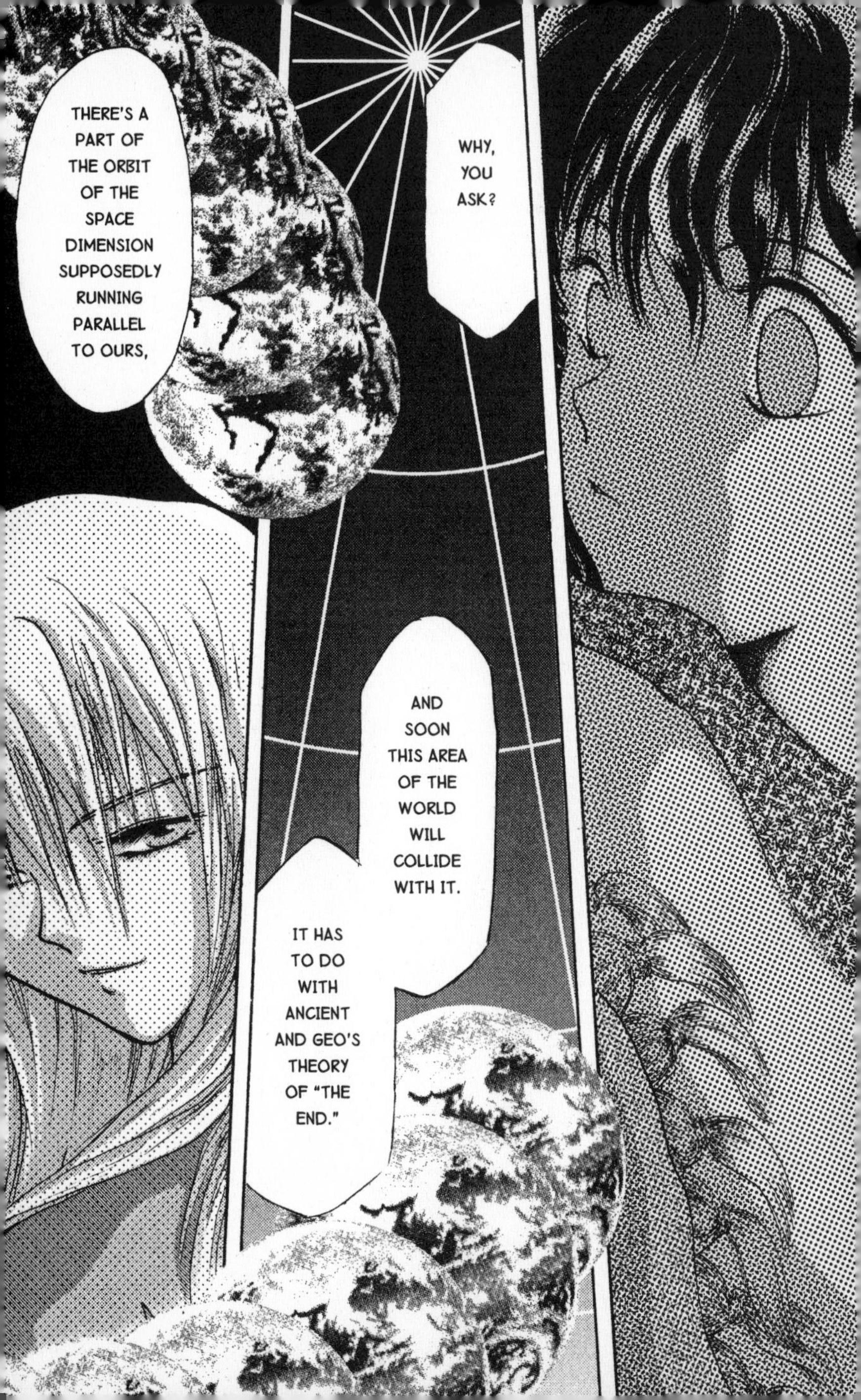
WHY, YOU ASK?
IT HAS TO DO WITH ANCIENT AND GEO'S THEORY OF "THE END."
THERE'S A PART OF THE ORBIT OF THE SPACE DIMENSION SUPPOSEDLY RUNNING PARALLEL TO OURS,
AND SOON THIS AREA OF THE WORLD WILL COLLIDE WITH IT.

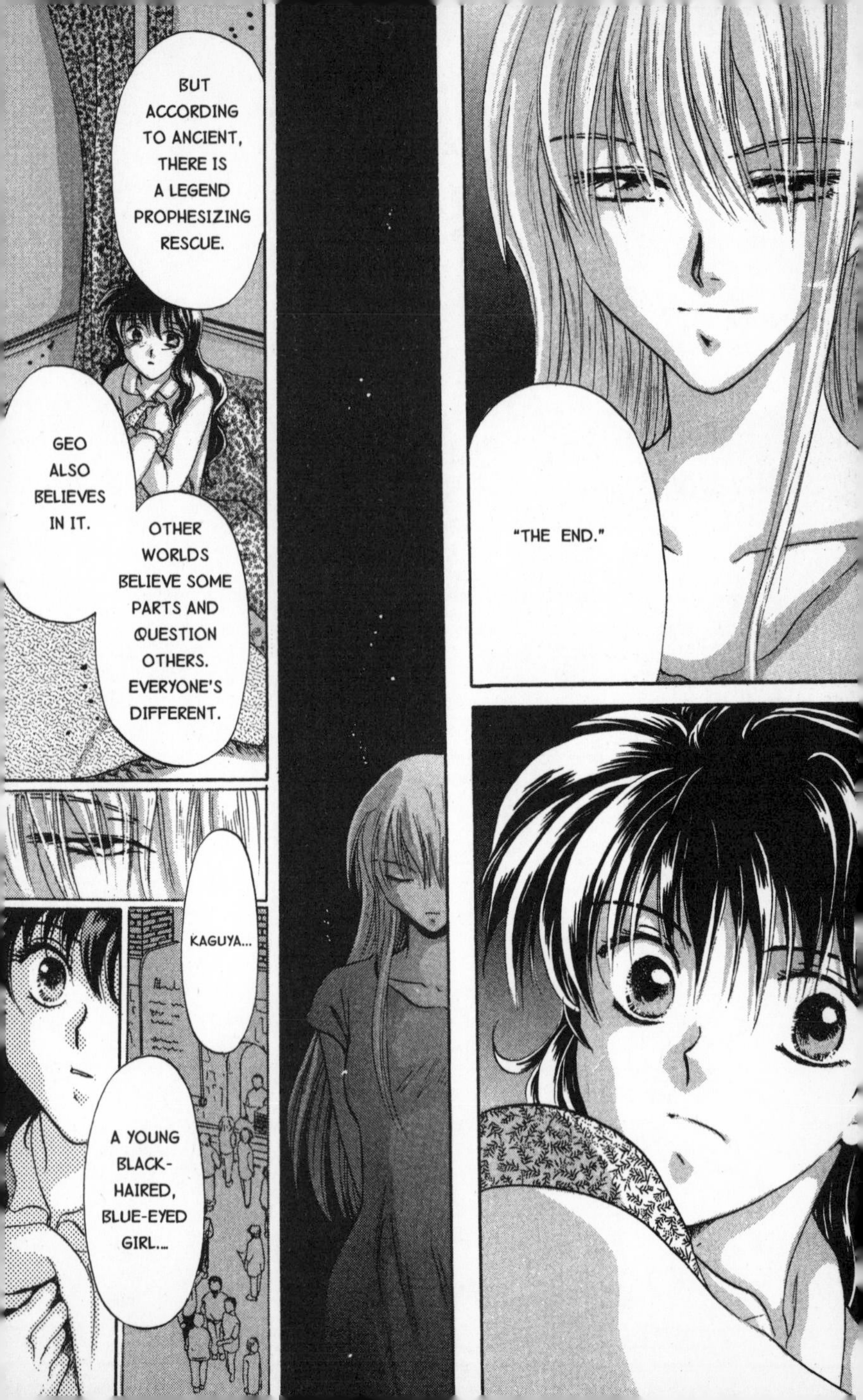
"THE END."
BUT ACCORDING TO ANCIENT, THERE IS A LEGEND PROPHESIZING RESCUE.
GEO ALSO BELIEVES IN IT.
OTHER WORLDS BELIEVE SOME PARTS AND QUESTION OTHERS. EVERYONE'S DIFFERENT.
KAGUYA...
A YOUNG BLACK-HAIRED, BLUE-EYED GIRL...

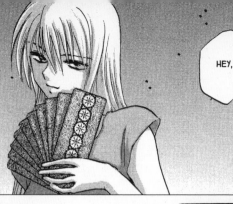

HEY,
I TURNED THESE CARDS OVER. WHY DON'T YOU SHUFFLE THEM?
CARDS...
カード
AFTER YOU SHUFFLE,
CHOOSE ONE.
I USED TO DO THIS WITH MY MOTHER.
HMMM, NOW LET'S SEE...
THAT GAME...
PACHA ....
I WAS TALKING ABOUT THE RESCUE IN THE LEGEND,
WASN'T I?
THERE'S ONE YOUNG GIRL...

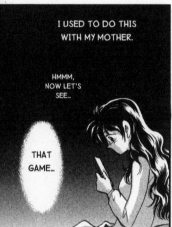

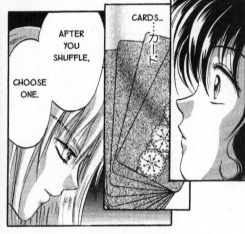

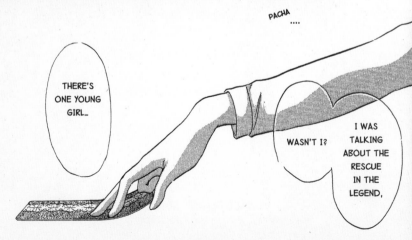

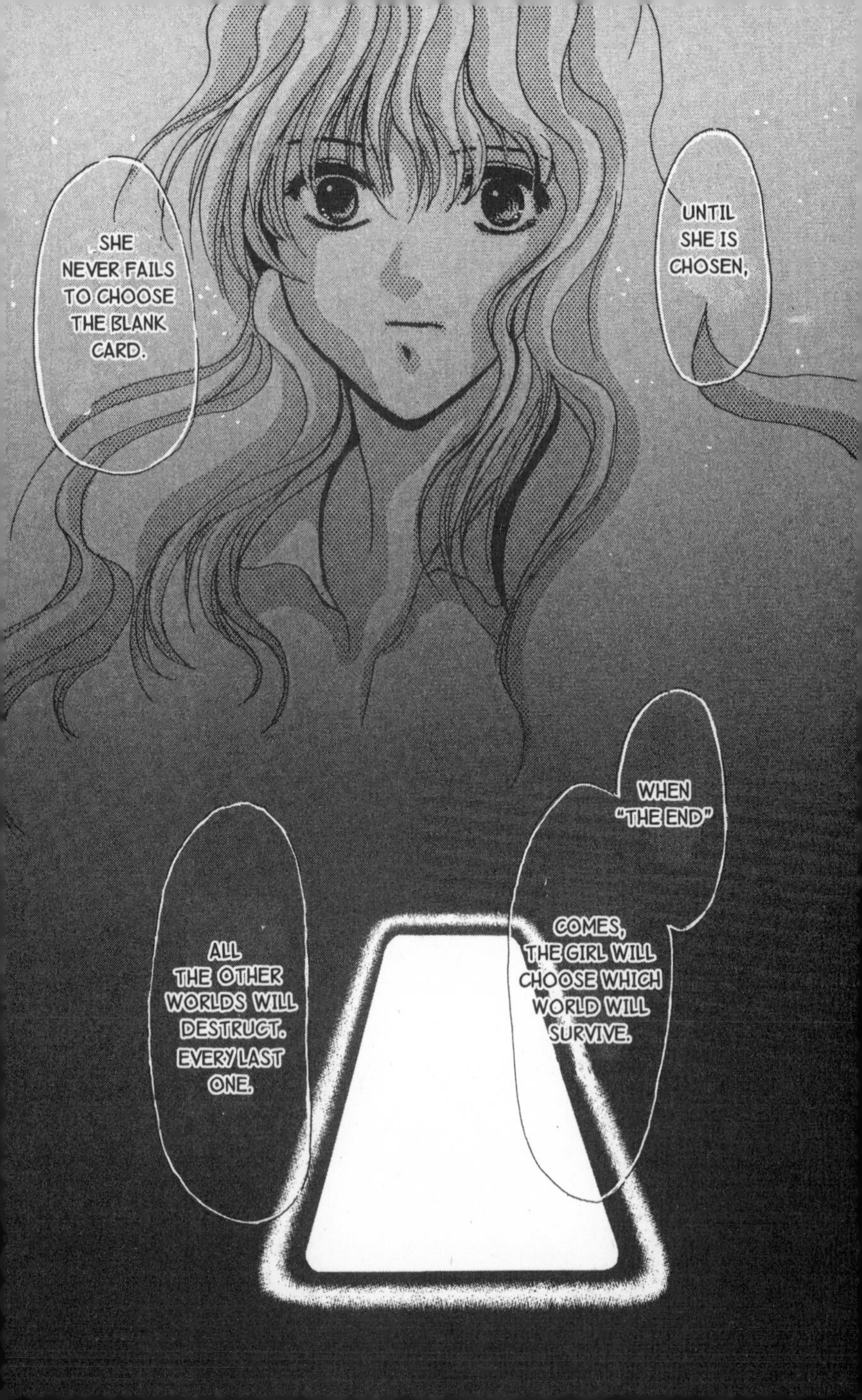
UNTIL SHE IS CHOSEN,
SHE NEVER FAILS TO CHOOSE THE BLANK CARD.
WHEN "THE END"
COMES, THE GIRL WILL CHOOSE WHICH WORLD WILL SURVIVE.
ALL THE OTHER WORLDS WILL DESTRUCT. EVERY LAST ONE.

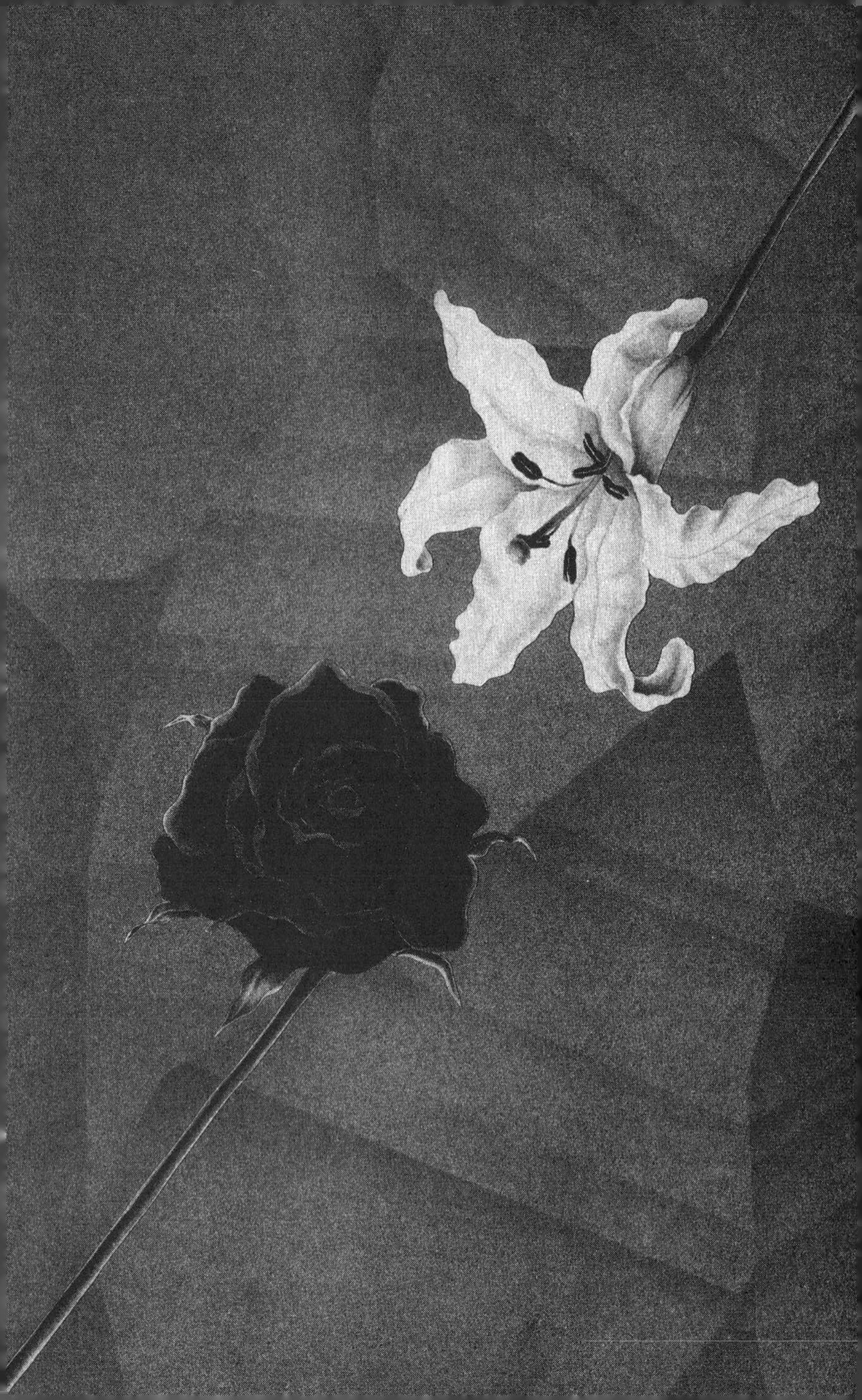

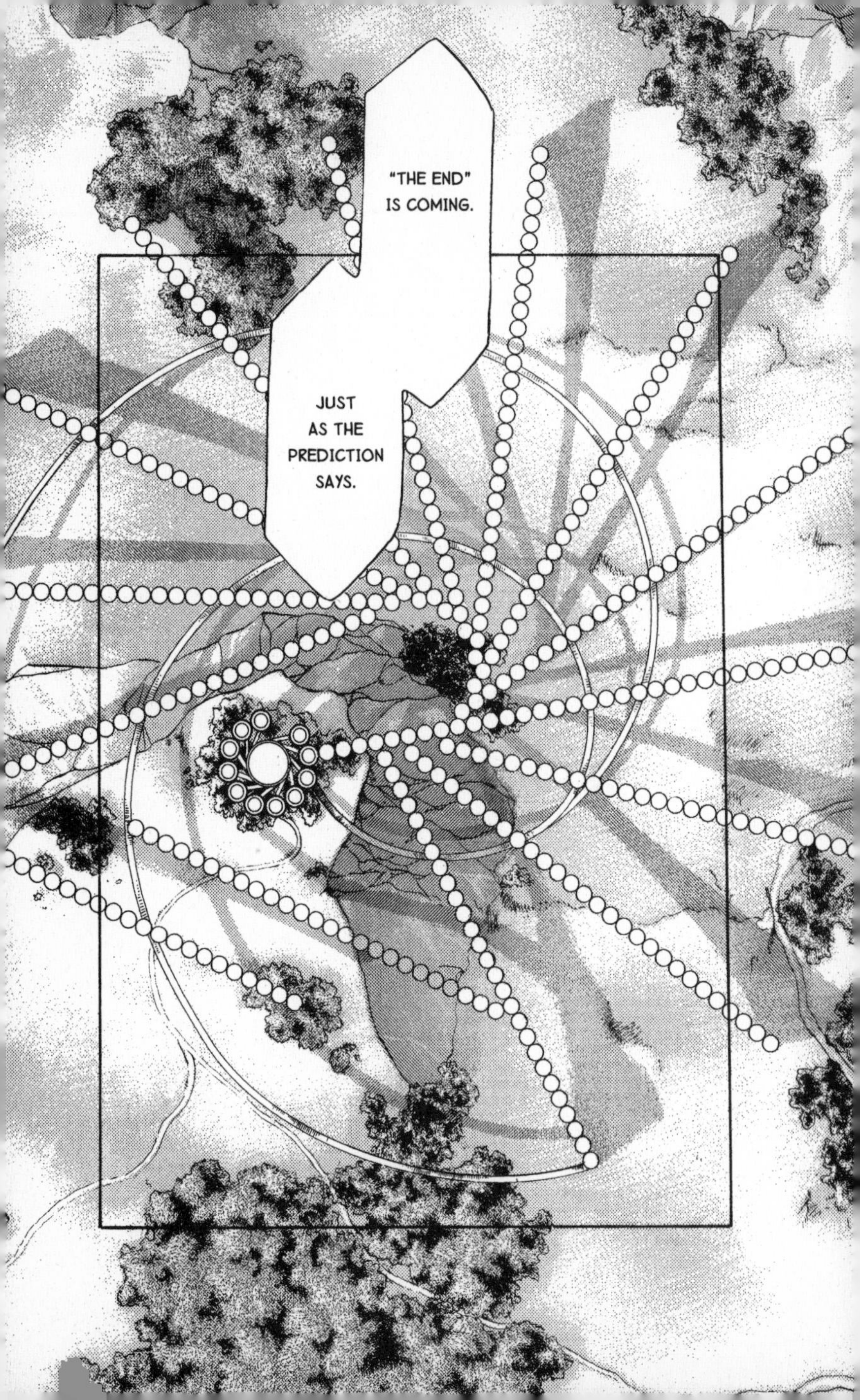
"THE END" IS COMING.
JUST AS THE PREDICTION SAYS.

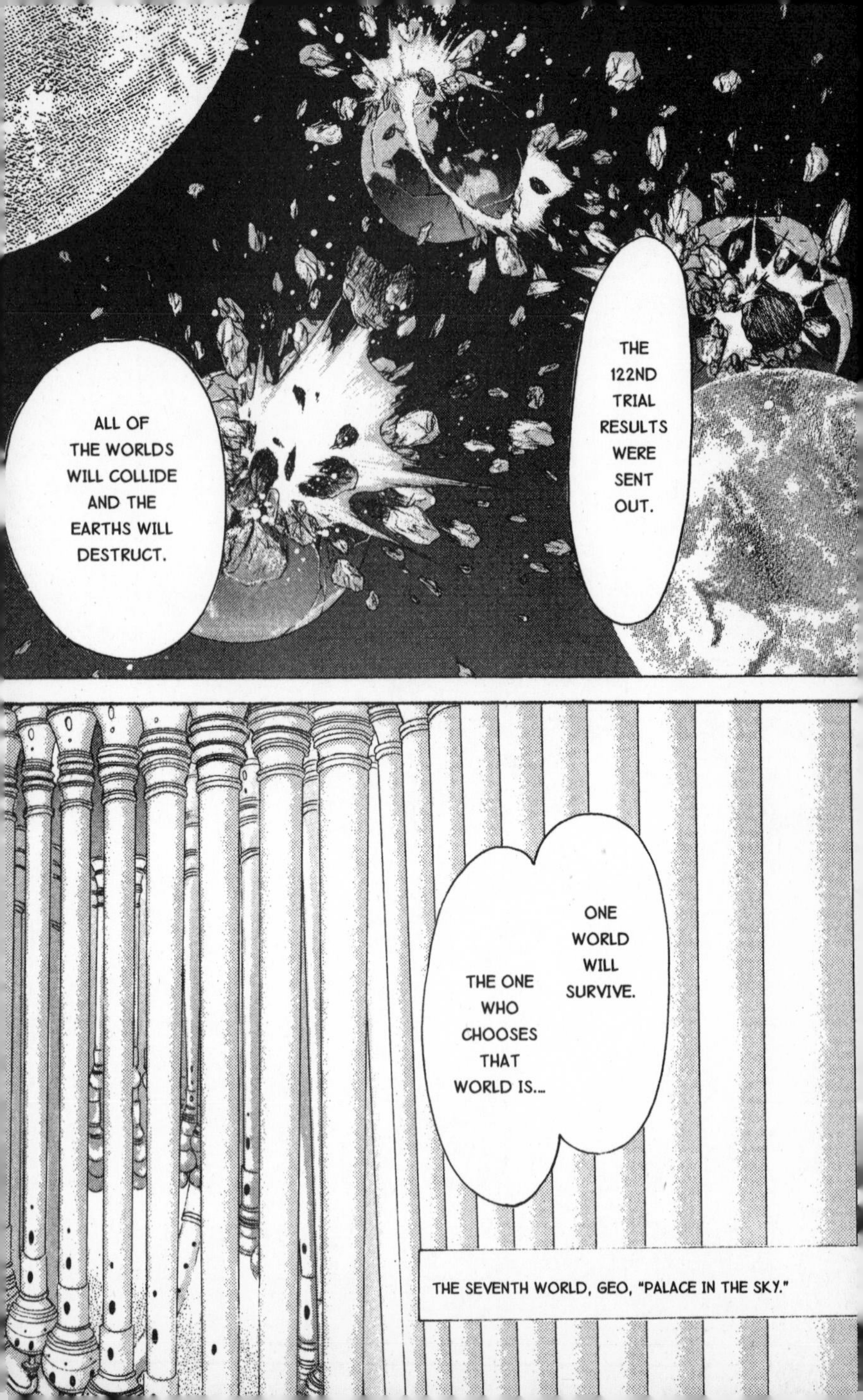
THE 122ND TRIAL RESULTS WERE SENT OUT.
ALL OF THE WORLDS WILL COLLIDE AND THE EARTHS WILL DESTRUCT.
ONE WORLD WILL SURVIVE.
THE ONE WHO CHOOSES THAT WORLD IS...
THE SEVENTH WORLD, GEO, "PALACE IN THE SKY."

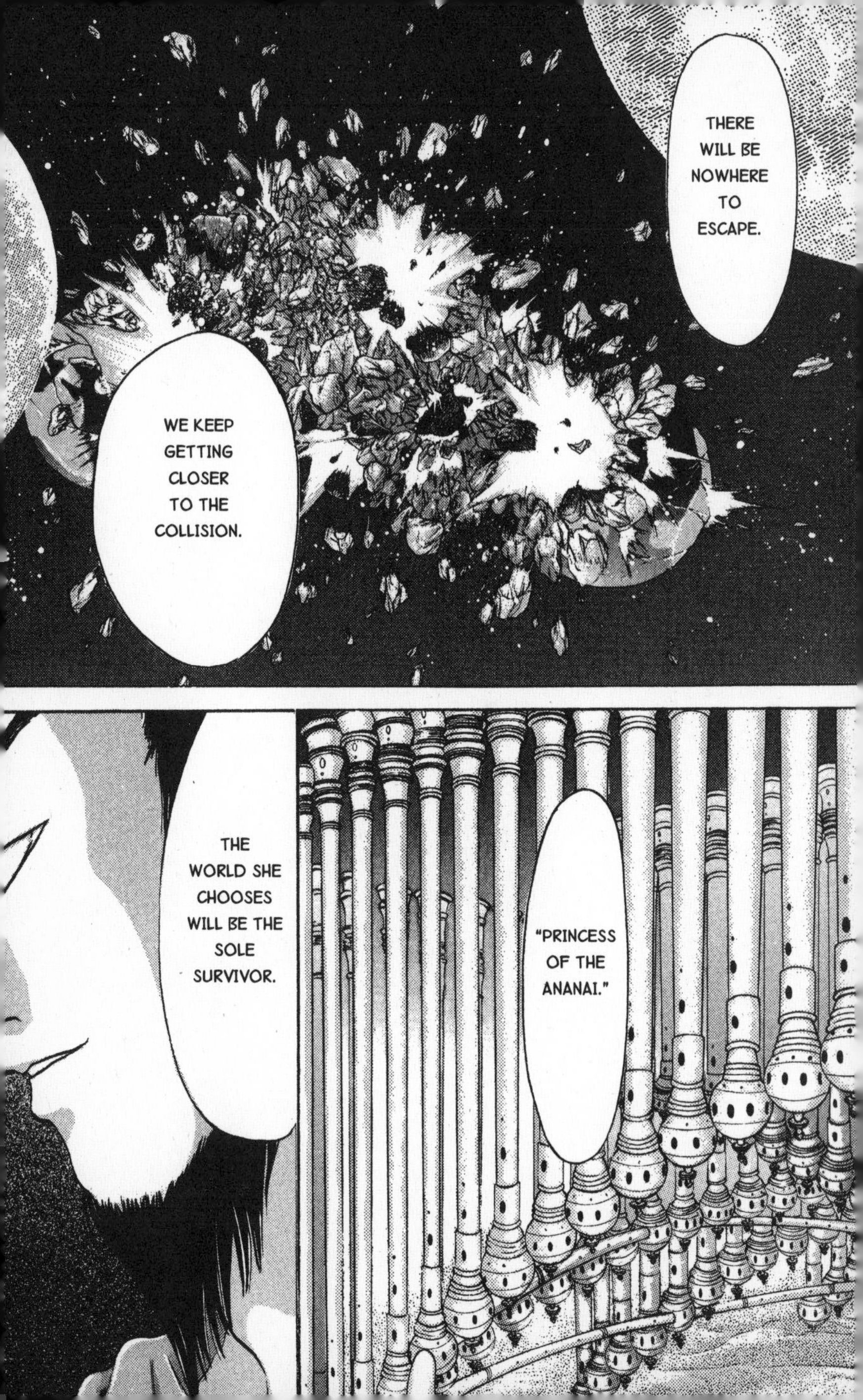
THERE WILL BE NOWHERE TO ESCAPE.
WE KEEP GETTING CLOSER TO THE COLLISION.
"PRINCESS OF THE ANANAI."
THE WORLD SHE CHOOSES WILL BE THE SOLE SURVIVOR.

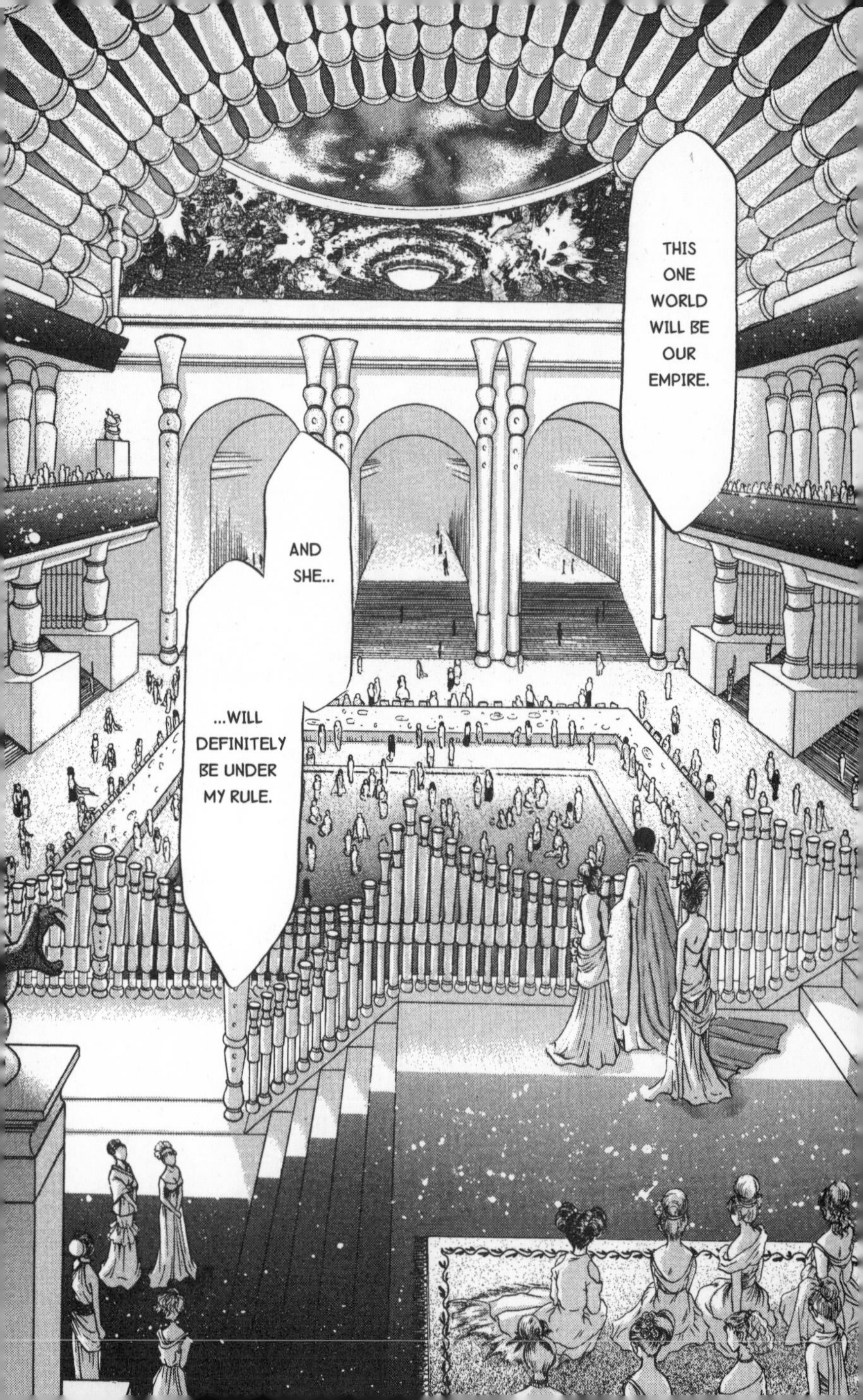
THIS ONE WORLD WILL BE OUR EMPIRE.
AND SHE...
...WILL DEFINITELY BE UNDER MY RULE.

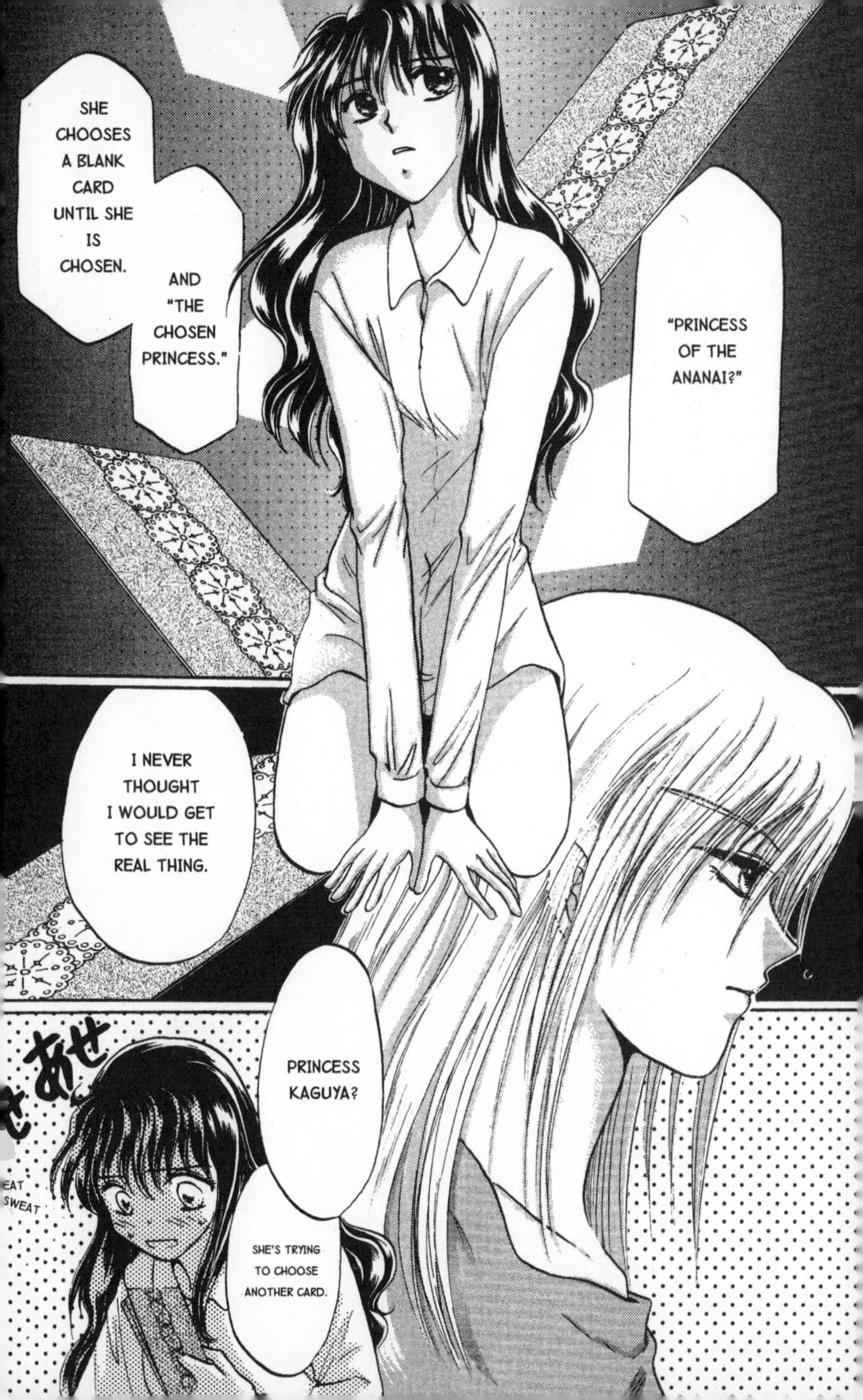
"PRINCESS OF THE ANANAI?"
AND "THE CHOSEN PRINCESS."
SHE CHOOSES A BLANK CARD UNTIL SHE IS CHOSEN.
I NEVER THOUGHT I WOULD GET TO SEE THE REAL THING.
PRINCESS KAGUYA?
SHE'S TRYING TO CHOOSE ANOTHER CARD.
あせ
SWEAT

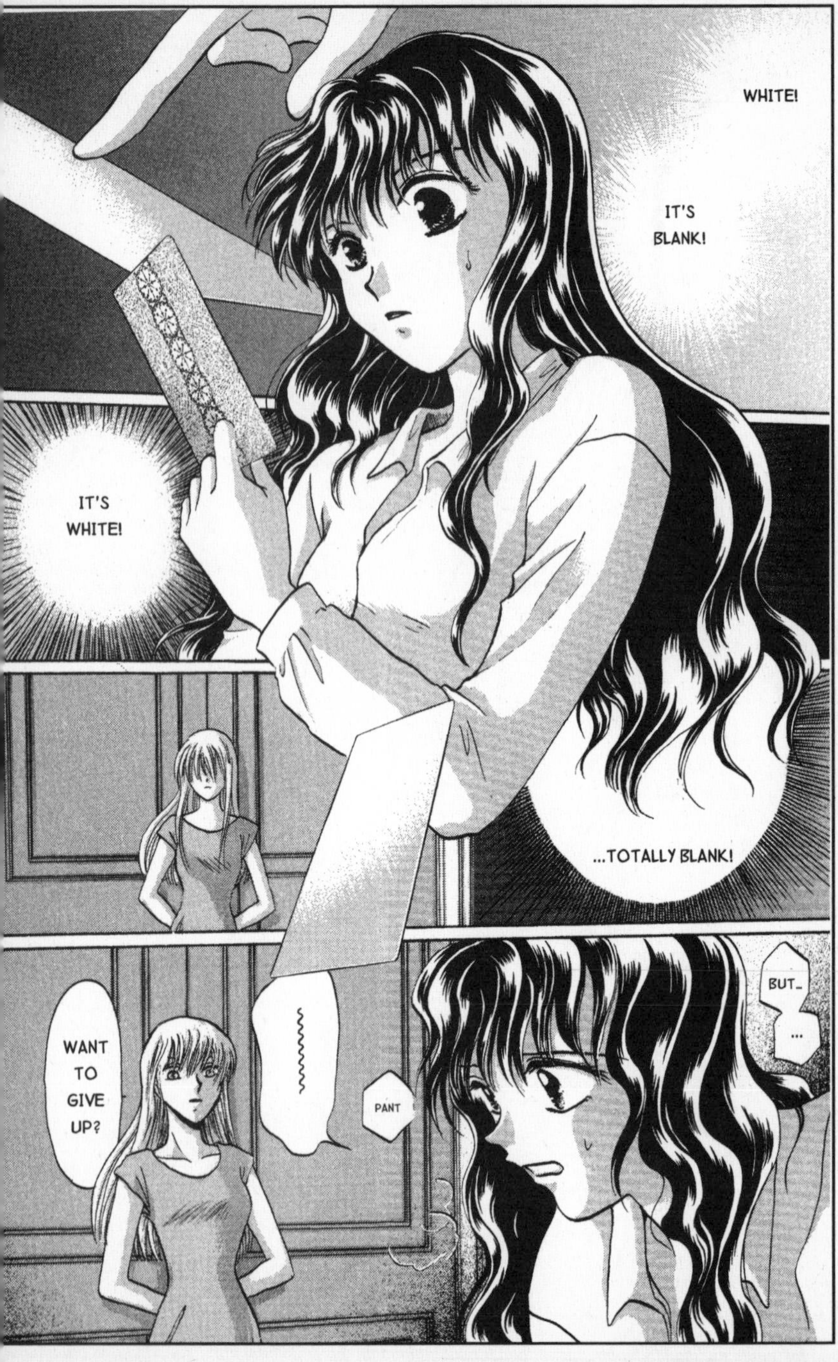
WHITE!
IT'S BLANK!
IT'S WHITE!
...TOTALLY BLANK!
BUT...
...
PANT
WANT TO GIVE UP?

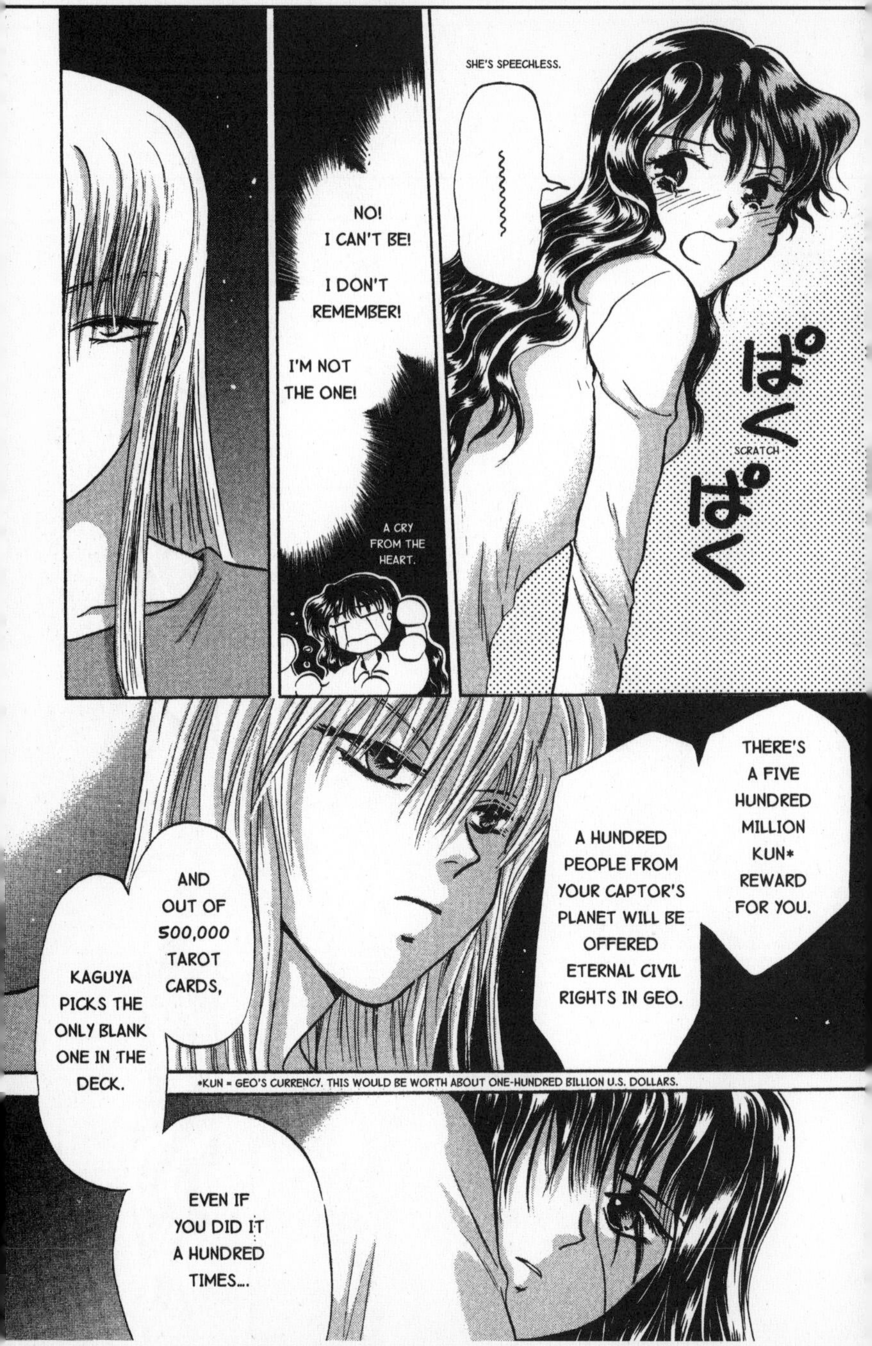
SHE'S SPEECHLESS.
ぱくぱく
SCRATCH
NO! I CAN'T BE!
I DON'T REMEMBER!
I'M NOT THE ONE!
A CRY FROM THE HEART.
THERE'S A FIVE HUNDRED MILLION KUN* REWARD FOR YOU.
A HUNDRED PEOPLE FROM YOUR CAPTOR'S PLANET WILL BE OFFERED ETERNAL CIVIL RIGHTS IN GEO.
AND OUT OF 500,000 TAROT CARDS,
KAGUYA PICKS THE ONLY BLANK ONE IN THE DECK.
*KUN = GEO'S CURRENCY. THIS WOULD BE WORTH ABOUT ONE-HUNDRED BILLION U.S. DOLLARS.
EVEN IF YOU DID IT A HUNDRED TIMES....

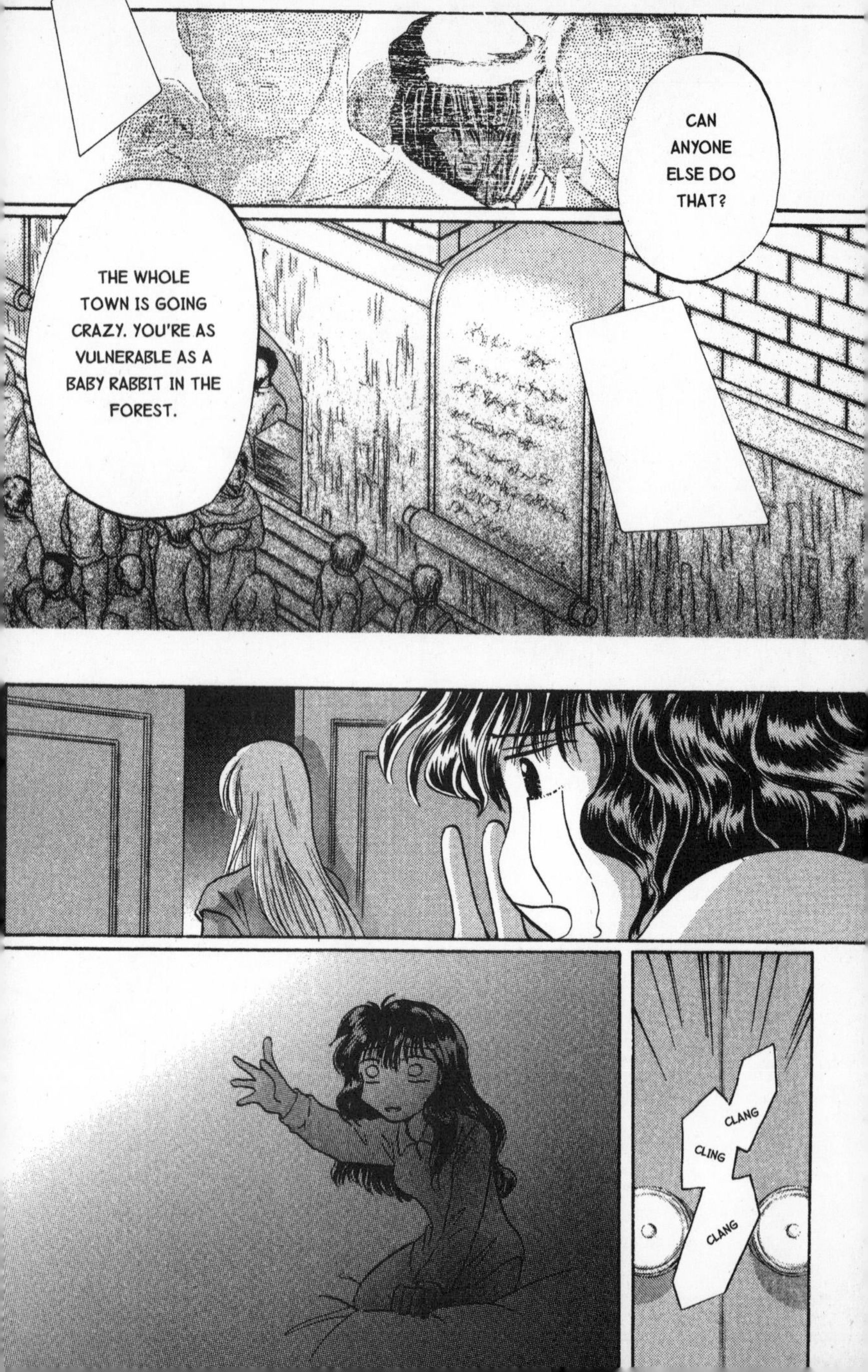
CAN ANYONE ELSE DO THAT?
THE WHOLE TOWN IS GOING CRAZY. YOU'RE AS VULNERABLE AS A BABY RABBIT IN THE FOREST.
CLANG
CLING
CLANG

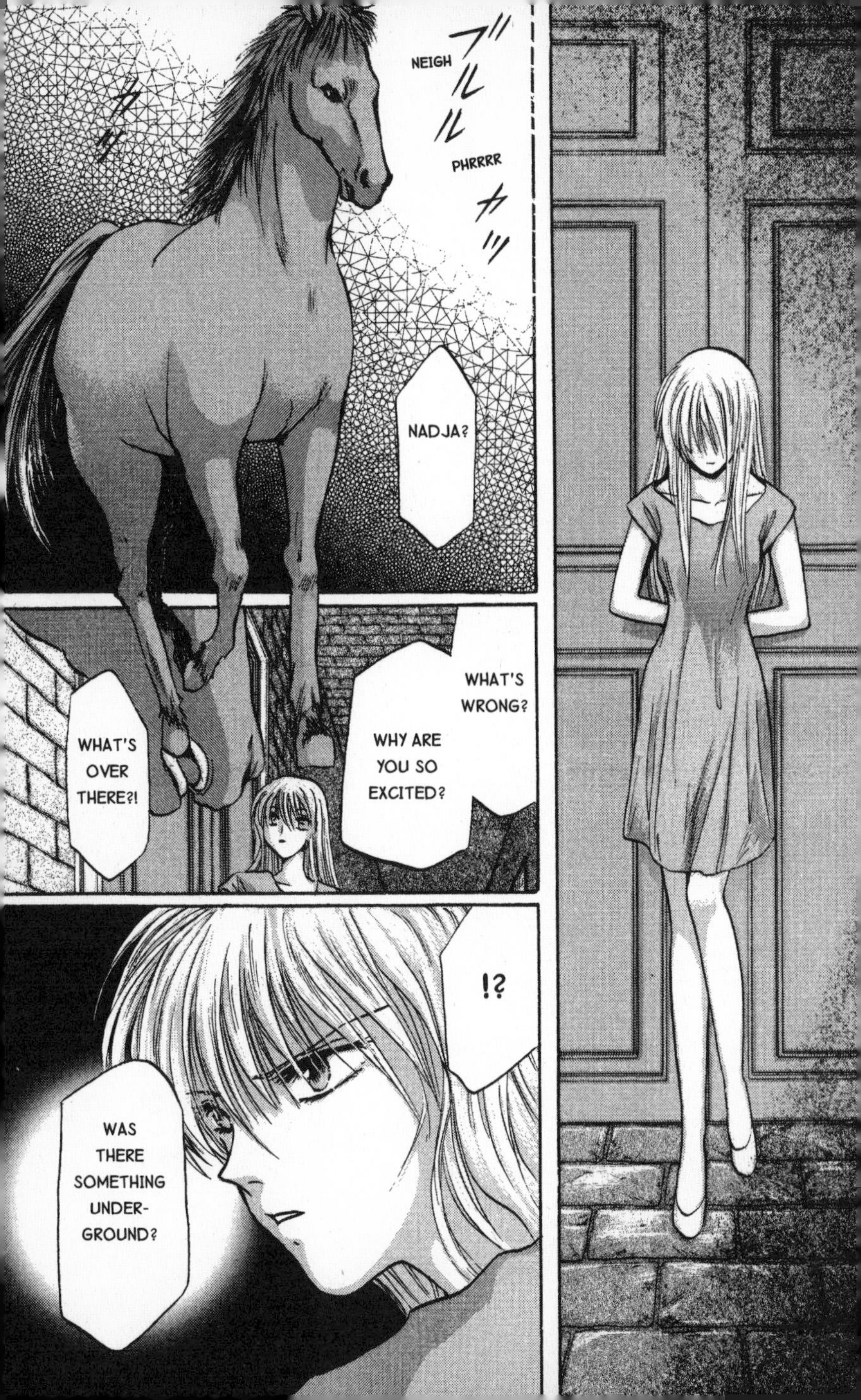
ブルル
NEIGH
PHRRRR
カッ
カッ
NADJA?
WHAT'S WRONG?
WHY ARE YOU SO EXCITED?
WHAT'S OVER THERE?!
!?
WAS THERE SOMETHING UNDER-GROUND?

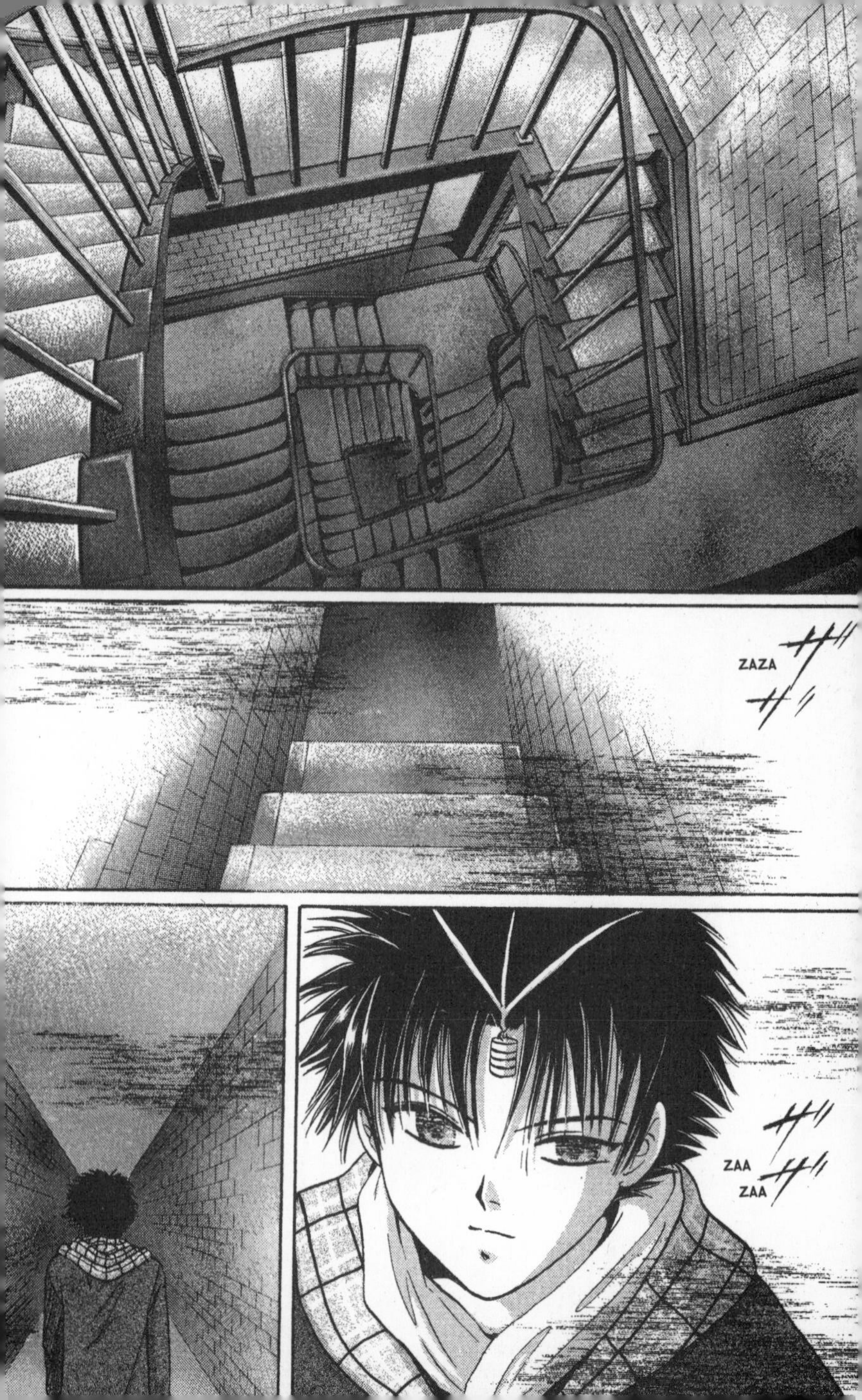
ZAZA
ZAA
ZAA

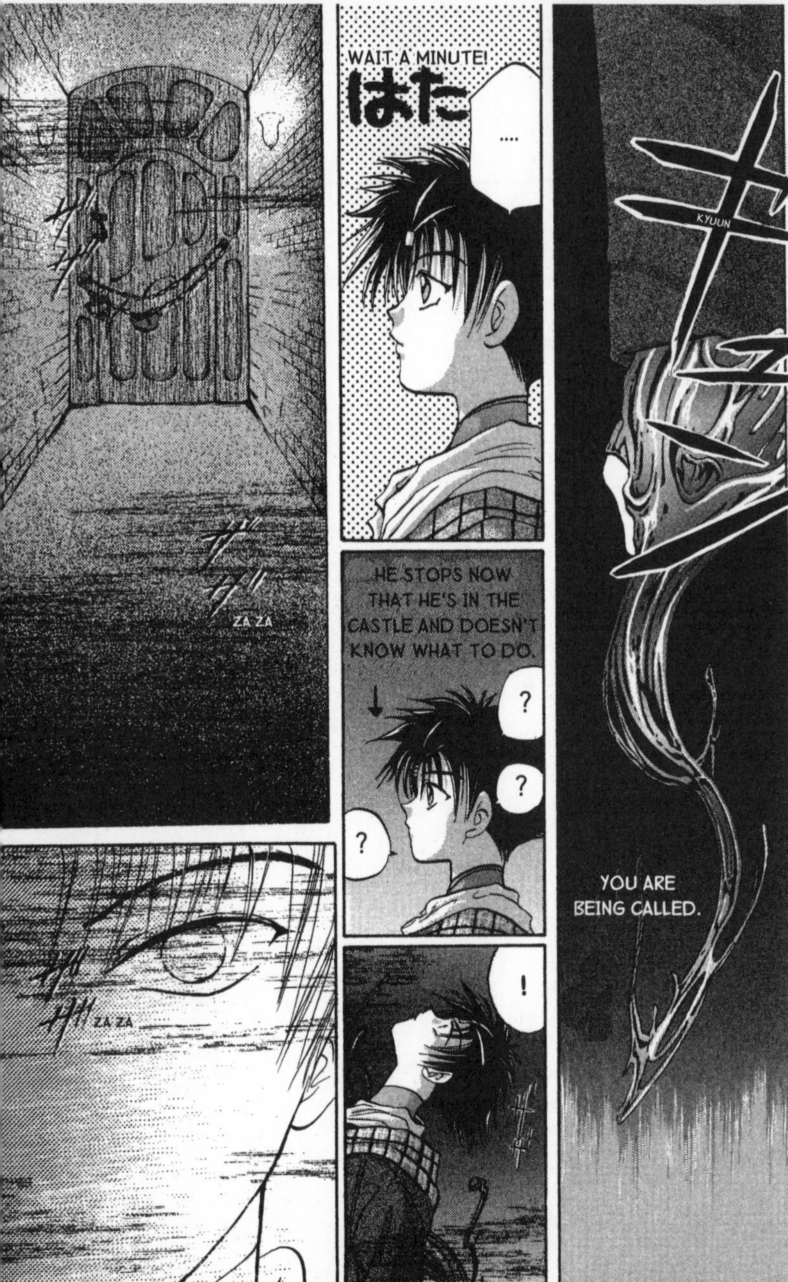
KYUUN
YOU ARE BEING CALLED.
WAIT A MINUTE!
はた
....
HE STOPS NOW THAT HE'S IN THE CASTLE AND DOESN'T KNOW WHAT TO DO.
?
?
?
!
ZA ZA
ZA ZA

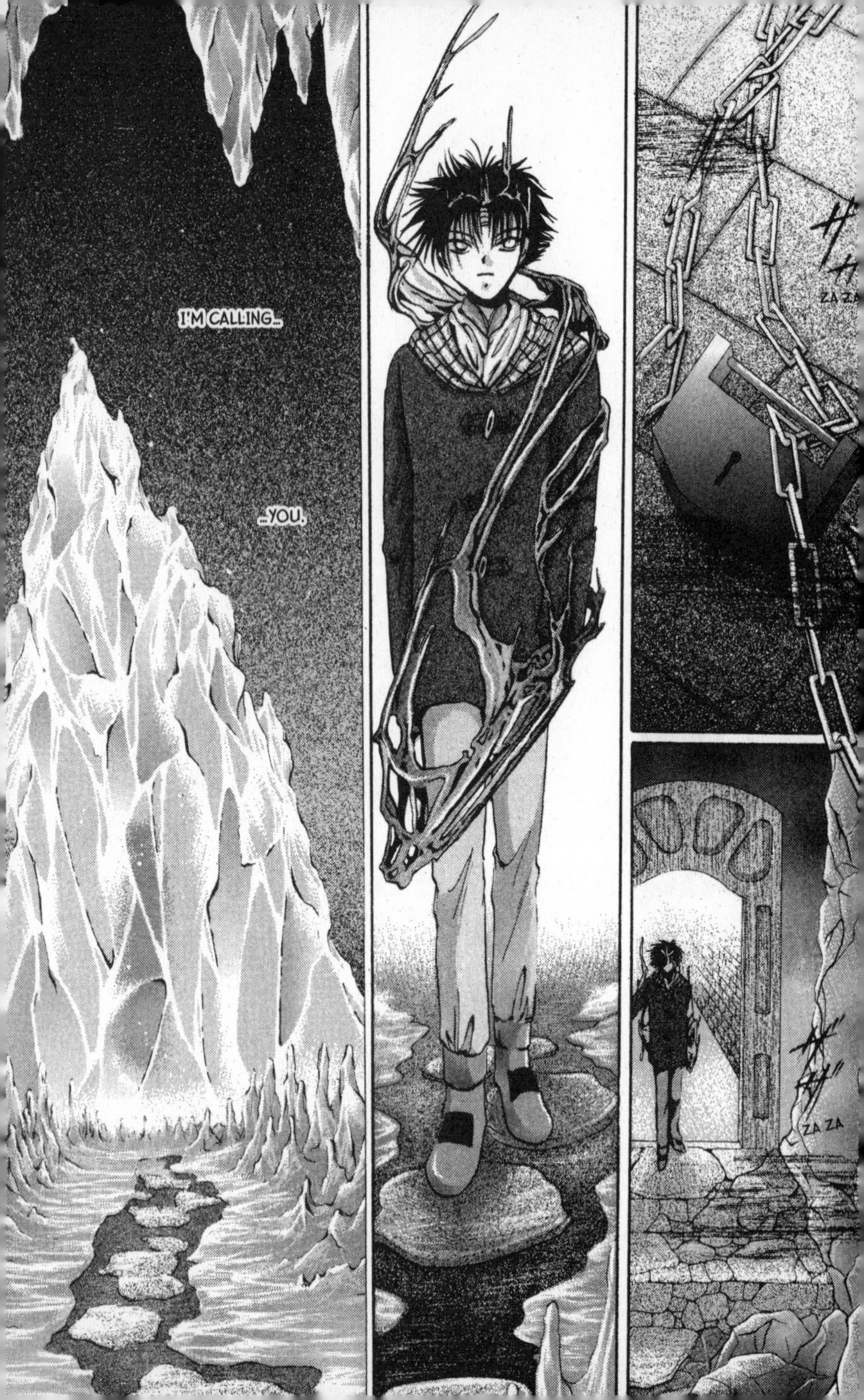
ZA ZA
ZA ZA
I'M CALLING...
...YOU.

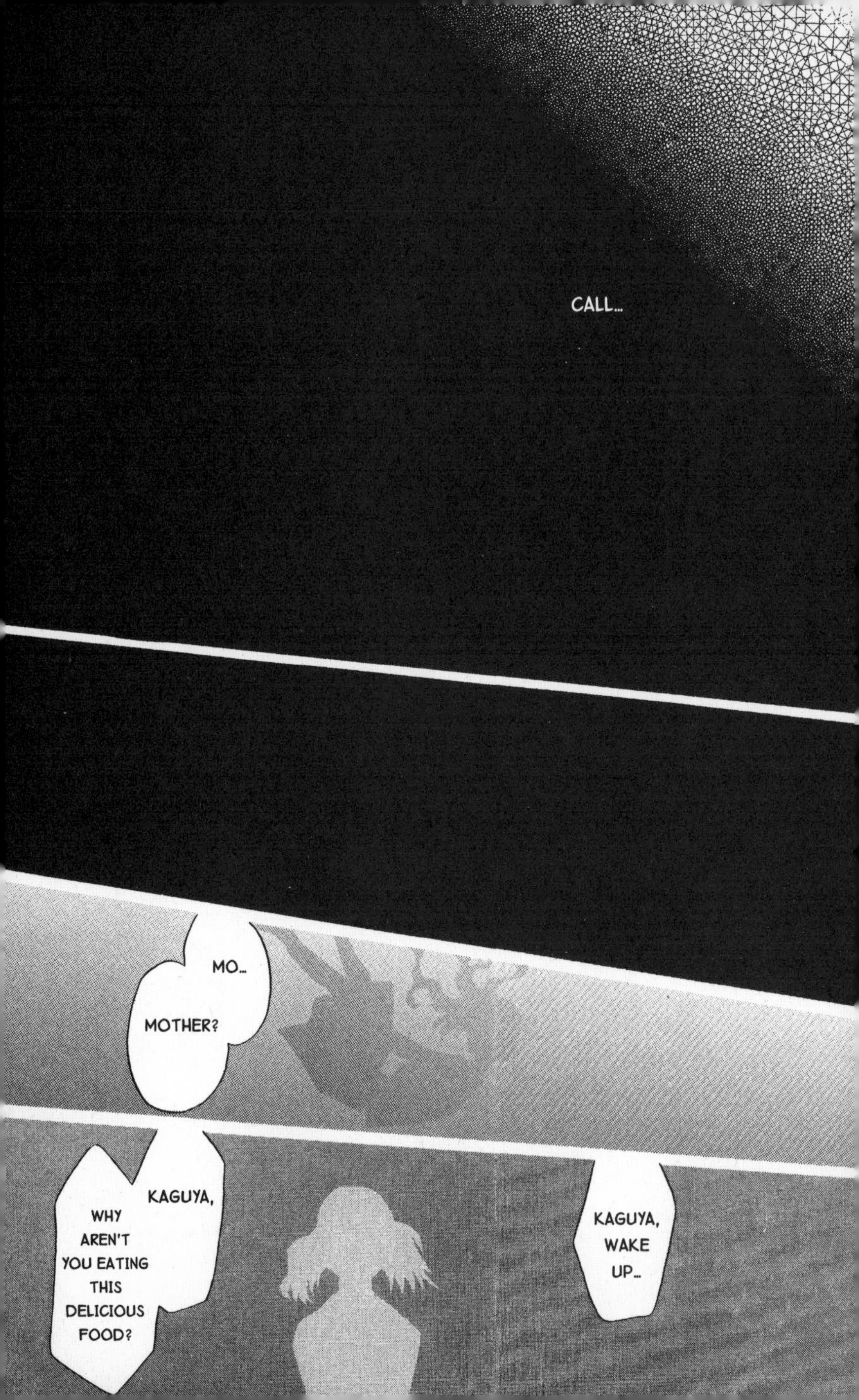
CALL...
MO... MOTHER?
KAGUYA, WAKE UP...
KAGUYA, WHY AREN'T YOU EATING THIS DELICIOUS FOOD?

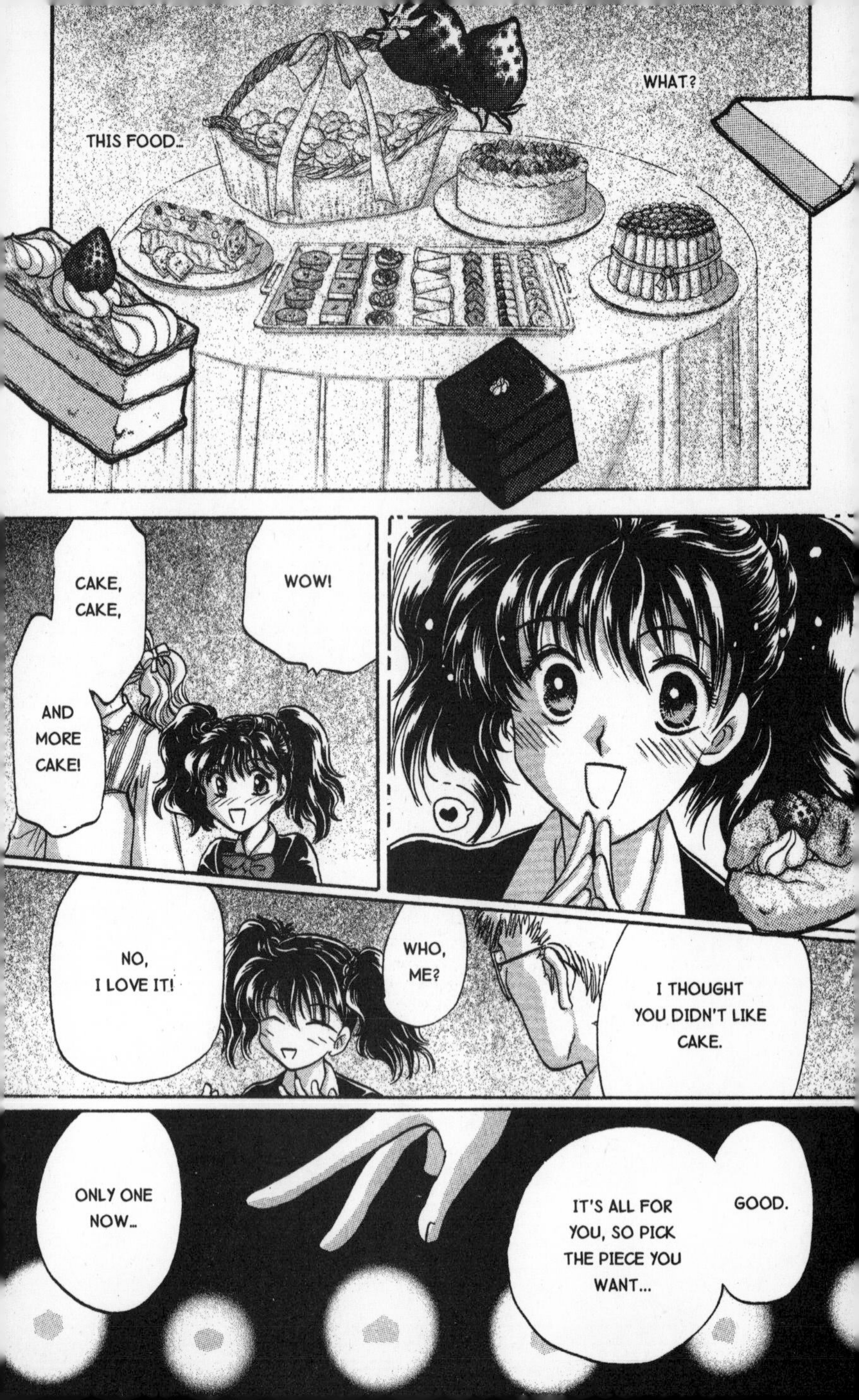
WHAT?
THIS FOOD...
WOW!
CAKE, CAKE,
AND MORE CAKE!
I THOUGHT YOU DIDN'T LIKE CAKE.
WHO, ME?
NO, I LOVE IT!
GOOD.
IT'S ALL FOR YOU, SO PICK THE PIECE YOU WANT...
ONLY ONE NOW...

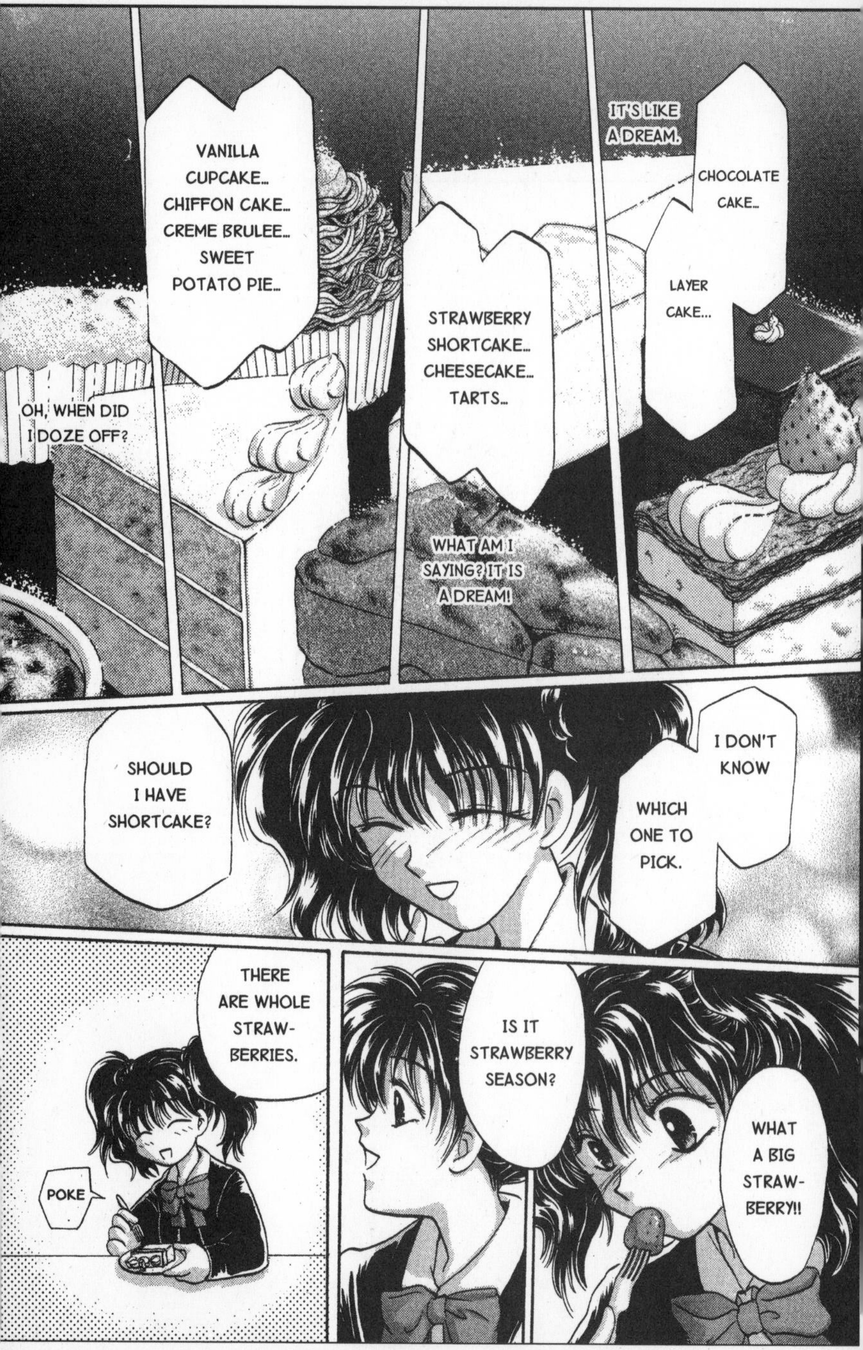
CHOCOLATE CAKE...
LAYER CAKE...
IT'S LIKE A DREAM.
STRAWBERRY SHORTCAKE... CHEESECAKE... TARTS...
WHAT AM I SAYING? IT IS A DREAM!
VANILLA CUPCAKE... CHIFFON CAKE... CREME BRULEE... SWEET POTATO PIE...
OH, WHEN DID I DOZE OFF?
I DON'T KNOW
WHICH ONE TO PICK.
SHOULD I HAVE SHORTCAKE?
IS IT STRAWBERRY SEASON?
WHAT A BIG STRAW-BERRY!!
THERE ARE WHOLE STRAW-BERRIES.
POKE

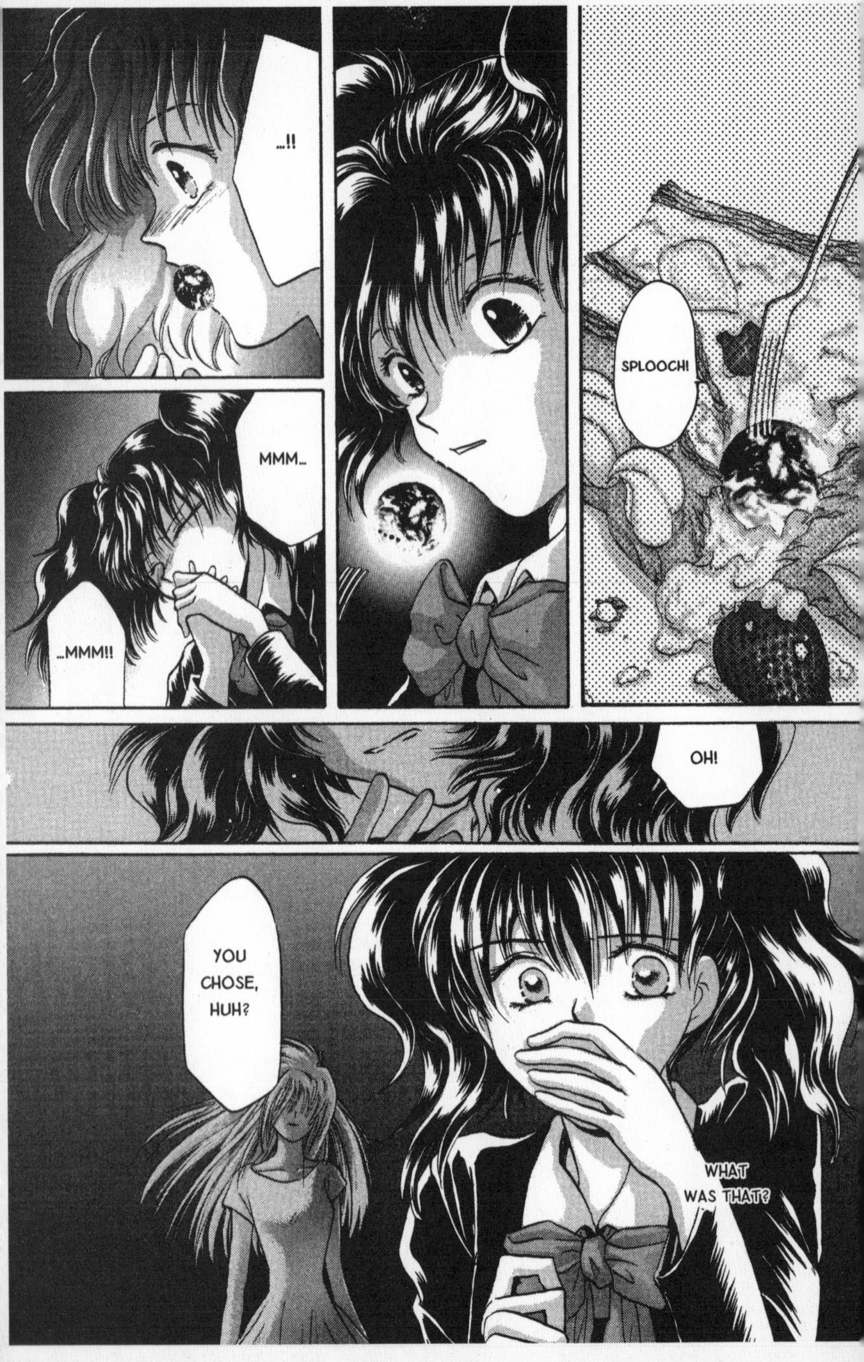
SPLOOCH!
...!!
MMM...
...MMM!!
OH!
YOU CHOSE, HUH?
WHAT WAS THAT?

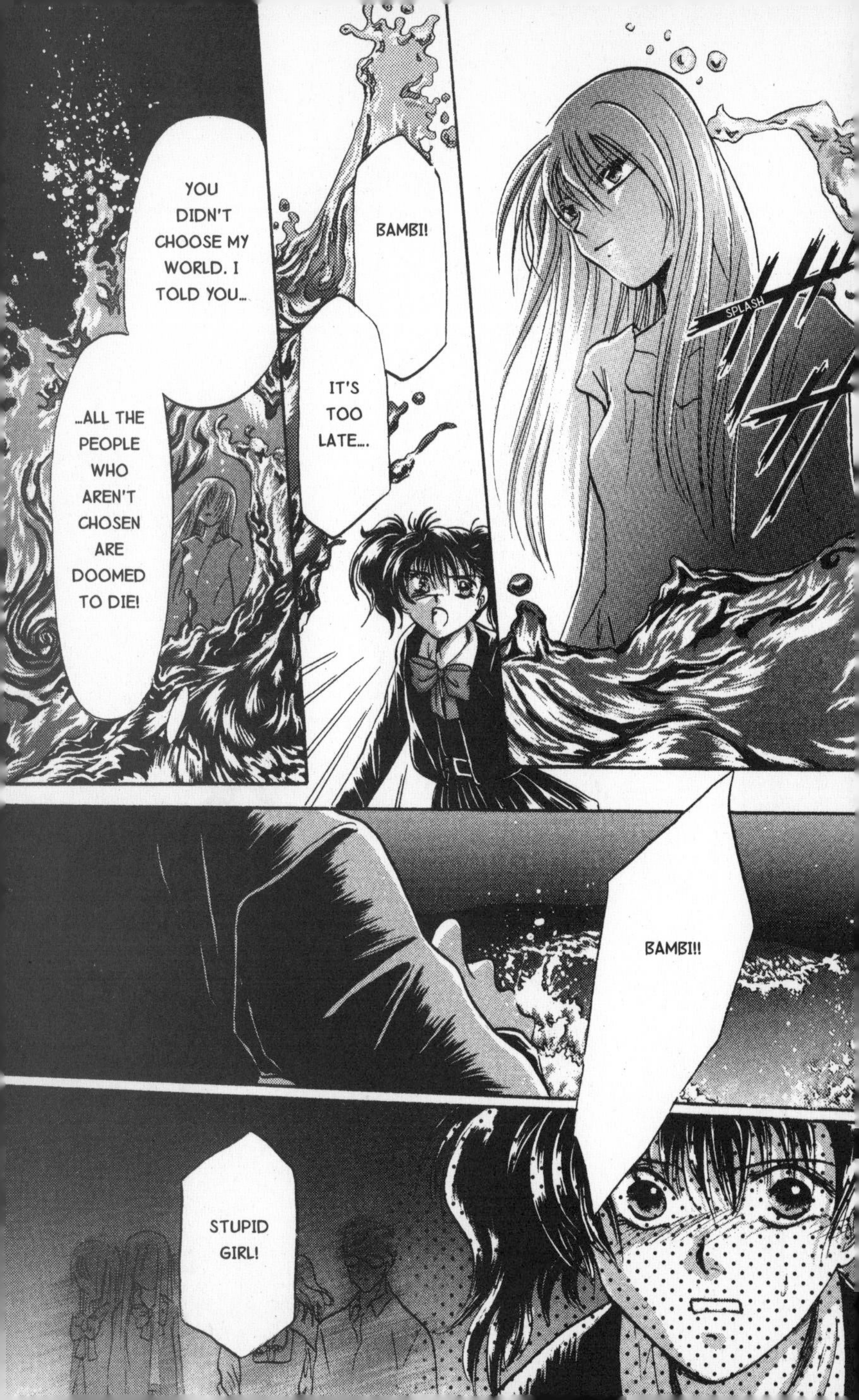
SPLASH
BAMBI!
IT'S TOO LATE....
YOU DIDN'T CHOOSE MY WORLD. I TOLD YOU...
...ALL THE PEOPLE WHO AREN'T CHOSEN ARE DOOMED TO DIE!
BAMBI!!
STUPID GIRL!

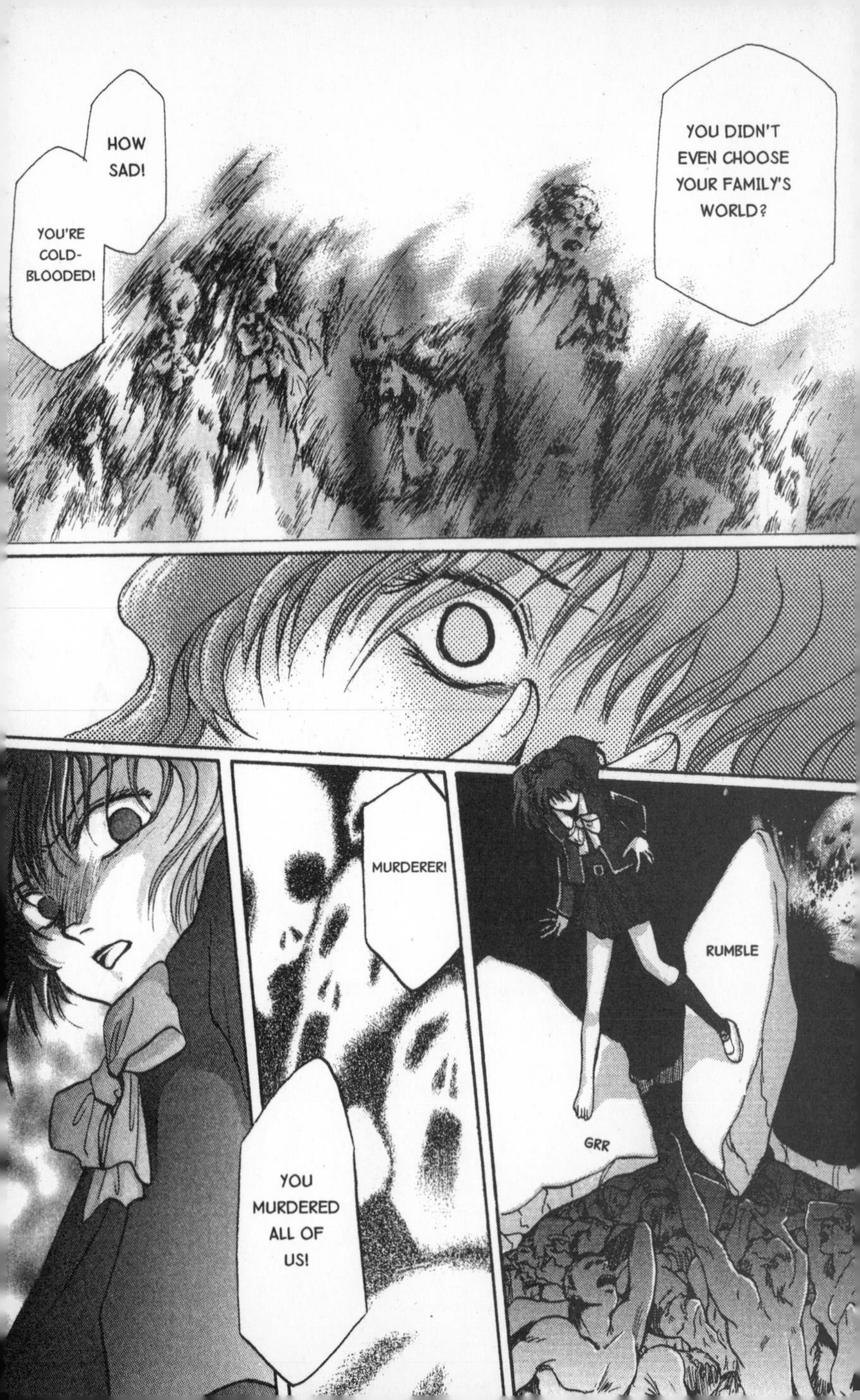
YOU DIDN'T EVEN CHOOSE YOUR FAMILY'S WORLD?
HOW SAD!
YOU'RE COLD-BLOODED!
RUMBLE
GRR
MURDERER!
YOU MURDERED ALL OF US!

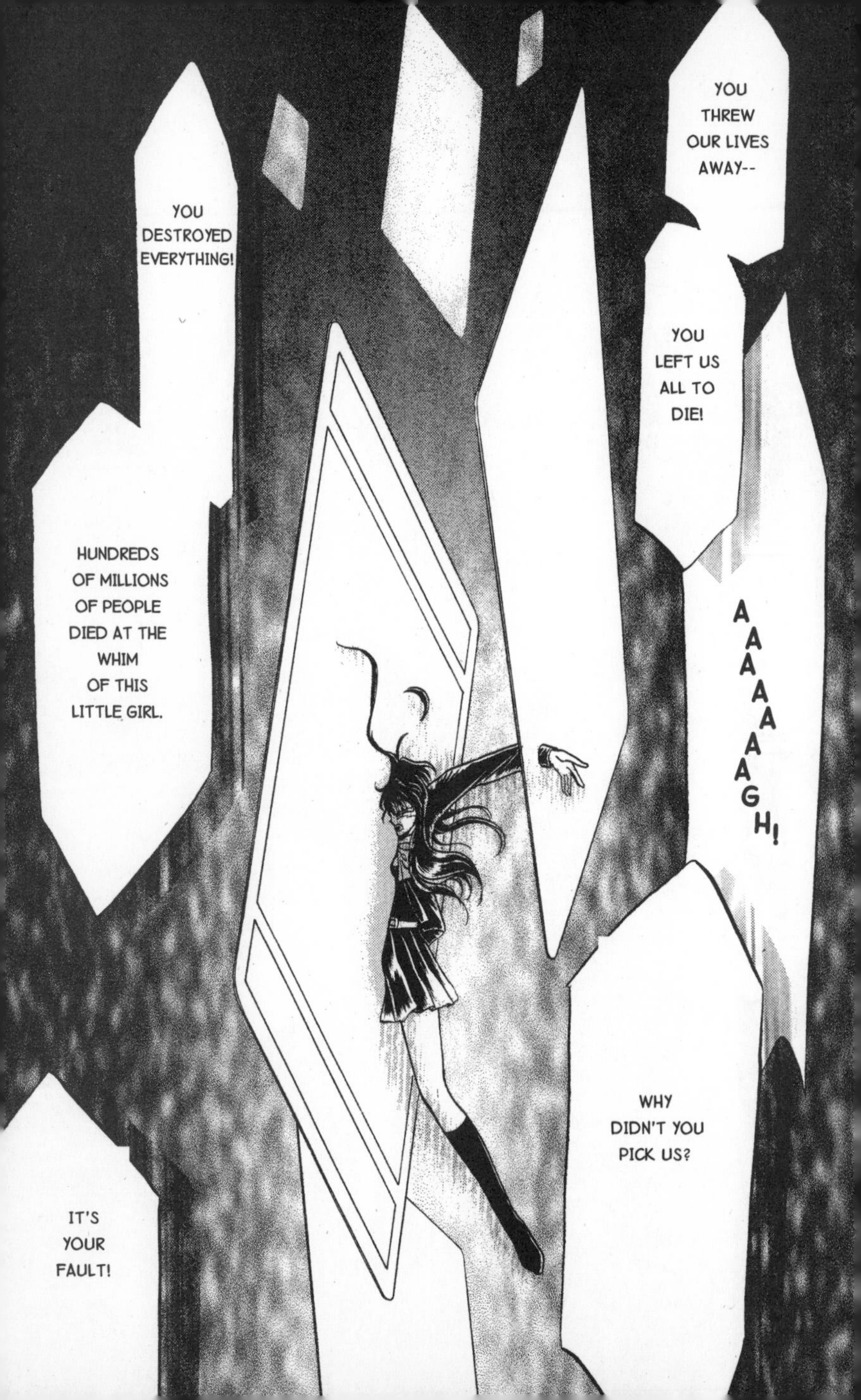
YOU THREW OUR LIVES AWAY--
YOU DESTROYED EVERYTHING!
YOU LEFT US ALL TO DIE!
HUNDREDS OF MILLIONS OF PEOPLE DIED AT THE WHIM OF THIS LITTLE GIRL.
AAAAAAAGH!
WHY DIDN'T YOU PICK US?
IT'S YOUR FAULT!

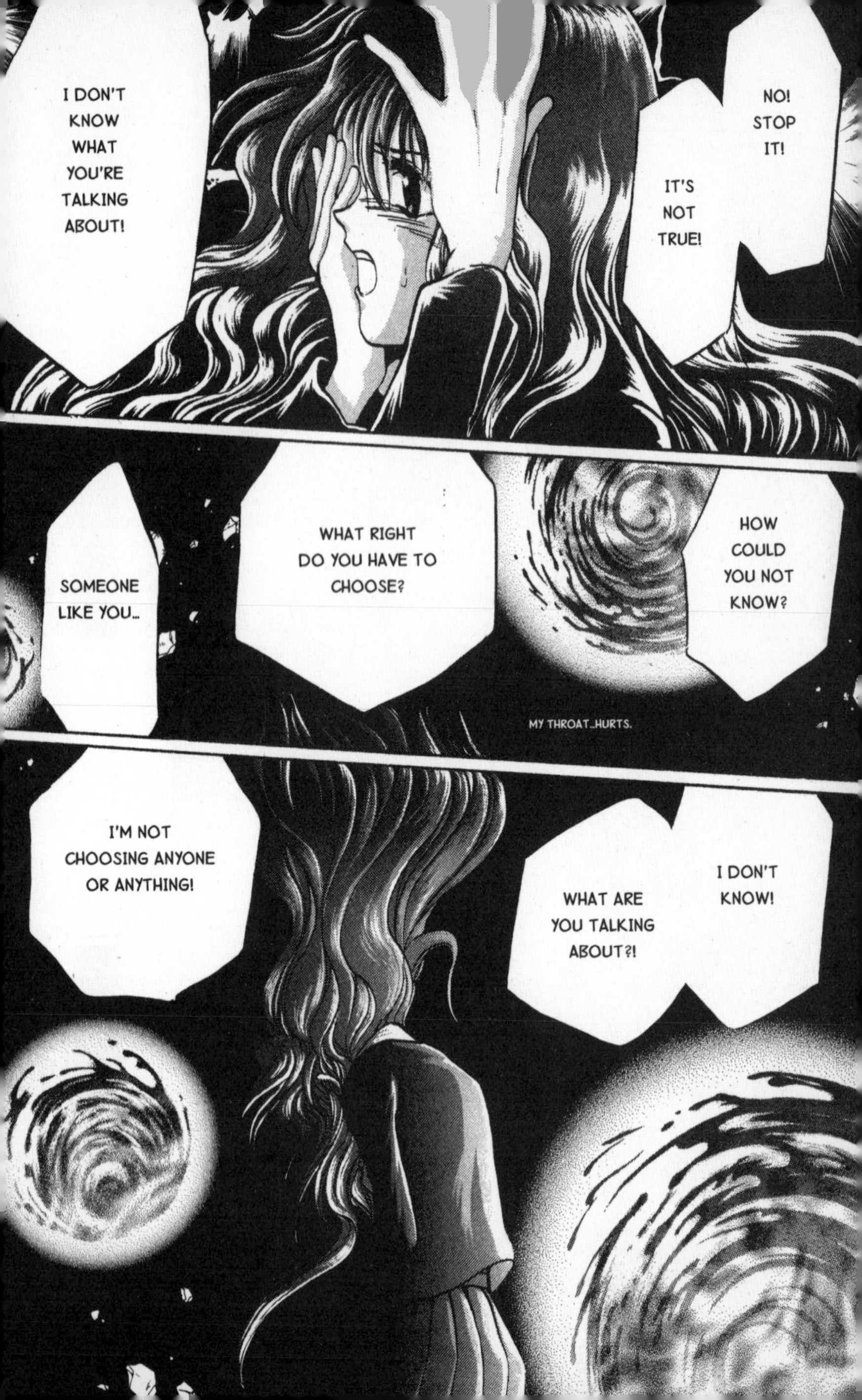
NO! STOP IT!
IT'S NOT TRUE!
I DON'T KNOW WHAT YOU'RE TALKING ABOUT!
HOW COULD YOU NOT KNOW?
WHAT RIGHT DO YOU HAVE TO CHOOSE?
SOMEONE LIKE YOU...
MY THROAT...HURTS.
I DON'T KNOW!
WHAT ARE YOU TALKING ABOUT?!
I'M NOT CHOOSING ANYONE OR ANYTHING!

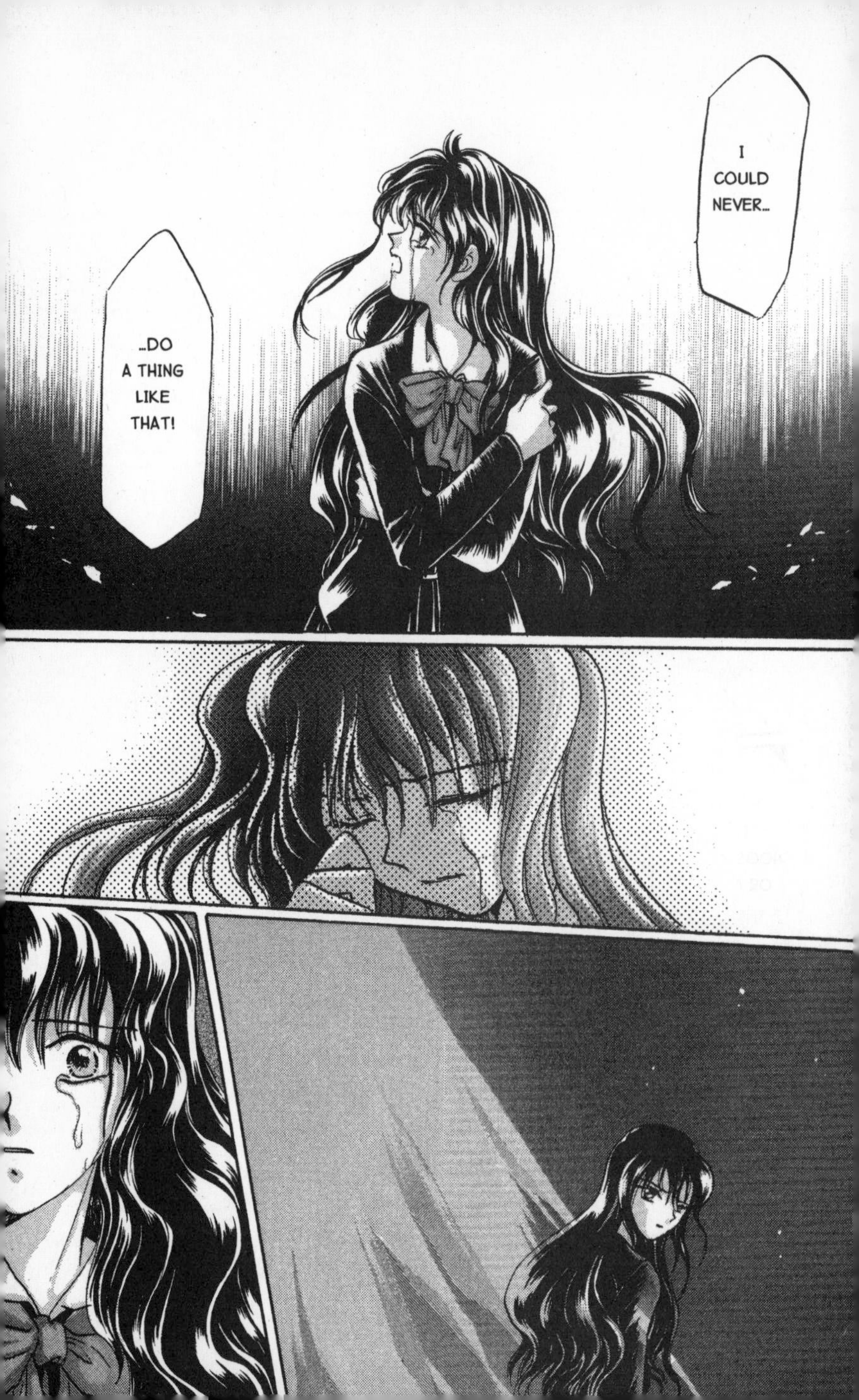

I COULD NEVER...
...DO A THING LIKE THAT!

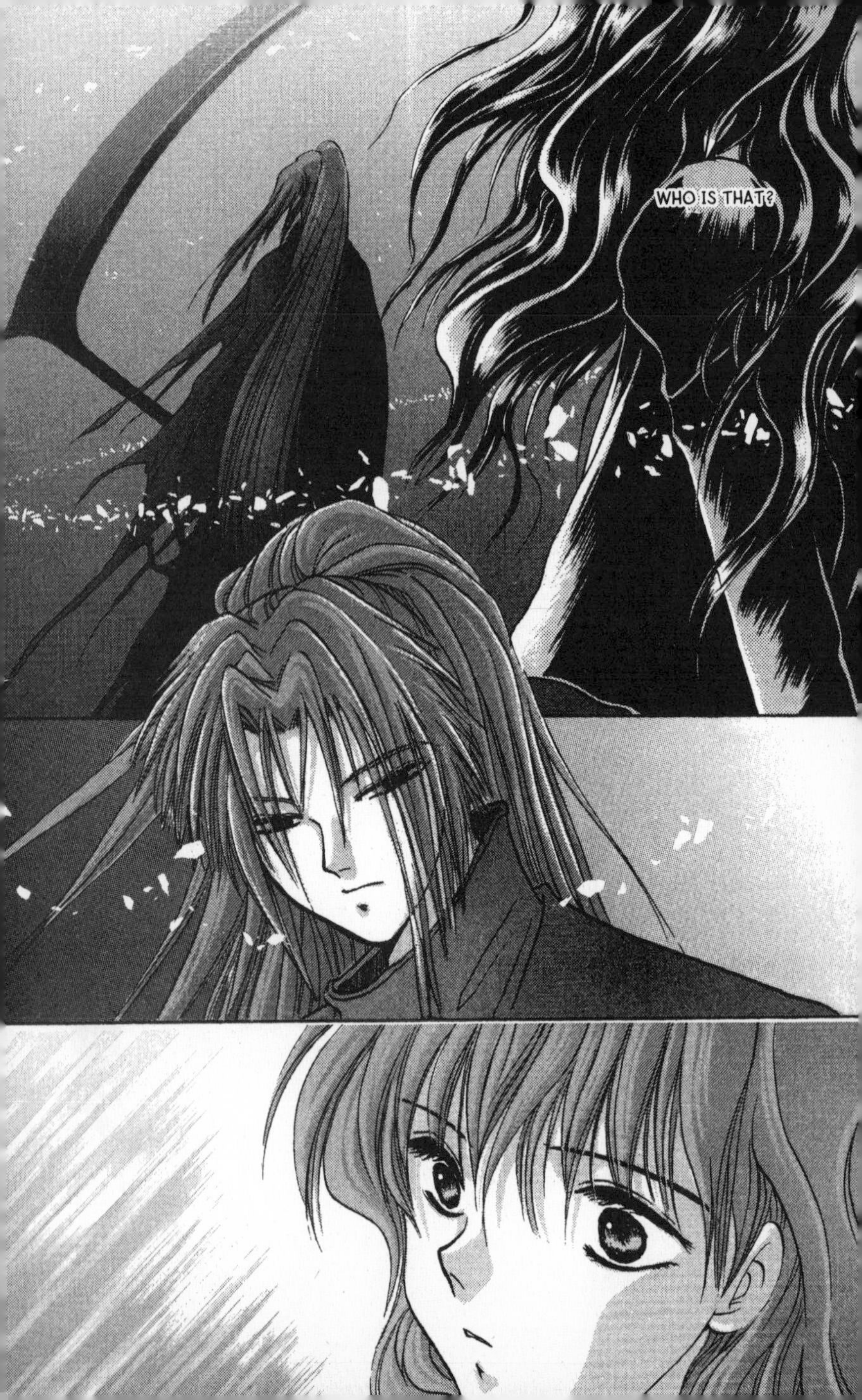
WHO IS THAT?

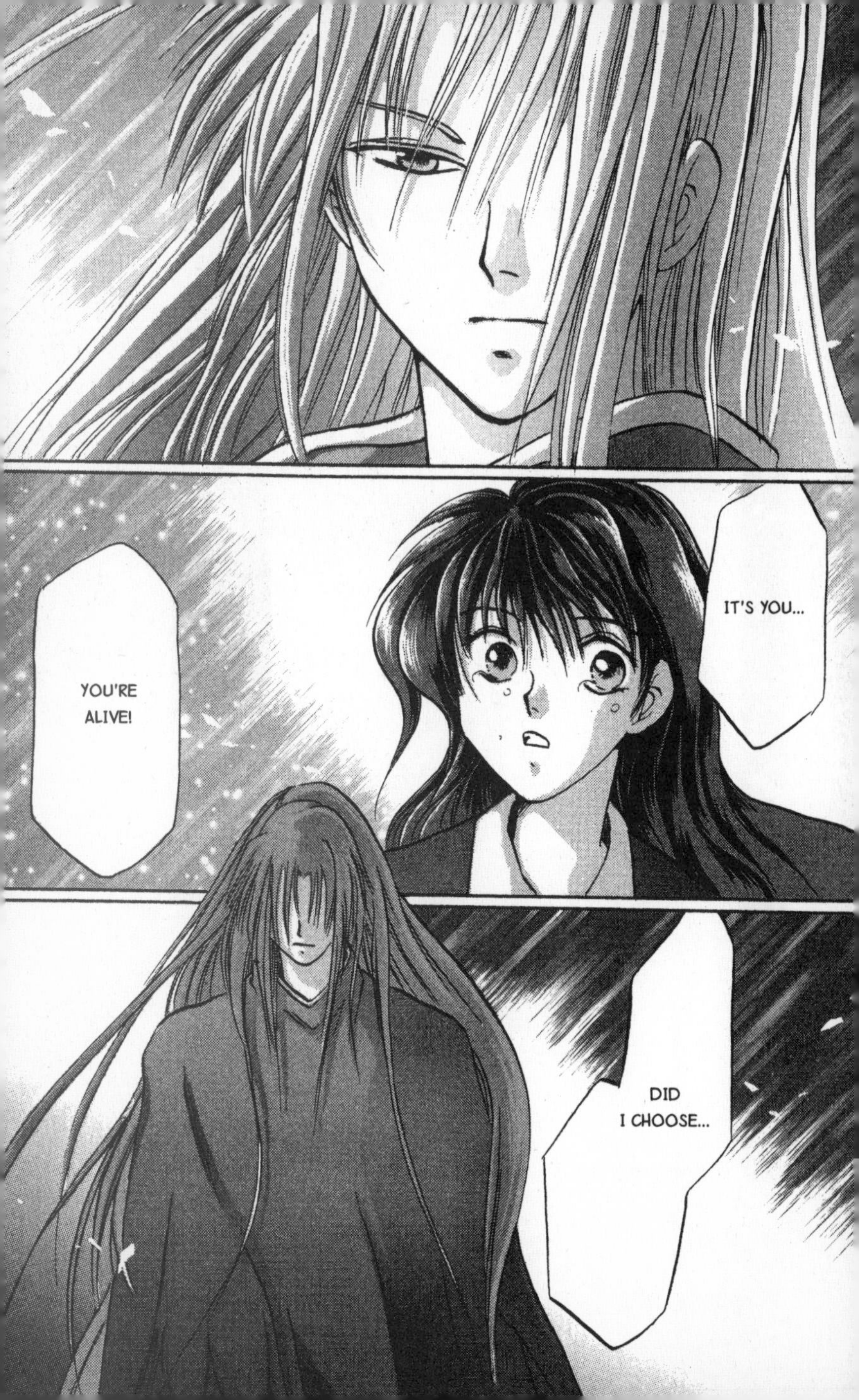
IT'S YOU...
YOU'RE ALIVE!
DID I CHOOSE...

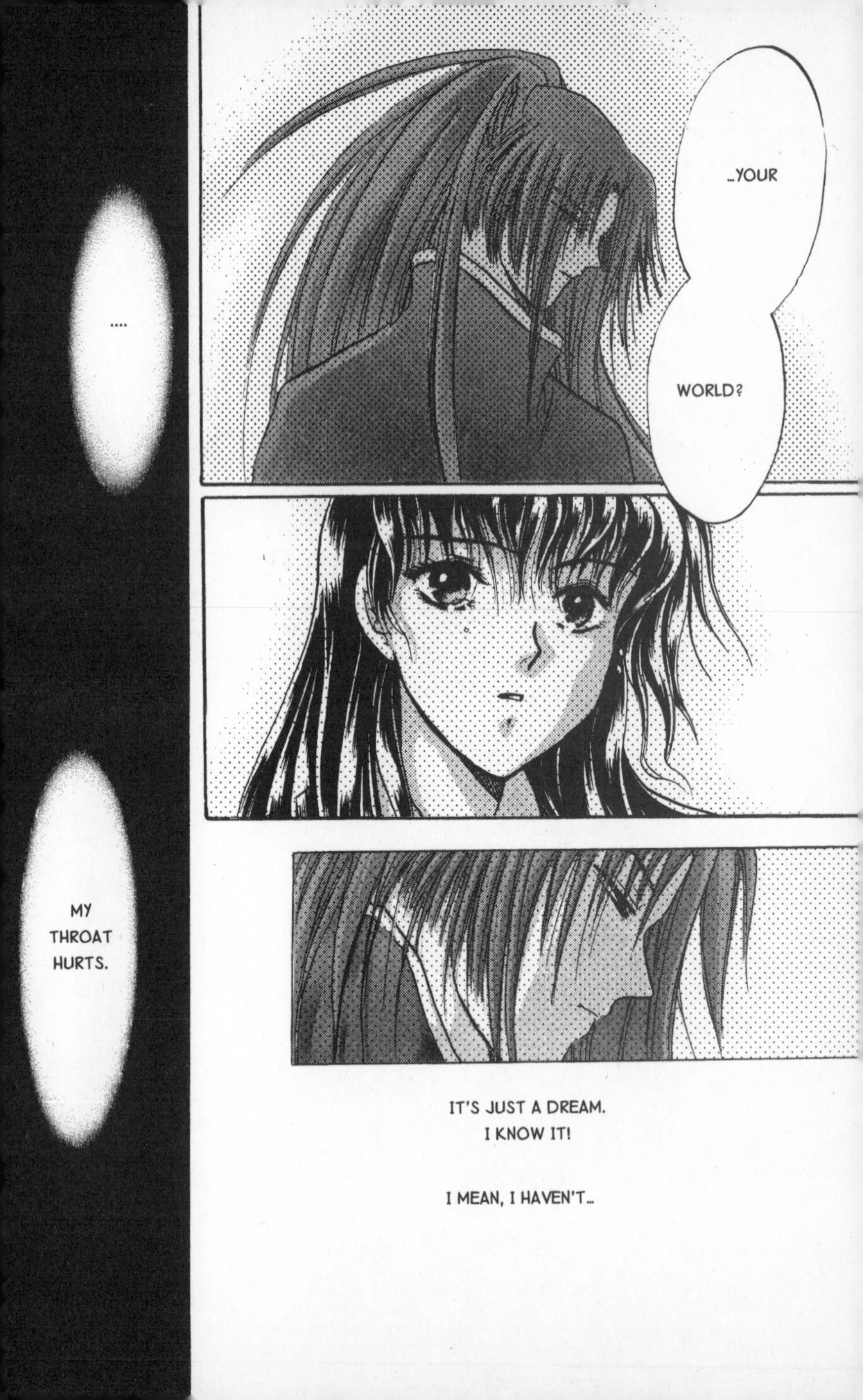
...YOUR
WORLD?
IT'S JUST A DREAM. I KNOW IT!
I MEAN, I HAVEN'T...
....
MY THROAT HURTS.

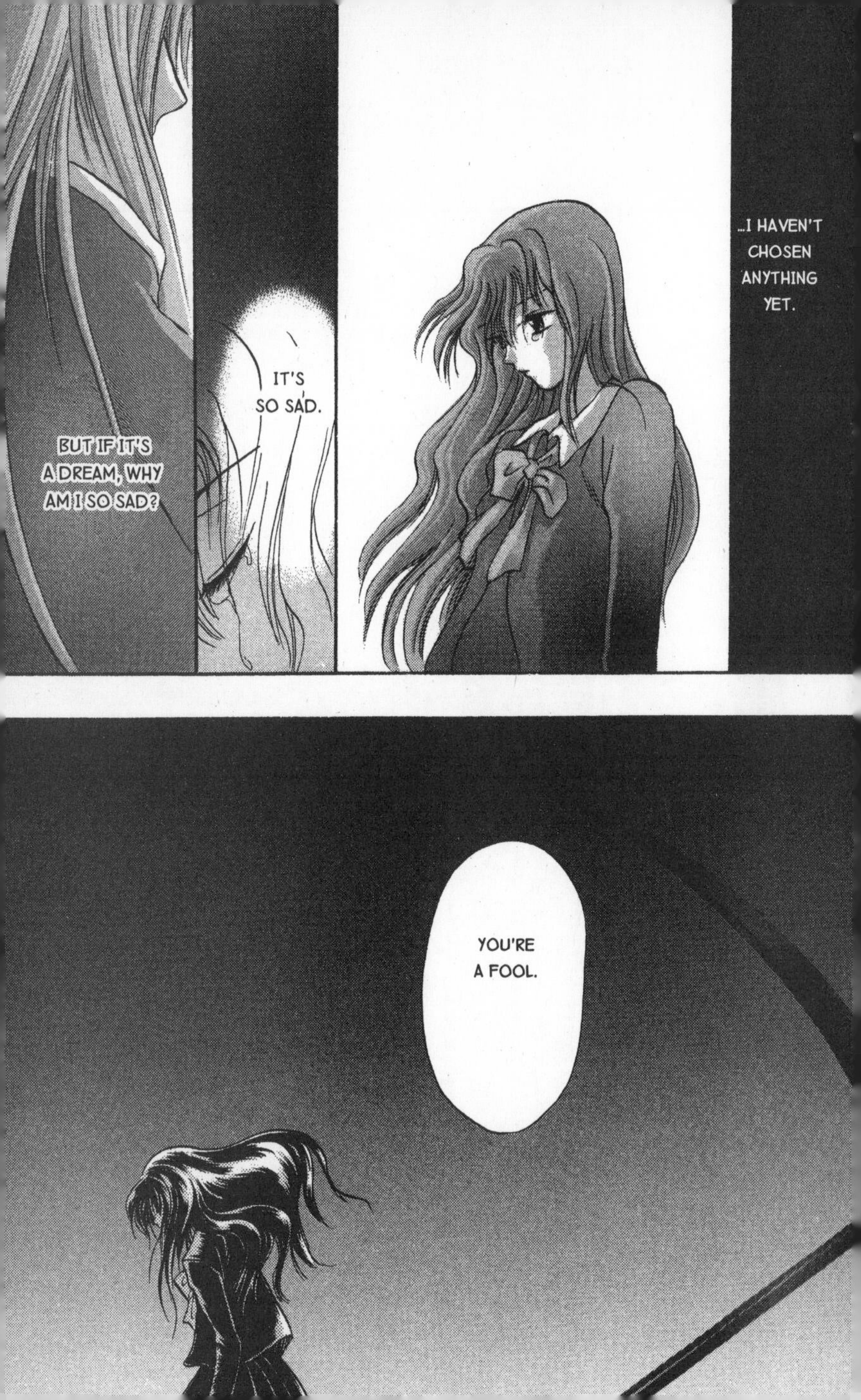
...I HAVEN'T CHOSEN ANYTHING YET.
IT'S SO SAD.
BUT IF IT'S A DREAM, WHY AM I SO SAD?
YOU'RE A FOOL.

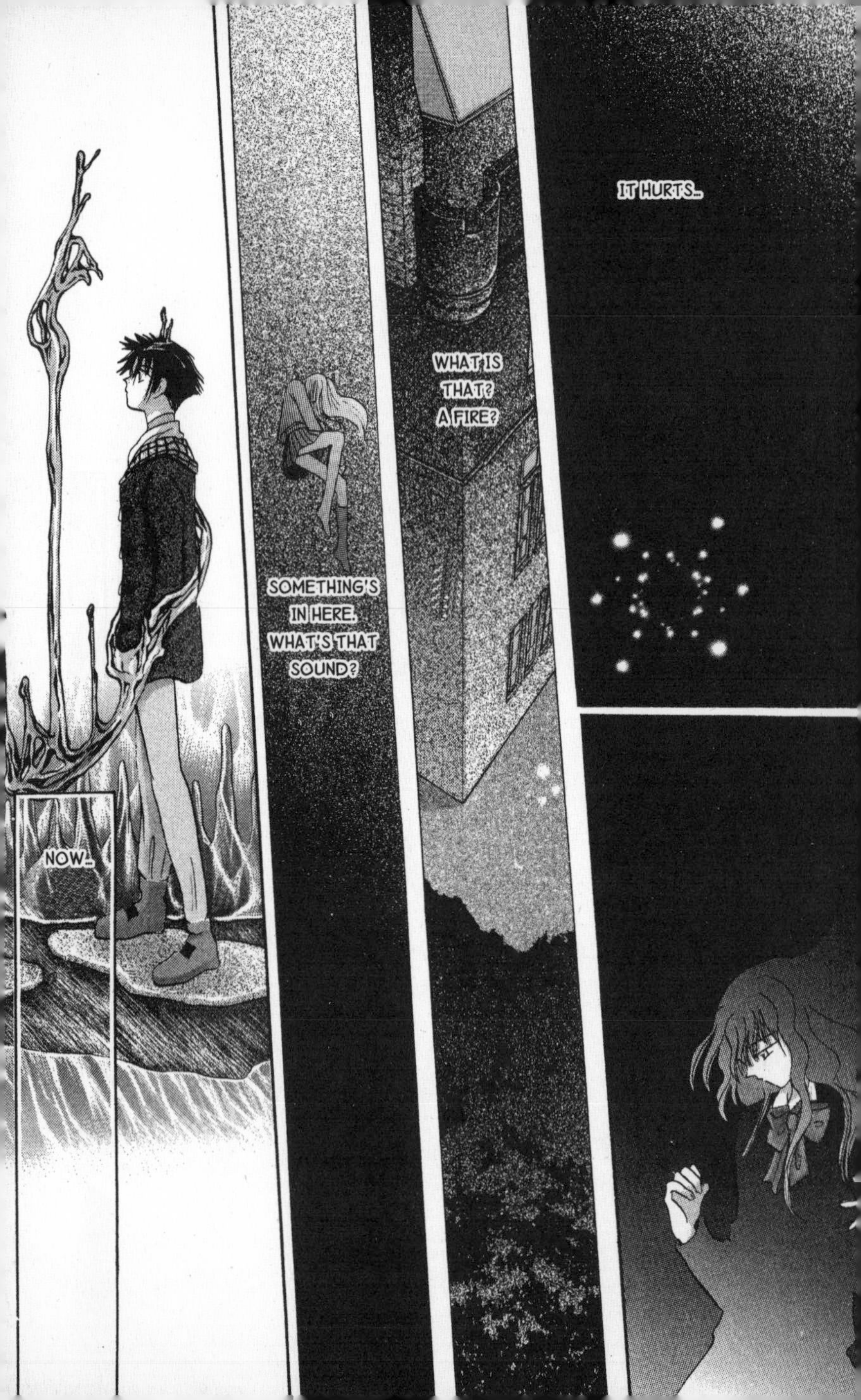
IT HURTS..
WHAT IS THAT? A FIRE?
SOMETHING'S IN HERE. WHAT'S THAT SOUND?
NOW..

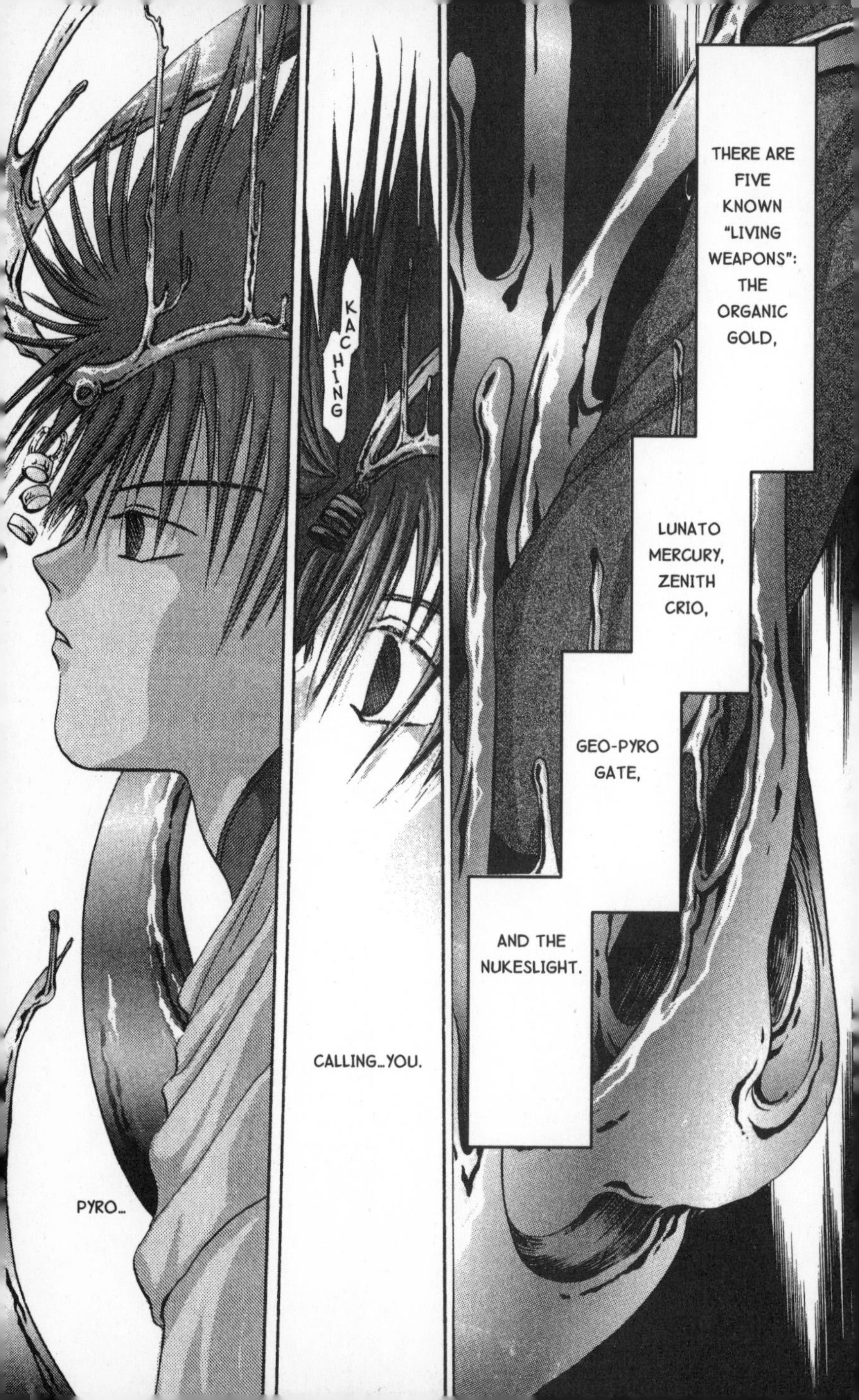
THERE ARE FIVE KNOWN "LIVING WEAPONS": THE ORGANIC GOLD,
LUNATO MERCURY, ZENITH CRIO,
GEO-PYRO GATE,
AND THE NUKESLIGHT.
KACHING
CALLING...YOU.
PYRO...

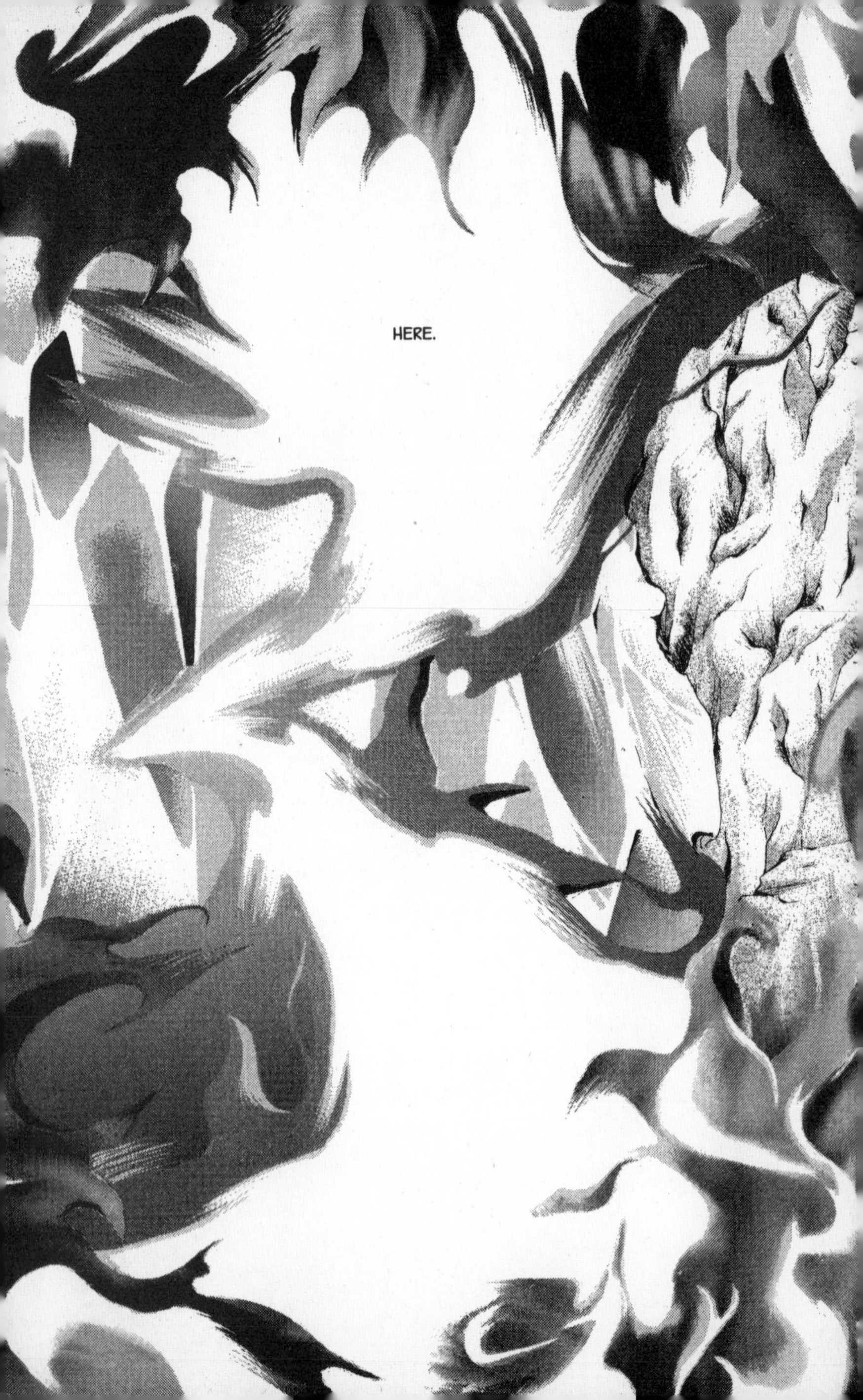
HERE.

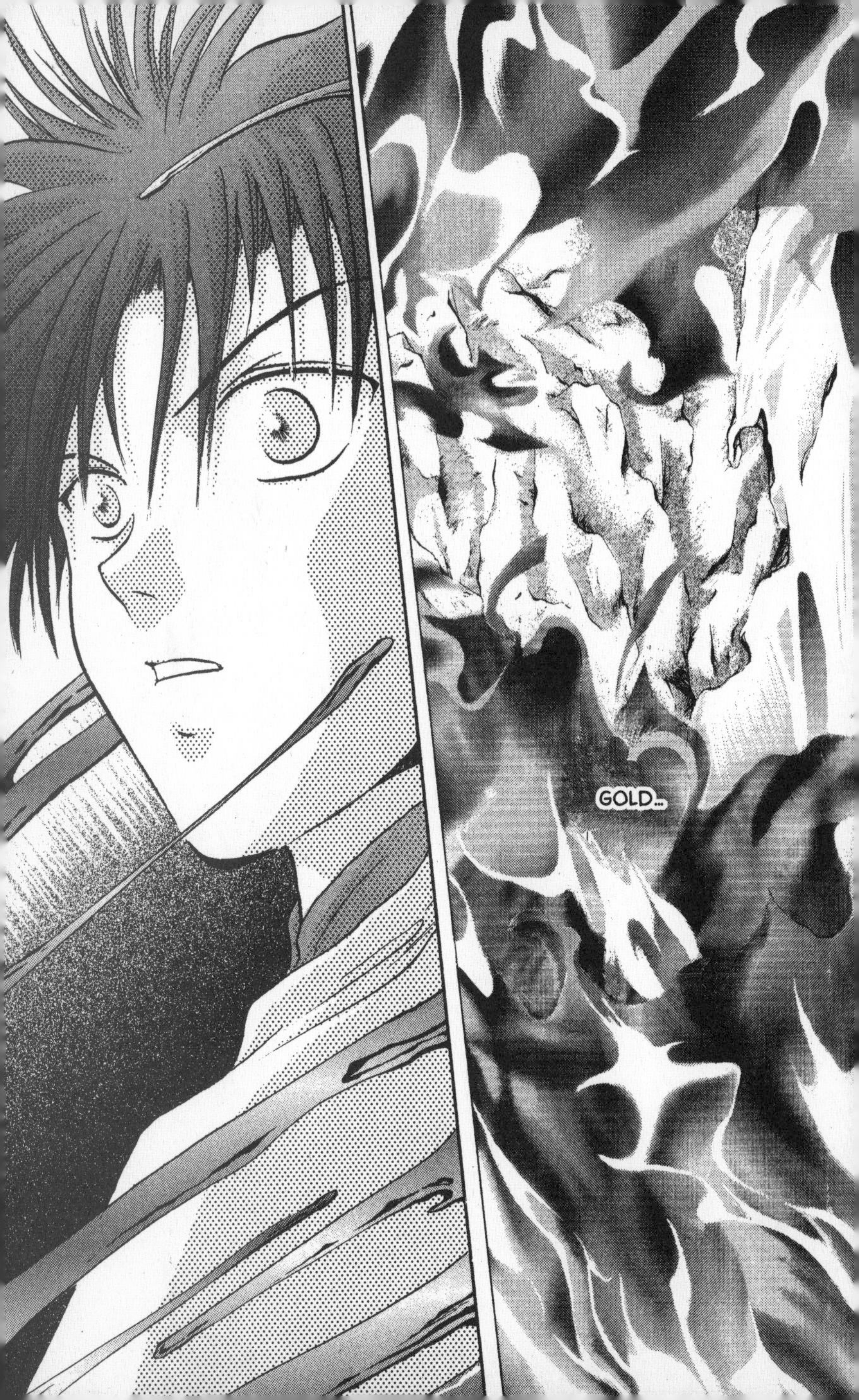
GOLD...

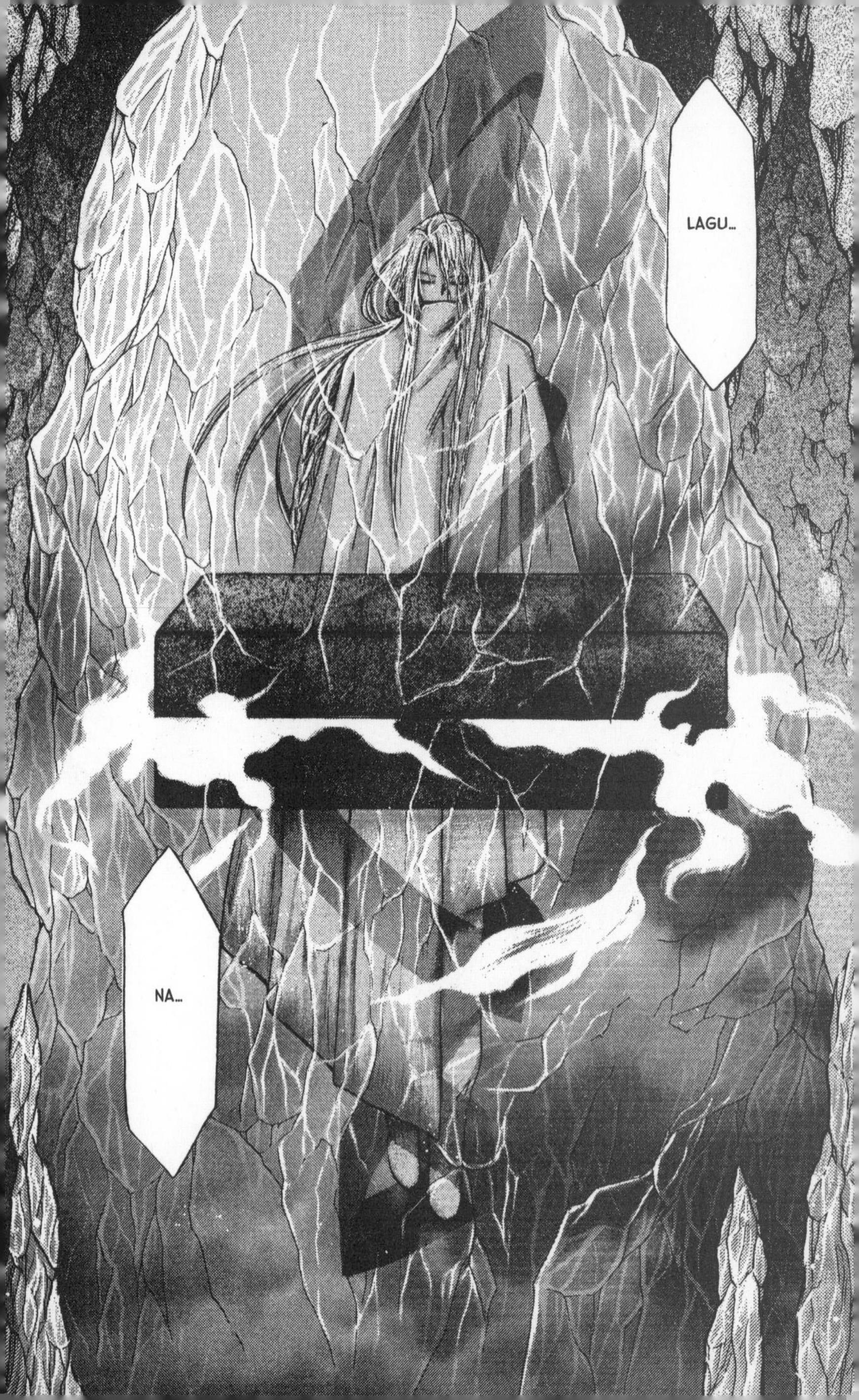
LAGU...
NA...

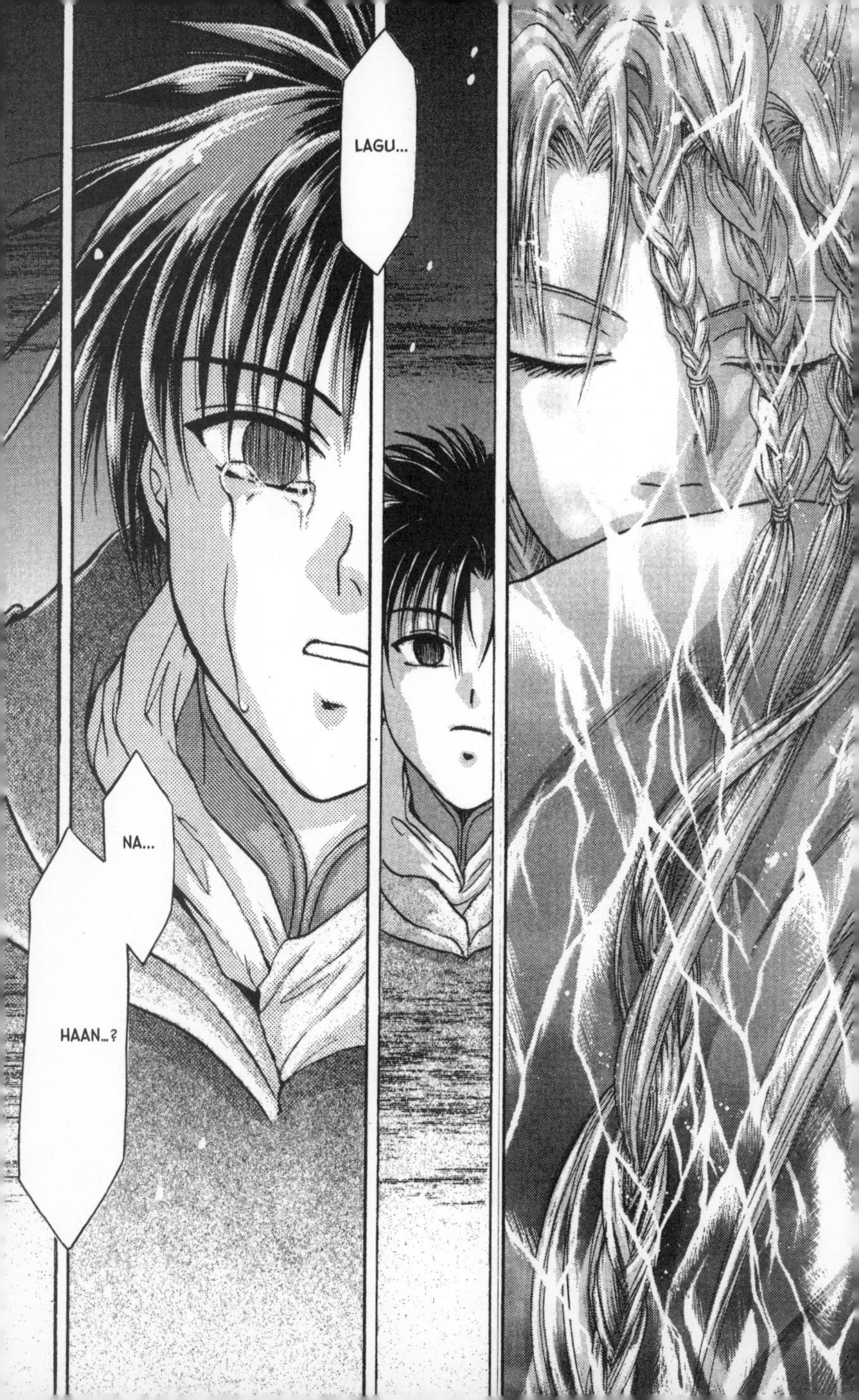
LAGU...
NA...
HAAN...?

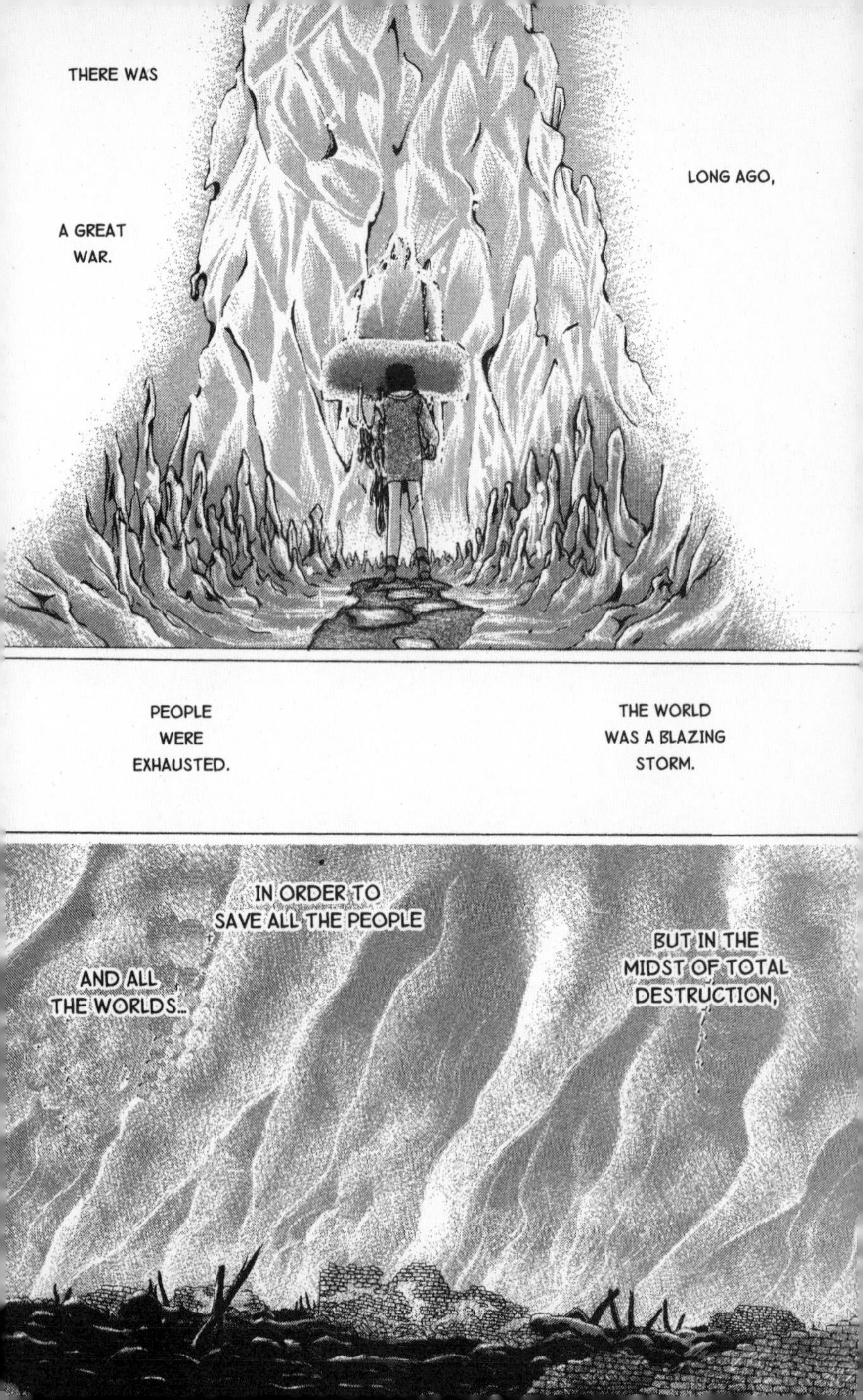
LONG AGO,
THERE WAS
A GREAT WAR.
THE WORLD WAS A BLAZING STORM.
PEOPLE WERE EXHAUSTED.
BUT IN THE MIDST OF TOTAL DESTRUCTION,
IN ORDER TO SAVE ALL THE PEOPLE
AND ALL THE WORLDS...

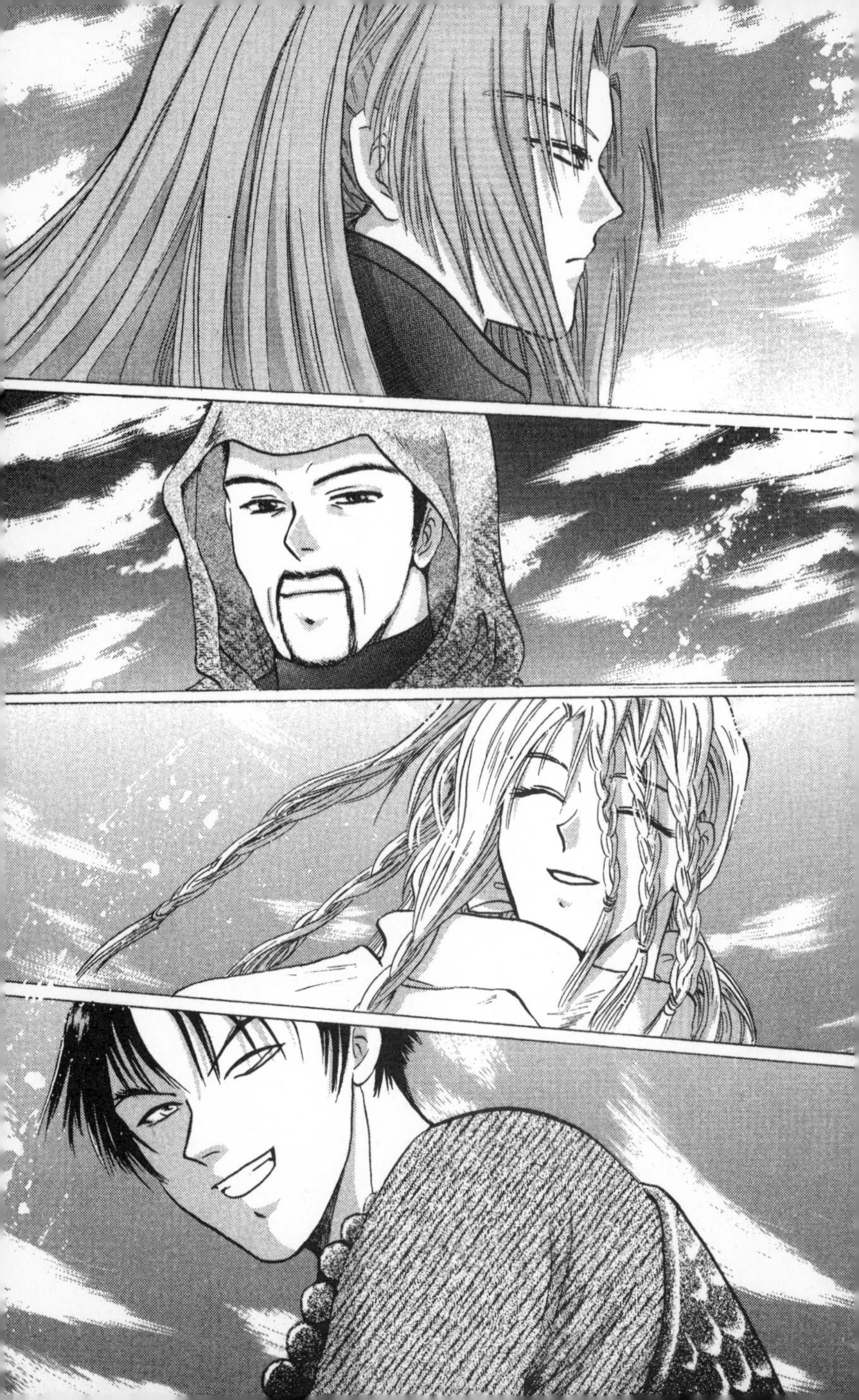

THERE ARE
LEGENDARY TALES ABOUT
THE MEN WHO FOUGHT
TOGETHER.

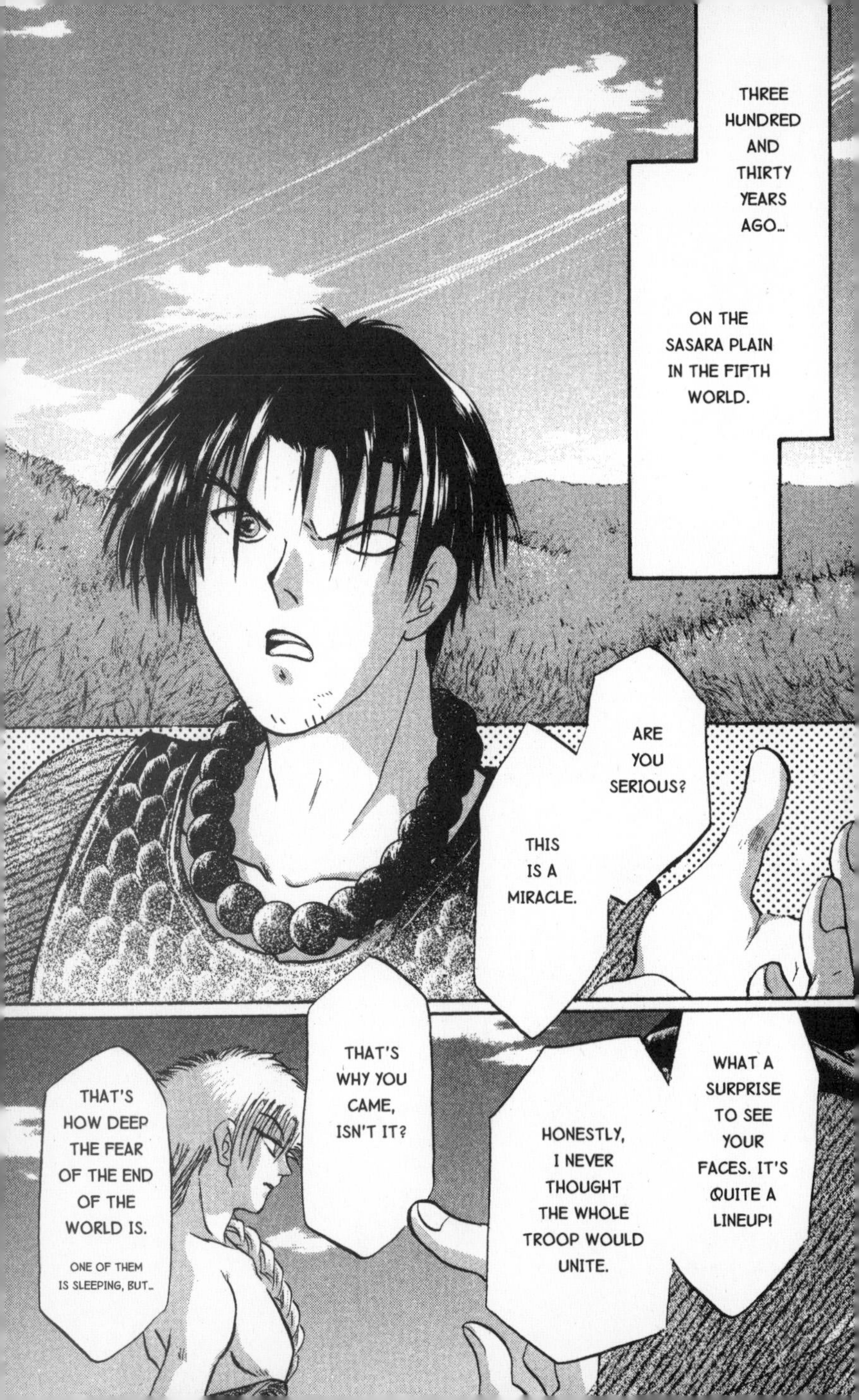
THREE HUNDRED AND THIRTY YEARS AGO...
ON THE SASARA PLAIN IN THE FIFTH WORLD.
ARE YOU SERIOUS?
THIS IS A MIRACLE.
WHAT A SURPRISE TO SEE YOUR FACES. IT'S QUITE A LINEUP!
HONESTLY, I NEVER THOUGHT THE WHOLE TROOP WOULD UNITE.
THAT'S WHY YOU CAME, ISN'T IT?
THAT'S HOW DEEP THE FEAR OF THE END OF THE WORLD IS.
ONE OF THEM IS SLEEPING, BUT...

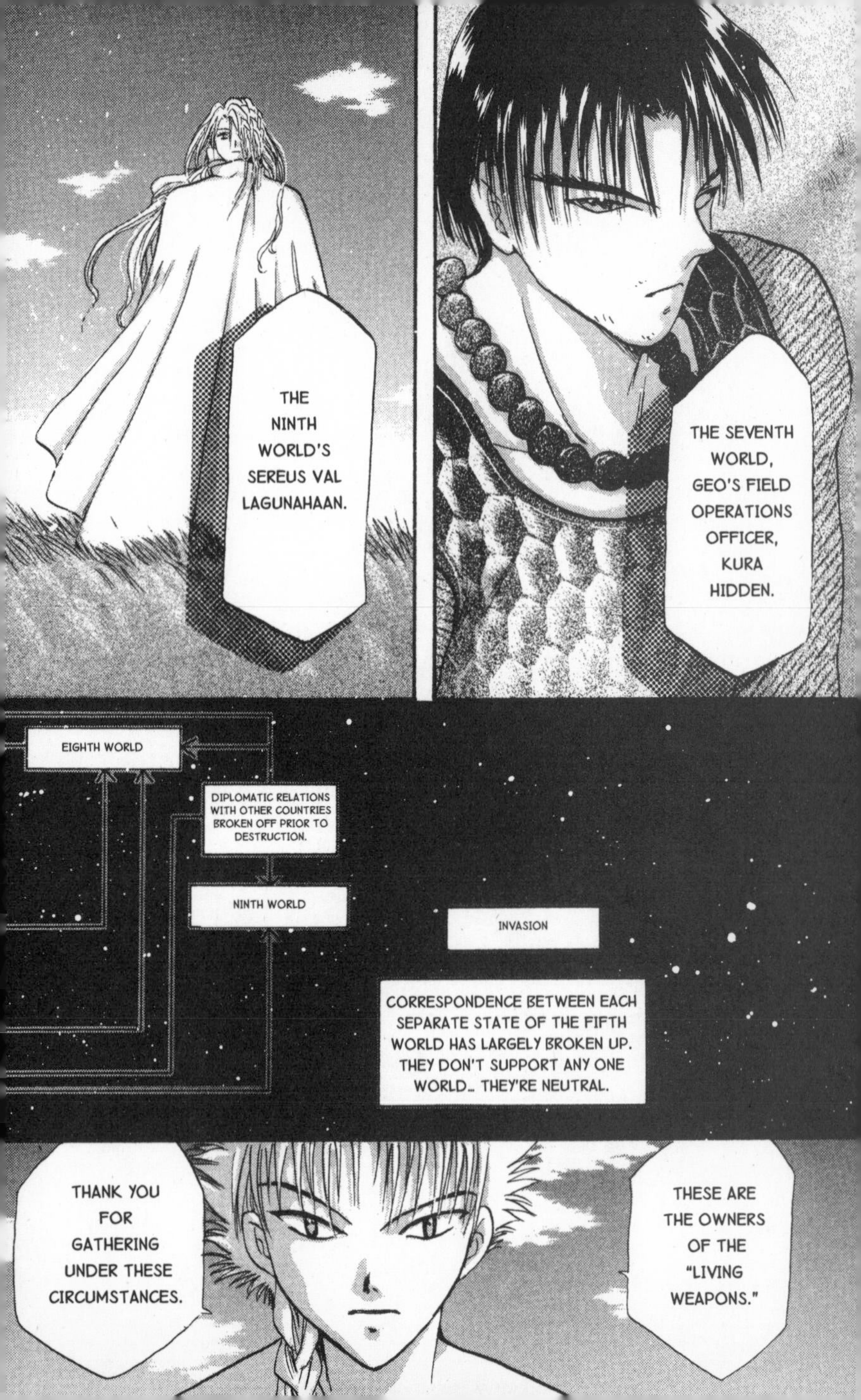
THE SEVENTH WORLD, GEO'S FIELD OPERATIONS OFFICER, KURA HIDDEN.
THE NINTH WORLD'S SEREUS VAL LAGUNAHAAN.
EIGHTH WORLD
DIPLOMATIC RELATIONS WITH OTHER COUNTRIES BROKEN OFF PRIOR TO DESTRUCTION.
NINTH WORLD
INVASION
CORRESPONDENCE BETWEEN EACH SEPARATE STATE OF THE FIFTH WORLD HAS LARGELY BROKEN UP. THEY DON'T SUPPORT ANY ONE WORLD... THEY'RE NEUTRAL.
THESE ARE THE OWNERS OF THE "LIVING WEAPONS."
THANK YOU FOR GATHERING UNDER THESE CIRCUMSTANCES.

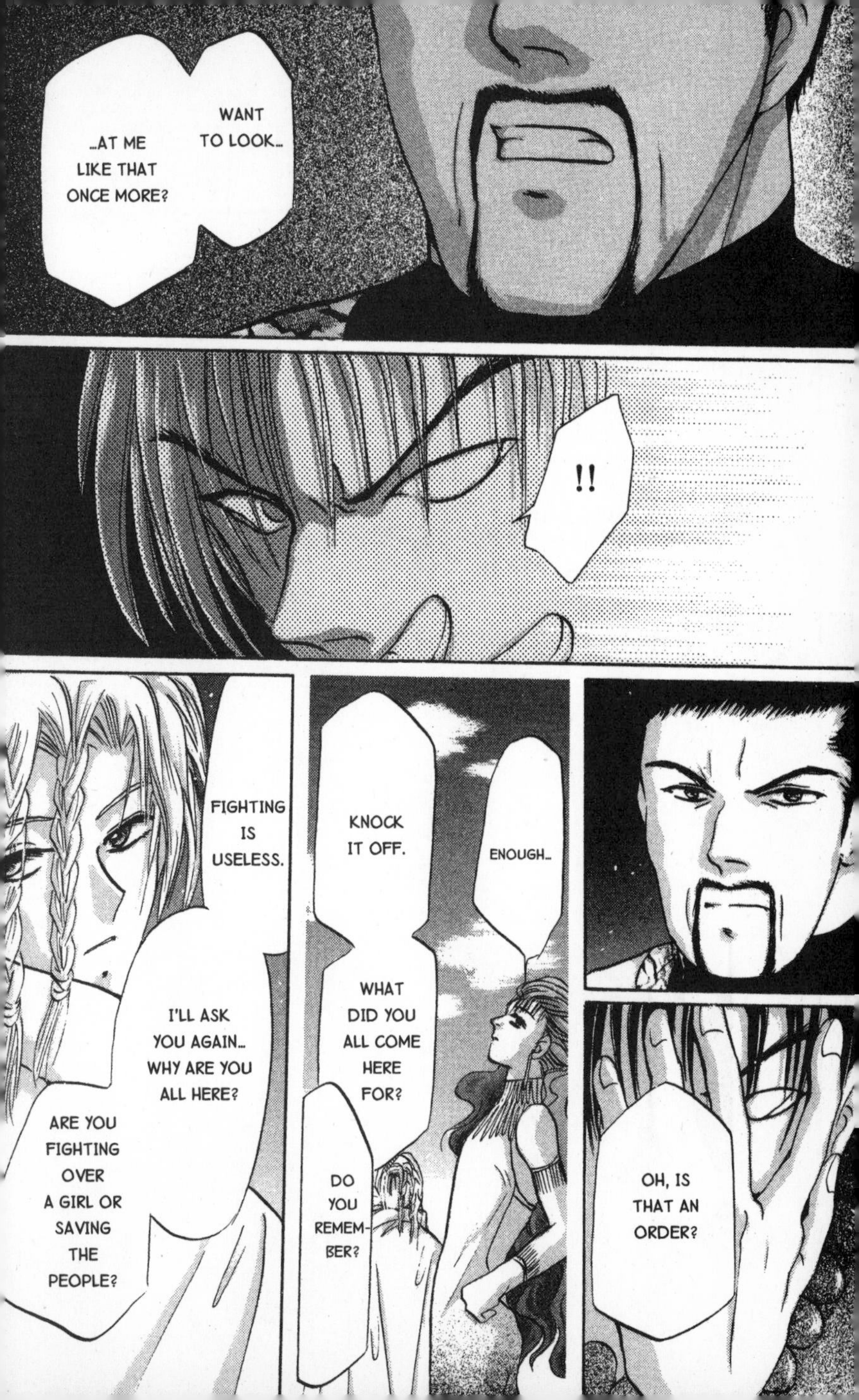
WANT TO LOOK...
...AT ME LIKE THAT ONCE MORE?
!!
OH, IS THAT AN ORDER?
ENOUGH...
KNOCK IT OFF.
WHAT DID YOU ALL COME HERE FOR?
DO YOU REMEM-BER?
FIGHTING IS USELESS.
I'LL ASK YOU AGAIN... WHY ARE YOU ALL HERE?
ARE YOU FIGHTING OVER A GIRL OR SAVING THE PEOPLE?

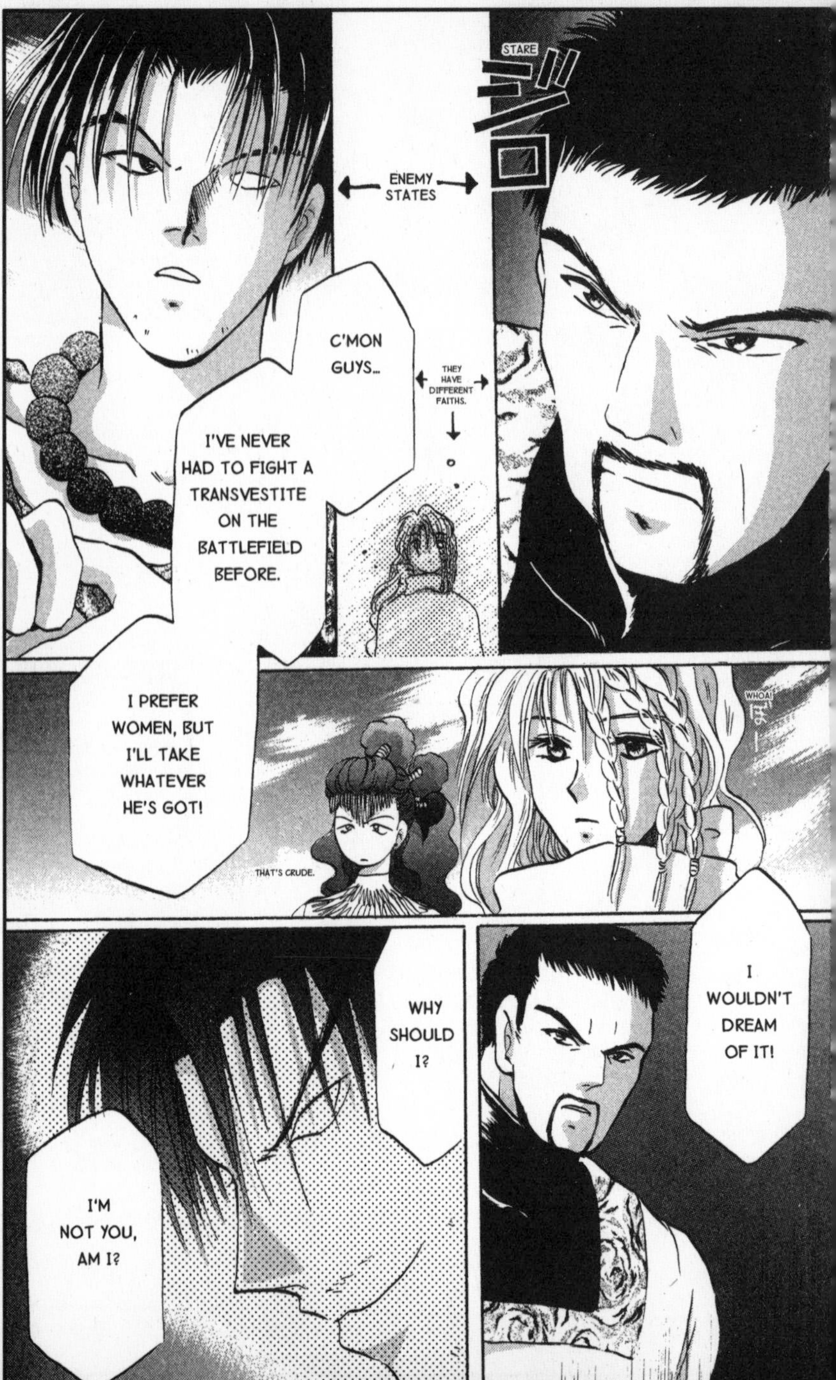
STARE
ENEMY STATES
C'MON GUYS...
THEY HAVE DIFFERENT FAITHS.
I'VE NEVER HAD TO FIGHT A TRANSVESTITE ON THE BATTLEFIELD BEFORE.
WHOA!
I PREFER WOMEN, BUT I'LL TAKE WHATEVER HE'S GOT!
THAT'S CRUDE.
I WOULDN'T DREAM OF IT!
WHY SHOULD I?
I'M NOT YOU, AM I?

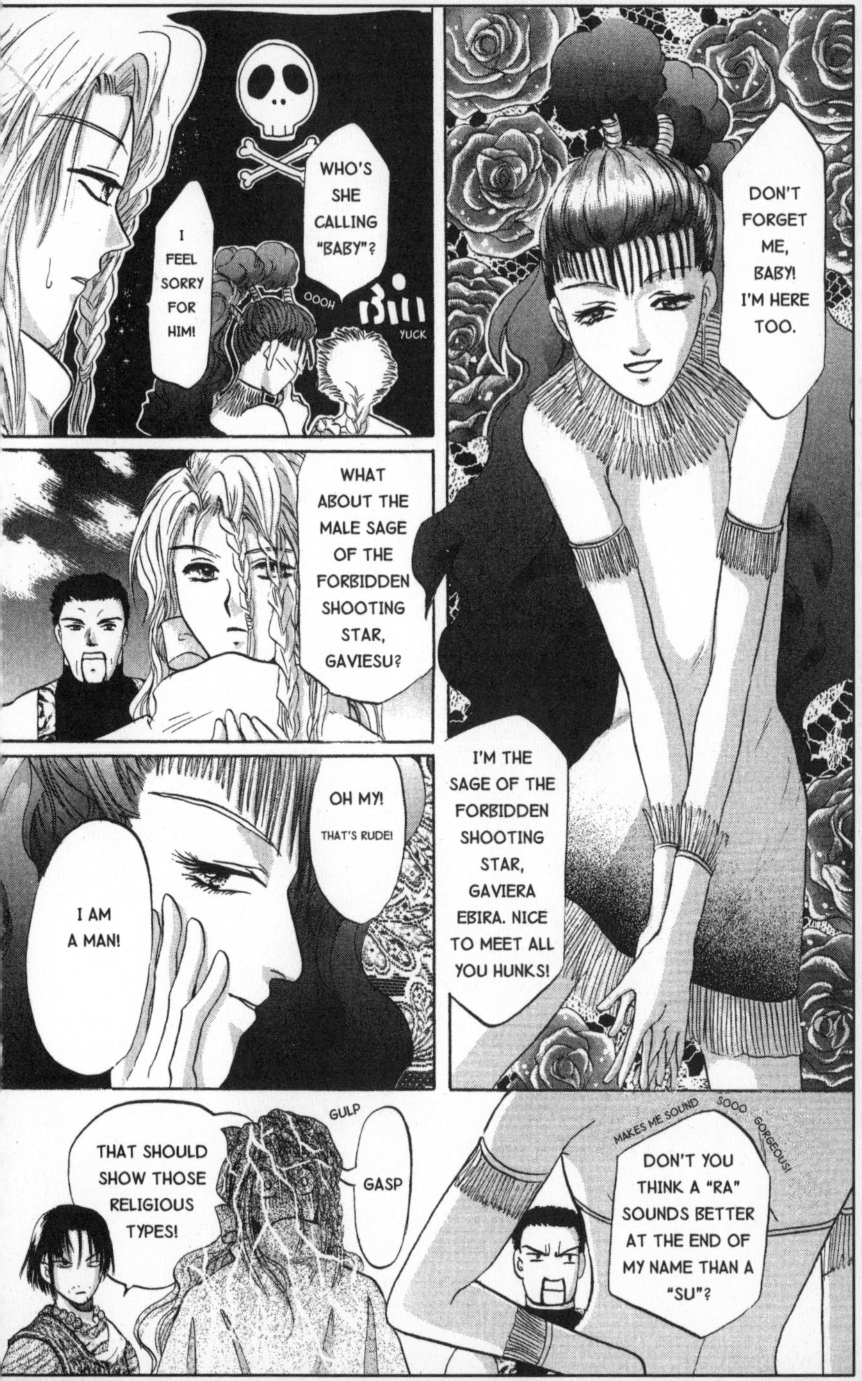
DON'T FORGET ME, BABY! I'M HERE TOO.
I'M THE SAGE OF THE FORBIDDEN SHOOTING STAR, GAVIERA EBIRA. NICE TO MEET ALL YOU HUNKS!
WHO'S SHE CALLING "BABY"?
I FEEL SORRY FOR HIM!
OOOH
YUCK
WHAT ABOUT THE MALE SAGE OF THE FORBIDDEN SHOOTING STAR, GAVIESU?
OH MY!
THAT'S RUDE!
I AM A MAN!
MAKES ME SOUND SOOO GORGEOUS!
DON'T YOU THINK A "RA" SOUNDS BETTER AT THE END OF MY NAME THAN A "SU"?
GULP
GASP
THAT SHOULD SHOW THOSE RELIGIOUS TYPES!

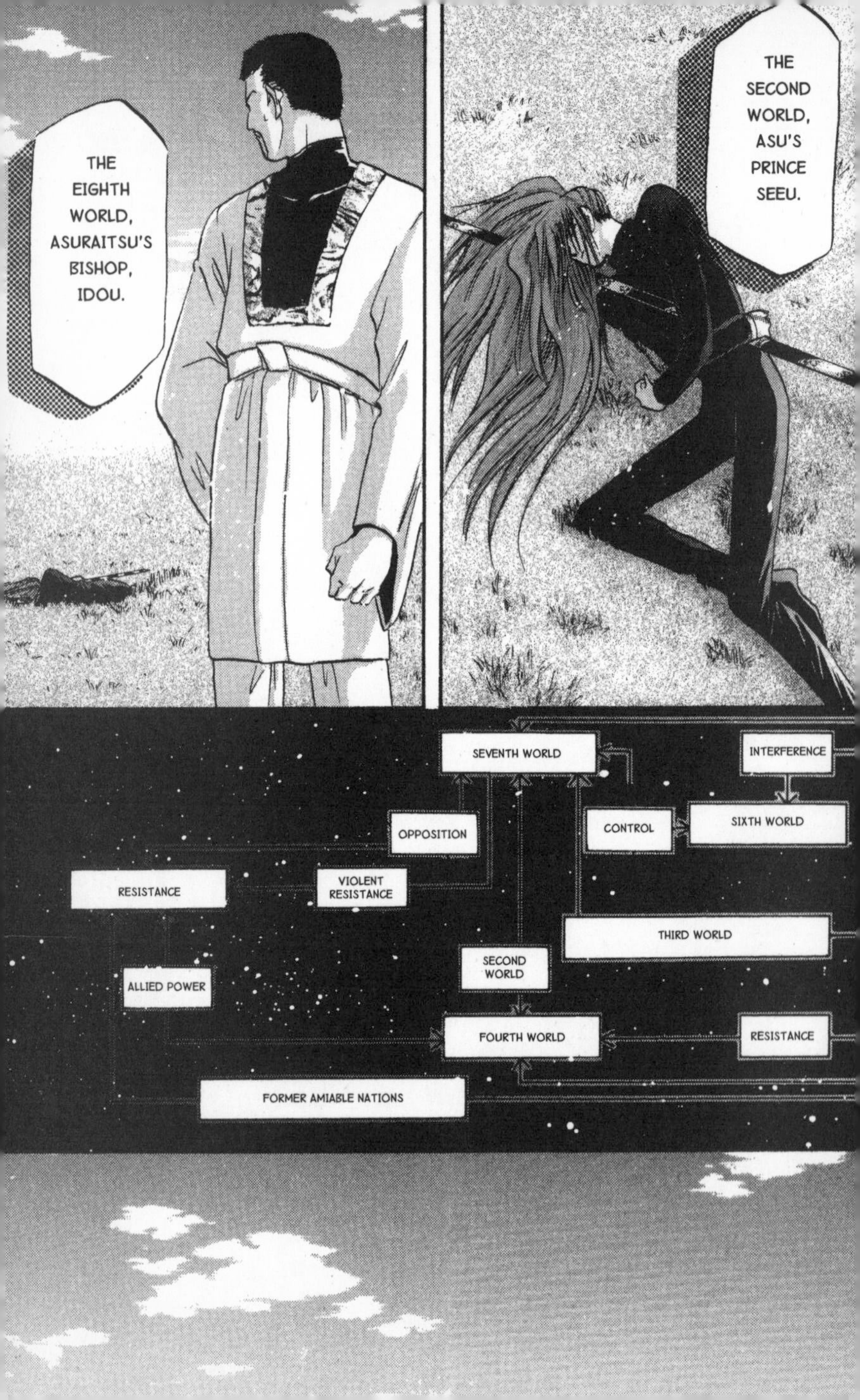
THE SECOND WORLD, ASU'S PRINCE SEEU.
THE EIGHTH WORLD, ASURAITSU'S BISHOP, IDOU.
SEVENTH WORLD
INTERFERENCE
OPPOSITION
CONTROL
SIXTH WORLD
RESISTANCE
VIOLENT RESISTANCE
THIRD WORLD
SECOND WORLD
ALLIED POWER
FOURTH WORLD
RESISTANCE
FORMER AMIABLE NATIONS

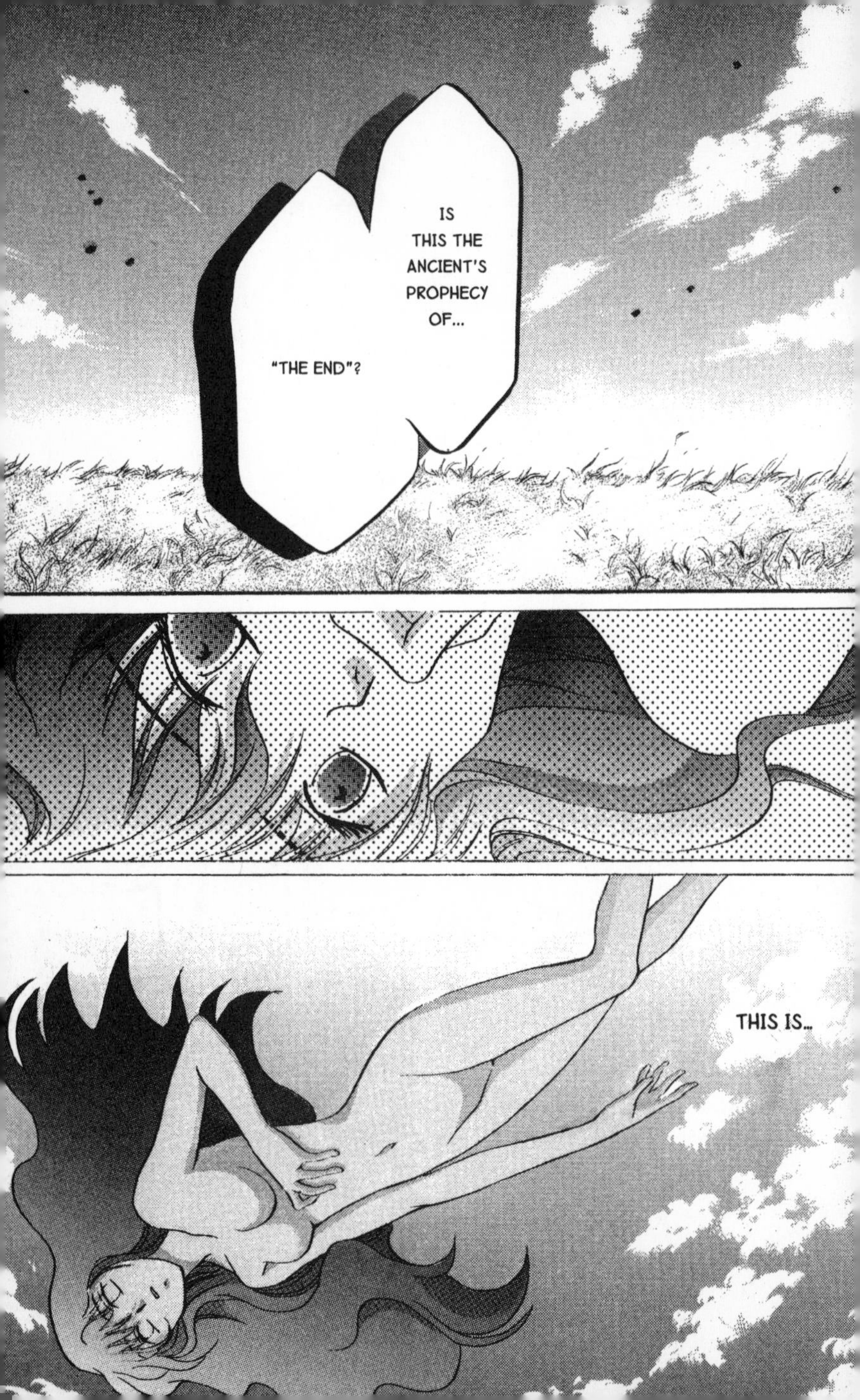
IS THIS THE ANCIENT'S PROPHECY OF...
"THE END"?
THIS IS...

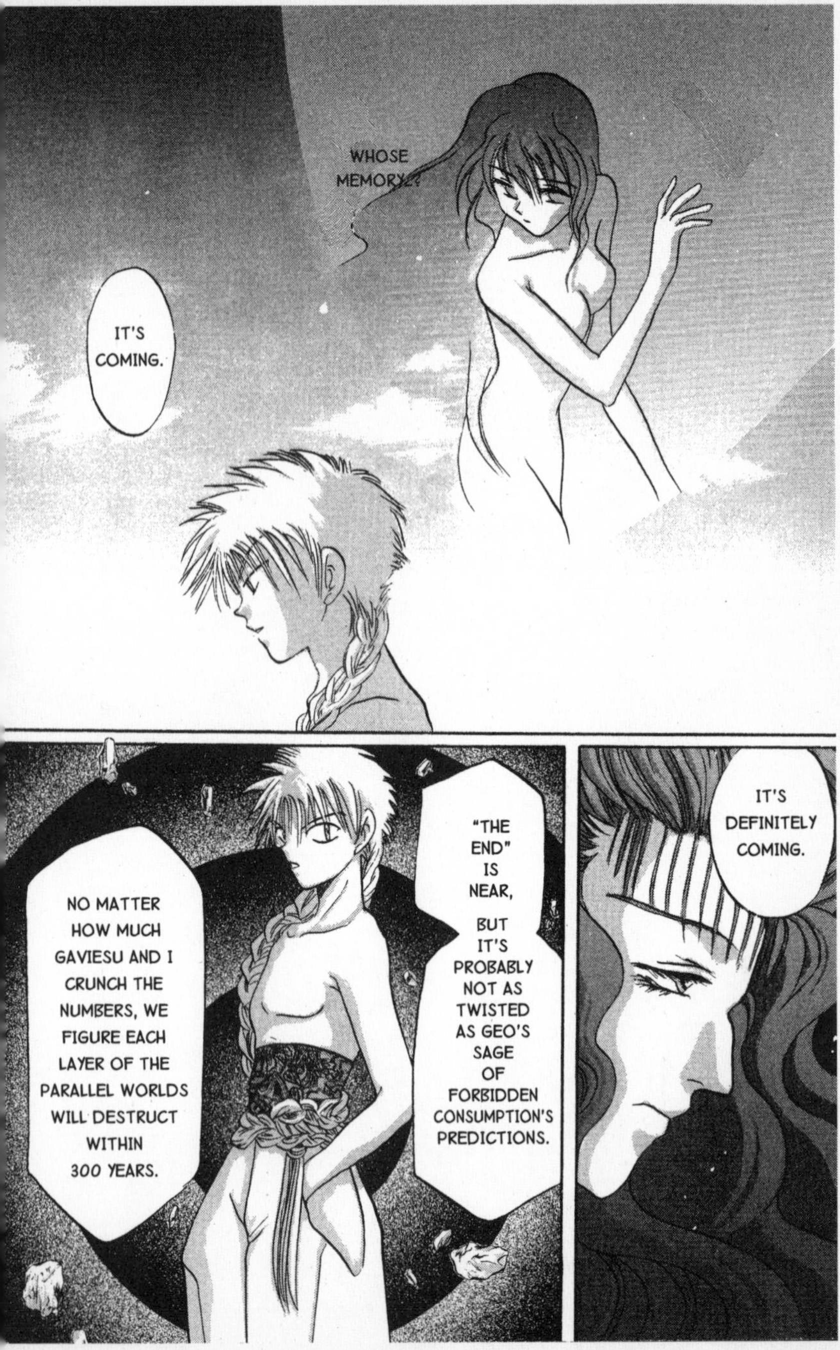
WHOSE MEMORY?
IT'S COMING.
IT'S DEFINITELY COMING.
"THE END" IS NEAR, BUT IT'S PROBABLY NOT AS TWISTED AS GEO'S SAGE OF FORBIDDEN CONSUMPTION'S PREDICTIONS.
NO MATTER HOW MUCH GAVIESU AND I CRUNCH THE NUMBERS, WE FIGURE EACH LAYER OF THE PARALLEL WORLDS WILL DESTRUCT WITHIN 300 YEARS.

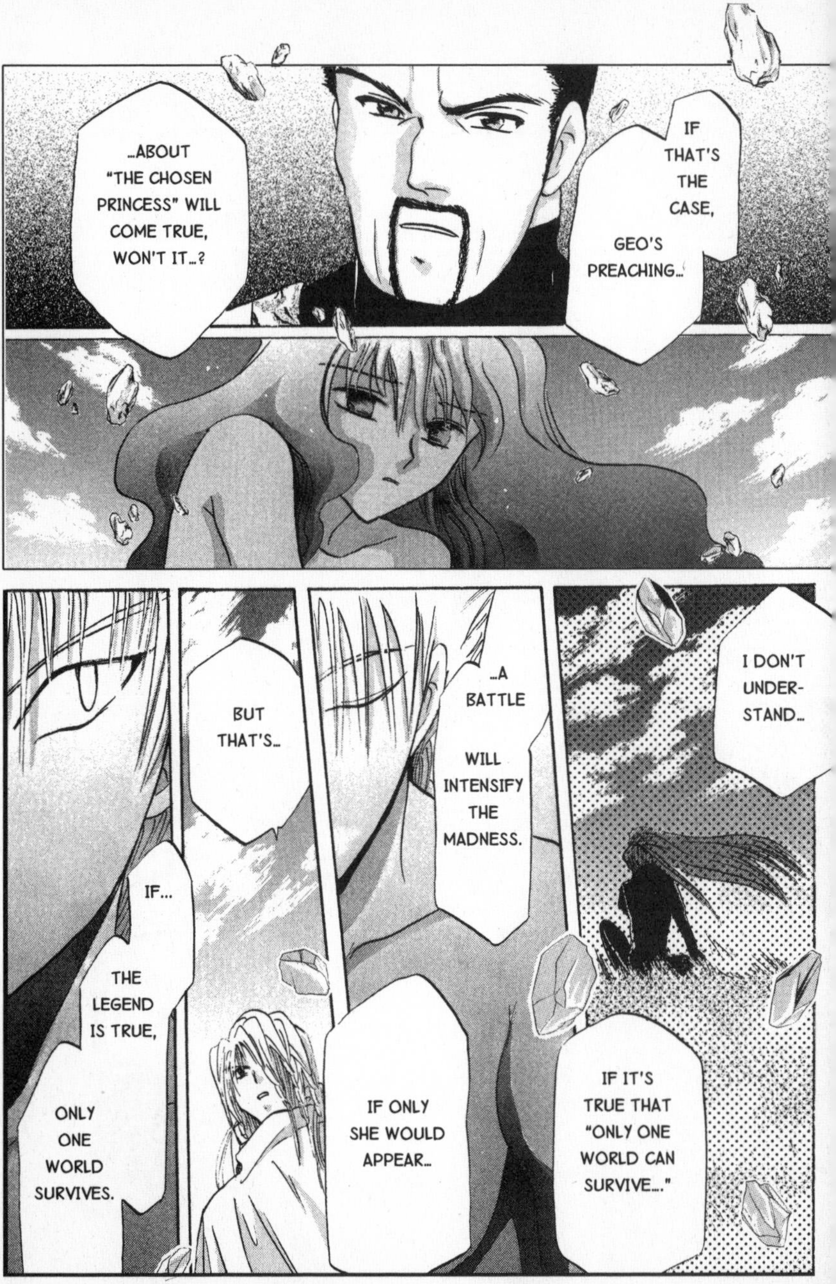
IF THAT'S THE CASE,
GEO'S PREACHING...
...ABOUT "THE CHOSEN PRINCESS" WILL COME TRUE, WON'T IT...?
I DON'T UNDER-STAND...
IF IT'S TRUE THAT "ONLY ONE WORLD CAN SURVIVE..."
...A BATTLE
WILL INTENSIFY THE MADNESS.
IF ONLY SHE WOULD APPEAR...
BUT THAT'S...
IF...
THE LEGEND IS TRUE,
ONLY ONE WORLD SURVIVES.

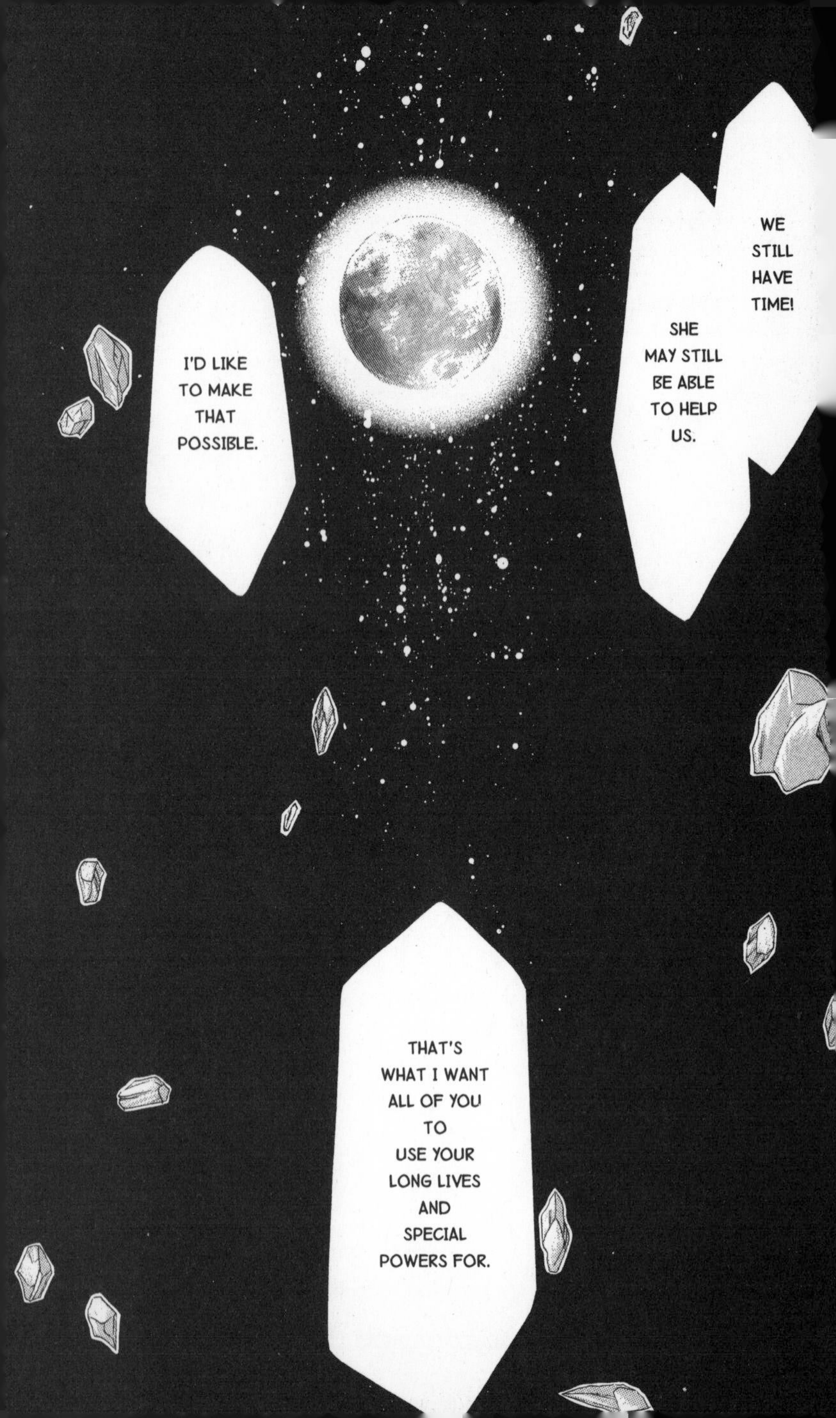
WE STILL HAVE TIME!
SHE MAY STILL BE ABLE TO HELP US.
I'D LIKE TO MAKE THAT POSSIBLE.
THAT'S WHAT I WANT ALL OF YOU TO USE YOUR LONG LIVES AND SPECIAL POWERS FOR.

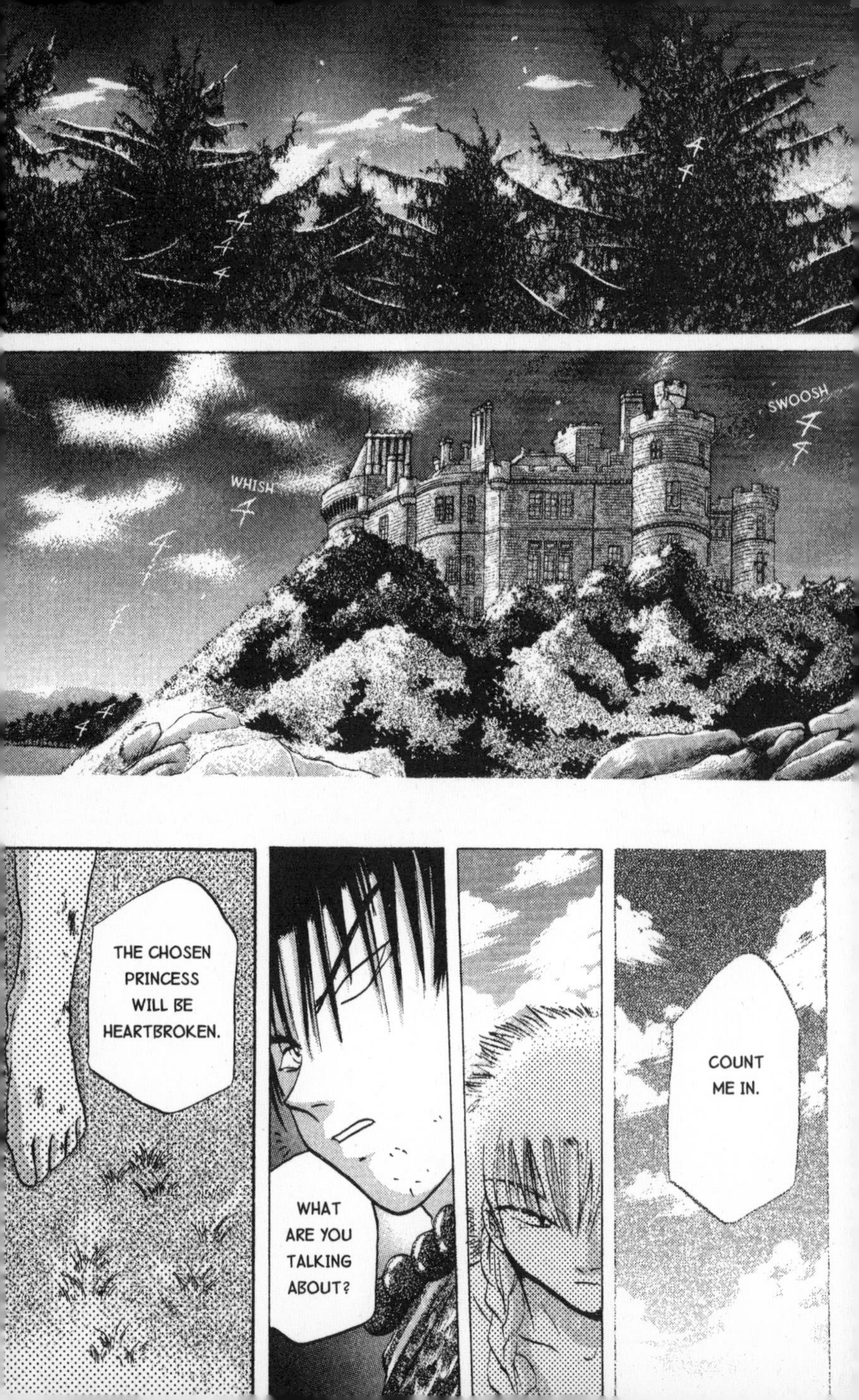
SWOOSH
WHISH
COUNT ME IN.
WHAT ARE YOU TALKING ABOUT?
THE CHOSEN PRINCESS WILL BE HEARTBROKEN.

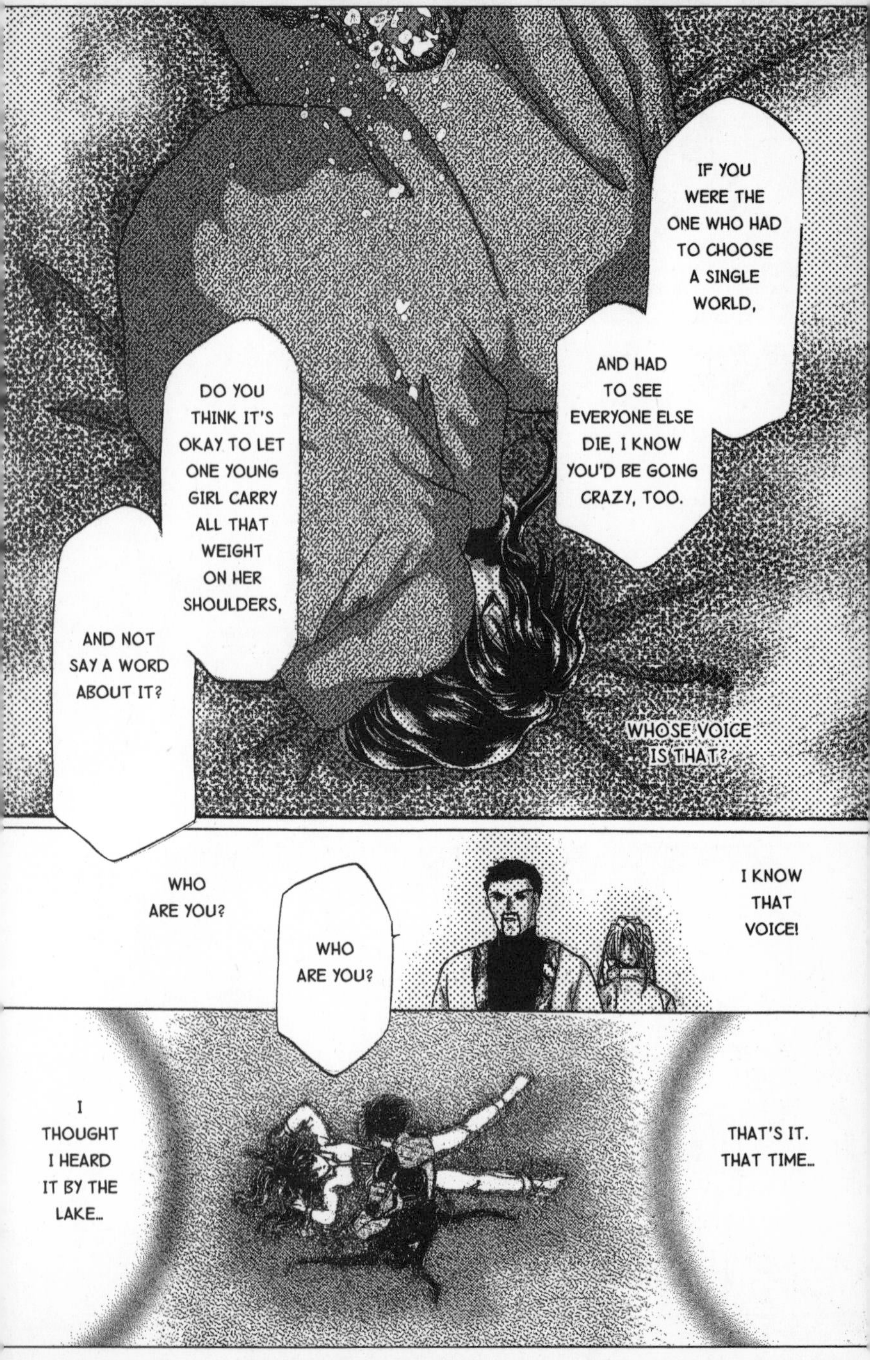
IF YOU WERE THE ONE WHO HAD TO CHOOSE A SINGLE WORLD,
AND HAD TO SEE EVERYONE ELSE DIE, I KNOW YOU'D BE GOING CRAZY, TOO.
DO YOU THINK IT'S OKAY TO LET ONE YOUNG GIRL CARRY ALL THAT WEIGHT ON HER SHOULDERS,
AND NOT SAY A WORD ABOUT IT?
WHOSE VOICE IS THAT?
I KNOW THAT VOICE!
WHO ARE YOU?
WHO ARE YOU?
THAT'S IT. THAT TIME...
I THOUGHT I HEARD IT BY THE LAKE...

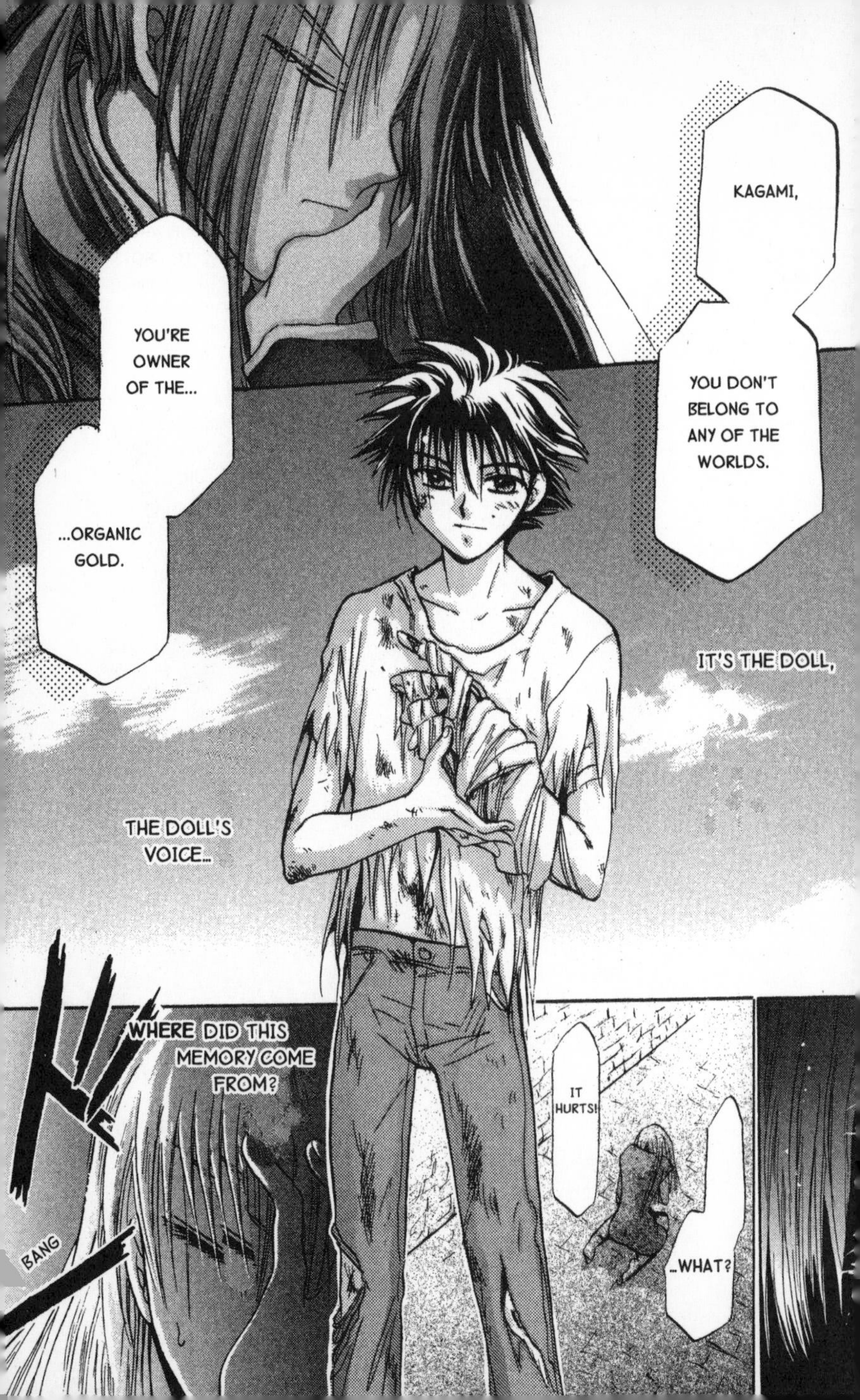
KAGAMI,
YOU DON'T BELONG TO ANY OF THE WORLDS.
YOU'RE OWNER OF THE...
...ORGANIC GOLD.
IT'S THE DOLL,
THE DOLL'S VOICE...
IT HURTS!
...WHAT?
WHERE DID THIS MEMORY COME FROM?
BANG

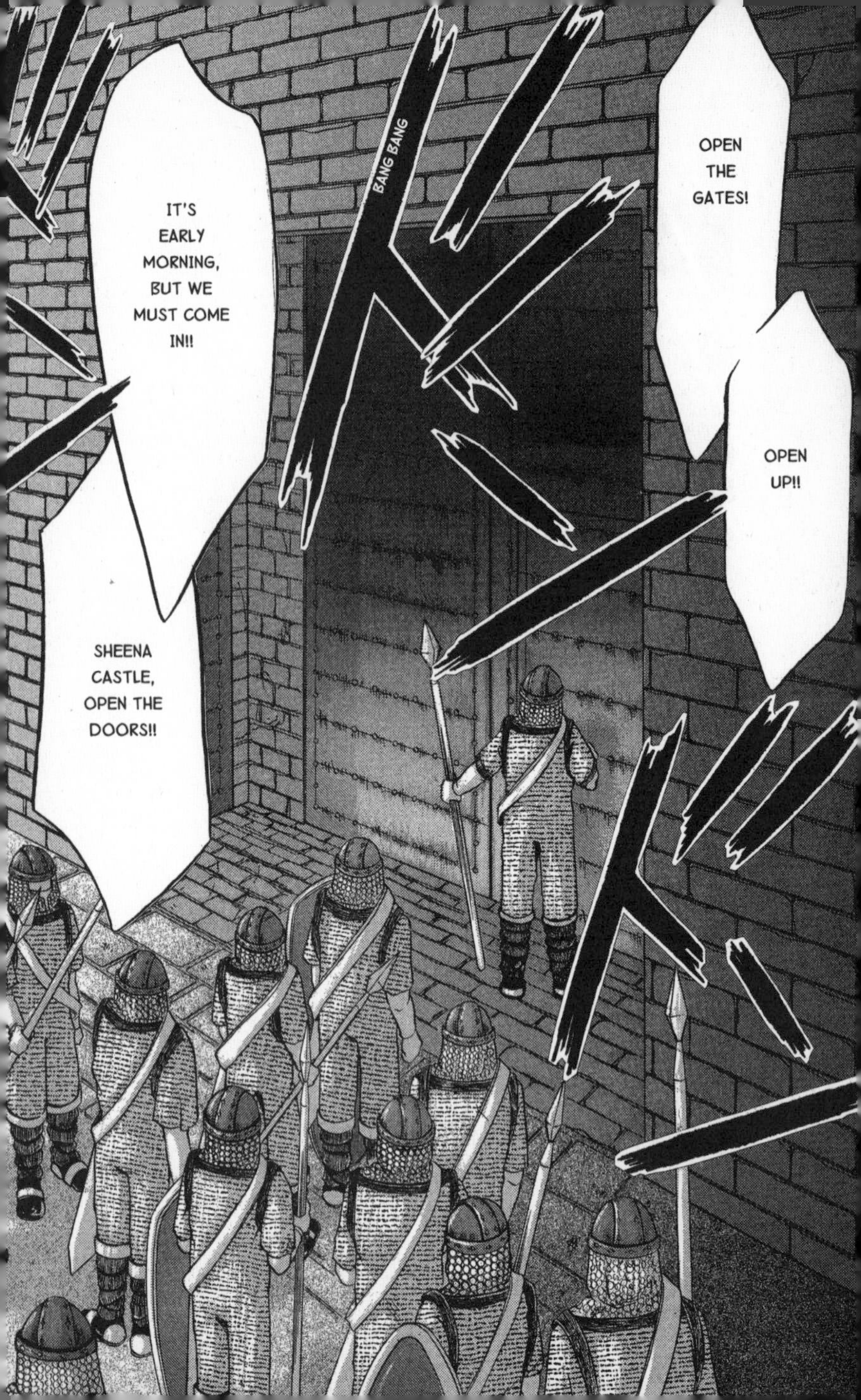
OPEN THE GATES!
OPEN UP!!
BANG BANG
IT'S EARLY MORNING, BUT WE MUST COME IN!!
SHEENA CASTLE, OPEN THE DOORS!!

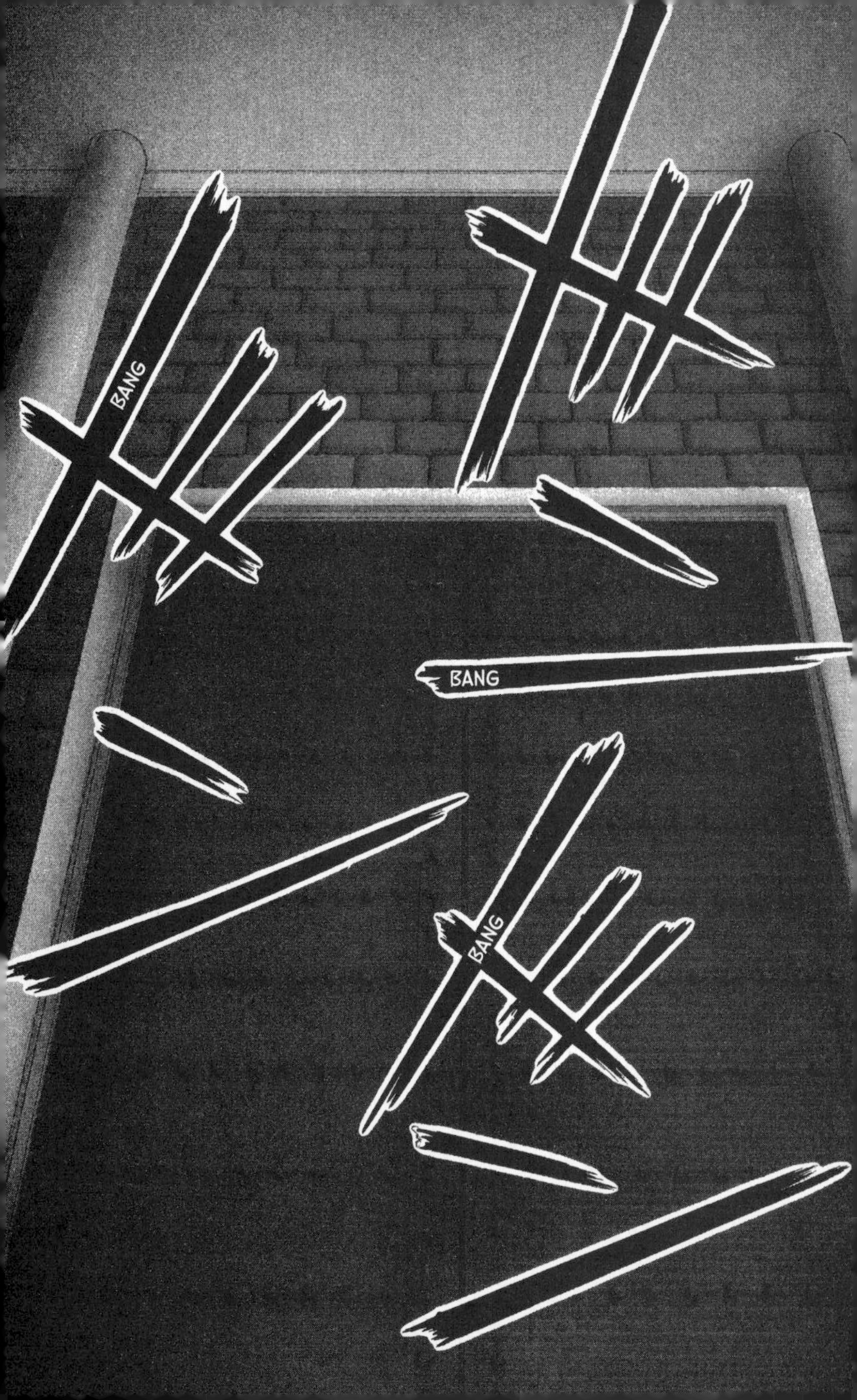
BANG
BANG
BANG

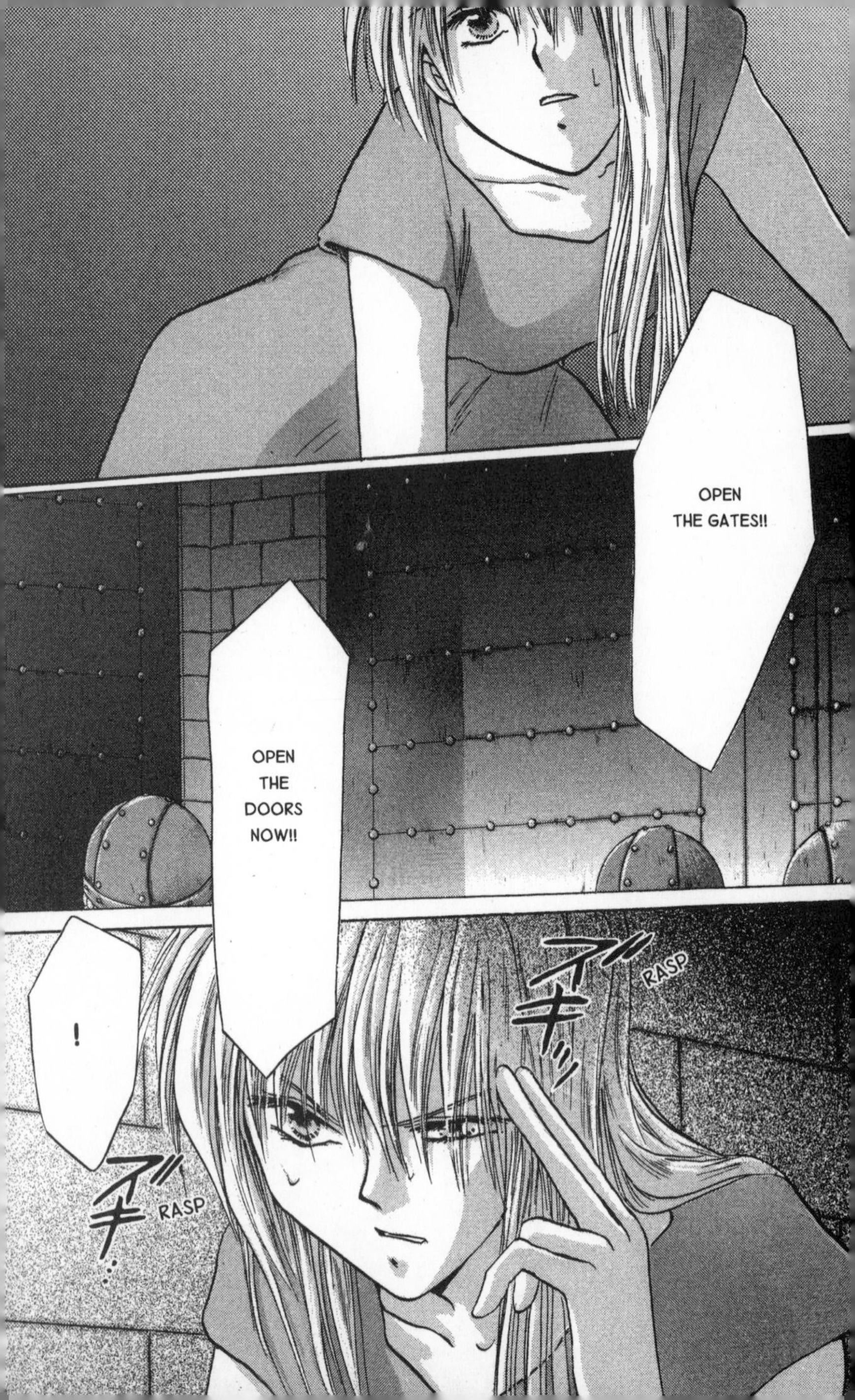
OPEN THE GATES!!
OPEN THE DOORS NOW!!
!
RASP
RASP

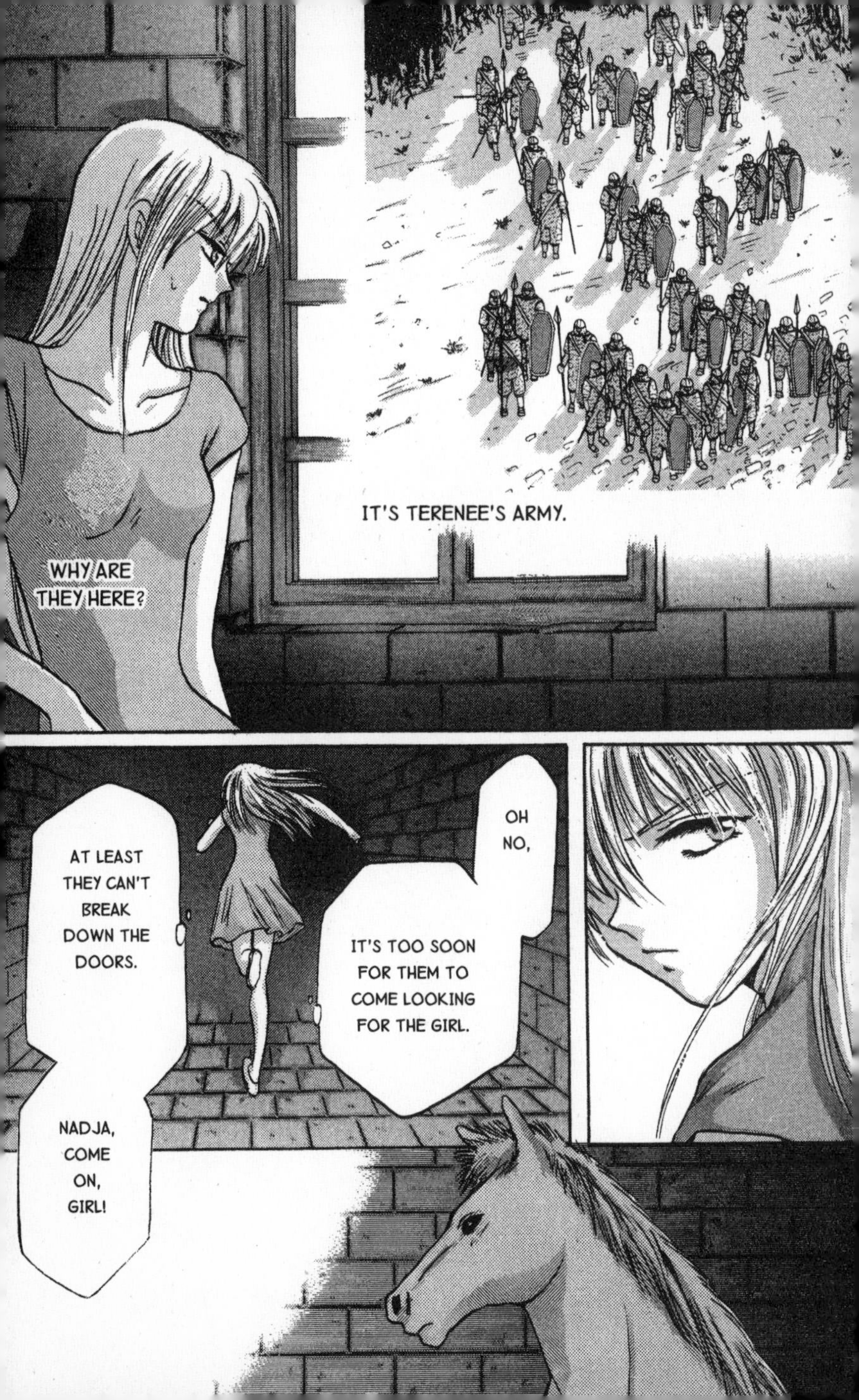
IT'S TERENEE'S ARMY.
WHY ARE THEY HERE?
OH NO,
IT'S TOO SOON FOR THEM TO COME LOOKING FOR THE GIRL.
AT LEAST THEY CAN'T BREAK DOWN THE DOORS.
NADJA, COME ON, GIRL!

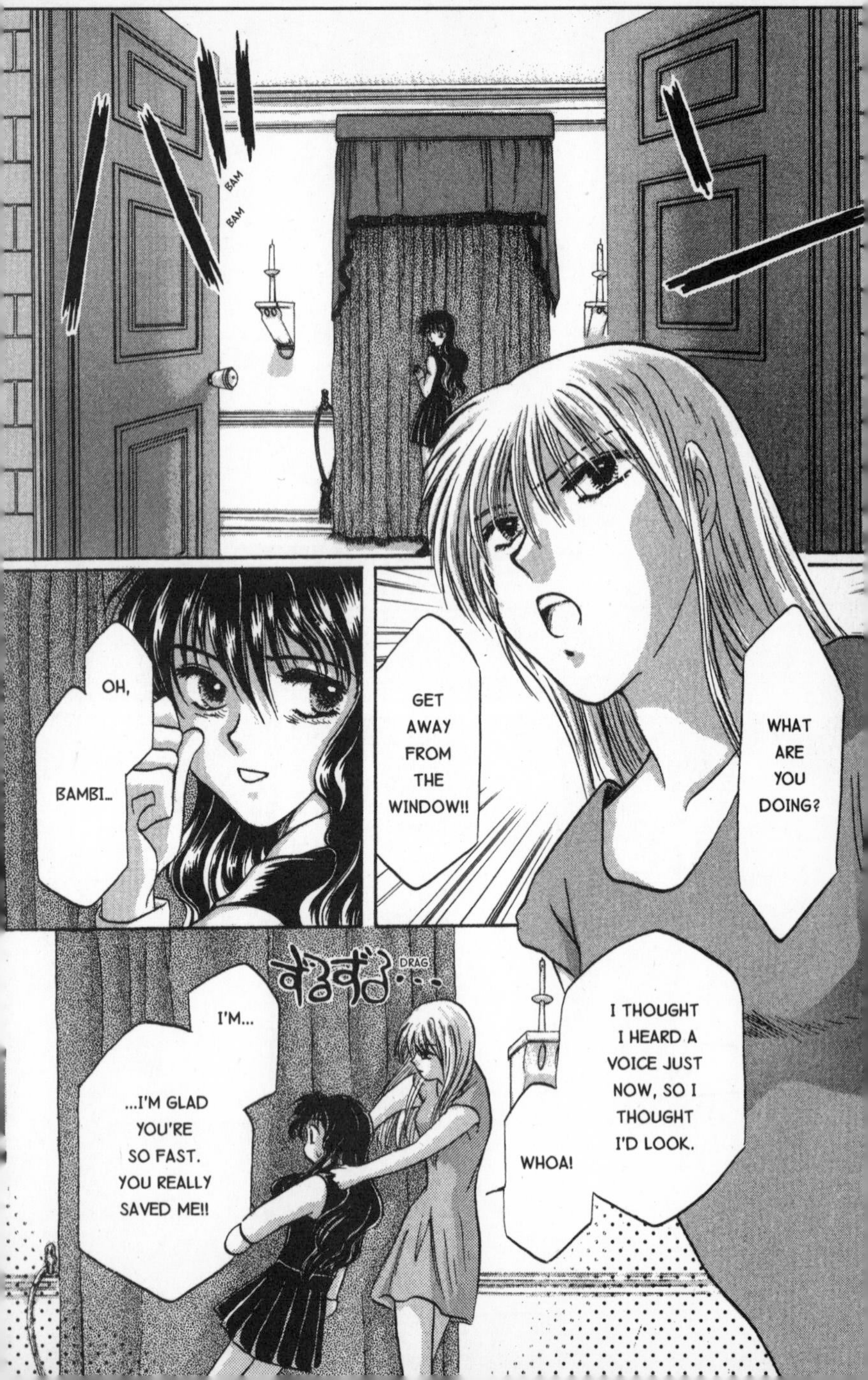

BAM
BAM
WHAT ARE YOU DOING?
GET AWAY FROM THE WINDOW!!
OH, BAMBI...
I THOUGHT I HEARD A VOICE JUST NOW, SO I THOUGHT I'D LOOK.
WHOA!
ずるずる DRAG
I'M...
...I'M GLAD YOU'RE SO FAST. YOU REALLY SAVED ME!!

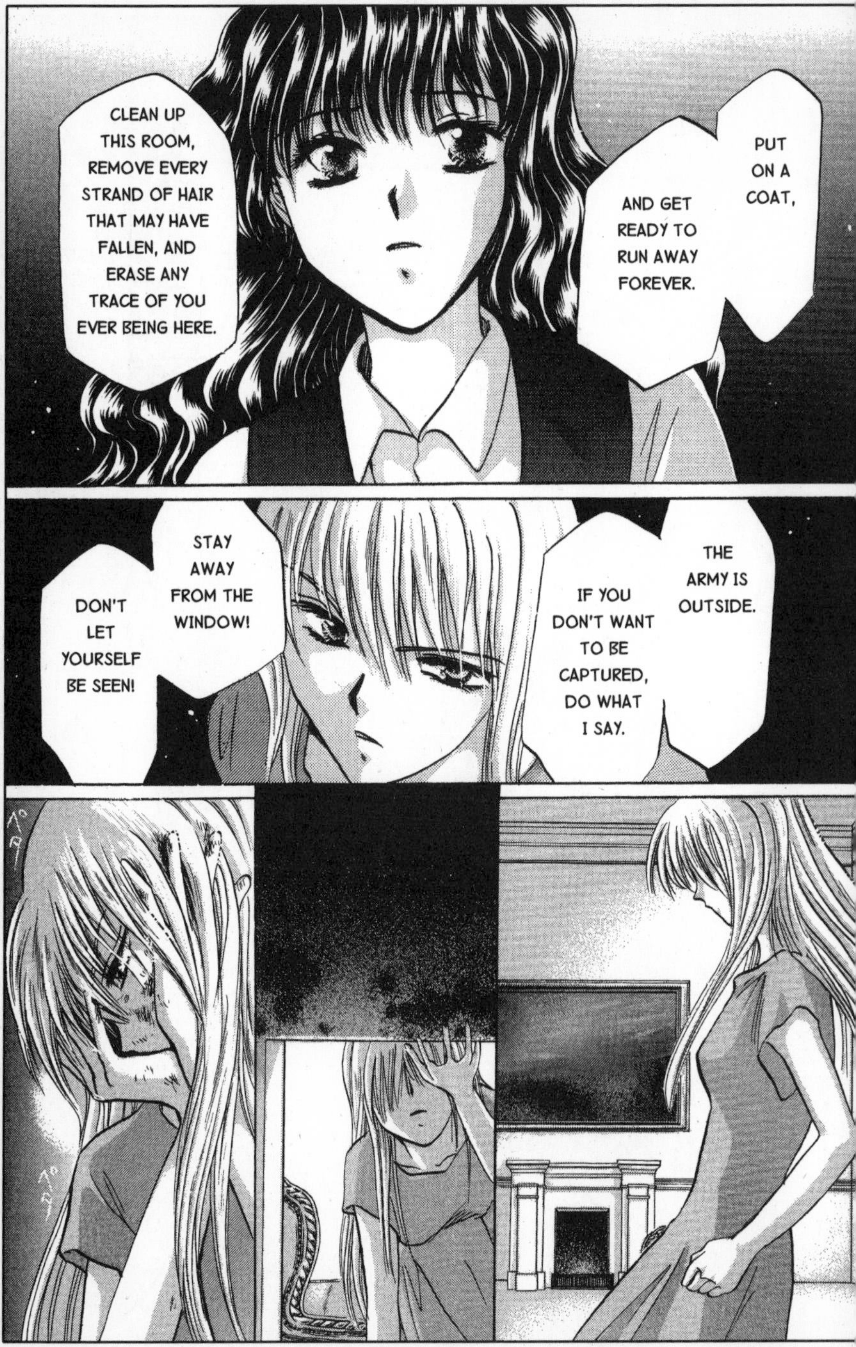
PUT ON A COAT,
AND GET READY TO RUN AWAY FOREVER.
CLEAN UP THIS ROOM, REMOVE EVERY STRAND OF HAIR THAT MAY HAVE FALLEN, AND ERASE ANY TRACE OF YOU EVER BEING HERE.
THE ARMY IS OUTSIDE.
IF YOU DON'T WANT TO BE CAPTURED, DO WHAT I SAY.
STAY AWAY FROM THE WINDOW!
DON'T LET YOURSELF BE SEEN!

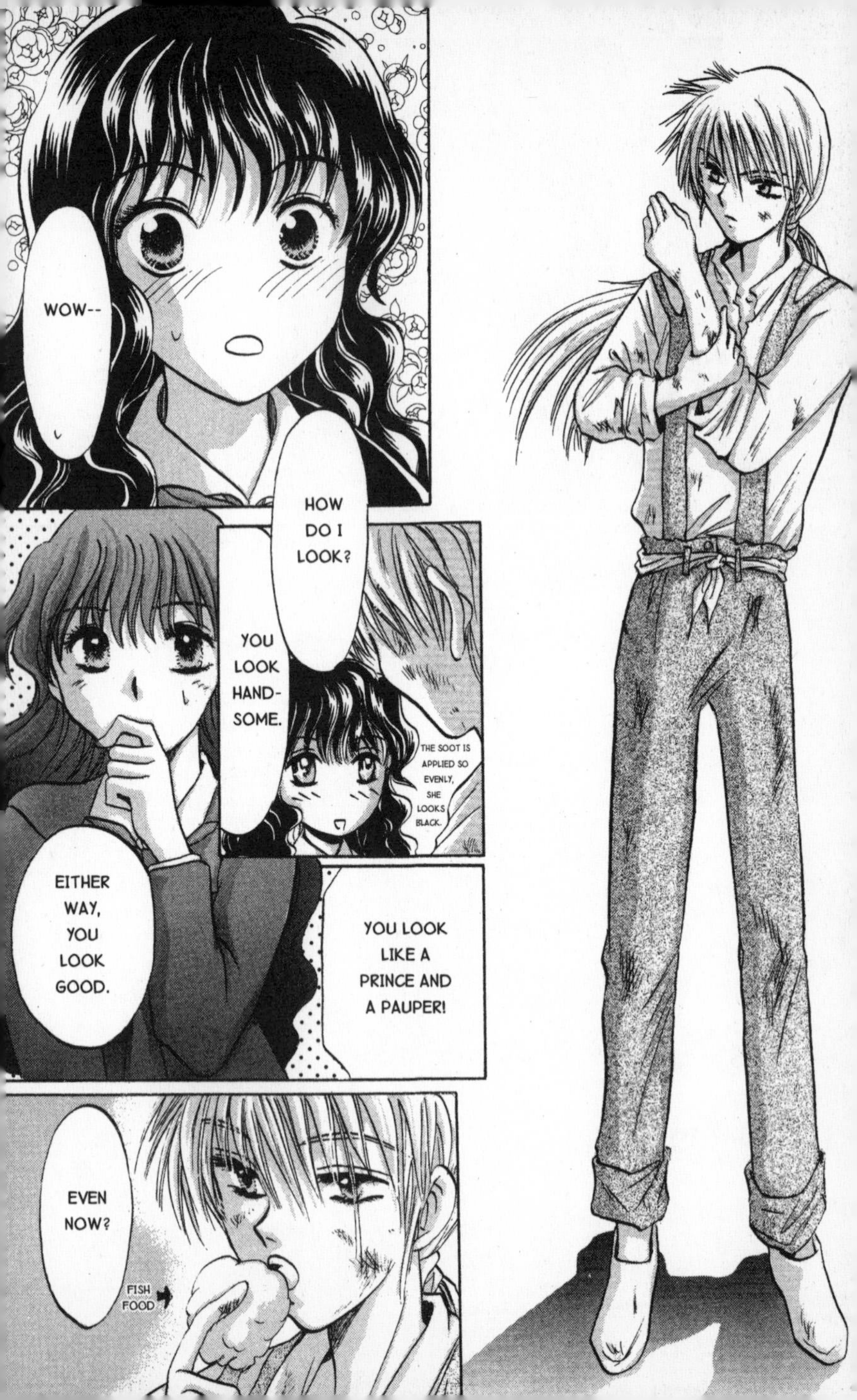
WOW--
HOW DO I LOOK?
YOU LOOK HANDSOME.
THE SOOT IS APPLIED SO EVENLY, SHE LOOKS BLACK.
YOU LOOK LIKE A PRINCE AND A PAUPER!
EITHER WAY, YOU LOOK GOOD.
EVEN NOW?
FISH FOOD

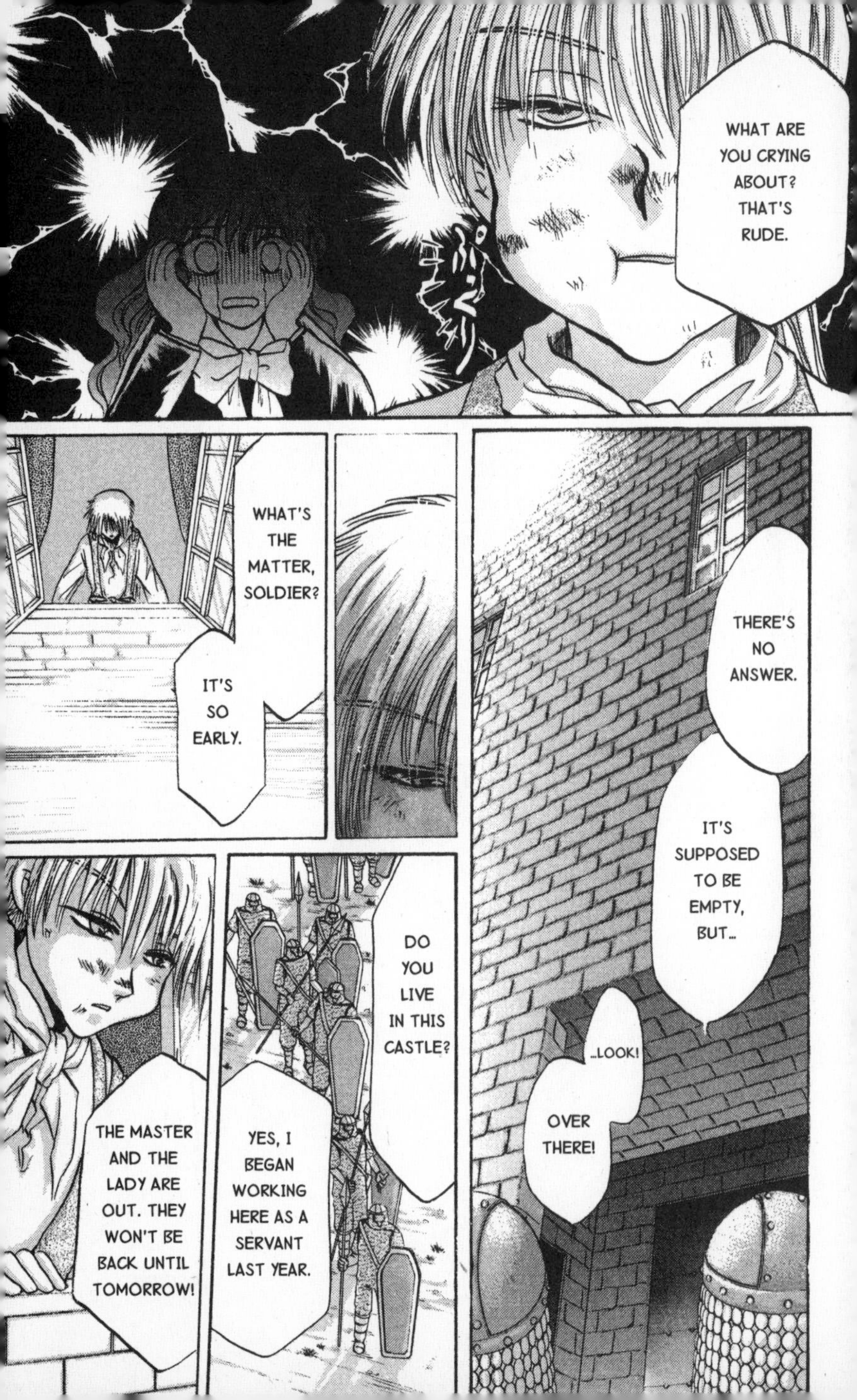
WHAT ARE YOU CRYING ABOUT? THAT'S RUDE.
THERE'S NO ANSWER.
IT'S SUPPOSED TO BE EMPTY, BUT...
...LOOK!
OVER THERE!
WHAT'S THE MATTER, SOLDIER?
IT'S SO EARLY.
DO YOU LIVE IN THIS CASTLE?
YES, I BEGAN WORKING HERE AS A SERVANT LAST YEAR.
THE MASTER AND THE LADY ARE OUT. THEY WON'T BE BACK UNTIL TOMORROW!

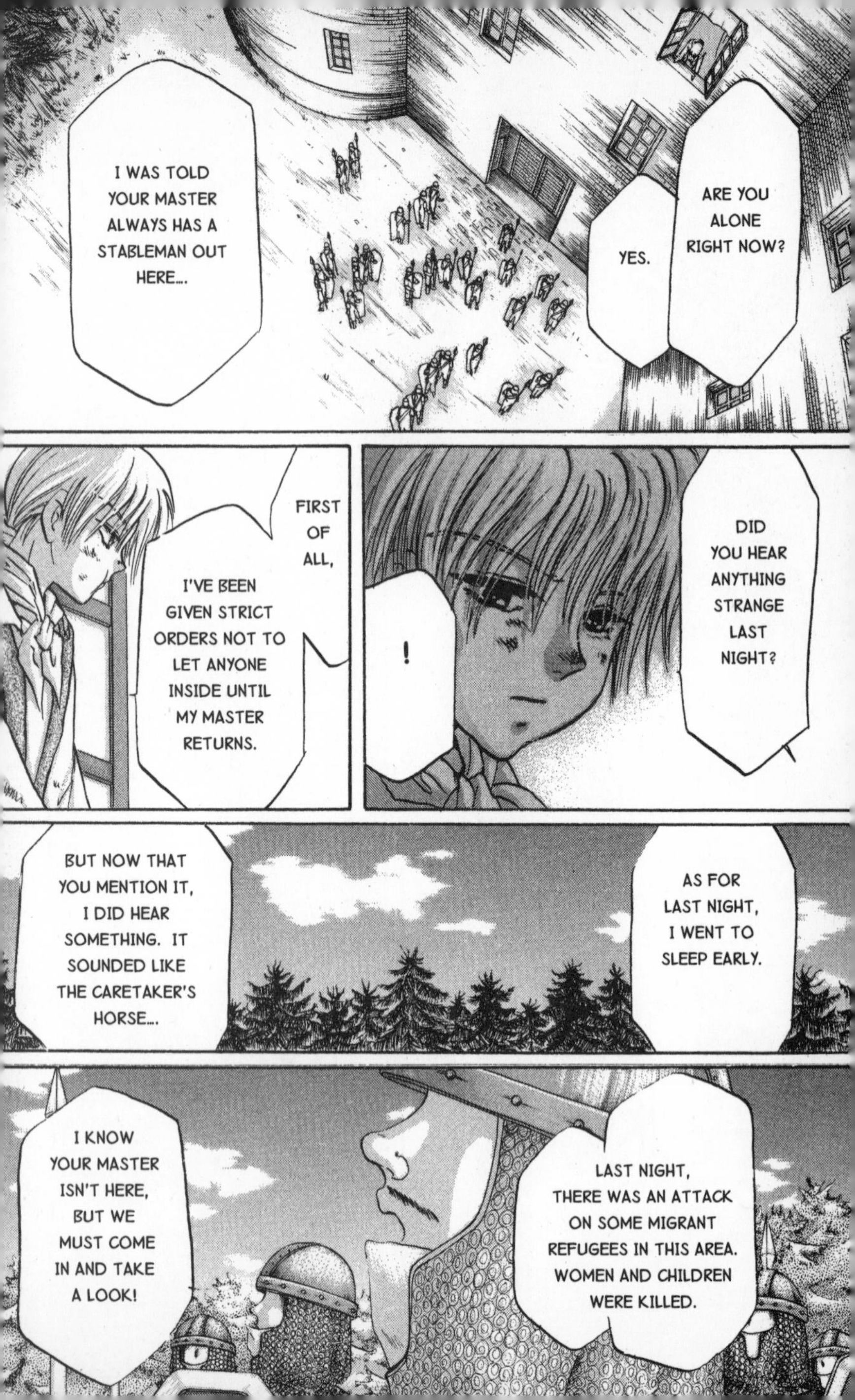
ARE YOU ALONE RIGHT NOW?
YES.
I WAS TOLD YOUR MASTER ALWAYS HAS A STABLEMAN OUT HERE....
DID YOU HEAR ANYTHING STRANGE LAST NIGHT?
!
FIRST OF ALL,
I'VE BEEN GIVEN STRICT ORDERS NOT TO LET ANYONE INSIDE UNTIL MY MASTER RETURNS.
AS FOR LAST NIGHT, I WENT TO SLEEP EARLY.
BUT NOW THAT YOU MENTION IT, I DID HEAR SOMETHING. IT SOUNDED LIKE THE CARETAKER'S HORSE....
LAST NIGHT, THERE WAS AN ATTACK ON SOME MIGRANT REFUGEES IN THIS AREA. WOMEN AND CHILDREN WERE KILLED.
I KNOW YOUR MASTER ISN'T HERE, BUT WE MUST COME IN AND TAKE A LOOK!

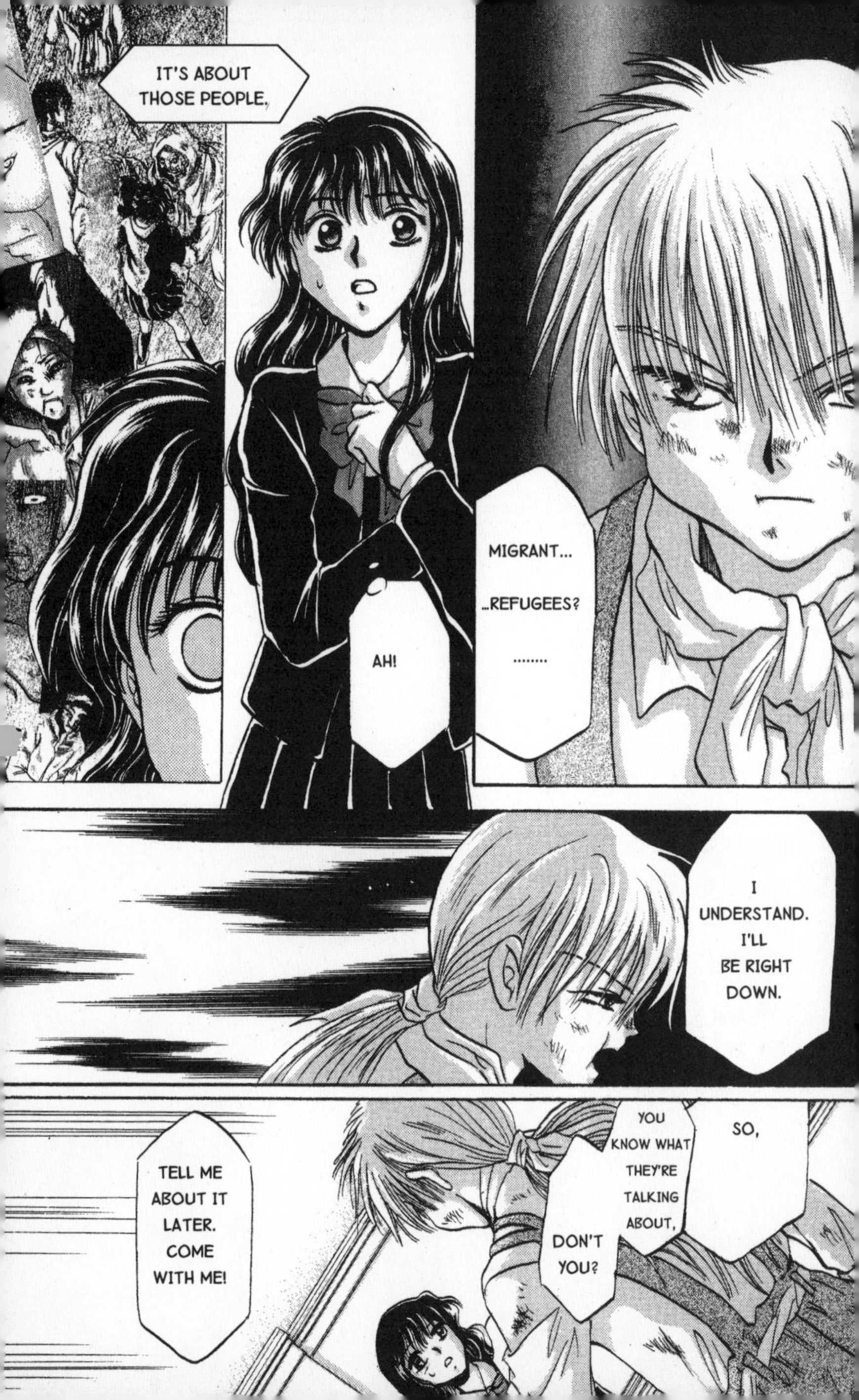
MIGRANT...
...REFUGEES?
....
AH!
IT'S ABOUT THOSE PEOPLE.
I UNDERSTAND. I'LL BE RIGHT DOWN.
SO,
YOU KNOW WHAT THEY'RE TALKING ABOUT,
DON'T YOU?
TELL ME ABOUT IT LATER. COME WITH ME!

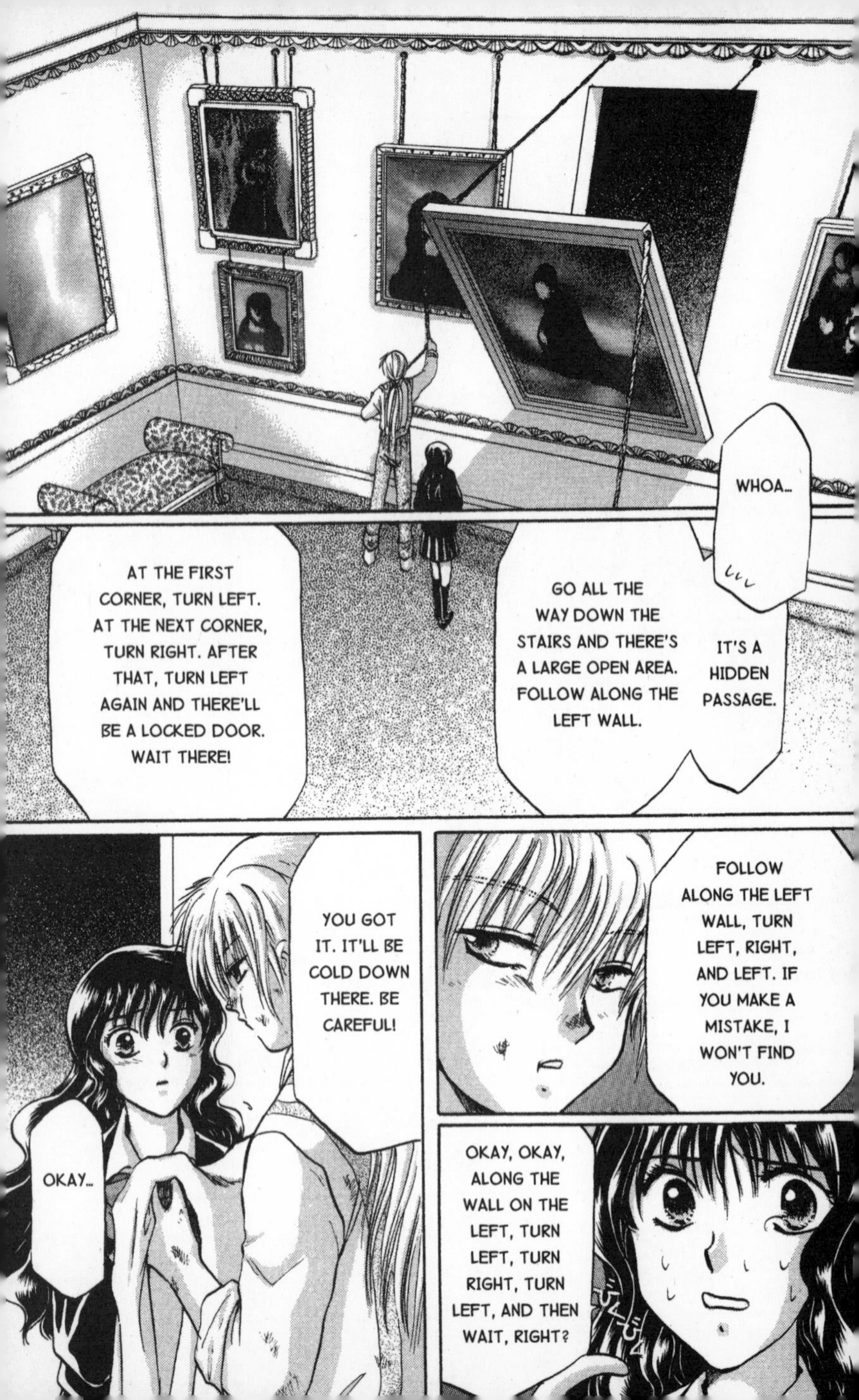
WHOA...
IT'S A HIDDEN PASSAGE.
GO ALL THE WAY DOWN THE STAIRS AND THERE'S A LARGE OPEN AREA. FOLLOW ALONG THE LEFT WALL.
AT THE FIRST CORNER, TURN LEFT. AT THE NEXT CORNER, TURN RIGHT. AFTER THAT, TURN LEFT AGAIN AND THERE'LL BE A LOCKED DOOR. WAIT THERE!
FOLLOW ALONG THE LEFT WALL, TURN LEFT, RIGHT, AND LEFT. IF YOU MAKE A MISTAKE, I WON'T FIND YOU.
OKAY, OKAY, ALONG THE WALL ON THE LEFT, TURN LEFT, TURN RIGHT, TURN LEFT, AND THEN WAIT, RIGHT?
YOU GOT IT. IT'LL BE COLD DOWN THERE. BE CAREFUL!
OKAY...

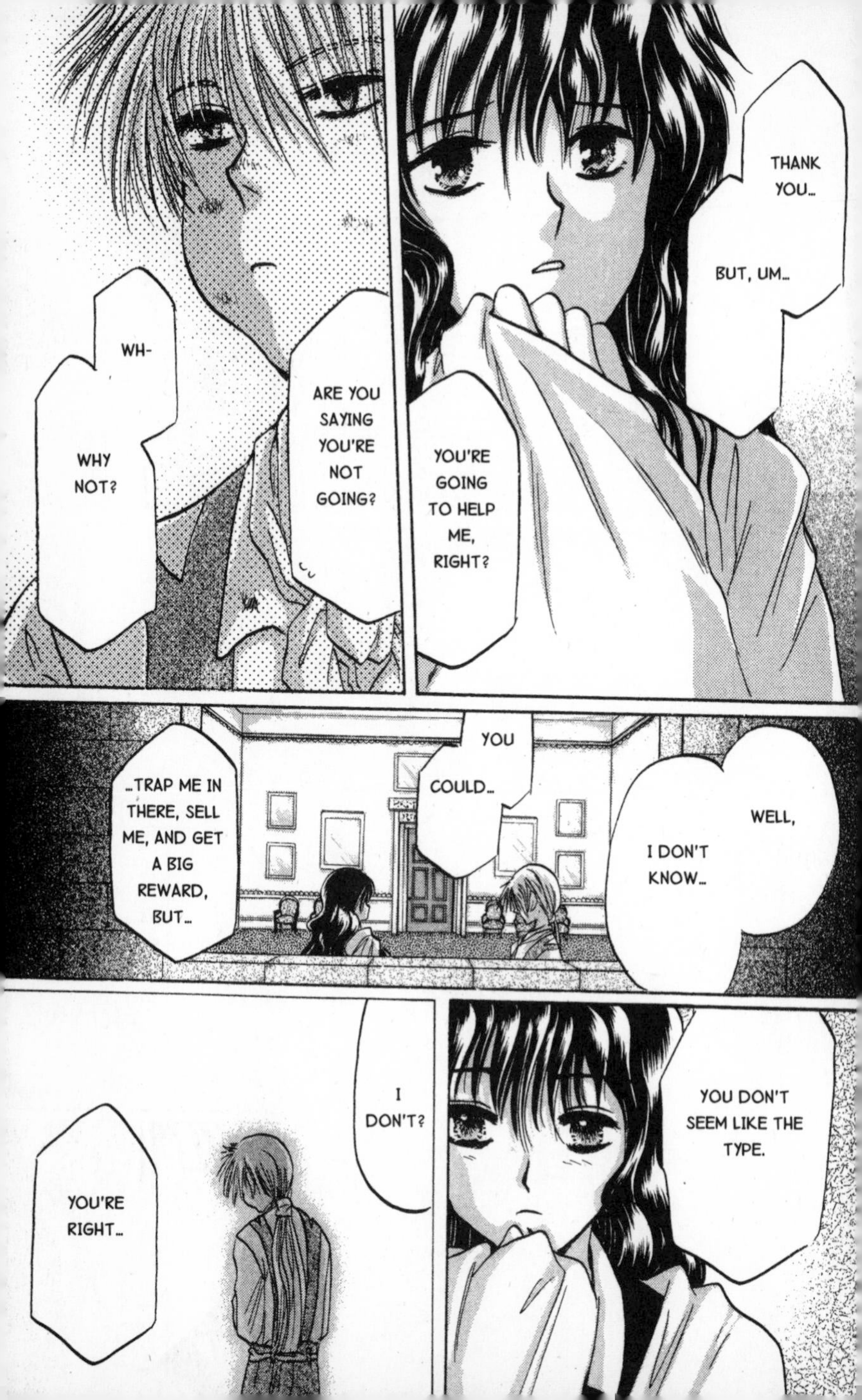
THANK YOU... BUT, UM...
YOU'RE GOING TO HELP ME, RIGHT?
ARE YOU SAYING YOU'RE NOT GOING?
WH- WHY NOT?
WELL, I DON'T KNOW...
YOU COULD...
...TRAP ME IN THERE, SELL ME, AND GET A BIG REWARD, BUT...
YOU DON'T SEEM LIKE THE TYPE.
I DON'T?
YOU'RE RIGHT...

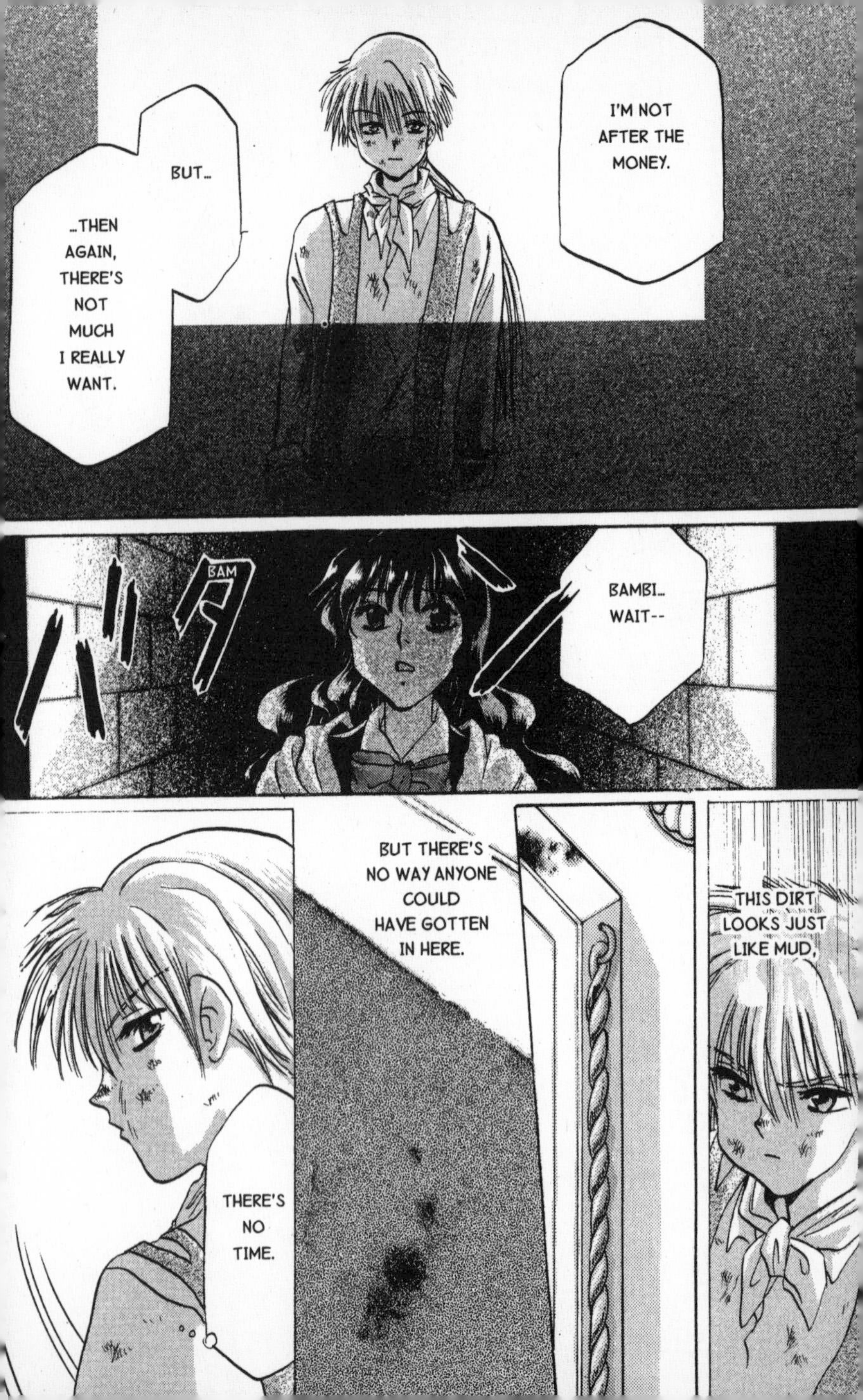
I'M NOT AFTER THE MONEY.
BUT...
...THEN AGAIN, THERE'S NOT MUCH I REALLY WANT.
BAMBI... WAIT--
BAM
THIS DIRT LOOKS JUST LIKE MUD,
BUT THERE'S NO WAY ANYONE COULD HAVE GOTTEN IN HERE.
THERE'S NO TIME.

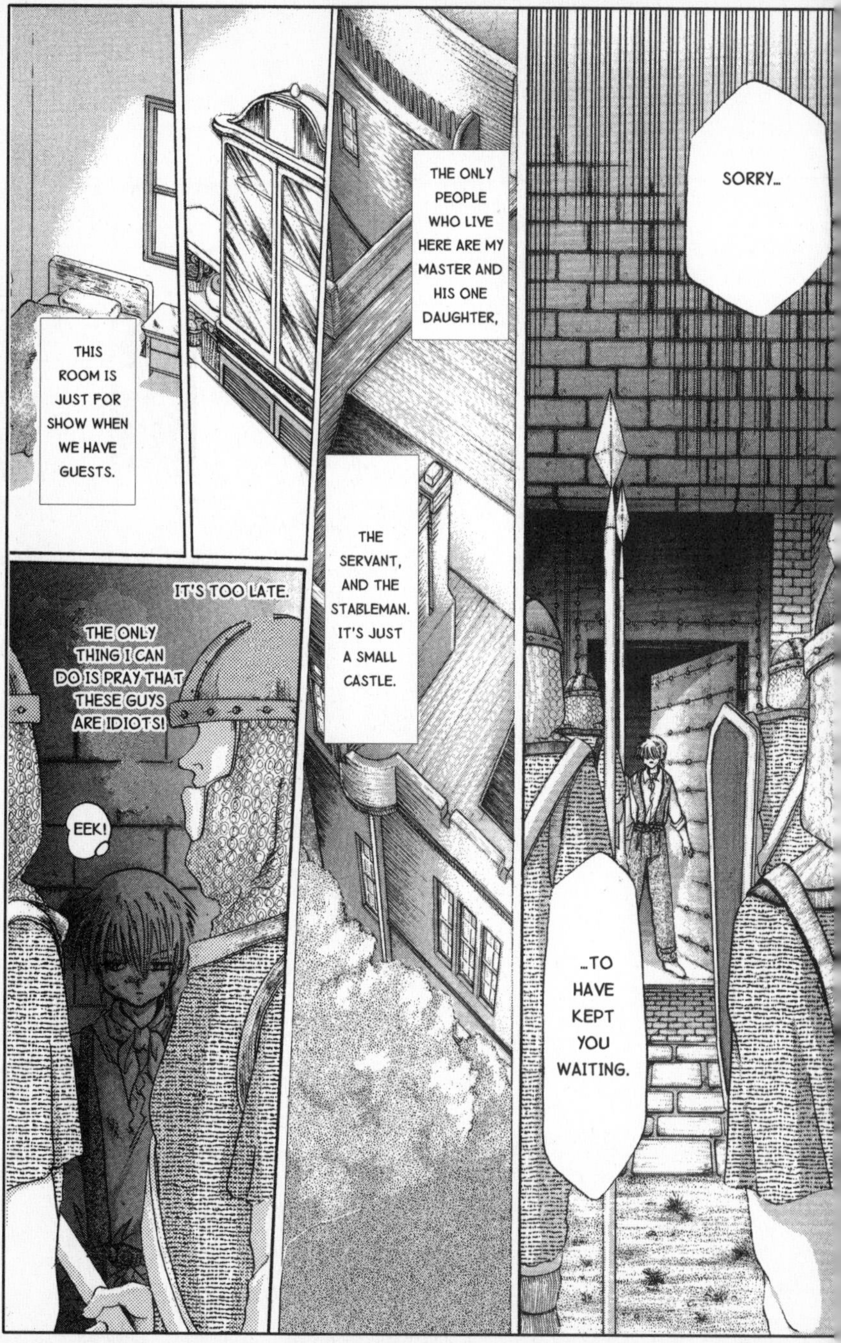
SORRY...
...TO HAVE KEPT YOU WAITING.
THE ONLY PEOPLE WHO LIVE HERE ARE MY MASTER AND HIS ONE DAUGHTER,
THE SERVANT, AND THE STABLEMAN. IT'S JUST A SMALL CASTLE.
THIS ROOM IS JUST FOR SHOW WHEN WE HAVE GUESTS.
IT'S TOO LATE.
THE ONLY THING I CAN DO IS PRAY THAT THESE GUYS ARE IDIOTS!
EEK!

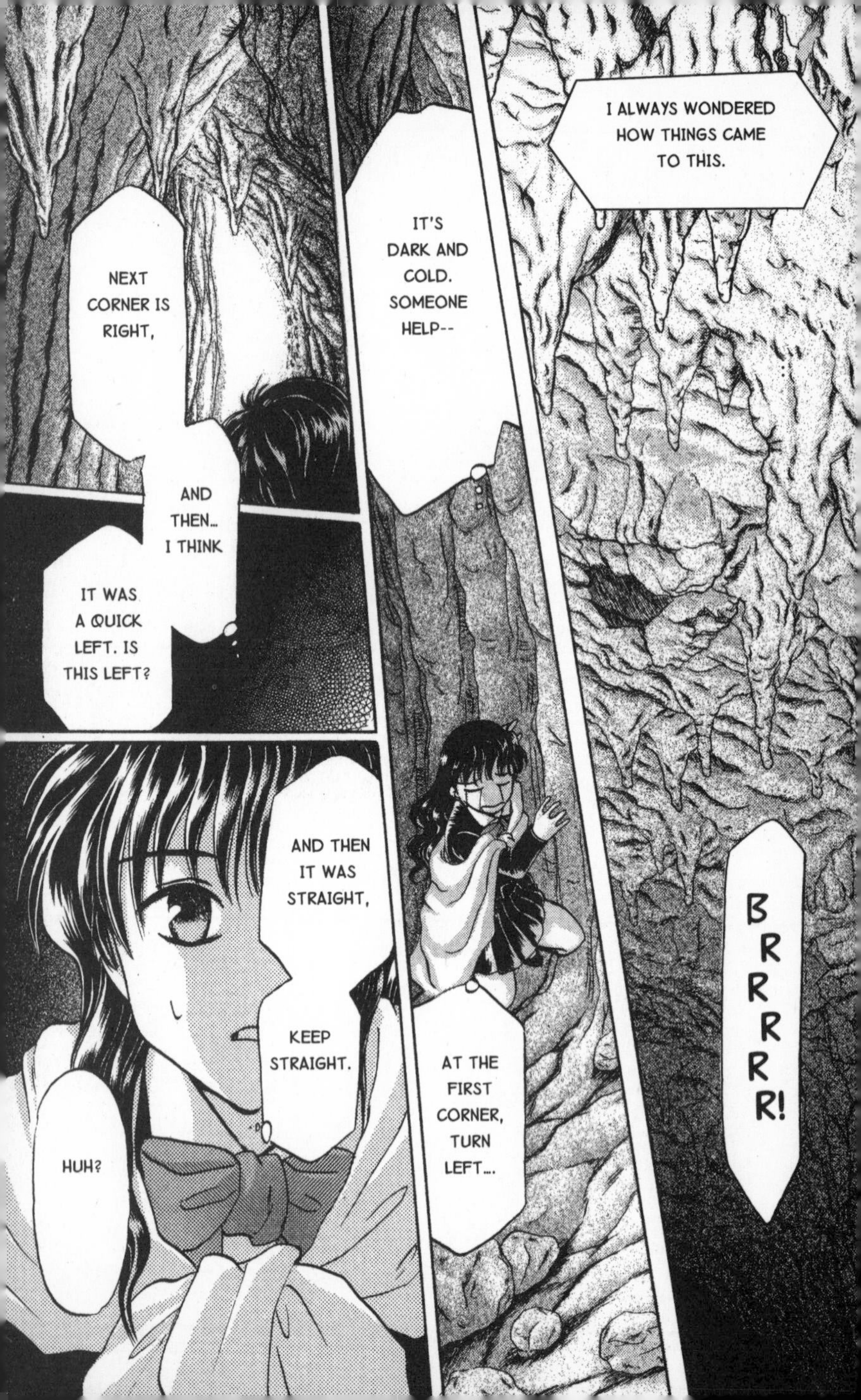
I ALWAYS WONDERED HOW THINGS CAME TO THIS.
BRRRRR!
IT'S DARK AND COLD. SOMEONE HELP--
AT THE FIRST CORNER, TURN LEFT....
NEXT CORNER IS RIGHT,
AND THEN... I THINK
IT WAS A QUICK LEFT. IS THIS LEFT?
AND THEN IT WAS STRAIGHT,
KEEP STRAIGHT.
HUH?

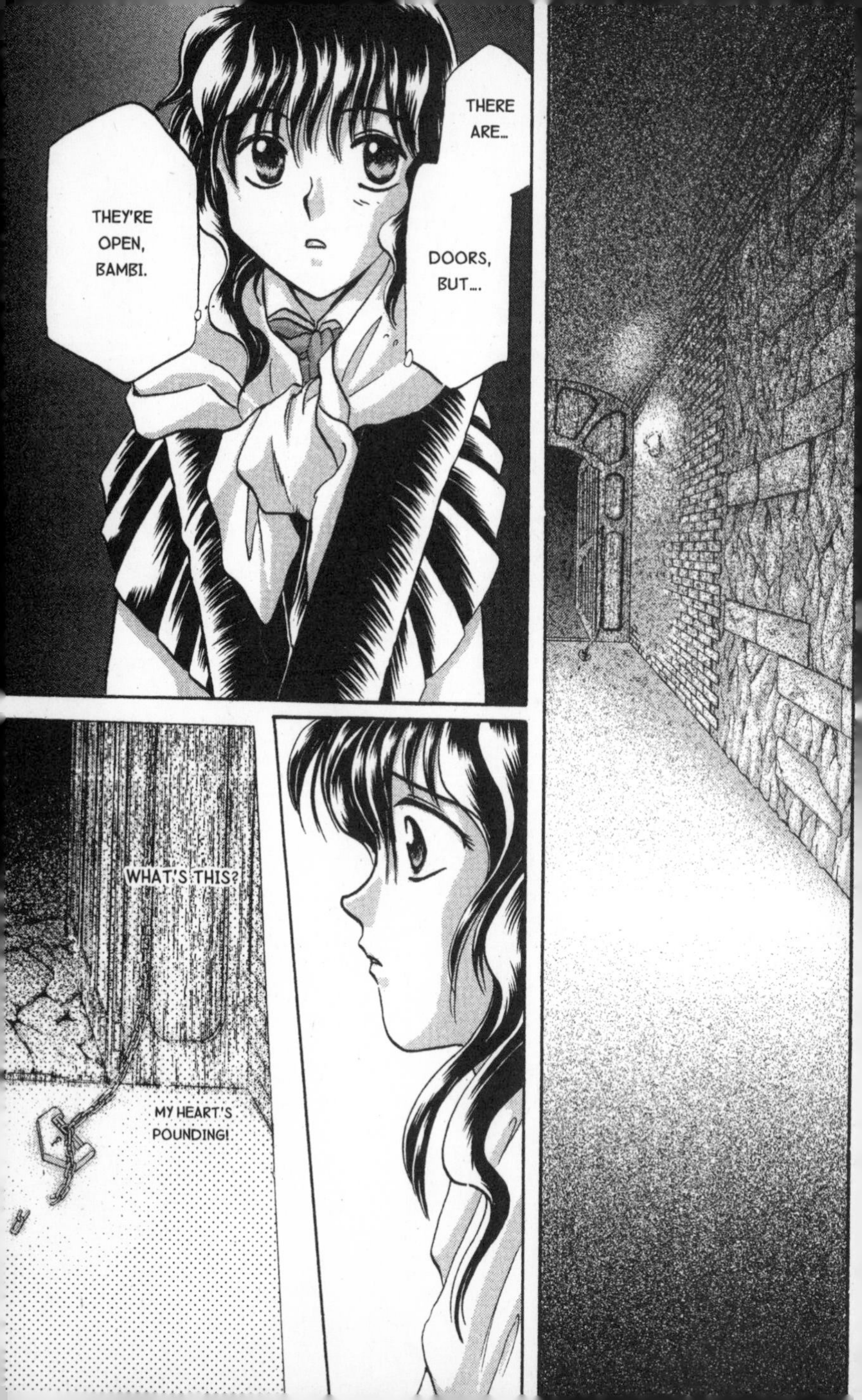
THERE ARE...
DOORS, BUT....
THEY'RE OPEN, BAMBI.
WHAT'S THIS?
MY HEART'S POUNDING!

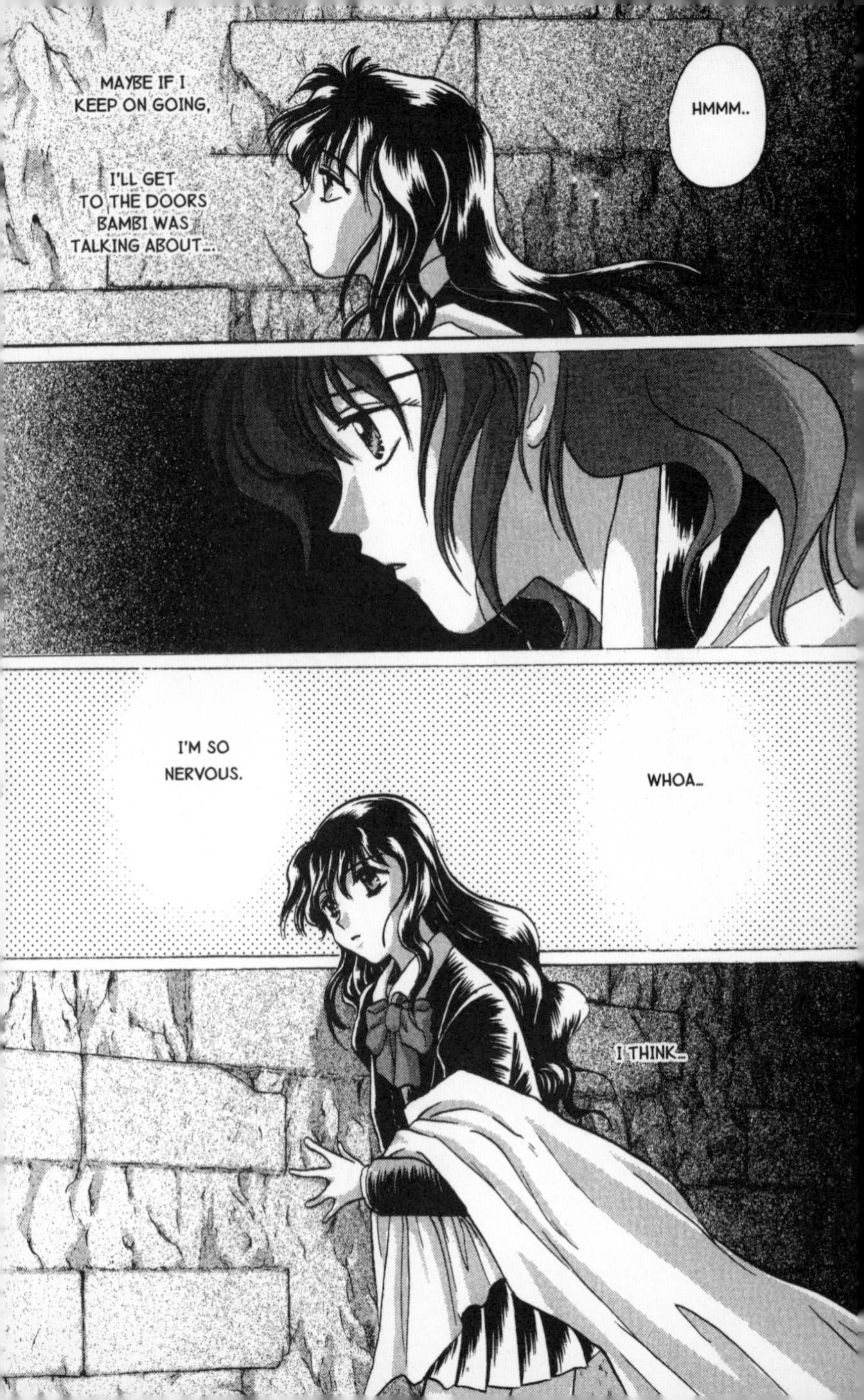
HMMM..
MAYBE IF I KEEP ON GOING,
I'LL GET TO THE DOORS BAMBI WAS TALKING ABOUT...
WHOA...
I'M SO NERVOUS.
I THINK...

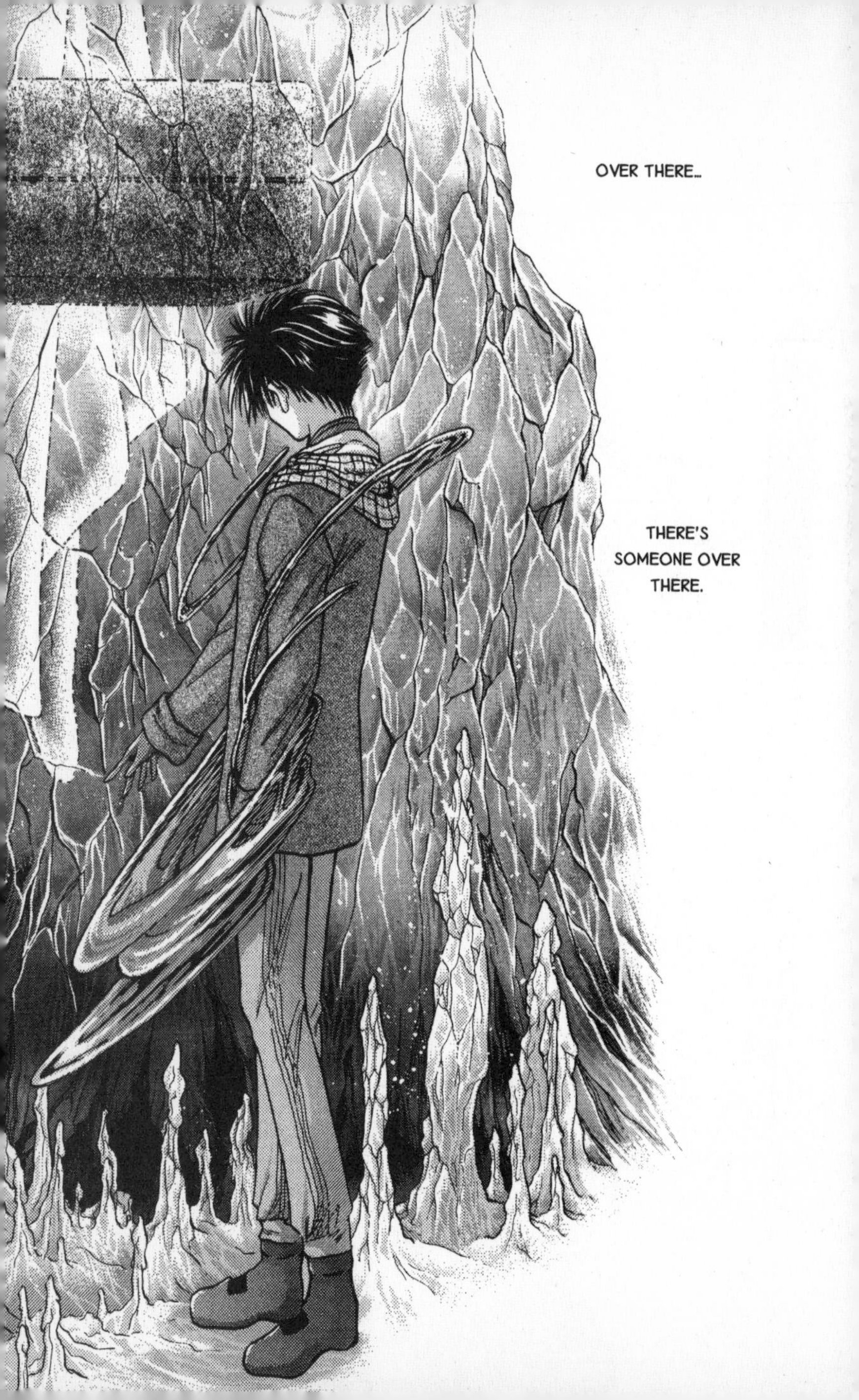
OVER THERE...
THERE'S SOMEONE OVER THERE.

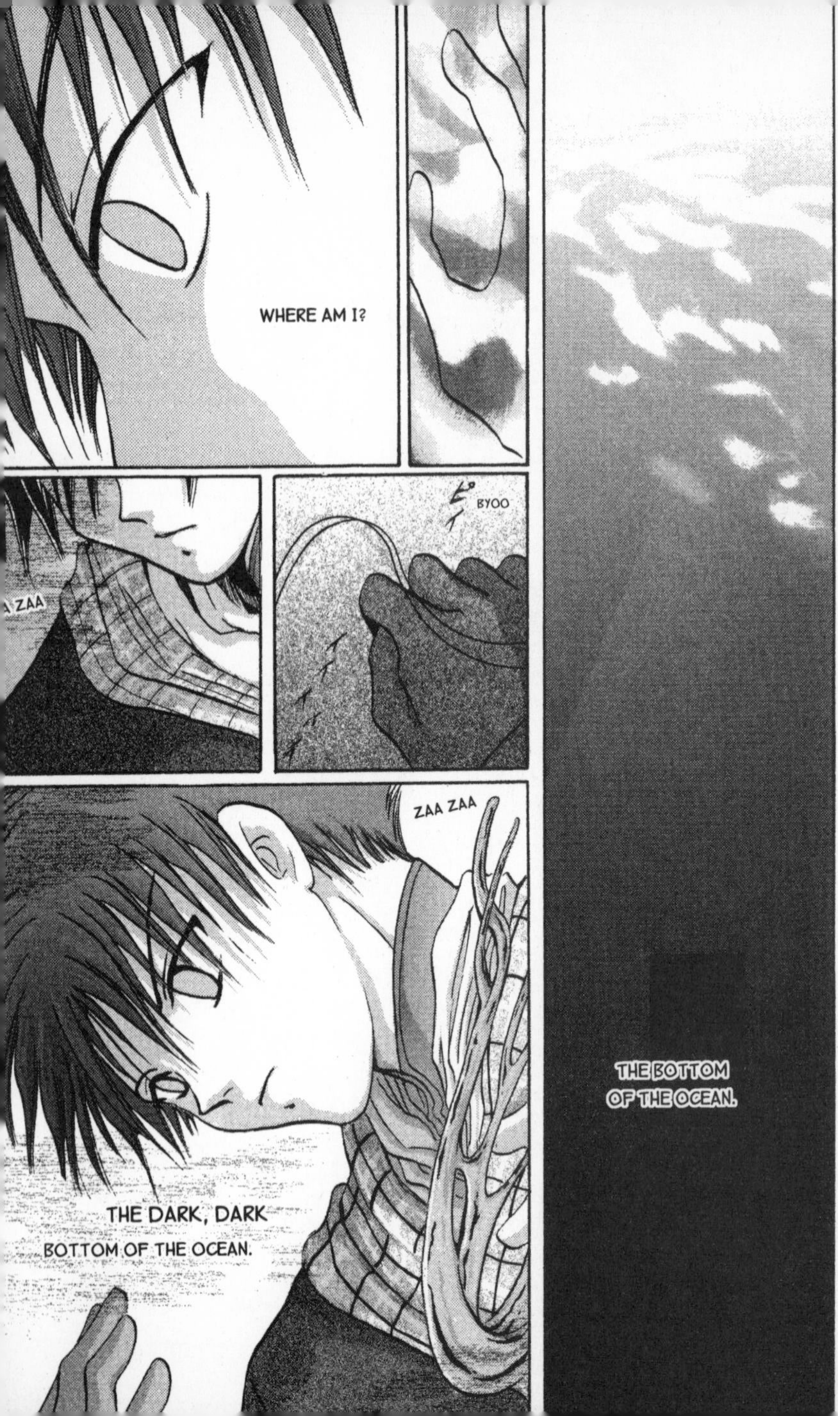
THE BOTTOM OF THE OCEAN.
WHERE AM I?
BYOO
ZAA
ZAA ZAA
THE DARK, DARK BOTTOM OF THE OCEAN.

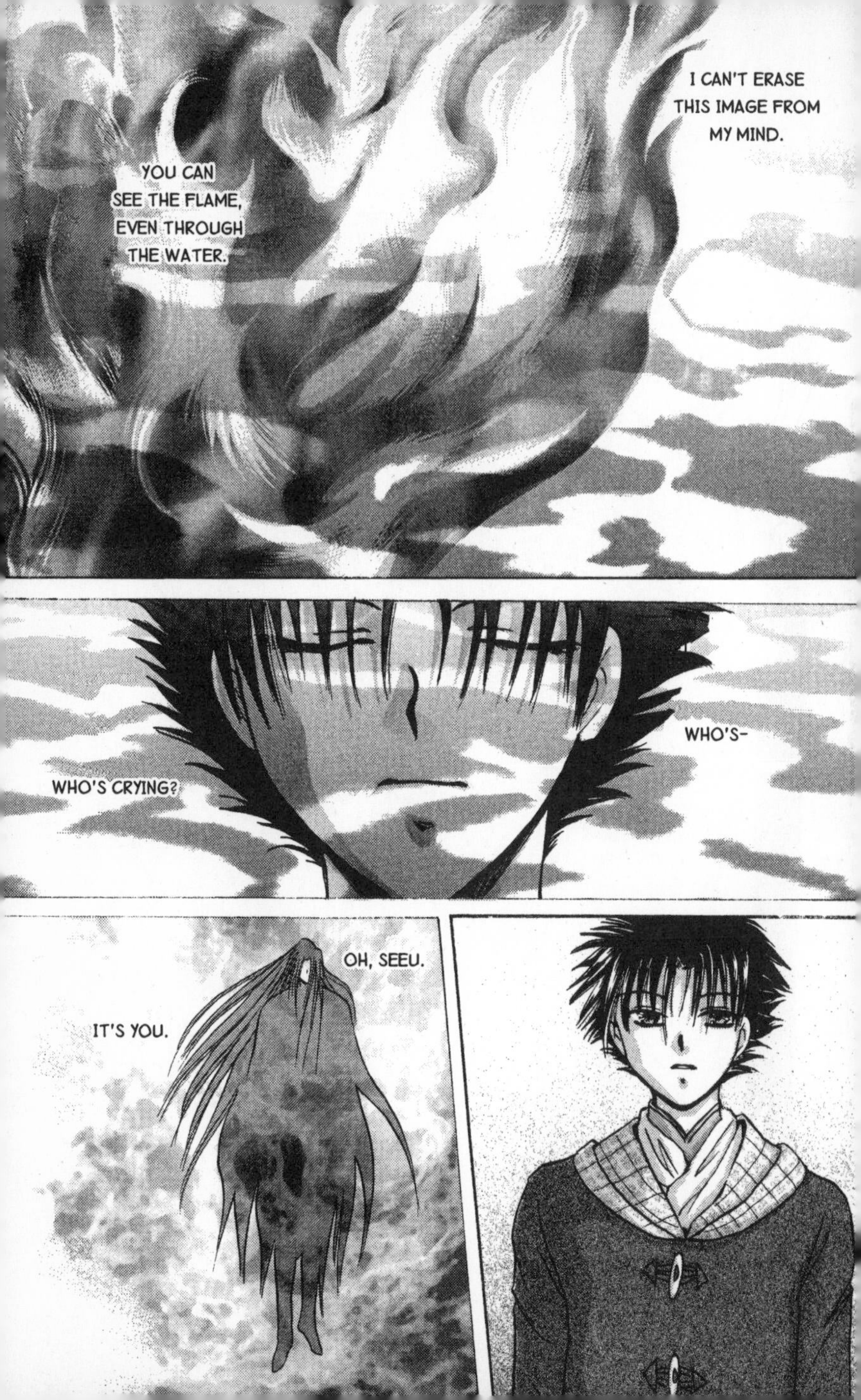
I CAN'T ERASE THIS IMAGE FROM MY MIND.
YOU CAN SEE THE FLAME, EVEN THROUGH THE WATER.
WHO'S-
WHO'S CRYING?
OH, SEEU.
IT'S YOU.

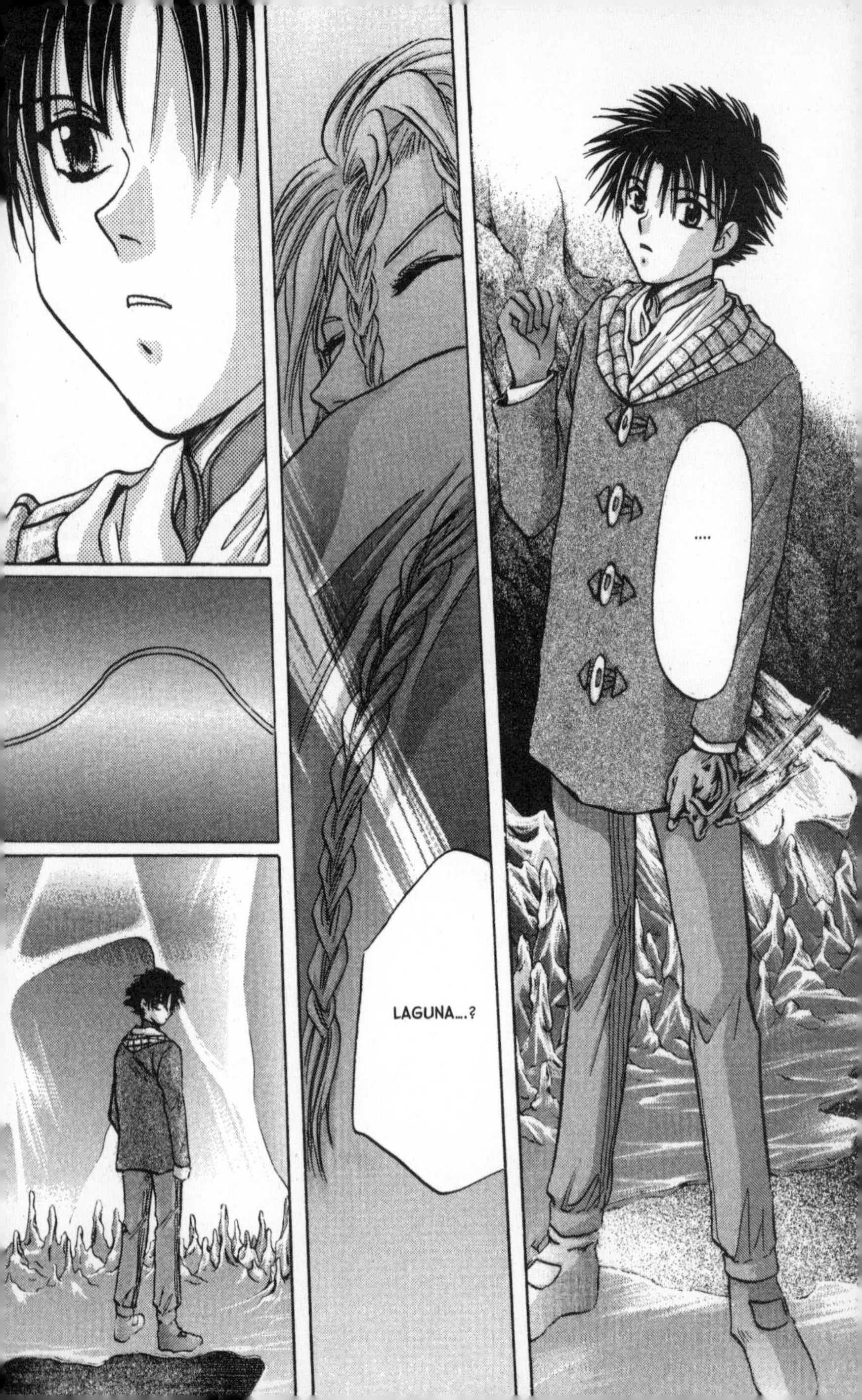
....
LAGUNA...?

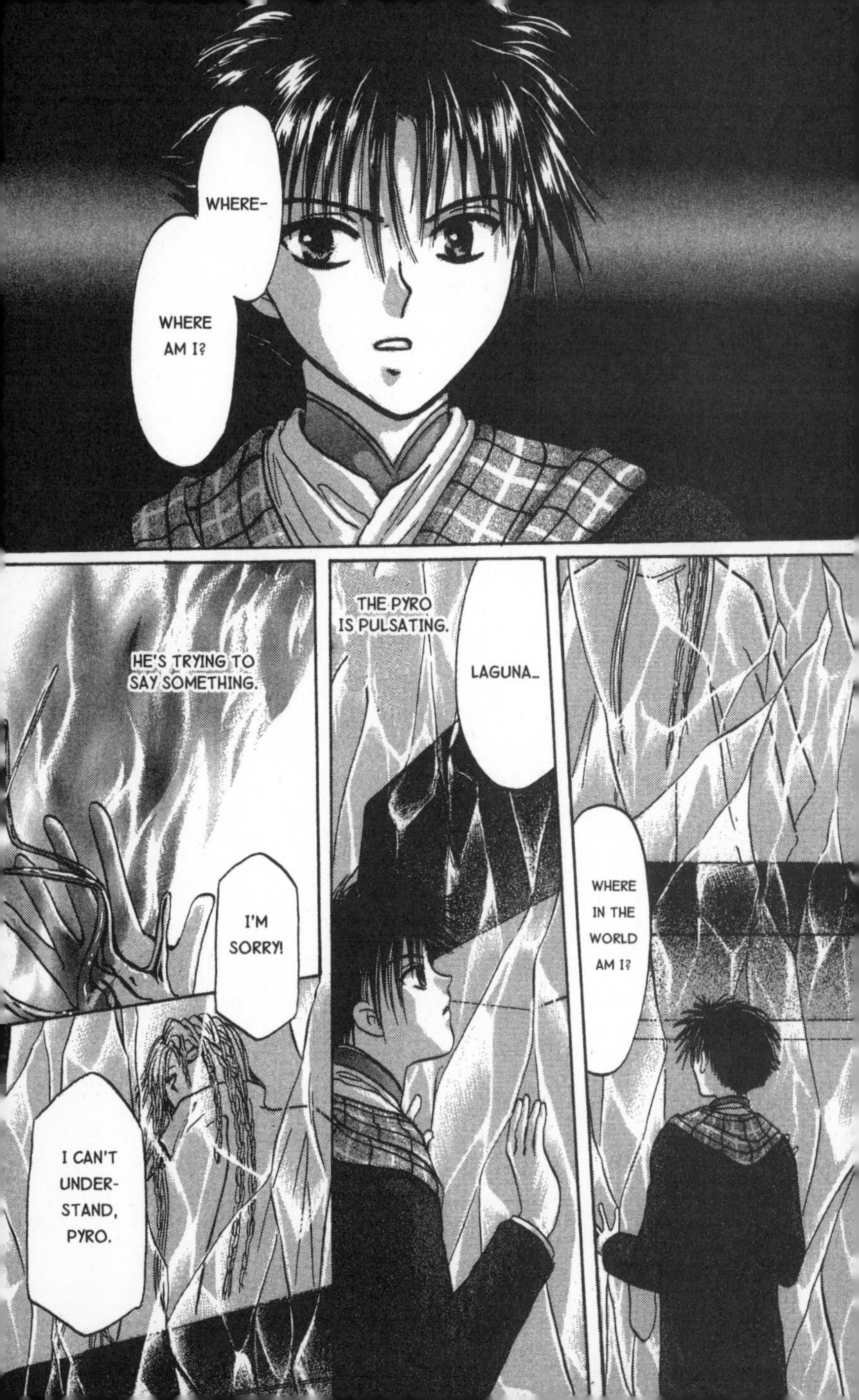
WHERE-
WHERE AM I?
WHERE IN THE WORLD AM I?
LAGUNA...
THE PYRO IS PULSATING.
HE'S TRYING TO SAY SOMETHING.
I'M SORRY!
I CAN'T UNDER-STAND, PYRO.

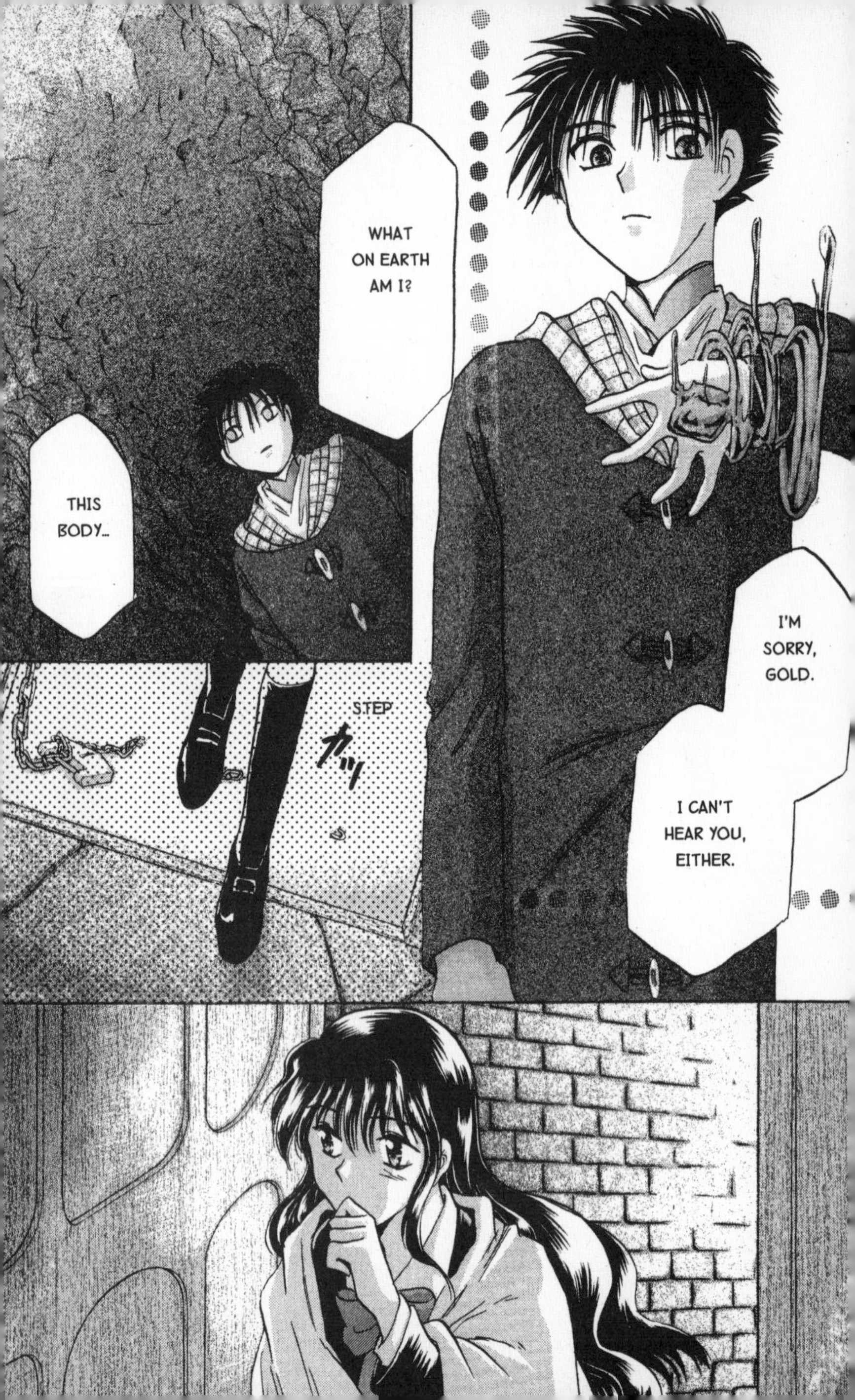
I'M SORRY, GOLD.
I CAN'T HEAR YOU, EITHER.
WHAT ON EARTH AM I?
THIS BODY...
STEP

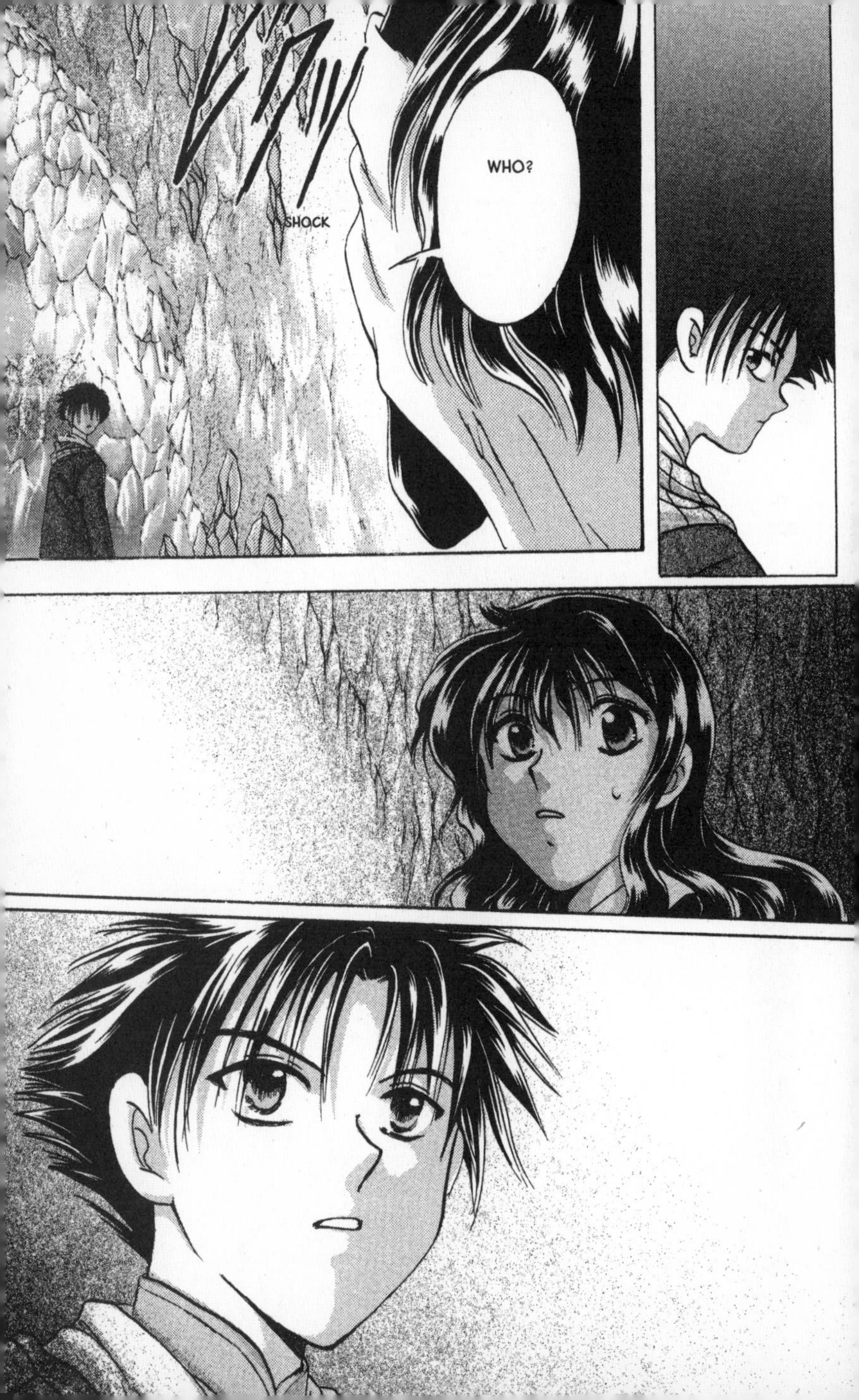
WHO?
SHOCK

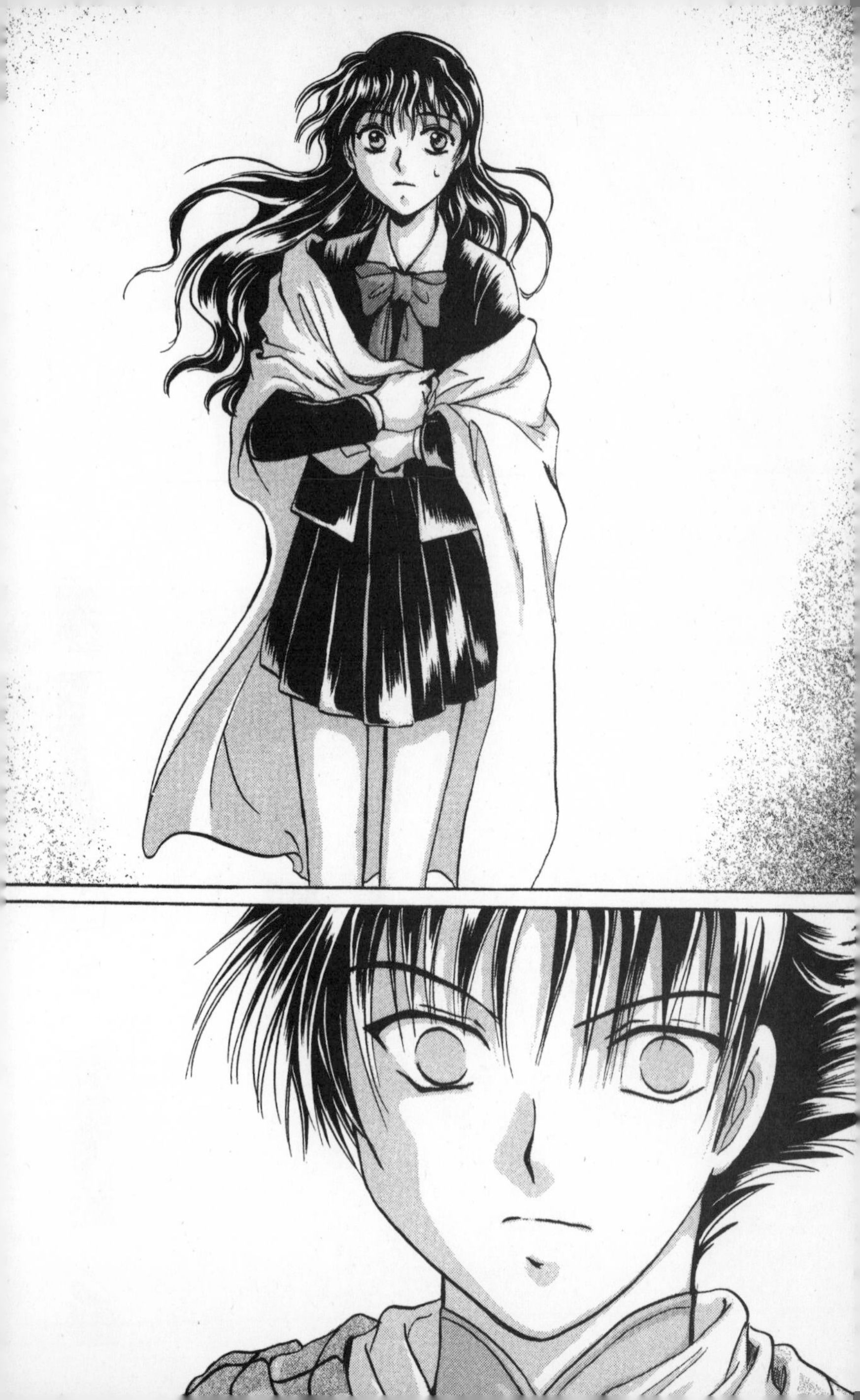

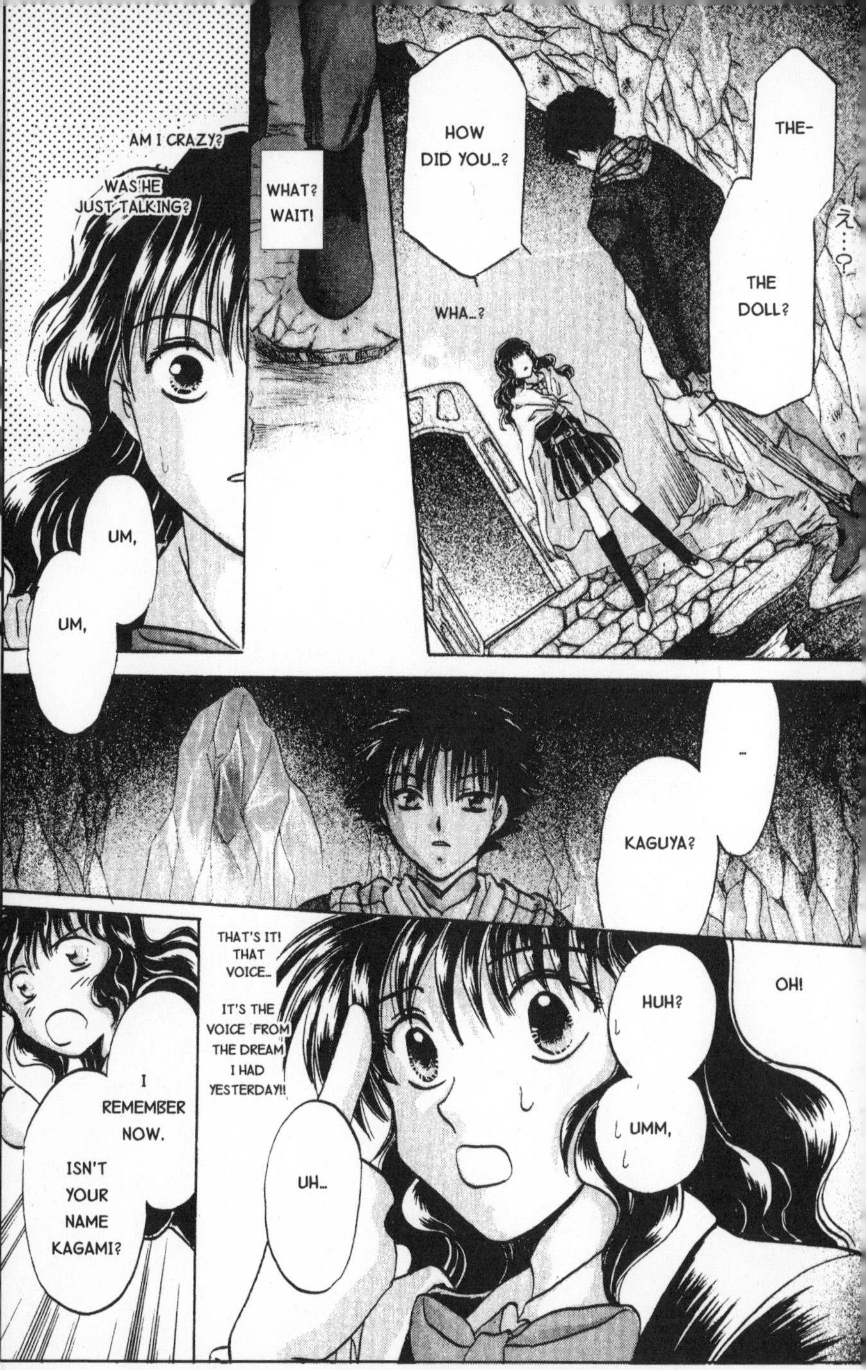
THE-
THE DOLL?
え…?
HOW DID YOU...?
WHA...?
WHAT? WAIT!
AM I CRAZY?
WAS HE JUST TALKING?
UM,
UM,
...
KAGUYA?
OH!
HUH?
UMM,
THAT'S IT! THAT VOICE...
IT'S THE VOICE FROM THE DREAM I HAD YESTERDAY!!
UH...
I REMEMBER NOW.
ISN'T YOUR NAME KAGAMI?

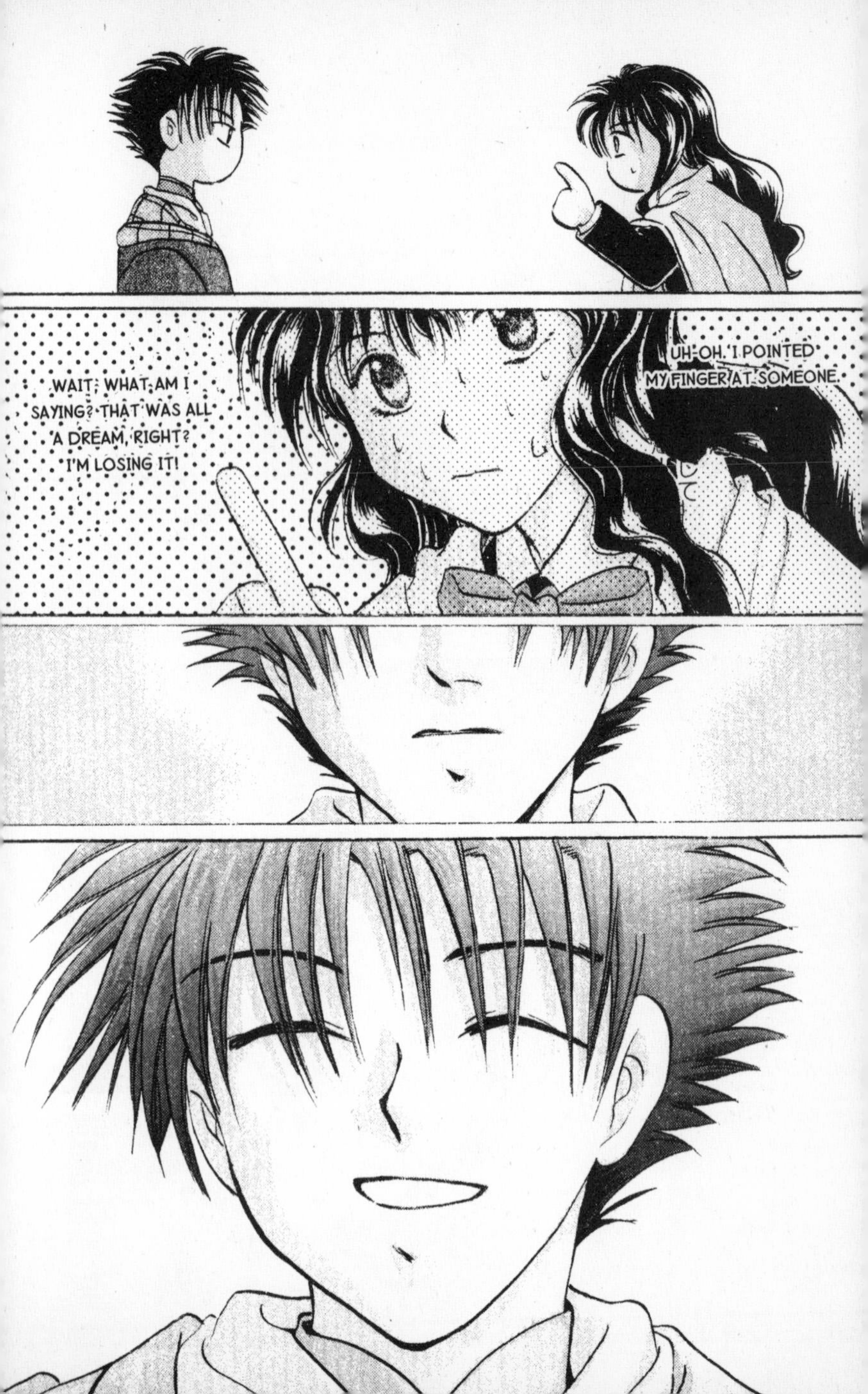
UH-OH. I POINTED MY FINGER AT SOMEONE.
WAIT, WHAT AM I SAYING? THAT WAS ALL A DREAM, RIGHT? I'M LOSING IT!

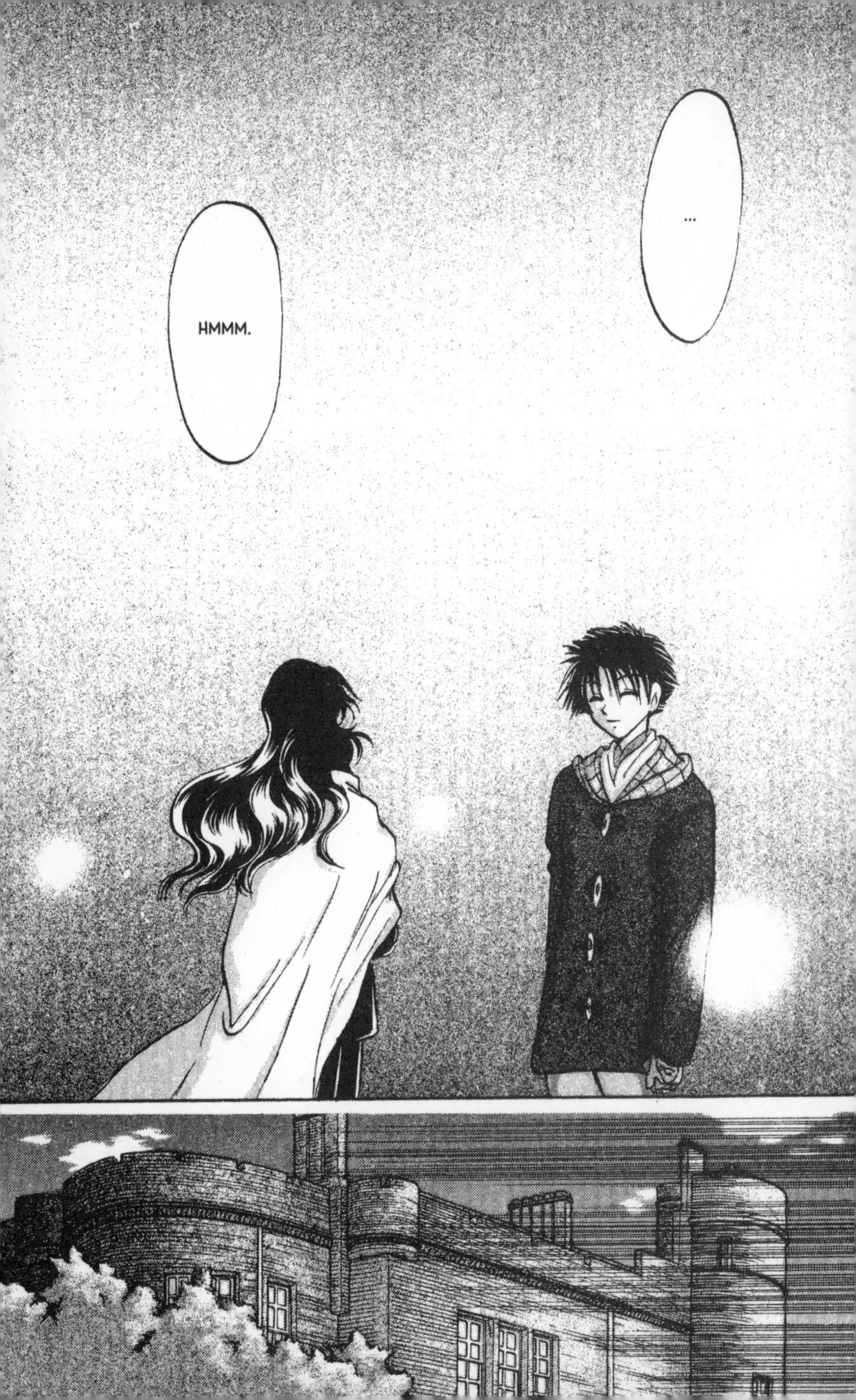
...
HMMM.

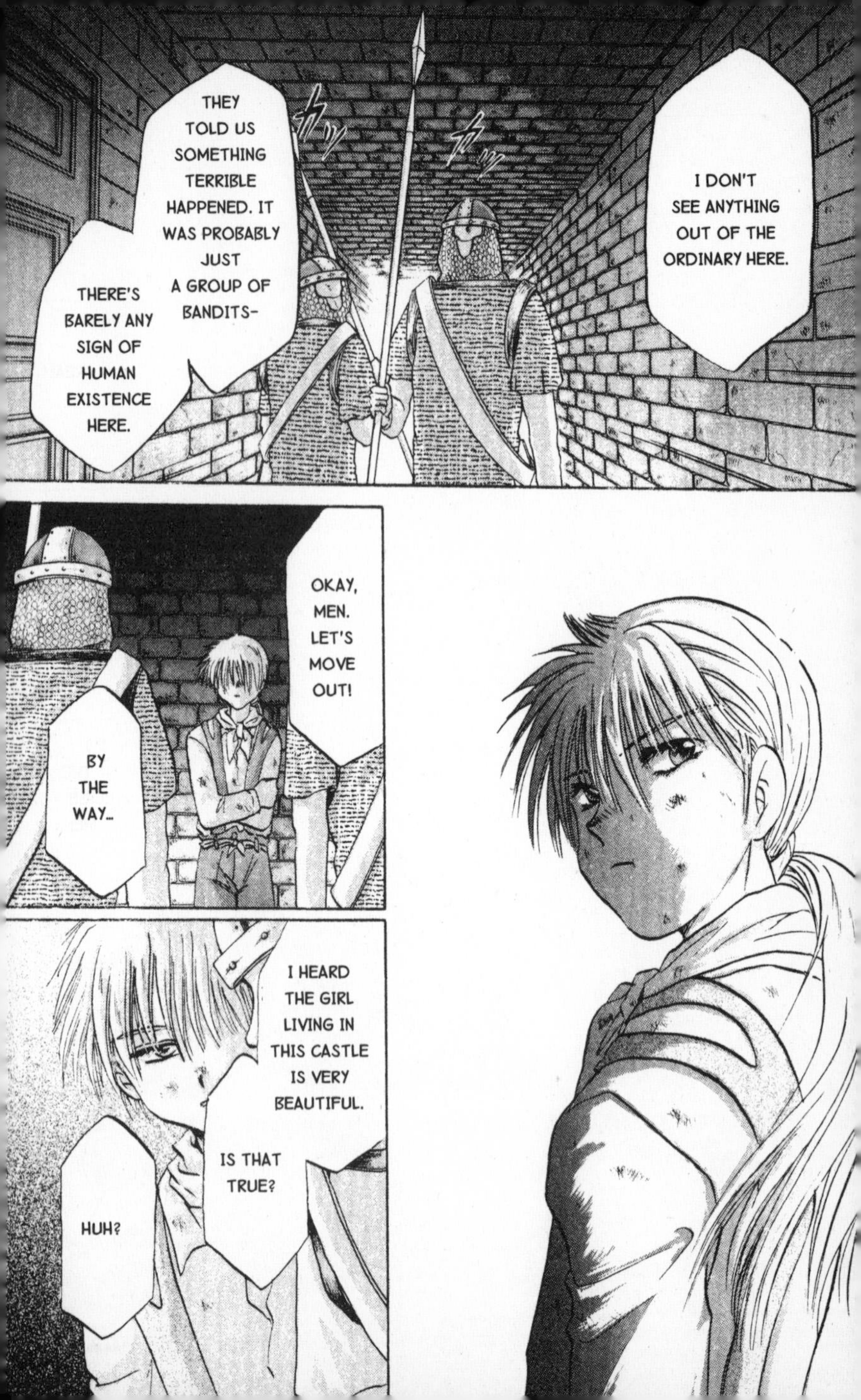
I DON'T SEE ANYTHING OUT OF THE ORDINARY HERE.
THEY TOLD US SOMETHING TERRIBLE HAPPENED. IT WAS PROBABLY JUST A GROUP OF BANDITS-
THERE'S BARELY ANY SIGN OF HUMAN EXISTENCE HERE.
OKAY, MEN. LET'S MOVE OUT!
BY THE WAY...
I HEARD THE GIRL LIVING IN THIS CASTLE IS VERY BEAUTIFUL.
IS THAT TRUE?
HUH?

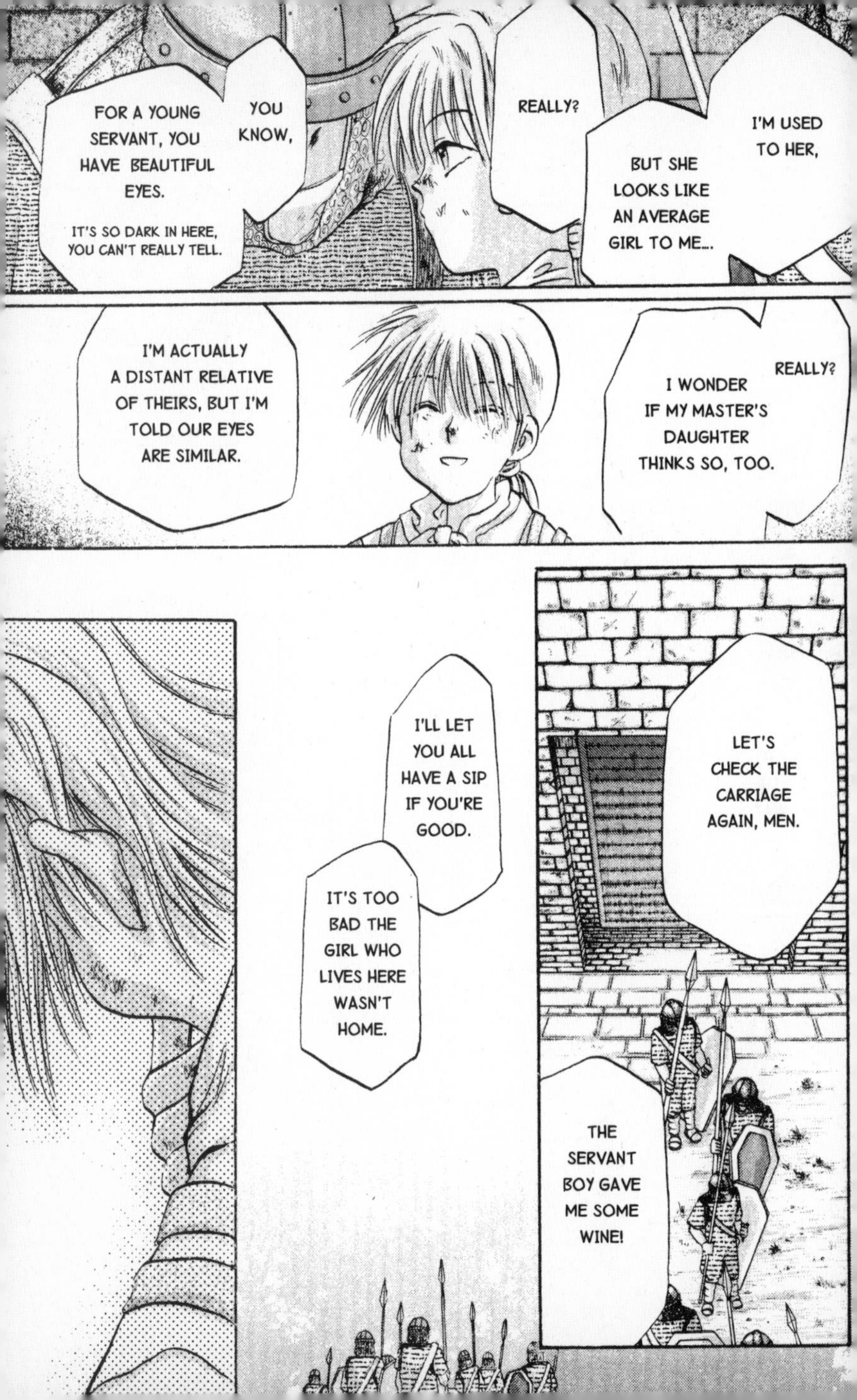
I'M USED TO HER,
BUT SHE LOOKS LIKE AN AVERAGE GIRL TO ME...
REALLY?
YOU KNOW,
FOR A YOUNG SERVANT, YOU HAVE BEAUTIFUL EYES.
IT'S SO DARK IN HERE, YOU CAN'T REALLY TELL.
REALLY?
I WONDER IF MY MASTER'S DAUGHTER THINKS SO, TOO.
I'M ACTUALLY A DISTANT RELATIVE OF THEIRS, BUT I'M TOLD OUR EYES ARE SIMILAR.
LET'S CHECK THE CARRIAGE AGAIN, MEN.
THE SERVANT BOY GAVE ME SOME WINE!
I'LL LET YOU ALL HAVE A SIP IF YOU'RE GOOD.
IT'S TOO BAD THE GIRL WHO LIVES HERE WASN'T HOME.

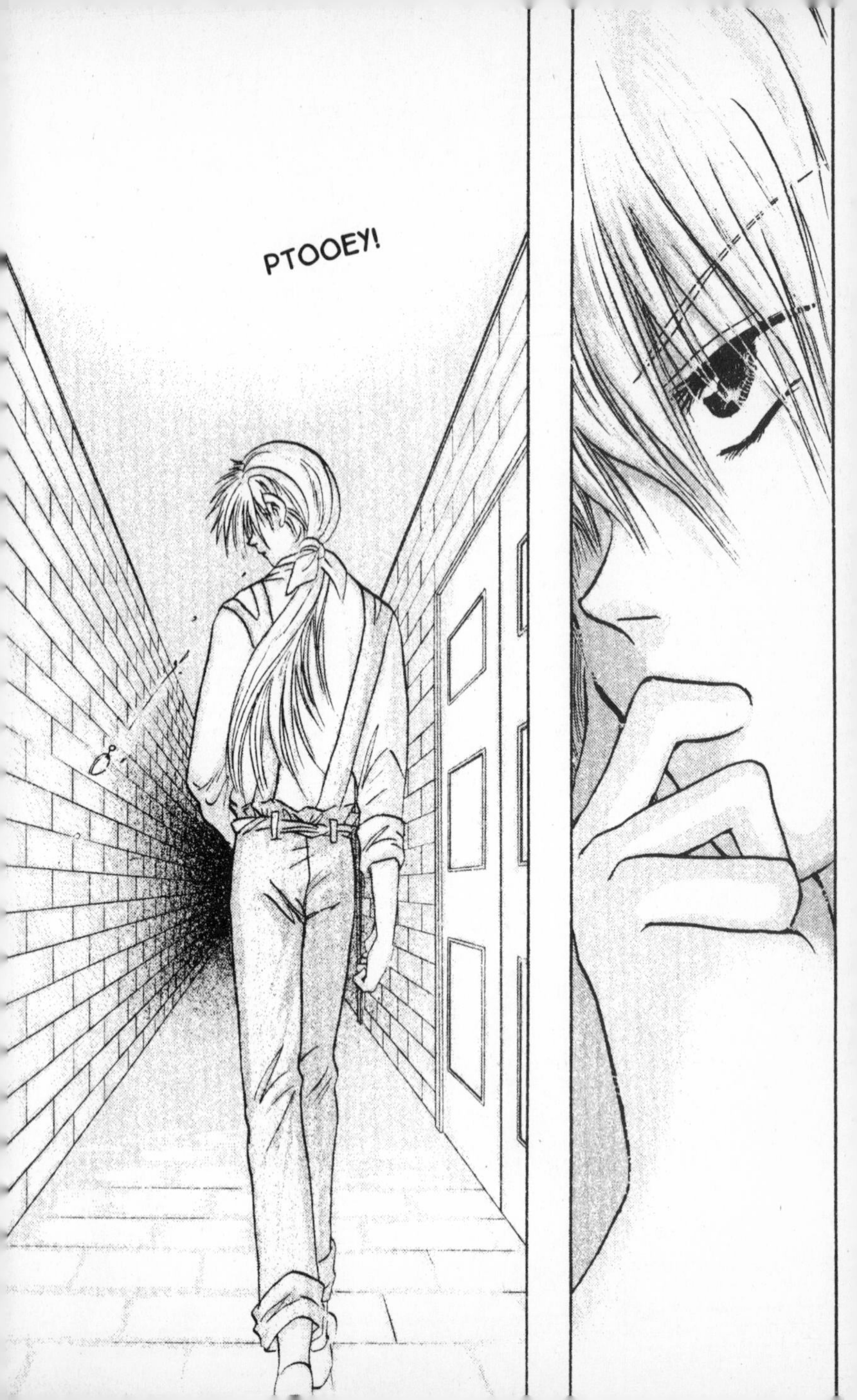
PTOOEY!

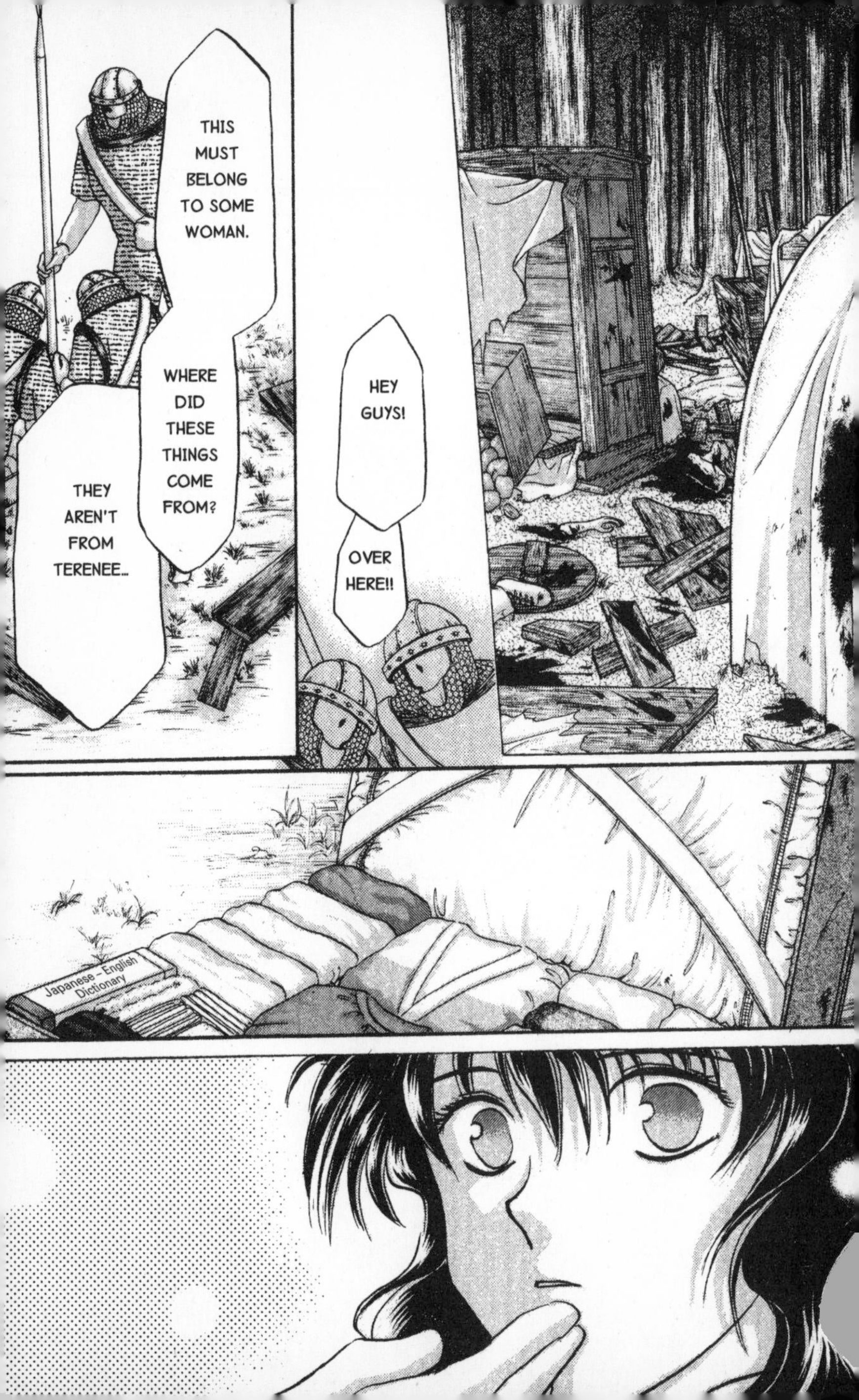
HEY GUYS!
OVER HERE!!
THIS MUST BELONG TO SOME WOMAN.
WHERE DID THESE THINGS COME FROM?
THEY AREN'T FROM TERENEE...
Japanese - English Dictionary

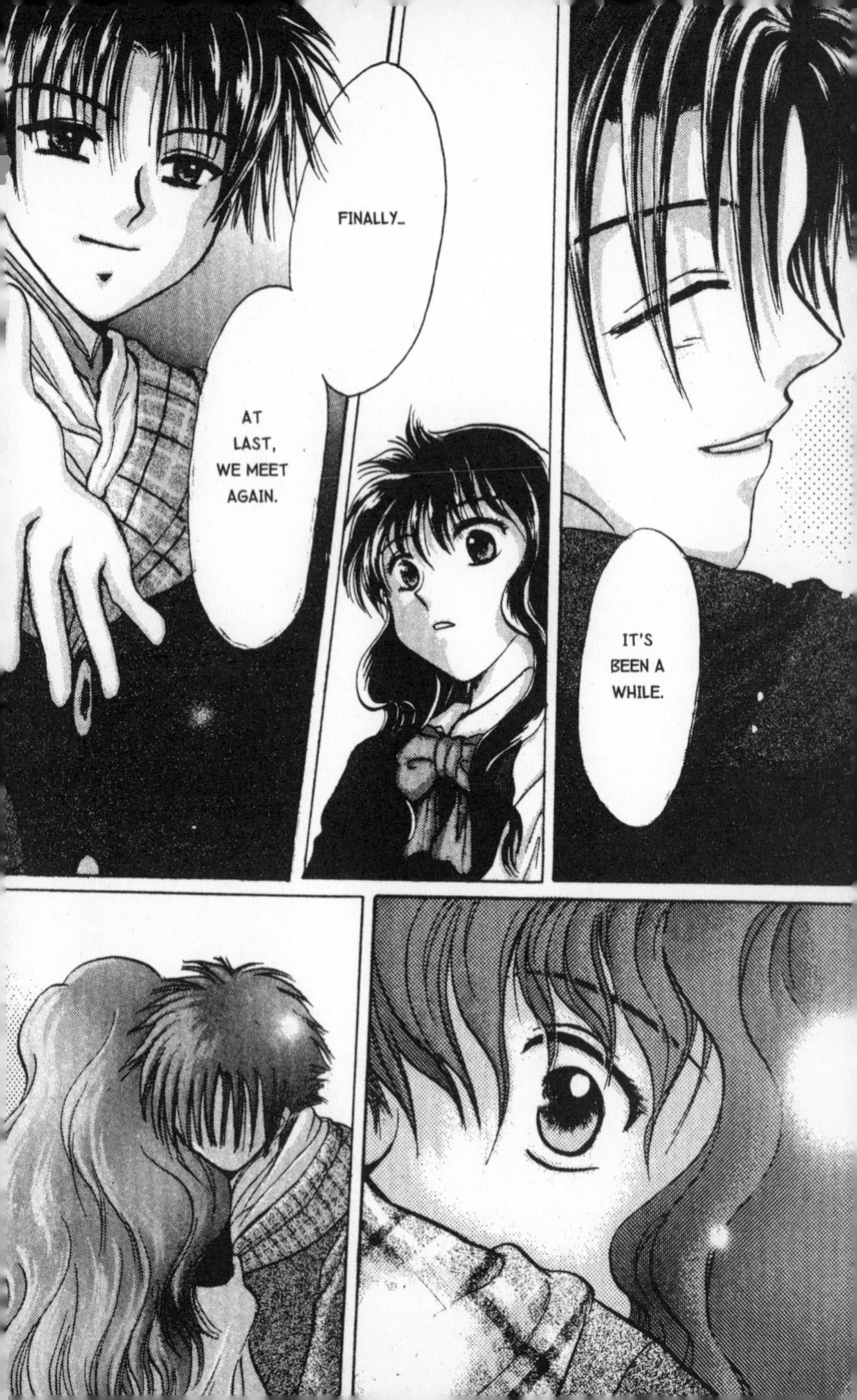
IT'S BEEN A WHILE.
FINALLY...
AT LAST, WE MEET AGAIN.

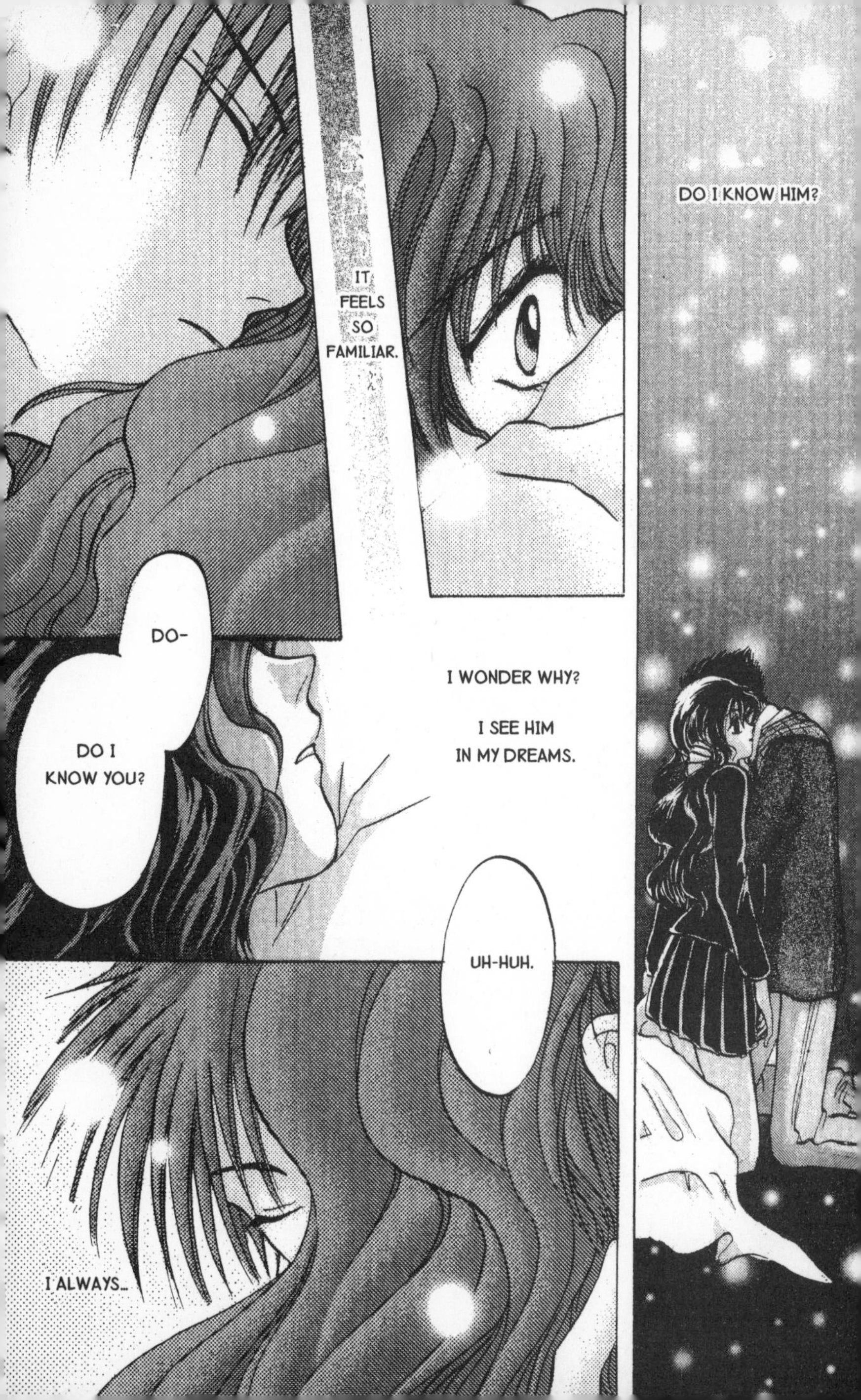
DO I KNOW HIM?
IT FEELS SO FAMILIAR.
I WONDER WHY?
I SEE HIM IN MY DREAMS.
DO-
DO I KNOW YOU?
UH-HUH.
I ALWAYS...

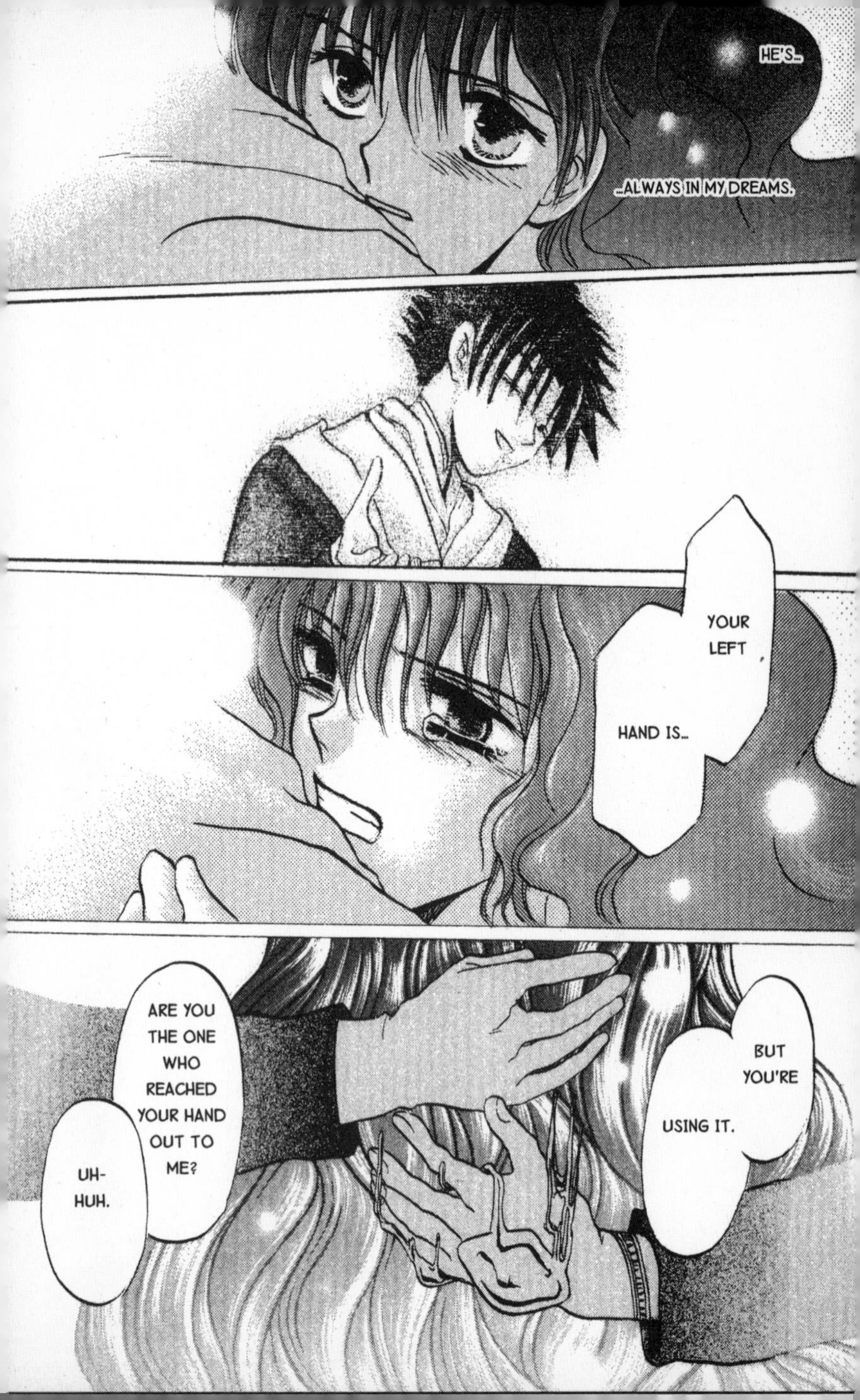
HE'S...
...ALWAYS IN MY DREAMS.
YOUR LEFT HAND IS...
BUT YOU'RE USING IT.
ARE YOU THE ONE WHO REACHED YOUR HAND OUT TO ME?
UH-HUH.

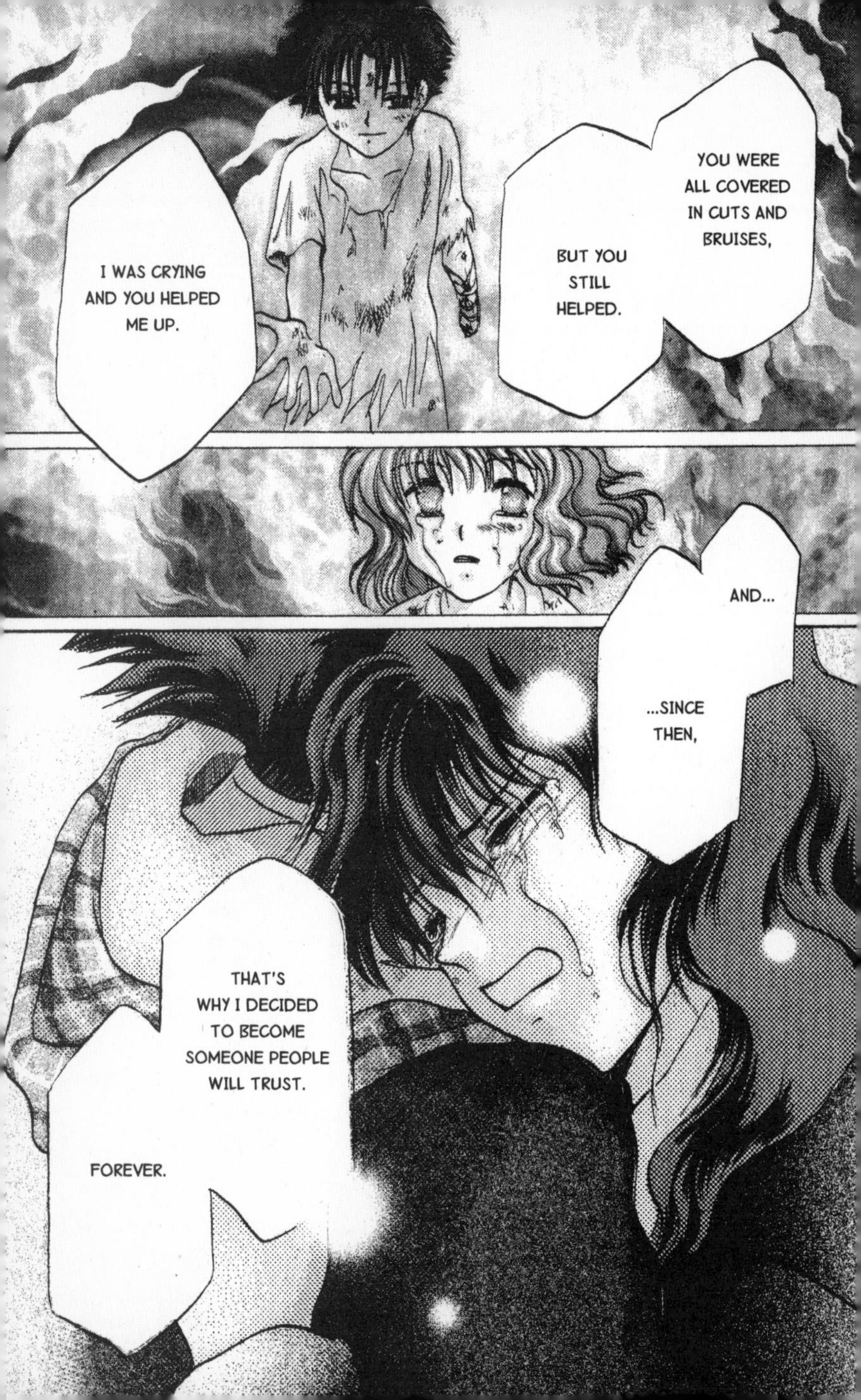
YOU WERE ALL COVERED IN CUTS AND BRUISES,
BUT YOU STILL HELPED.
I WAS CRYING AND YOU HELPED ME UP.
AND...
...SINCE THEN,
THAT'S WHY I DECIDED TO BECOME SOMEONE PEOPLE WILL TRUST.
FOREVER.

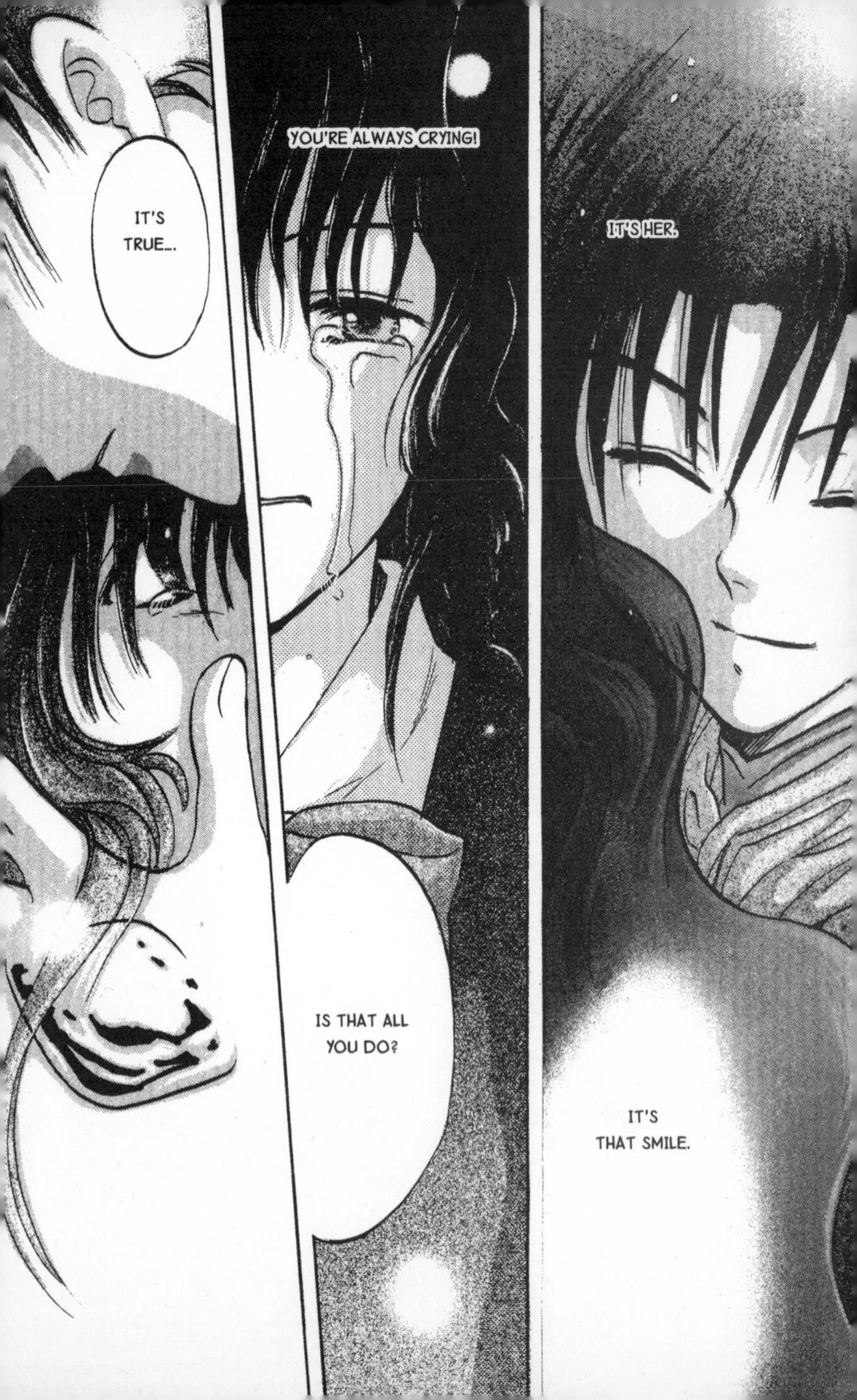
IT'S HER.
IT'S THAT SMILE.
YOU'RE ALWAYS CRYING!
IS THAT ALL YOU DO?
IT'S TRUE...

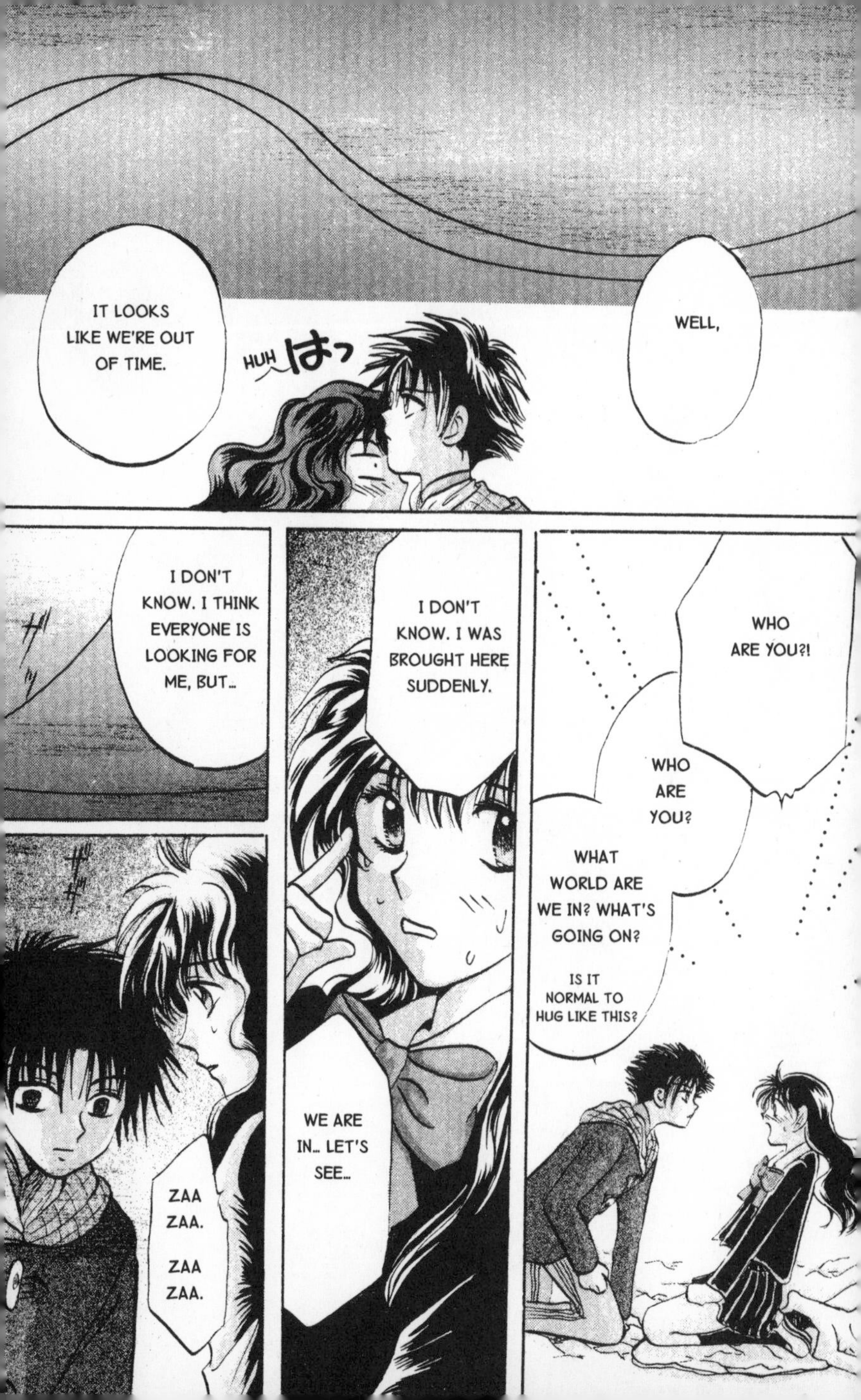
WELL,
IT LOOKS LIKE WE'RE OUT OF TIME.
HUH はっ
WHO ARE YOU?!
WHO ARE YOU?
WHAT WORLD ARE WE IN? WHAT'S GOING ON?
IS IT NORMAL TO HUG LIKE THIS?
I DON'T KNOW. I WAS BROUGHT HERE SUDDENLY.
WE ARE IN... LET'S SEE...
I DON'T KNOW. I THINK EVERYONE IS LOOKING FOR ME, BUT...
ZAA ZAA.
ZAA ZAA.

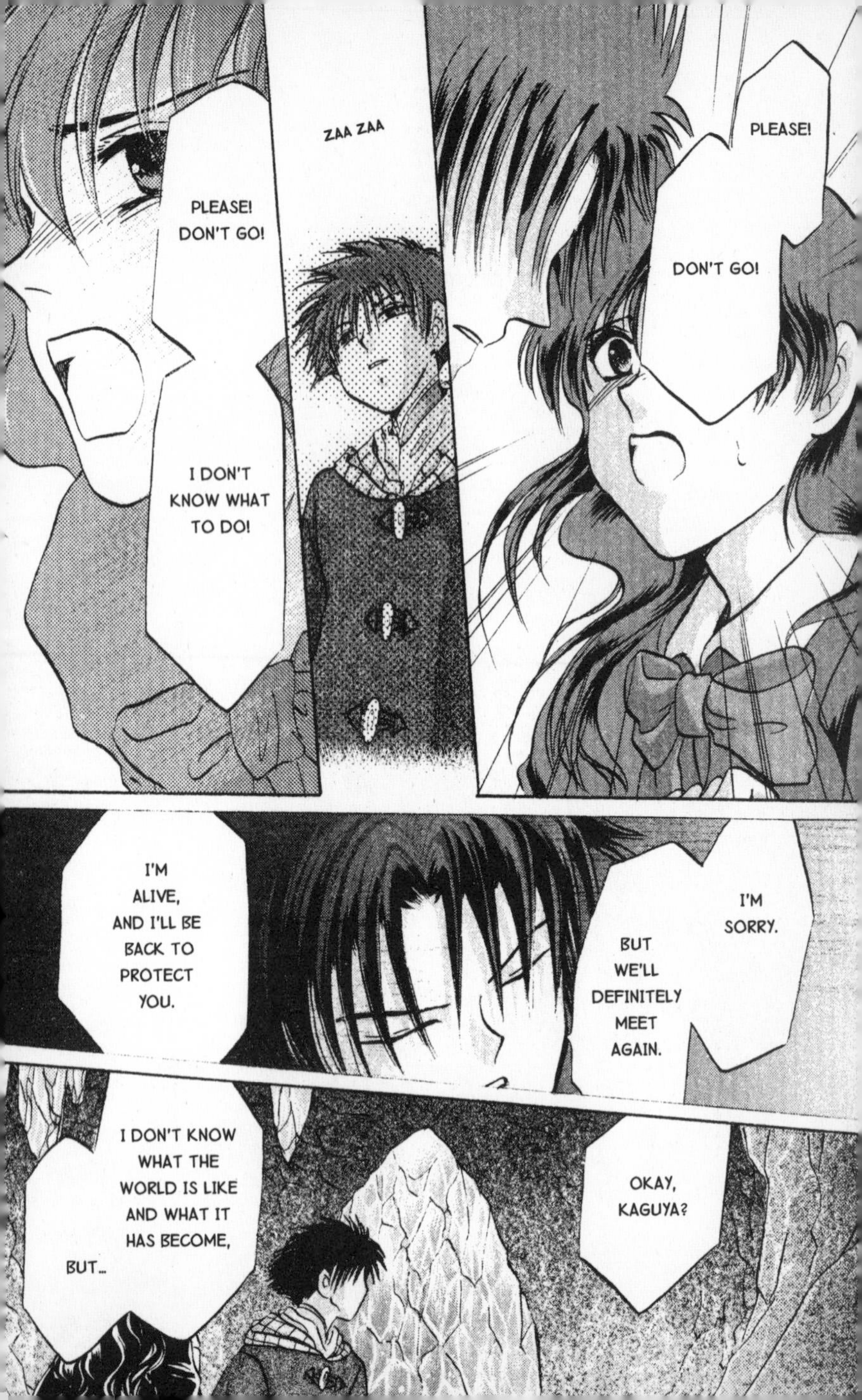
PLEASE!
DON'T GO!
ZAA ZAA
PLEASE! DON'T GO!
I DON'T KNOW WHAT TO DO!
I'M SORRY.
BUT WE'LL DEFINITELY MEET AGAIN.
I'M ALIVE, AND I'LL BE BACK TO PROTECT YOU.
OKAY, KAGUYA?
I DON'T KNOW WHAT THE WORLD IS LIKE AND WHAT IT HAS BECOME,
BUT...

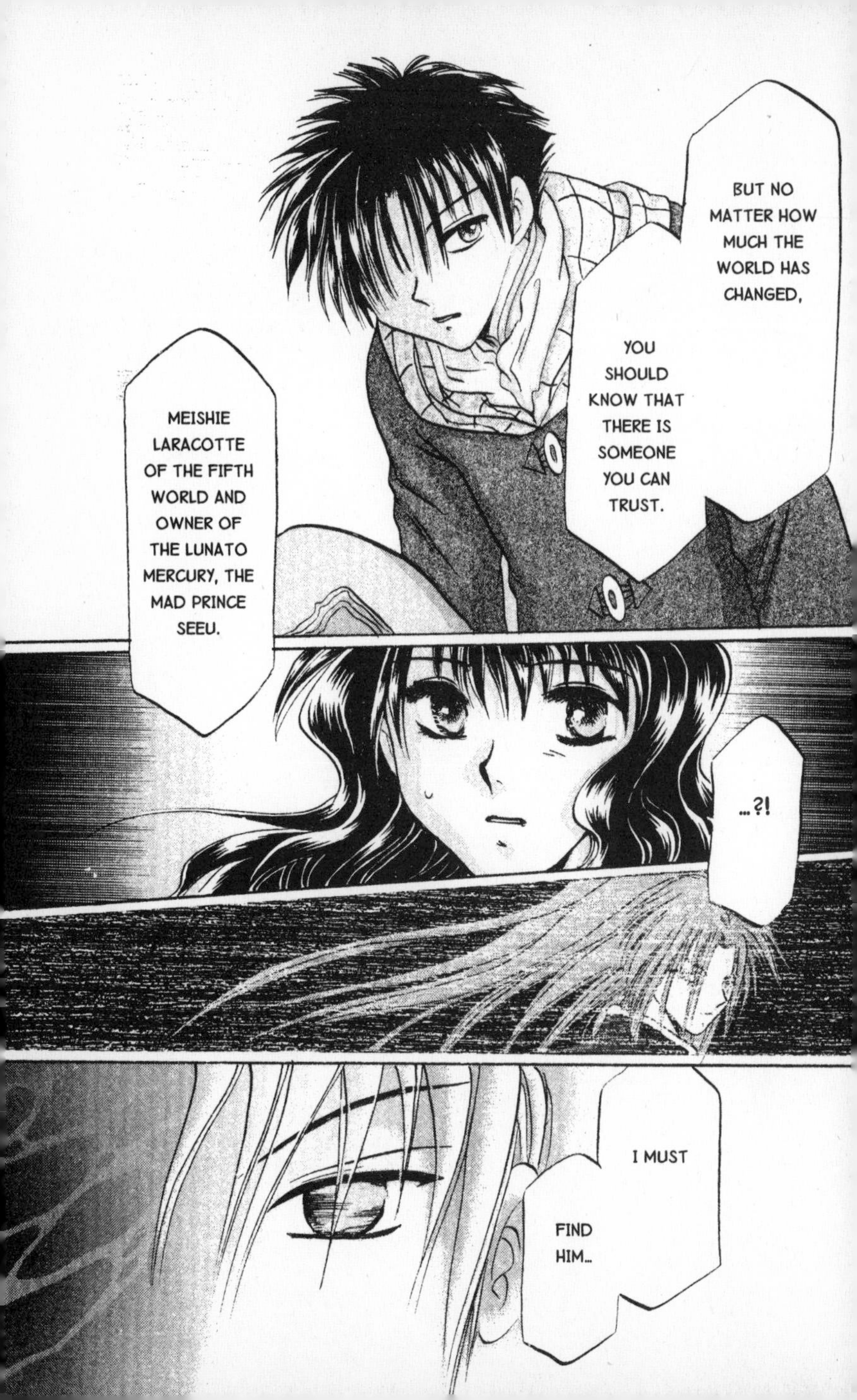
BUT NO MATTER HOW MUCH THE WORLD HAS CHANGED,
YOU SHOULD KNOW THAT THERE IS SOMEONE YOU CAN TRUST.
MEISHIE LARACOTTE OF THE FIFTH WORLD AND OWNER OF THE LUNATO MERCURY, THE MAD PRINCE SEEU.
...?!
I MUST
FIND HIM...

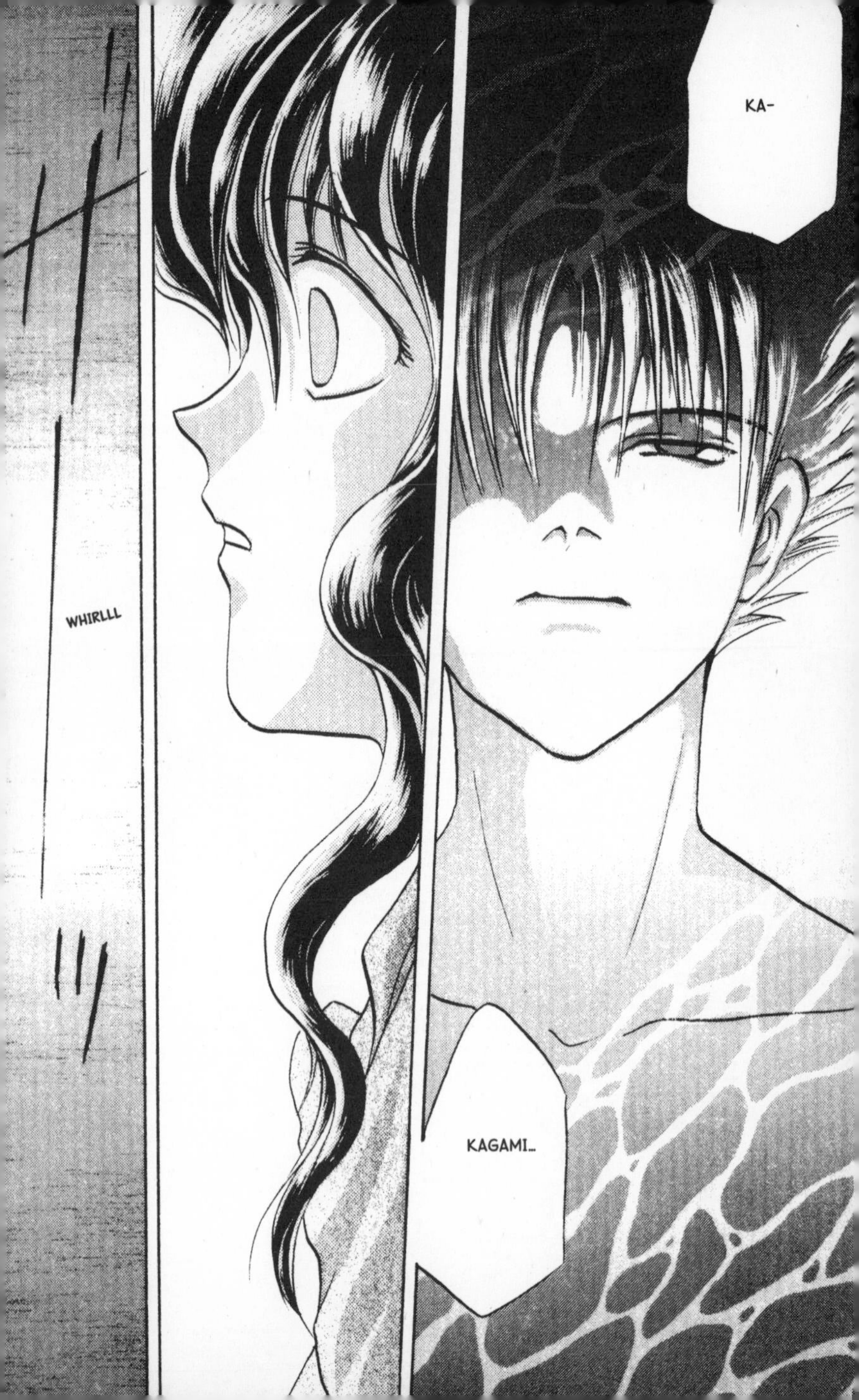
KA-
KAGAMI...
WHIRLLL

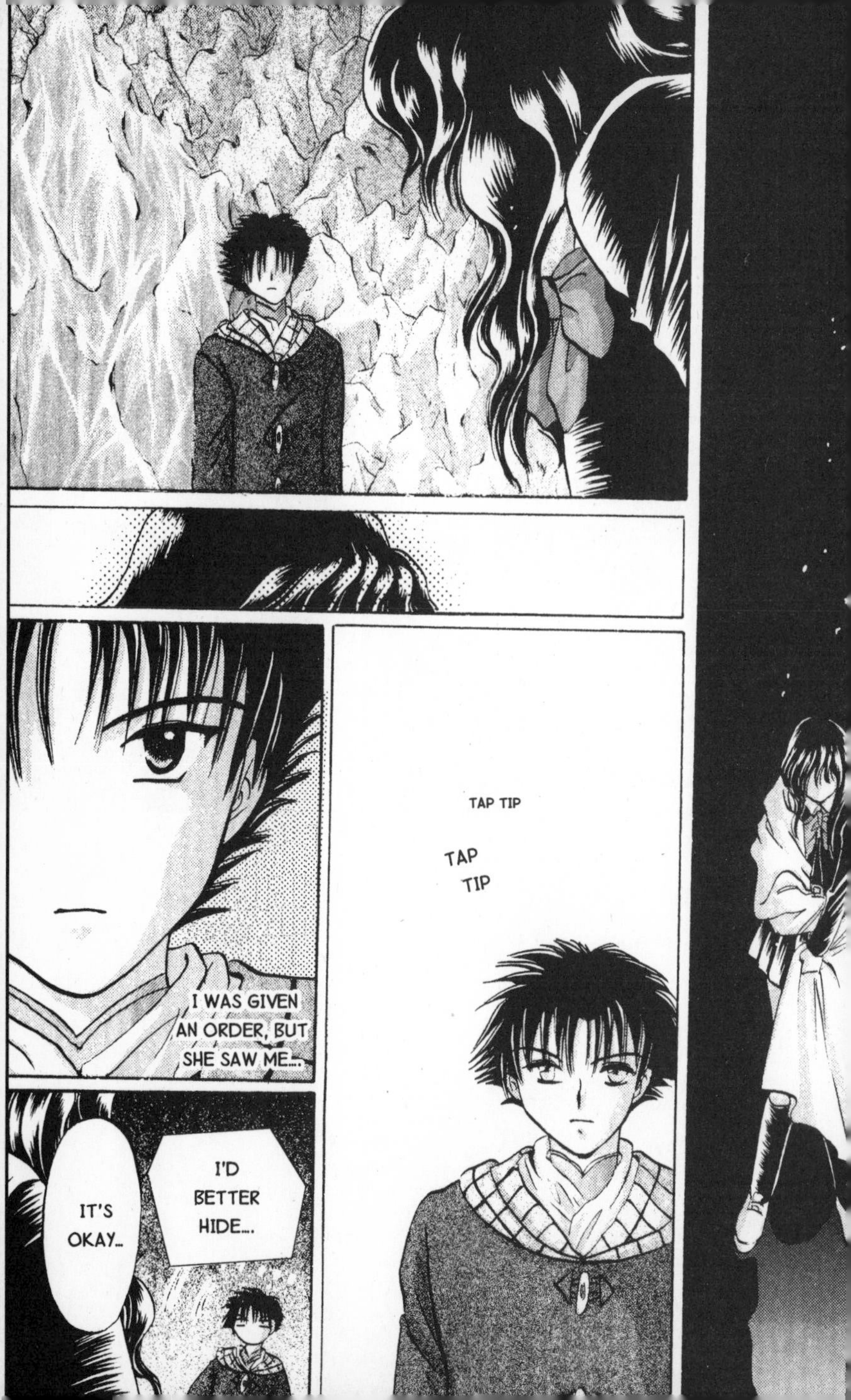
TAP TIP
TAP
TIP
I WAS GIVEN AN ORDER, BUT SHE SAW ME....
I'D BETTER HIDE....
IT'S OKAY...

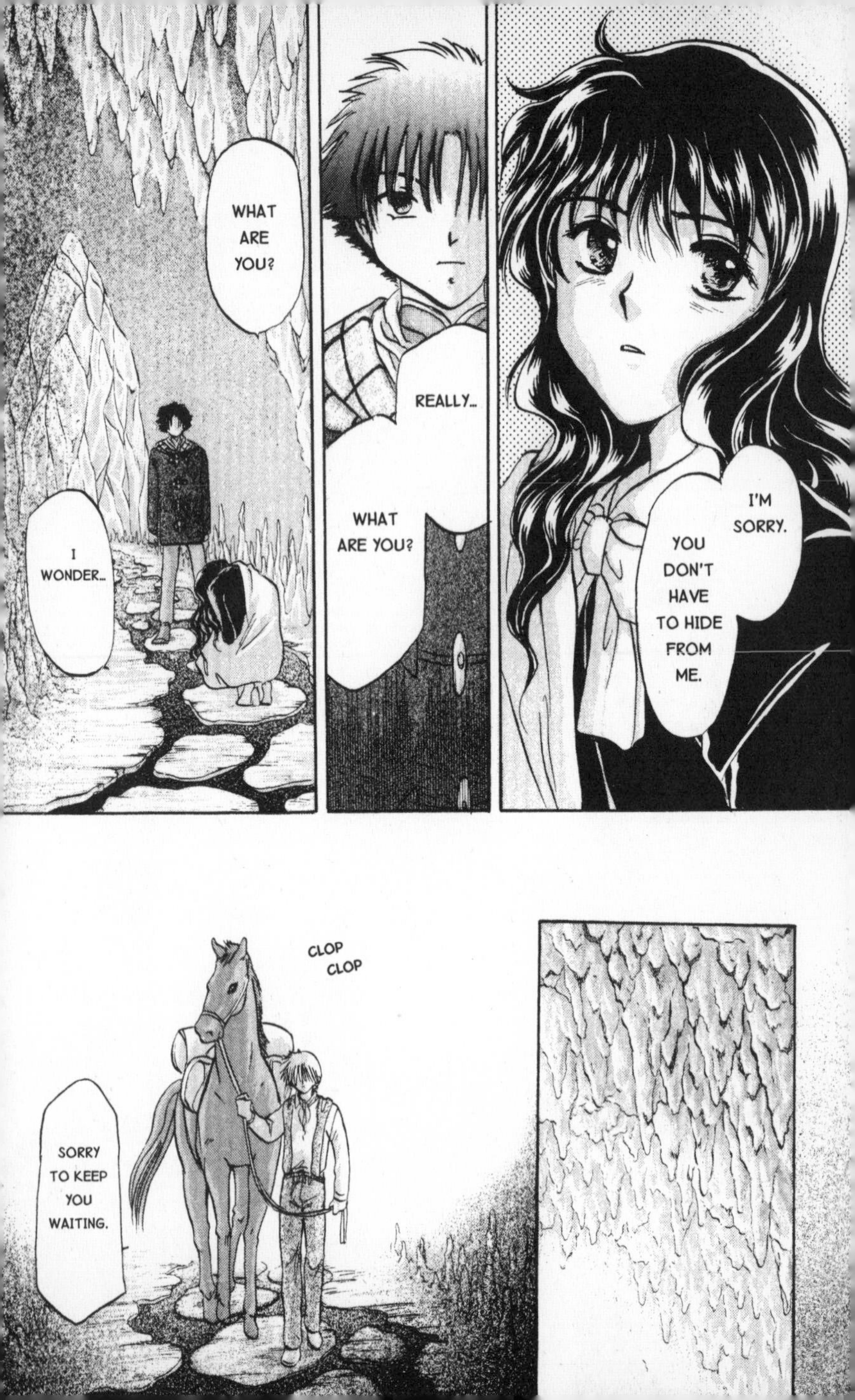
I'M SORRY.
YOU DON'T HAVE TO HIDE FROM ME.
REALLY...
WHAT ARE YOU?
WHAT ARE YOU?
I WONDER...
CLOP CLOP
SORRY TO KEEP YOU WAITING.

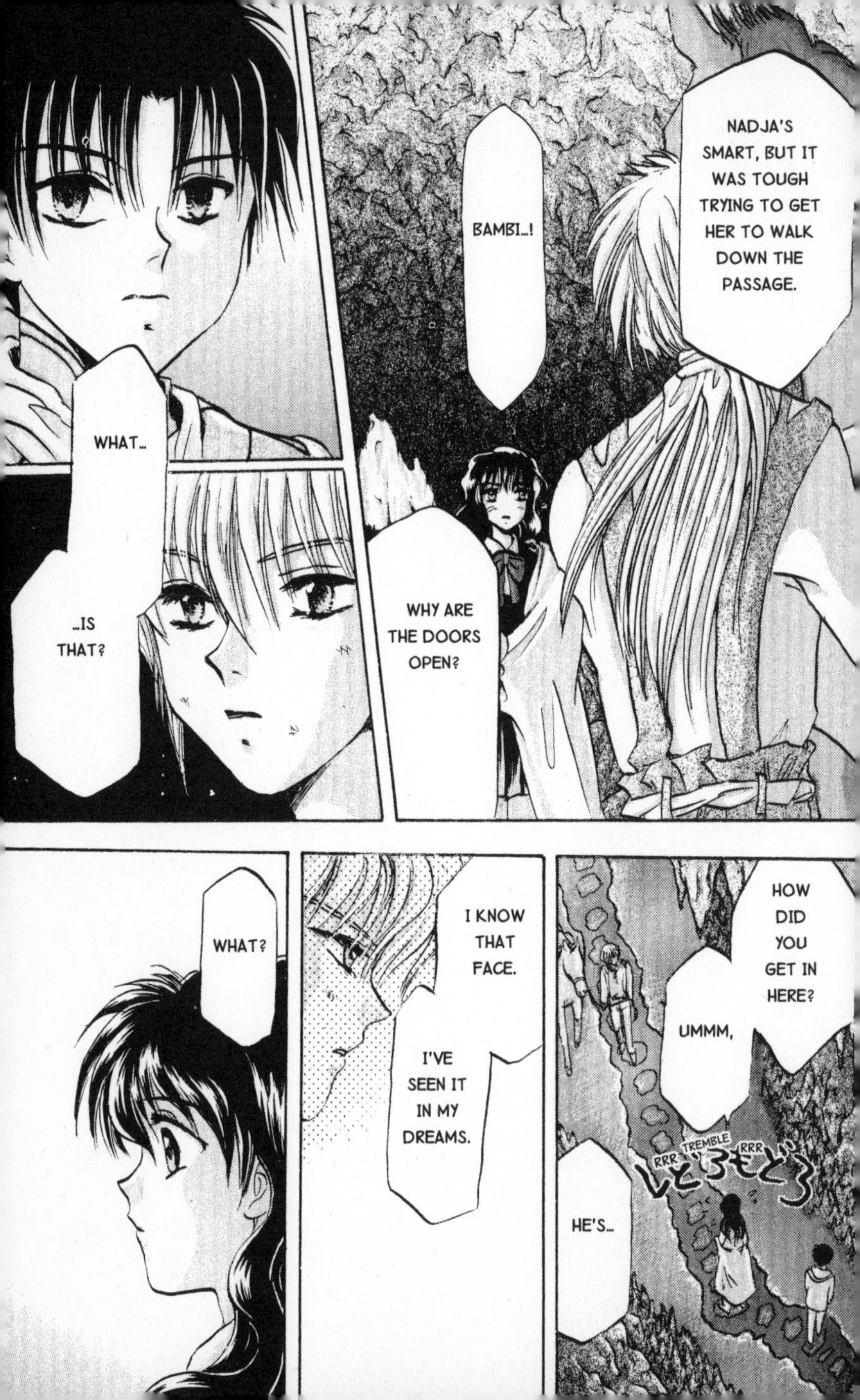
NADJA'S SMART, BUT IT WAS TOUGH TRYING TO GET HER TO WALK DOWN THE PASSAGE.
BAMBI...!
WHY ARE THE DOORS OPEN?
WHAT...
...IS THAT?
HOW DID YOU GET IN HERE?
UMMM,
RRR TREMBLE RRR
しどろもどろ
HE'S...
I KNOW THAT FACE.
I'VE SEEN IT IN MY DREAMS.
WHAT?

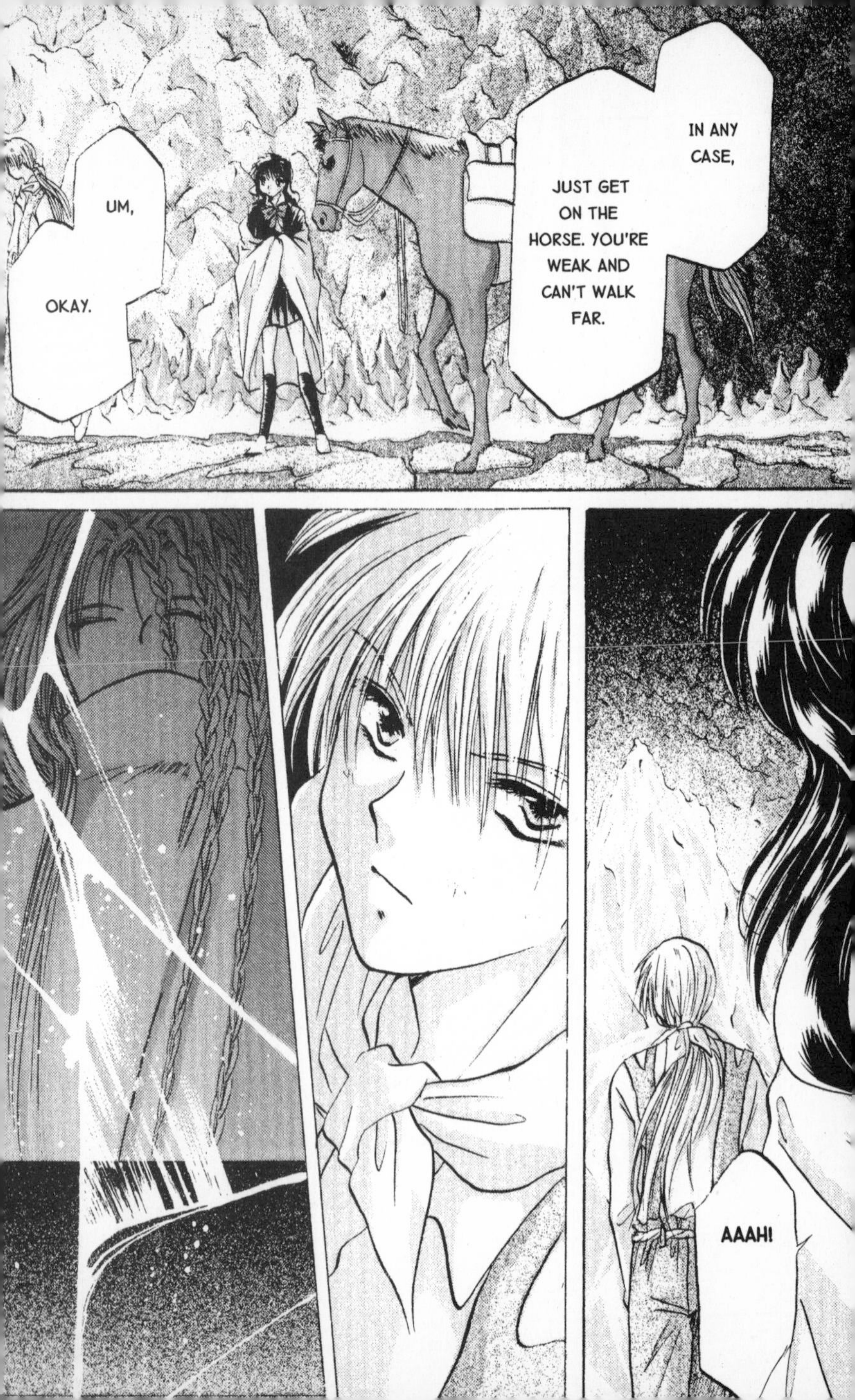
IN ANY CASE, JUST GET ON THE HORSE. YOU'RE WEAK AND CAN'T WALK FAR.
UM, OKAY.
AAAH!

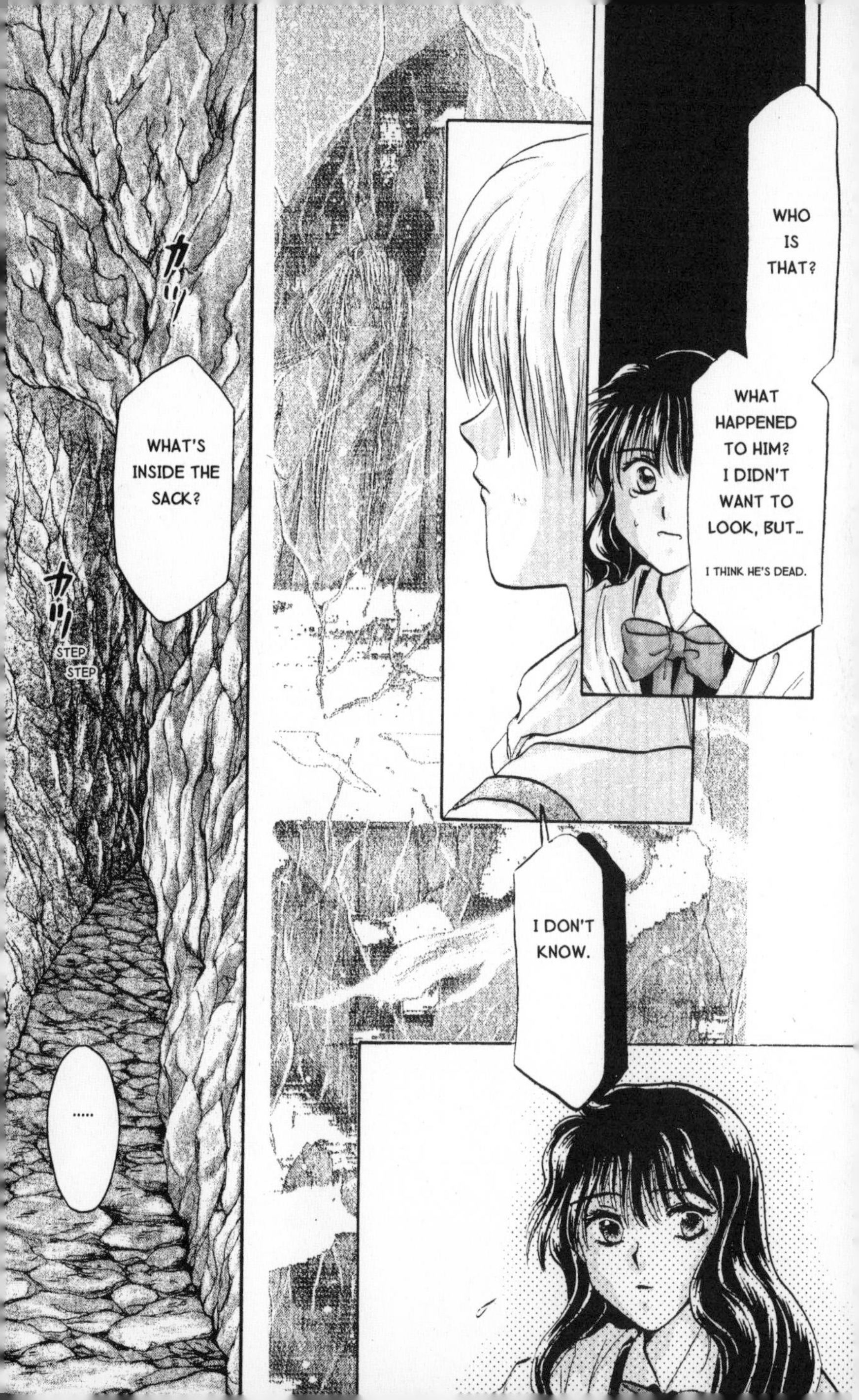
WHO IS THAT?
WHAT HAPPENED TO HIM? I DIDN'T WANT TO LOOK, BUT...
I THINK HE'S DEAD.
I DON'T KNOW.
カッ
WHAT'S INSIDE THE SACK?
カッ
STEP STEP
......

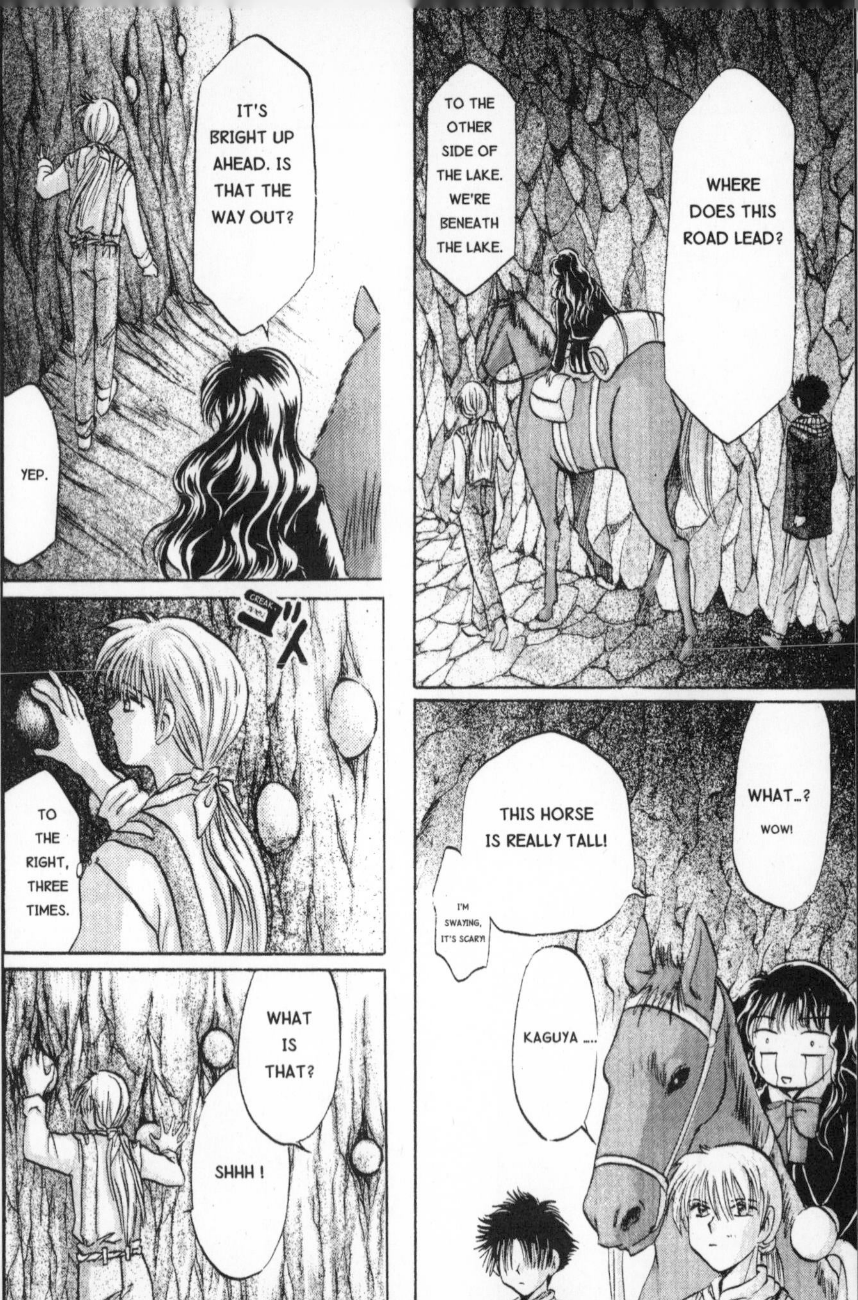
WHERE DOES THIS ROAD LEAD?
TO THE OTHER SIDE OF THE LAKE. WE'RE BENEATH THE LAKE.
WHAT...?
WOW!
THIS HORSE IS REALLY TALL!
I'M SWAYING, IT'S SCARY!
KAGUYA ....
IT'S BRIGHT UP AHEAD. IS THAT THE WAY OUT?
YEP.
CREAK
TO THE RIGHT, THREE TIMES.
WHAT IS THAT?
SHHH !

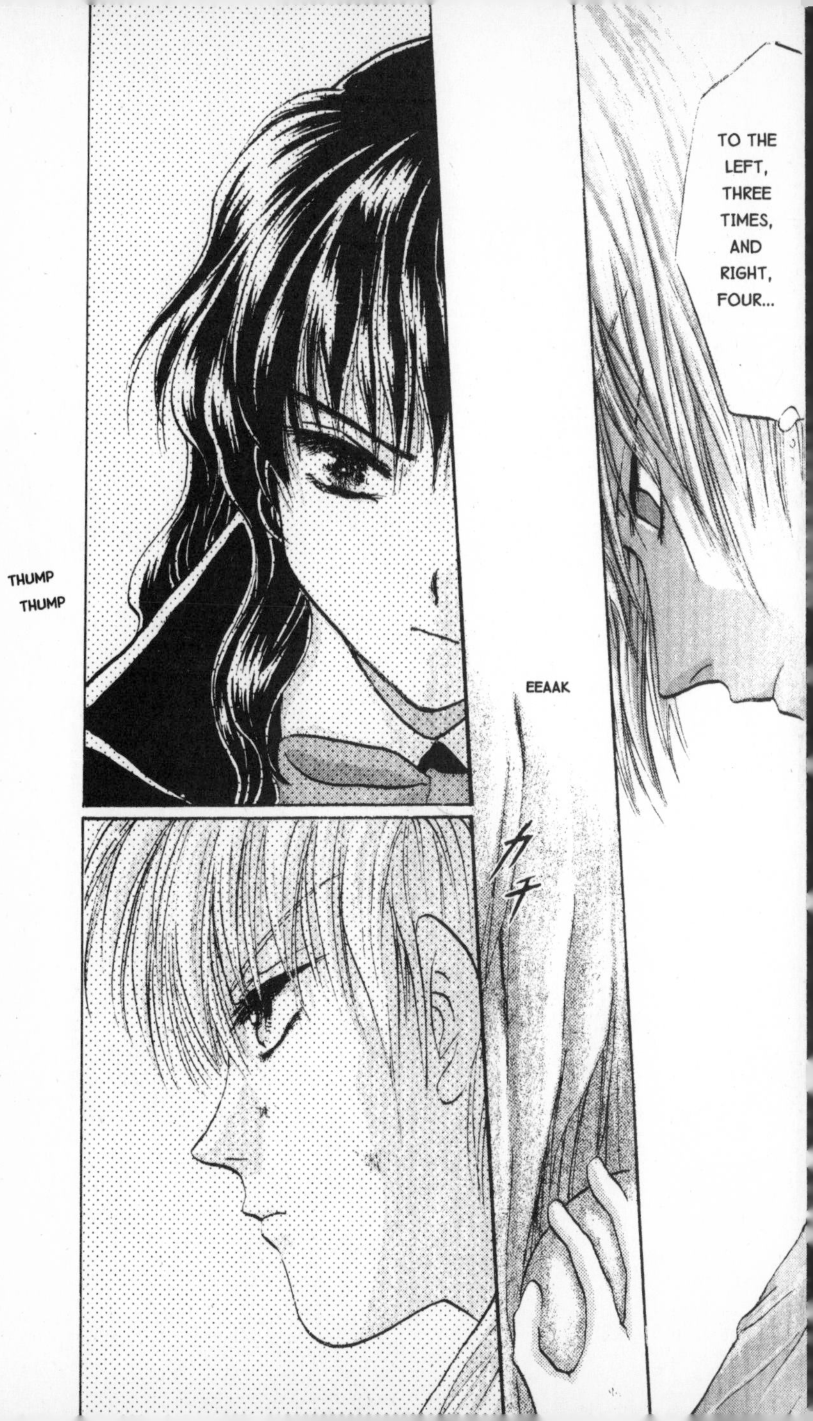
TO THE LEFT, THREE TIMES, AND RIGHT, FOUR...
EEAAK
カチ
THUMP THUMP

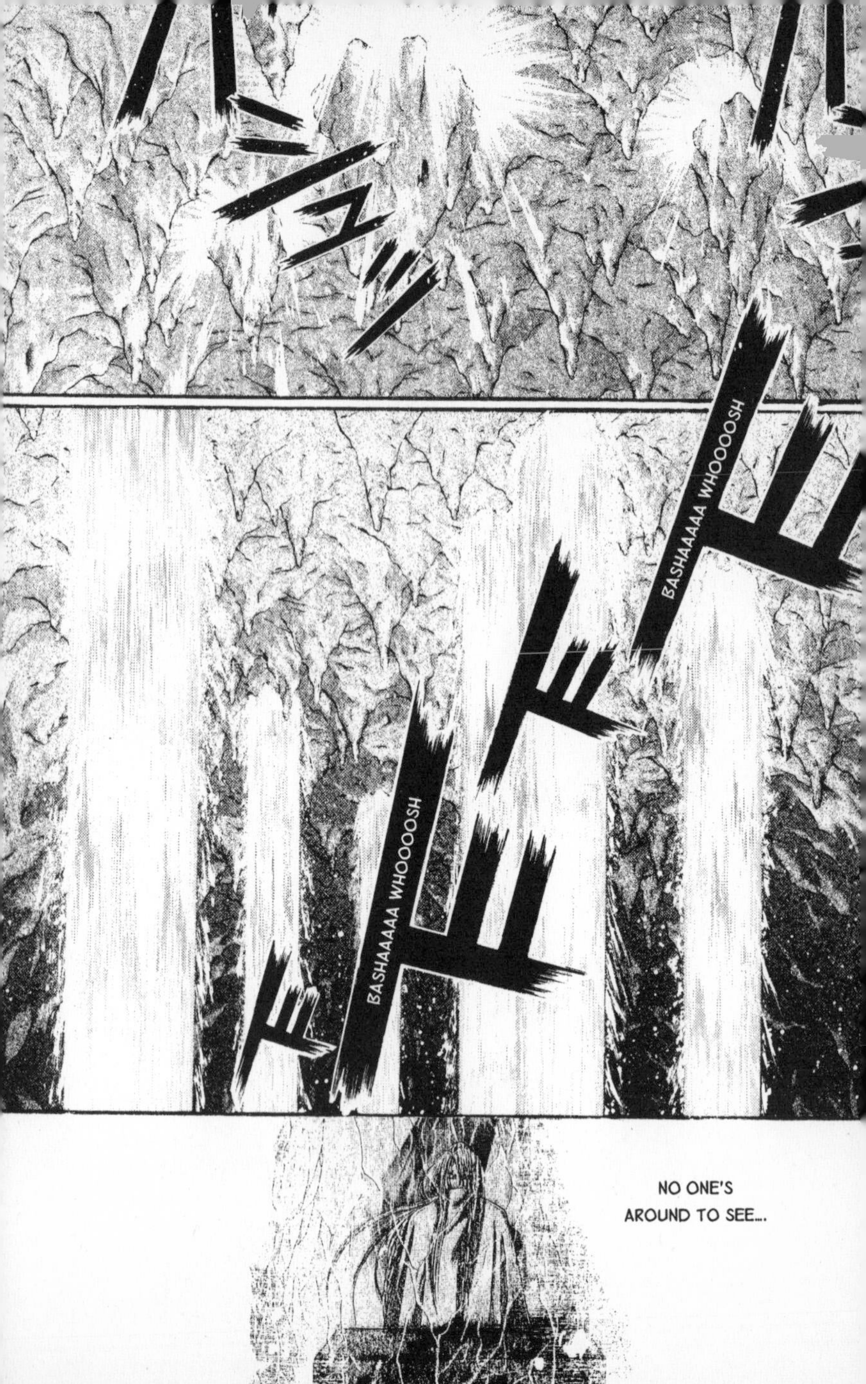
BASHAAAAA WHOOOOSH
BASHAAAAA WHOOOOSH
NO ONE'S AROUND TO SEE...

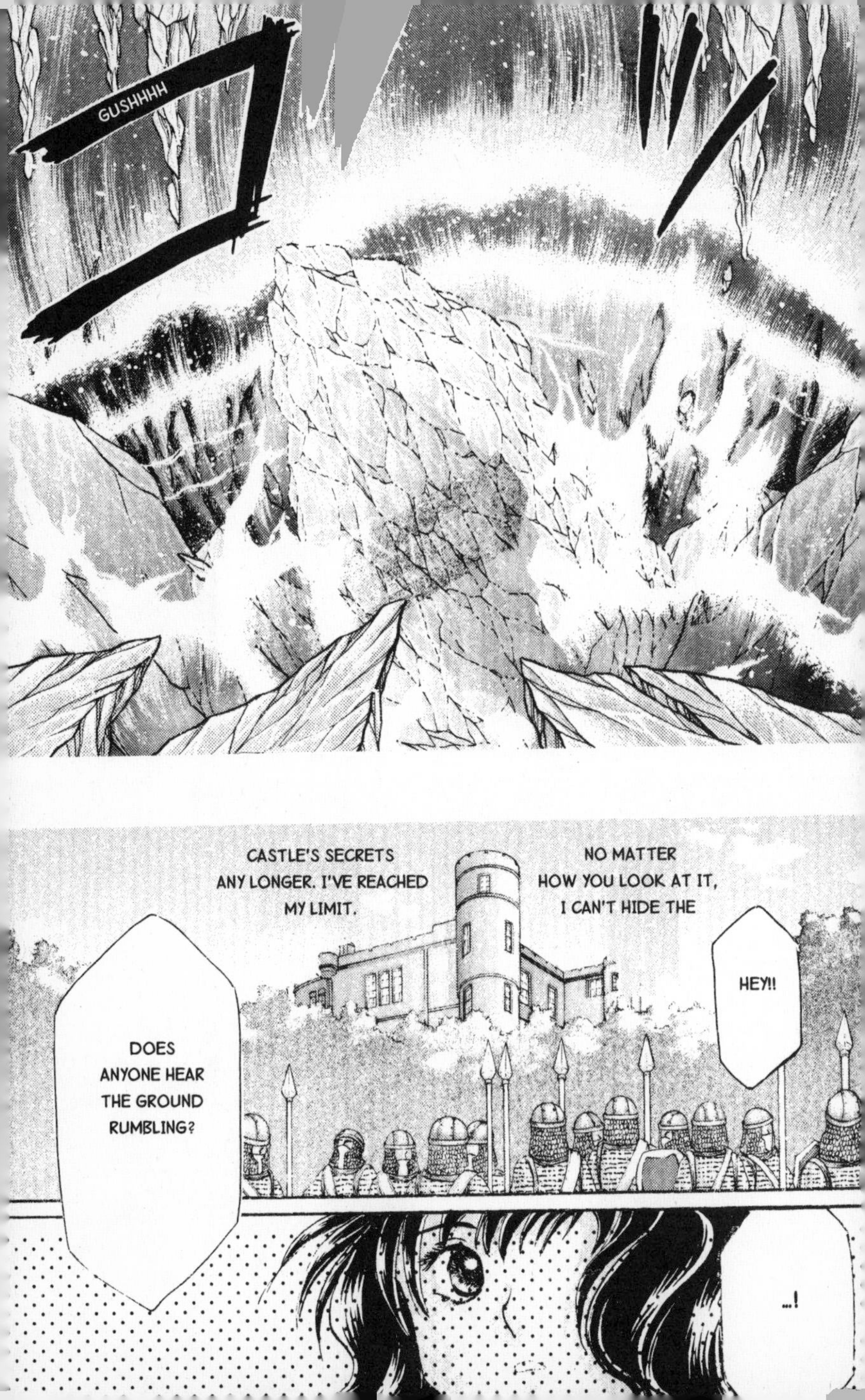
GUSHHHH
NO MATTER HOW YOU LOOK AT IT, I CAN'T HIDE THE
CASTLE'S SECRETS ANY LONGER. I'VE REACHED MY LIMIT.
HEY!!
DOES ANYONE HEAR THE GROUND RUMBLING?
...!

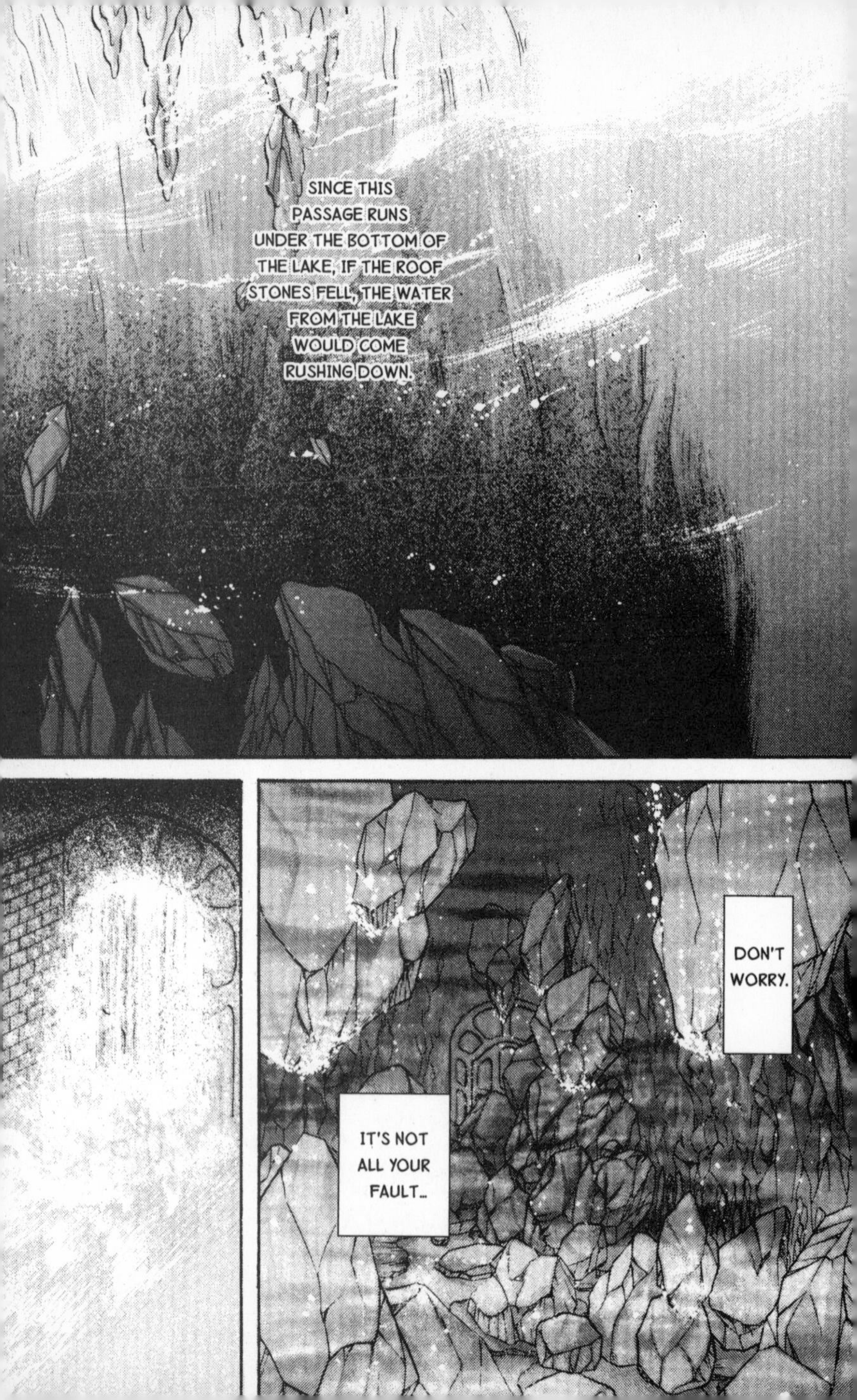
SINCE THIS PASSAGE RUNS UNDER THE BOTTOM OF THE LAKE, IF THE ROOF STONES FELL, THE WATER FROM THE LAKE WOULD COME RUSHING DOWN.
DON'T WORRY.
IT'S NOT ALL YOUR FAULT...

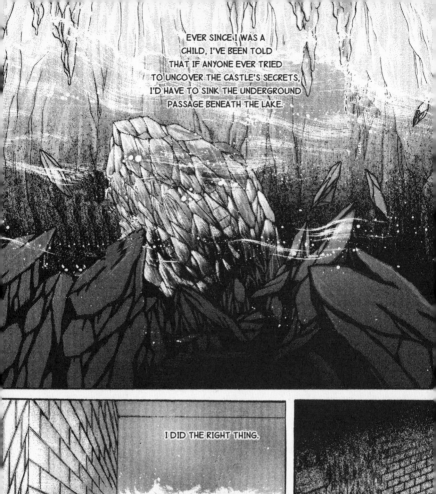

EVER SINCE I WAS A
CHILD, I'VE BEEN TOLD
THAT IF ANYONE EVER TRIED
TO UNCOVER THE CASTLE'S SECRETS,
I'D HAVE TO SINK THE UNDERGROUND
PASSAGE BENEATH THE LAKE.

I DID THE RIGHT THING.

BAMBI SAID QUIETLY.

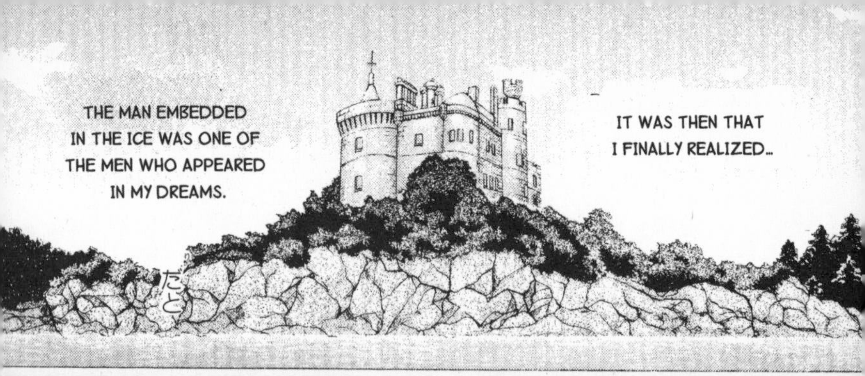
IT WAS THEN THAT I FINALLY REALIZED...
THE MAN EMBEDDED IN THE ICE WAS ONE OF THE MEN WHO APPEARED IN MY DREAMS.
だと

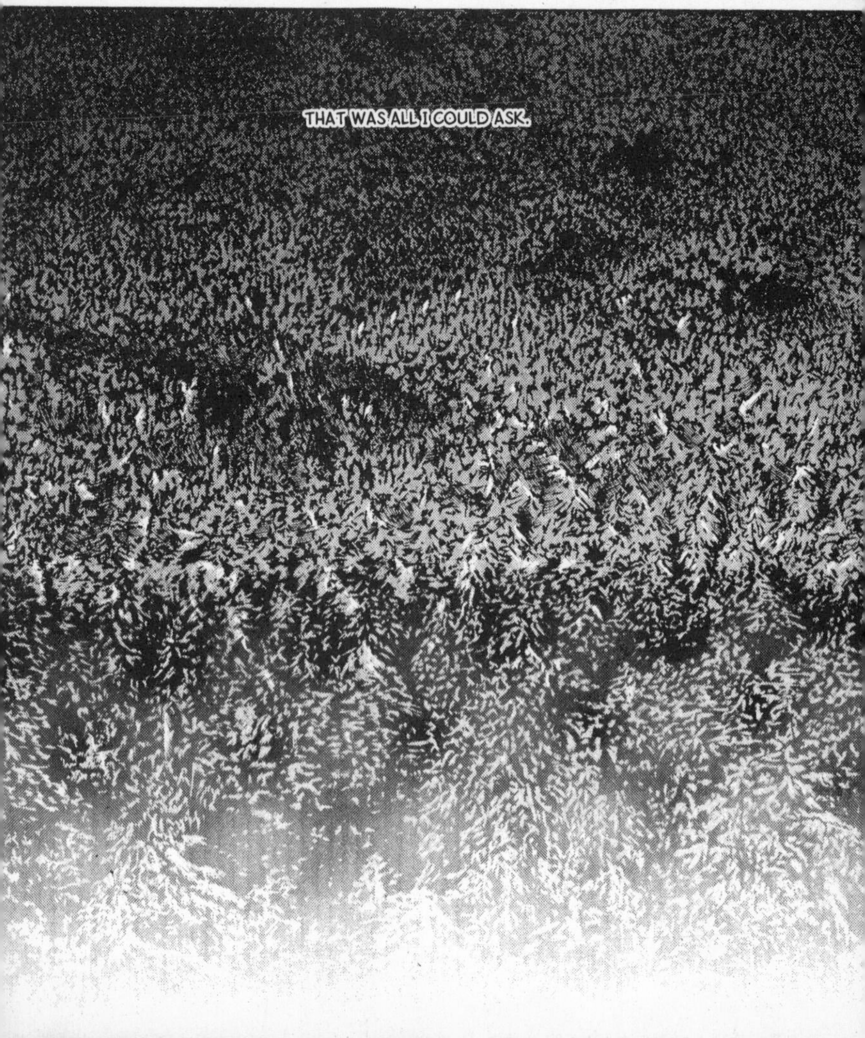
THAT WAS ALL I COULD ASK.

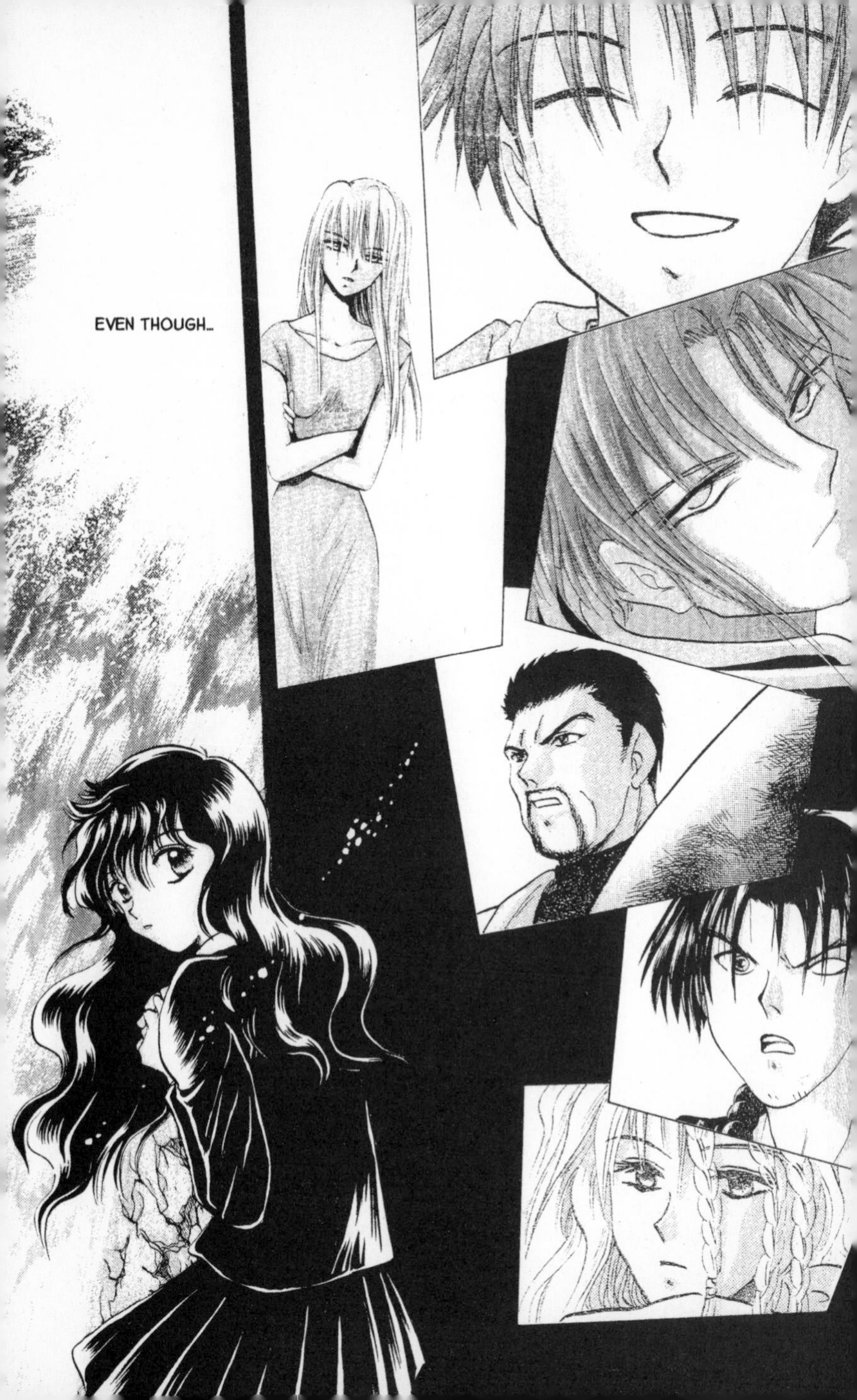
EVEN THOUGH...

...ON THE OTHER SIDE OF THOSE DOORS,
I KNOW THERE IS A WORLD BREWING WITH TURMOIL .
BUT I KNOW I'VE GOT TO OPEN THOSE
DOORS BY MYSELF, WITH MY OWN TWO HANDS.

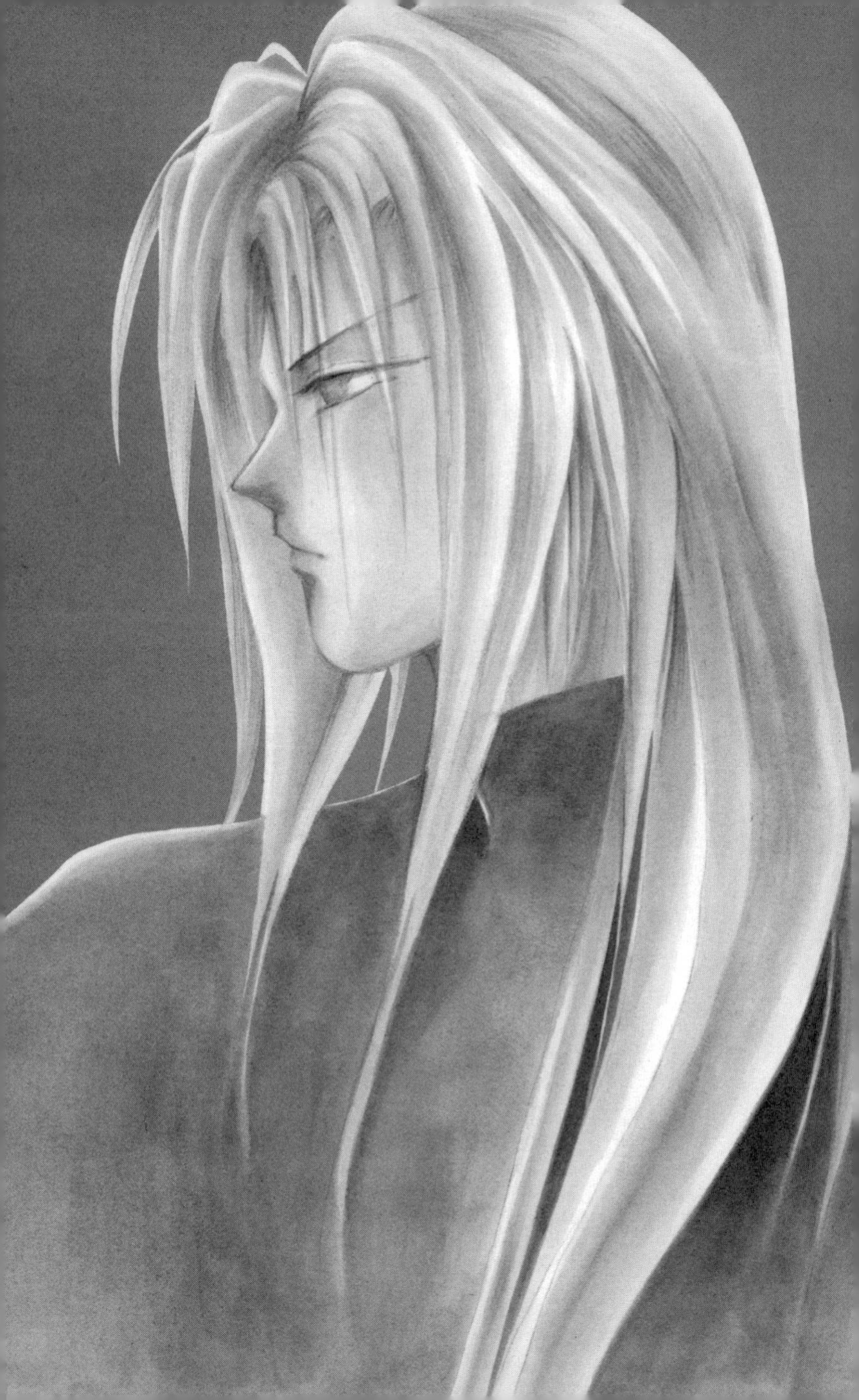

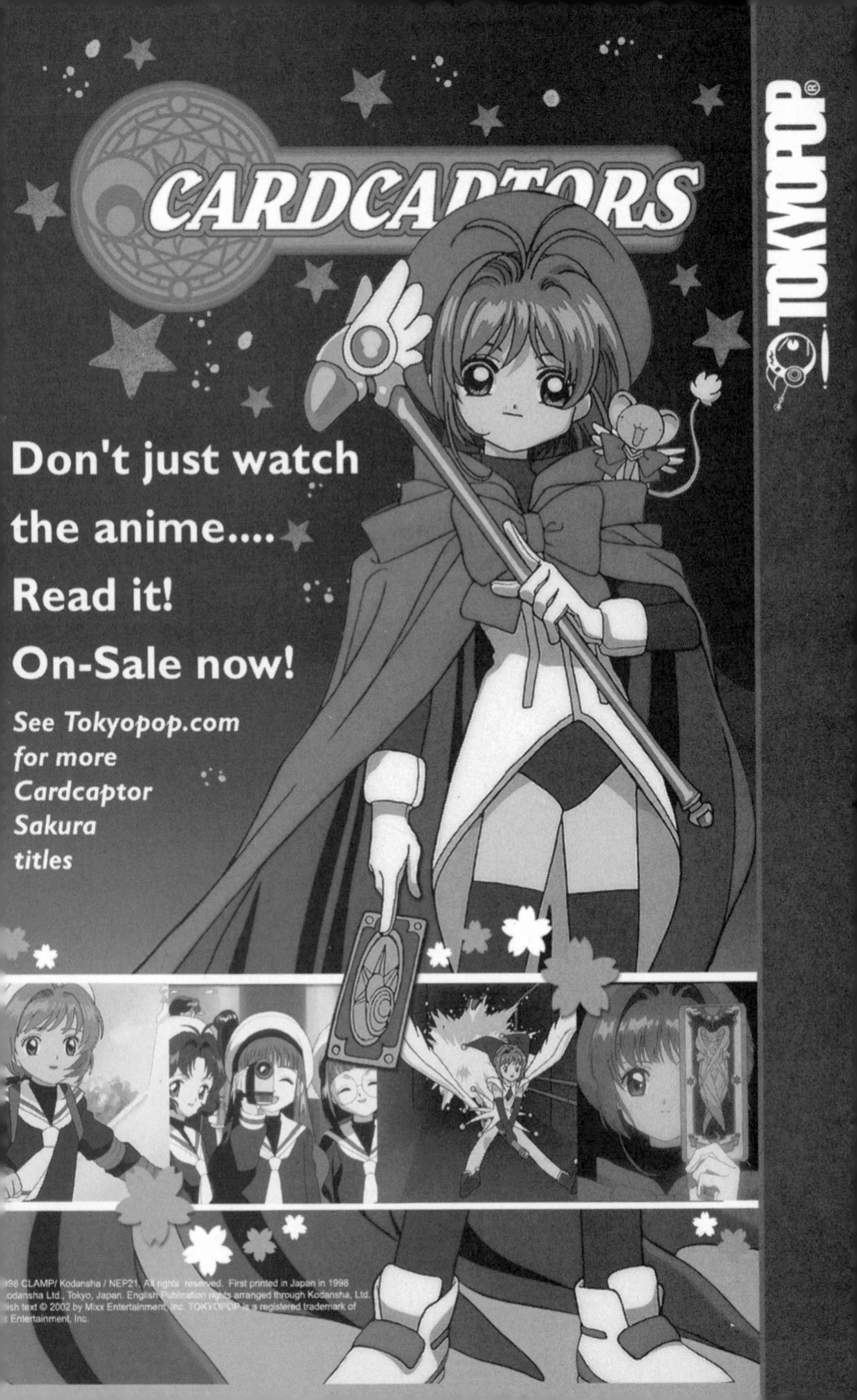
CARDCAPTORS
Don't just watch the anime.... Read it! On-Sale now!
See Tokyopop.com for more Cardcaptor Sakura titles
TOKYOPOP
98 CLAMP/ Kodansha / NEP21. All rights reserved. First printed in Japan in 1998
odansha Ltd., Tokyo, Japan. English Publication rights arranged through Kodansha, Ltd.
ish text © 2002 by Mixx Entertainment, Inc. TOKYOPOP is a registered trademark of
Entertainment, Inc.

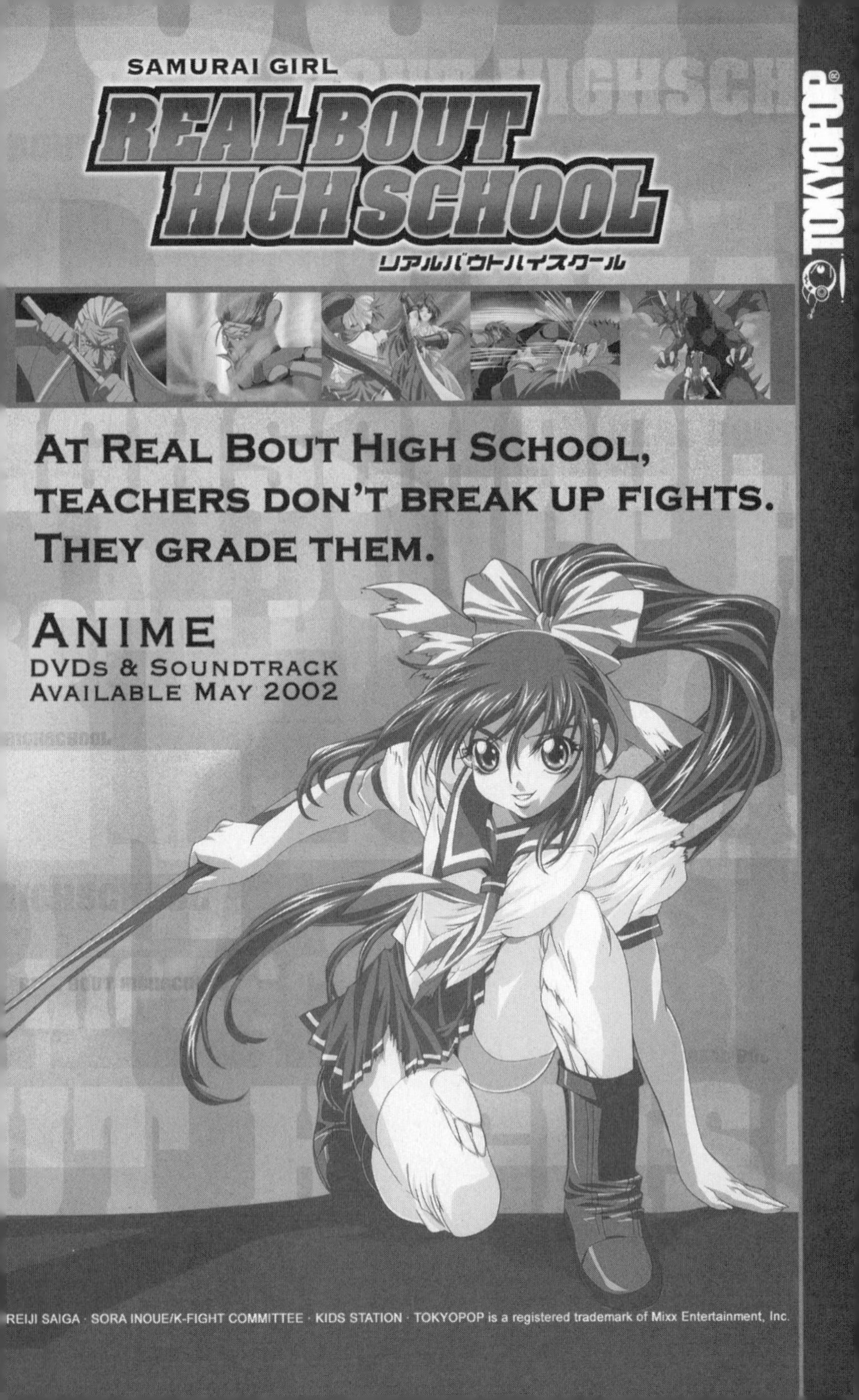
SAMURAI GIRL
REAL BOUT HIGH SCHOOL
リアルバウトハイスクール
AT REAL BOUT HIGH SCHOOL, TEACHERS DON'T BREAK UP FIGHTS. THEY GRADE THEM.
ANIME
DVDs & SOUNDTRACK
AVAILABLE MAY 2002
REIJI SAIGA · SORA INOUE/K-FIGHT COMMITTEE · KIDS STATION · TOKYOPOP is a registered trademark of Mixx Entertainment, Inc.
TOKYOPOP®

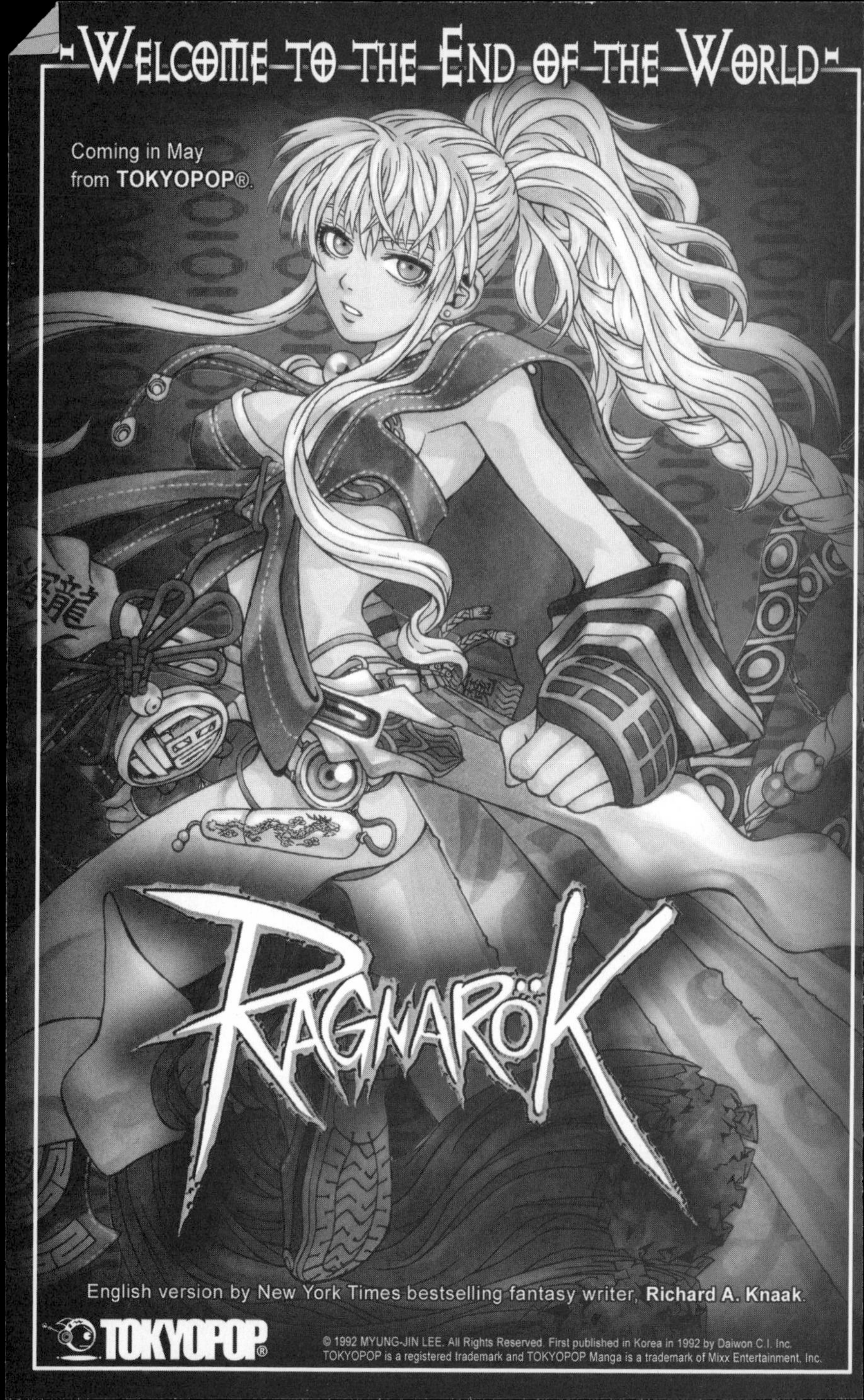
WELCOME TO THE END OF THE WORLD
Coming in May
from TOKYOPOP®.
RAGNARÖK
English version by New York Times bestselling fantasy writer, Richard A. Knaak.
TOKYOPOP®
© 1992 MYUNG-JIN LEE. All Rights Reserved. First published in Korea in 1992 by Daiwon C.I. Inc.
TOKYOPOP is a registered trademark and TOKYOPOP Manga is a trademark of Mixx Entertainment, Inc.

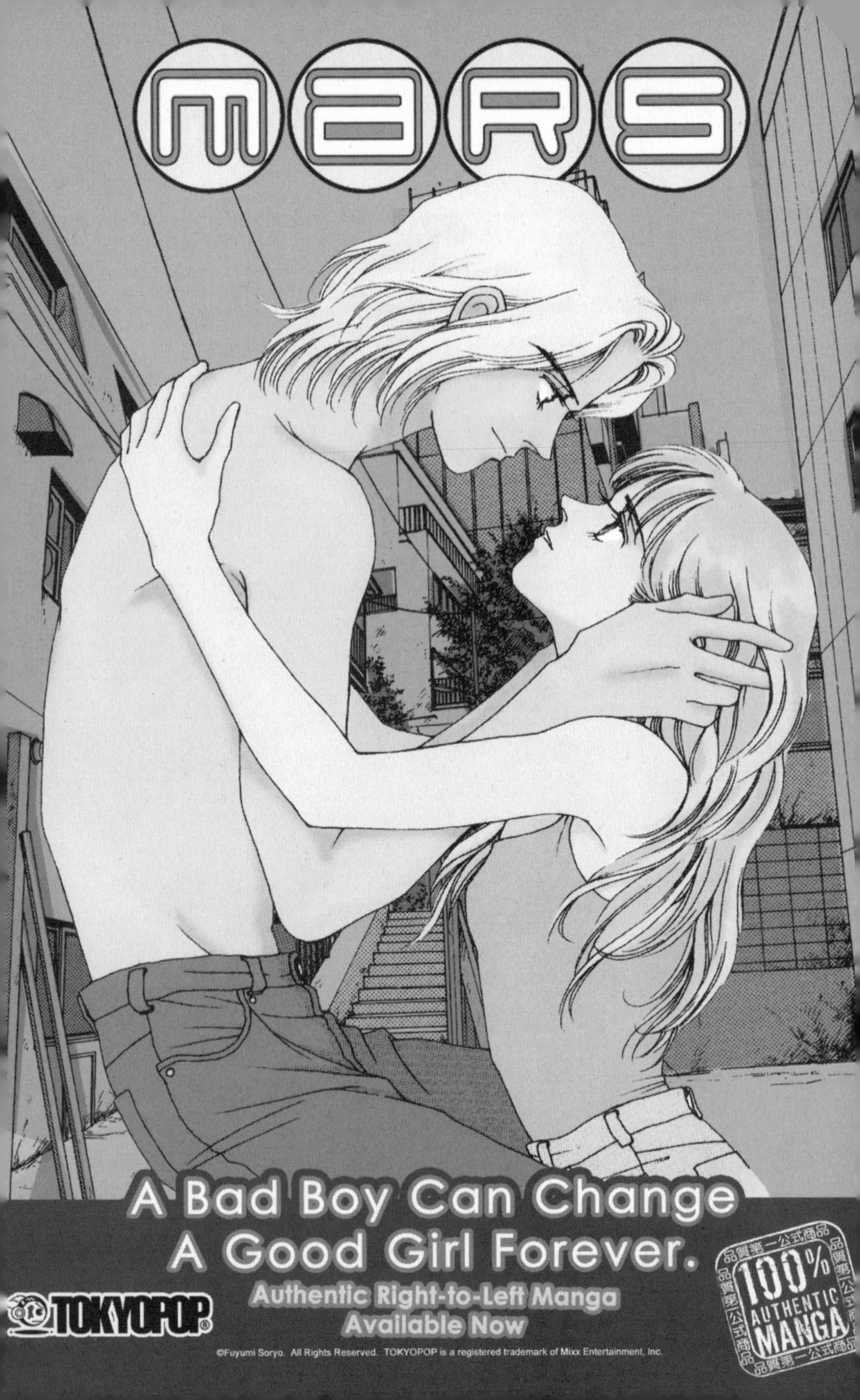
MARS
A Bad Boy Can Change
A Good Girl Forever.
Authentic Right-to-Left Manga
Available Now
TOKYOPOP
100% AUTHENTIC MANGA
©Fuyumi Soryo. All Rights Reserved. TOKYOPOP is a registered trademark of Mixx Entertainment, Inc.

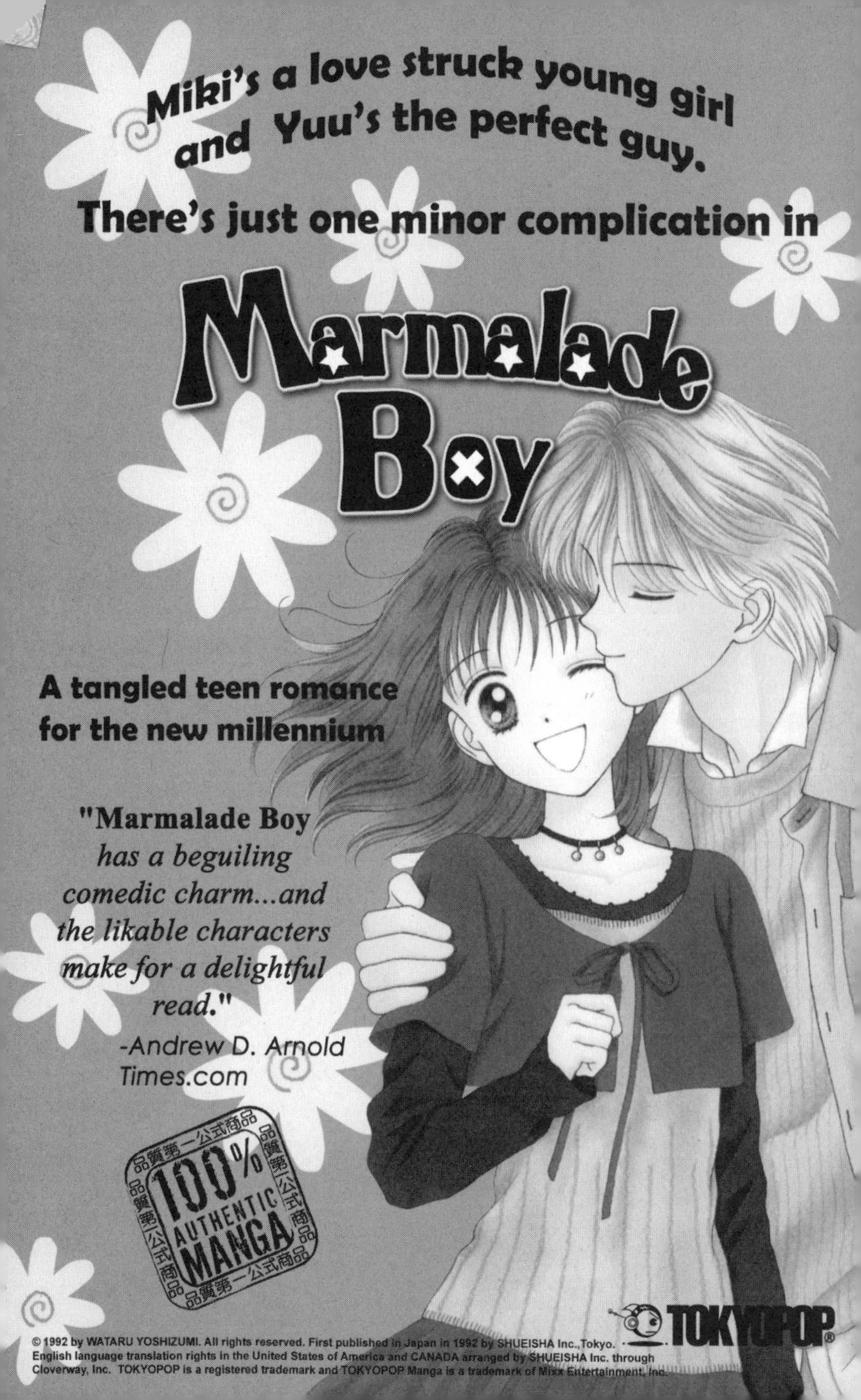
Miki's a love struck young girl
and Yuu's the perfect guy.
There's just one minor complication in
Marmalade Boy
A tangled teen romance
for the new millennium
"Marmalade Boy
has a beguiling
comedic charm...and
the likable characters
make for a delightful
read."
-Andrew D. Arnold
Times.com
100% AUTHENTIC MANGA
品質第一公式商品
TOKYOPOP
© 1992 by WATARU YOSHIZUMI. All rights reserved. First published in Japan in 1992 by SHUEISHA Inc.,Tokyo.
English language translation rights in the United States of America and CANADA arranged by SHUEISHA Inc. through
Cloverway, Inc. TOKYOPOP is a registered trademark and TOKYOPOP Manga is a trademark of Mixx Entertainment, Inc.

STOP!

This is the back of the book.
You wouldn't want to spoil a great ending!

This book is printed "manga-style," in the authentic Japanese right-to-left format. Since none of the artwork has been flipped or altered, readers get to experience the story just as the creator intended. You've been asking for it, so TOKYOPOP® delivered: authentic, hot-off-the-press, and far more fun!

DIRECTIONS

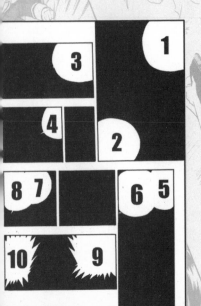

If this is your first time reading manga-style, here's a quick guide to help you understand how it works.

It's easy... just start in the top right panel and follow the numbers. Have fun, and look for more 100% authentic manga from TOKYOPOP®!